April 2012   *Adolf Grünbaum*

FREUD, THE RELUCTANT PHILOSOPHER

FREUD, THE RELUCTANT PHILOSOPHER

Alfred I. Tauber

PRINCETON UNIVERSITY PRESS   PRINCETON AND OXFORD

Published by Princeton University Press, 41 William Street,
Princeton, New Jersey 08540

In the United Kingdom: Princeton University Press, 6 Oxford Street,
Woodstock, Oxfordshire OX20 1TW
press.princeton.edu

Library of Congress Cataloging-in-Publication Data

Tauber, Alfred I.
Freud, the reluctant philosopher / Alfred I. Tauber.
p.   cm.
Includes bibliographical references (p.   ) and index.
ISBN 978-0-691-14551-8 (hardcover : alk. paper)
ISBN 978-0-691-14552-5 (pbk.: alk. paper)
1. Freud, Sigmund, 1856–1939—Philosophy. 2. Psychoanalysis
and philosophy. I. Title.
BF109.F74T38 2010
150.19′52092—dc22   2010001612

British Library Cataloging-in-Publication Data is available

This book has been composed in Sabon

Printed on acid-free paper. ∞

Printed in the United States of America

1   3   5   7   9   10   8   6   4   2

for Jane

The voice of the intellect is a soft one, but it does not rest till it has gained a hearing. Finally, after a countless succession of rebuffs, it succeeds. This is one of the few points on which one may be optimistic about the future of mankind, but it is in itself a point of no small importance. And from it one can derive yet other hopes.
— Sigmund Freud, *Future of an Illusion* (1927, 53)

... freedom in human beings—against: there is no freedom, rather everything is natural necessity; it was this that first woke me from my dogmatic slumber and drove me to the critique of reason itself to dissolve the scandal of the contradiction of reason with itself.
— Immanuel Kant, letter to Christian Garve,
September 21, 1798

My discoveries are not primarily a heal-all. My discoveries are a basis for a very grave philosophy. There are very few who understand this, *there are very few who are capable of understanding this.*
— Sigmund Freud (1933 conversation, quoted
by Hilda Doolittle 1971, 25)

Contents

We shall one day recognize in Freud's life-work the cornerstone
for the building of a new anthropology and therewith of a new
structure, to which many stones are being brought up today, which
shall be the future dwelling of a wiser and freer humanity. This
physicianly psychologist will, I make no doubt at all, be honoured
as the path-finder towards a humanism of the future, which we
dimly divine and which will have experienced much that the earlier
humanism knew not of. It will be a humanism ... bolder, freer,
blither, productive of a riper art than any possible in our neurotic,
fear-ridden, hate ridden-world. ... The analytic revelation is a
revolutionary force.
    —Thomas Mann (1947, 427)

THIS BOOK, PERHAPS INEVITABLY, began as a fantasy: If Sigmund Freud
had remained faithful to both domains in which he had studied as a university student (philosophy and medicine [Bernfeld 1951]), how would
he then have argued the case for psychoanalysis? More specifically, instead of steadfastly holding to a narrow scientific orientation, how would
he have responded to philosophers who might have posed questions that
probed the conceptual infrastructure of his theory? Since philosophy was
in a particularly rich ferment during the fin de siècle and into the first
decades of the twentieth century, ample opportunity for debate against
a rich variety of positions suggests robust and enlightening arguments.
His disputants, given the opportunity (and inclination), would have undoubtedly offered biting criticism of his philosophical assumptions and,
perhaps more generously, encouragement for his larger mission. Those
dialogues would have initially drawn in neo-Kantians, Nietzscheans, historicists, phenomenologists, materialists, and hermeneutists, and later
Heideggerians, existentialists, Wittgensteinians, and logical positivists.
And if Freud had seriously engaged William James (who was ill during
their brief encounter in 1909) or John Dewey, then pragmatism would
have been thrown into the mix. Each tribe would have challenged Freud's

positions as suspect, even highly dubious, given their own commitments. I further imagined that Freud might well have responded with a mixture of robust defenses and reluctant admissions. In the end he would undoubtedly have maintained that psychoanalysis was not philosophy and that it had no pretense of engaging in philosophical discourse. Yet, if pushed, he might have responded along the lines that he did have a philosophical platform: a philosophy of science founded on positivist principles, a mind-body parallelism, and a particular form of naturalism. And here the debate would begin, not only in challenges to his self-declared positions, but also in critiques that would expose Freud's unacknowledged philosophical debts. Indeed, these hidden conceptual sources comprise the heart of my own interpretation of Freud's psychoanalytic theory.

Each of Freud's interrogators, at least according to my initial script, would have chastised him for his reluctance to forthrightly admit his philosophical liabilities and to acknowledge how certain positivist assumptions gnawed at psychoanalytic theory to its detriment.[1] From the neo-Kantian perspective (particularly as advocated by Friedrich Lange and Wilhelm Windelband), Freud's failing to recognize the metaphysical character of his theory not only miscast the unconscious as a scientific object, but also robbed psychoanalysis of its full philosophical character. Accordingly, if Freud left his philosophy undeveloped, he would jeopardize the entire project. The neo-Kantians could then turn the psychoanalytic table and accuse Freud of repression, denial, and worse! The question remains for us, the observers of this imagined interlocutory, how we might better understand psychoanalytic theory when subject to such criticism.

Placing Freud in this postulated dialogue is not entirely contrived, because he knew the basic outline of the philosophical tradition as taught in the 1870s. Moreover, we have evidence that he continued to entertain the relation of psychoanalytic theory to Kant and to other philosophers as he also took pains to convince himself and his readers that he was not doing philosophy. And then, with some inconsistency, he played to the philosopher's band by imagining that instead of rejection, the new theory "would be all the more likely to meet with applause from philosophers" (Freud 1925b, 216), as he hoped to direct them towards a new understanding. By and large he failed, and in frustration he would rant throughout his career against the consciousness-oriented philosophies of mind as misdirected.

While Freud's critique focused on the centrality of unconsciousness as an alternative to other philosophies of mind, his disdain for philosophy extended to a general rejection. As late as his *New Introductory Lectures* of 1933, he sounded his repeated refrain about "philosophers" and his own philosophy:

> Philosophy is not opposed to science, it behaves like a science and works in part by the same methods; it departs from it, however, by clinging to the illusion of being able to present a picture of the universe which is without gaps and is coherent, though one which is bound to collapse with every fresh advance of our knowledge. It goes astray in its method of over-estimating the epistemological value of our logical operations and by accepting other sources of knowledge such as intuition. (Freud 1933, 160–61)

Freud's rejection of philosophy rested upon his diagnosis of three weaknesses: (1) philosophy represents an encompassing mode of knowledge (or perhaps a metaphysics) that cannot respond to new empirical findings; (2) beyond its blindness to empiricism (sic, science), philosophy's logic is closed and limited; and (3) philosophers elevate nonscientific forms of knowledge to an epistemological level that is rightly reserved for positivist findings. That this characterization distorts "philosophy" requires little comment, other than to note the irony that Freud accepted his own positivism without the same critical appraisal that he applied to other philosophies. He associated philosophy with religion and with what was already a widely rejected Hegelianism; he avoided exploring the logic of his own science and its presumptive claim on true knowledge; and finally, he seemingly ignored the metaphysical foundations of his own efforts to devise an encompassing philosophy of human nature.

These seemingly naïve points are not my primary interest, but as they fit into Freud's own construction of a particular philosophy, they serve my greater themes: (1) The phases of Freud's relationship to philosophy—application, denial, and rejection—each constitute an aspect of his own concern about the veracity of psychoanalysis, which he sought to establish as a scientific discipline; (2) he employed specific philosophical positions for his own theoretical purposes, and these philosophical elements form the grounding of his thought, both scientific and humanistic; (3) he founded his own philosophy of human nature on both an empirically based psychology and a humanistic philosophy of human freedom coupled to a vision of moral self-responsibility; (4) this mixture of objective empiricism and subjective interpretation challenges the scientific basis of psychoanalysis and points to its ultimate ethical mission; and finally, (5) Freud's inconsistent antagonism to philosophy coupled with the active extrapolations of psychoanalysis to hypotheses about human history, culture, and religion reveals his persistent underlying efforts to produce a social philosophy.[2]

We witness this tension between an empirical science and a moral philosophy throughout Freud's opus. That philosophy combines two elements, a biological conception of human behavior (justifying the empiricism) and a humanistic understanding of the soul (a more accurate translation of *psyche* [Bettelheim 1982]). But Freud never explicitly describes these postions in his publications and in his correspondence, for in the express rejection of formal philosophy, he eschewed significant self-reflection on his own intellectual commitments. Yet on several occasions, Freud privately admitted that in his retreat from philosophy he never completely abandoned the musings of his youth. Shortly after receiving his medical degree, he wrote his fiancée that philosophy, "which I have always pictured as my goal and refuge in my old age, gains every day in attraction . . . but the fear of the supreme uncertainty of all political [anti-Semitism] and local matters [economic] keeps me from that sphere" (letter to Martha Bernays of August 16, 1882. quoted by Jones 1953–57, 3:41). However, philosophy was not easily dispelled, and writing to Wilhelm Fliess (in 1896), Freud observed, "As a young man I knew no longing other than for philosophical knowledge, and now I am about to fulfill it as I move from medicine to psychology. I became a therapist against my will" (1985, 180). Putting aside for now how psychology might have been construed as a form of philosophy, Freud's "against my will" seems, at the very least, ironic, for while Freud never admitted his own deviance from the science of psychoanalysis, his very silence doth protest too much. Indeed, his proclivities for philosophy suffered repression until his maturity, when he freely speculated about culture and history, and thus I agree with Patricia Herzog (1988) that the "myth of Freud as an anti-philosopher" is exactly that, a myth.[3]

The intellectual portrait presented here regards Freud, the reluctant philosopher, expending considering intellectual (and psychic) energy in defining himself as an empirical scientist at the expense of a competing, seemingly repressed passion, and that this subordinated desire to philosophize finally emerged upon writing *Totem and Taboo* (1913b) and the meta-psychological papers shortly thereafter. Why he made this shift has prompted much speculation (e.g., a crisis centered on Jewish identity [Paul 1996] or in response to the conflict with Jung [Breger 2000]), but suffice it to summarize my claim here: I broadly regard such extensions of psychology as representing the expression of a frustrated philosopher, and while these speculations may have many sources, each contributes to a more general humanist commitment whose origins are evident from Freud's youth.

I suggest we image Freud in a triptych: a physician, sitting by a couch, listening to his patient; a studious scientist, sitting at his desk composing his theory; an intellectual entering the halls of the humanities through a side door, hoping to remain inconspicuous. We can easily imagine the first two figures, but how do we see the third? That one—nebulous, and consequently elusive—ducks through the portal. But this shadow figure appears most clearly if the proper light is applied, and indeed, two kinds of illumination are required, because Freud, in adopting the scientist's mantle, melded two apparently disparate forms of knowledge: a rigorous empiricism tempered by a broad humane appreciation of the complexity of the human soul, so psychoanalysis becomes a chimera of rationalities, in which two kinds of reason—positivist and hermeneutic—complement one another to fulfill distinctive demands.

So *Freud, the Reluctant Philosopher* builds upon Freud's own acknowledgments that the psychoanalytic approach to human behavior represented a "backdoor" entry into the speculative problems that originally intrigued him as a university student. In assuming this position, I employ a lesson from the master himself: "An important element in the theory of repression is the view that repression is not an event that occurs once but that it requires a permanent expenditure [of energy]" Freud (1926c, 157). This personal aspect of Freud's biography only complements my main argument. Although I respect the biographical evidence that would distance Freud from philosophy, I nevertheless maintain that his thinking borrowed philosophical premises that would prove integral to his venture at all points of its development. The reader will thus find here a philosophical interpretation of psychoanalysis inspired by Freud's own tantalizing hints of indebtedness to a background of modern philosophy.

That Freud repressed "philosophy" seems obvious to me, and thus I will use the plot of that obscured story to help explicate his defense of psychoanalysis and elucidate the underpinnings of the theory. To make that case, I will outline certain philosophical positions that serve as the foundation of his thought, and explain, first, how Freud built his science upon a challenge offered by his philosophical mentor, Franz Brentano (1838–1917) with whom he studied as a university student and then show how Freud's basic interpretative strategy rested upon Kant's argument about the transcendental relation of mind and nature. On my view, Freud's thinking was deeply influenced by Kantianism, inasmuch as the seer of Königsberg set the agenda for nineteenth-century thought, either by enlisting those in general support of his transcendental strategy or by summoning detractors arrayed in opposition to it. Freud too was caught in these currents of thought. By employing arguments and assertions of several nineteenth-century philosophers (Hegel, Schopenhauer, Nietzsche, Lange, and Windelband—themselves also reacting to Kant), I will highlight how Freud's theory refracts Freud's own relationship to Kant. That discussion offers an assessment both of the ethical structure of psychoanalysis and of the understanding of personal identity that psychoanalytic theory presents. We end with Freud's moral philosophy.

I do not endeavor to defend Freud, but I hope to rescue him from battles that no longer compel attention by deflecting the argument about his scientific claims (an issue I believe settled against psychoanalysis in terms of ordinary understandings of science), and more appropriately define his project as a mode of interpreting human experience, human emotion, and human history. After all, from radically different perspectives, psychoanalysis has inspired myriad contemporary interpretations of culture, history, personal identity, and moral discourse. For example, plucking from my bookcase most handily, on sexual and gender identity, Brown (1959), Kristeva (1987), and Gilman (1993a); on spirituality, Rieff (1966) and Küng (1990); on the nature of civilization, Marcuse (1955) and Paul (1996); on death, Dollimore (1998), von Unwerth (2005), Volberg (2007), and so forth. Whether in support or opposition, all would concede that Freud bequeathed theories and methods that have deeply influenced Western self-conceptions of personhood, subjectivity, and interpersonal relations. At the very least, we can no longer think of ourselves independently of a Freudian self-consciousness, in which insight into unconscious influences and the suspicions of self-knowledge have molded Western notions of individualism and moral self-identity. From this broad appreciation, Freud may fairly be credited as a key architect of the social and psychological markings of contemporary Westerners.

Given these cultural *facts,* philosophers cannot ignore Freud's work, for the philosophical study of psychoanalysis contributes both to comprehending Freudianism—its continued strengths and discarded fictions—and to enriching contemporary philosophy in diverse areas of common interest. I rest my study on these shared interests. In short, this book explores why Freud's ideas and opinions are profitably understood within the philosophical context of his age, and why psychoanalysis has had continued philosophical importance in our own era.[4] When viewed from this vantage, Freud's exposed intellectual commitments lead us not only to appreciate the philosophical basis of psychoanalytic theory, but also to understand more deeply how Freudianism has organized contemporary comprehension of human agency

This book addresses at least three groups of readers: Those who still believe Freud made an abiding contribution to our understanding of human being and who seek philosophical guidance on how his project might be so configured; others who have an interest in a case example of philosophy's influence on psychology during the period spanning Freud's productive career; and then a third group interested in the clash of philosophical systems that occurred during fifty years (1880–1930) of extraordinary intellectual ferment and creativity. So while this study is about Freud and the philosophical structure of psychoanalysis, it also considers relevant post-Kantian depictions of human nature. Because some readers may not have a thorough knowledge of the key philosophical positions surveyed here—from Kant to Wittgenstein—I have provided perhaps more expository background than expert philosophers require, but I hope that even the cognoscente will appreciate explicit descriptions of the philosophical positions that have led me to the interpretations offered here. To that end, I trust the two discourses—psychoanalytic and philosophical—support each other adequately for my thematic purposes.

Acknowledgments

THIS WORK CONTINUES several themes I have explored over the past 20 years: the enigmatic status of selfhood; the moral character of personal identity; the relationship of objective science and subjective ways of knowing; and the interplay of facts and values in positivist and postpositivist science. To integrate these concerns, I have argued for a "moral epistemology," which endeavors to redraw the borders that traditionally have demarcated these topics (1994a; 1999; 2001; 2005; 2009). Following this philosophical path, moral epistemology frames my approach to Freud and his theory, and thus I have extensively drawn on my previous scholarship to make the argument of this book.

Of those with whom I have had the opportunity to discuss my ideas about Freud and psychoanalytic theory directly, Jurgen Reeder (a Swedish psychoanalyst) must be singled out. After completing the first draft of this book, I read his *Reflecting Psychoanalysis* (2002), a work that deserves a wide readership. Since recognizing his book as a companion to my own, we have engaged in a dialogue that has enriched my own interpretation, and I thank him for his critical support of my efforts. To help complete this project, I also gratefully acknowledge the helpful suggestions made by Kevin Amidon, Klaus Brinkman, José Brunner, Antonio Casado da Rocha, Daniel Dahlstrom, Eliahu Ellman, Miriam Ellman, Menachem Fisch, Gideon Freudenthal, Philip Hill, Moshe Halbertal, Yoram Hazony, Moshe Idel, Dani Kremer, W. W. Meissner, Andre Schonberg, Roger Smith, Benjamin Tauber, Dylan Tauber, Josh Weinstein, and David Wiggins. Further, I appreciate the research assistance of Frederick Nitsch. I salute Rob Tempio's good judgment and steadfast support of this project, as well as offer my appreciation to the other staff of Princeton University Press who brought this book through production with admirable professionalism. Most especially, I thank my wife, Paula Fredriksen, who calmly and steadfastly encourages all my efforts in the impatient search for the words of my thoughts and the thought of my words. More, she has been my loving partner in living the interpretation recounted here.

I hereby acknowledge permission to reprint edited portions of previously published papers: sections of chapters 1 and 7, "Freud's Philosophical Path: From a Science of the Mind to a Philosophy of Human Being," *Scandinavian Psychoanalytic Review* 32:32–49 (2009); a segment of chapter 2 dealing with Wittgenstein, as well as note #1, chapter 7 and note #6, chapter 3 have been adopted from my book, *Science and the Quest for Meaning,* Baylor University Press (2009); part of chapter 4, "Freud's Dreams of Reason: The Kantian Structure of Psychoanalysis," *History of the Human Sciences* 22:1–29 (2009); and sections of chapter 6, "The Reflexive Project: Reconstructing the Moral Agent," *History of the Human Sciences* 18:49–75 (2006).

Boscawen, New Hampshire
October 2009

FREUD, THE RELUCTANT PHILOSOPHER

Introduction

Psychoanalysis as Philosophy

Where are the new physicians of the soul?
—Friedrich Nietzsche, *Daybreak* (1982, 33)

FREUD'S CONCEPT—WHEREBY "man lives with his unconscious, not by it" (Meissner 2003, 214)—has vexed critics since its inception. That humans possess a vast reservoir of memories, perceptions, and forms of judgment cannot be denied. Indeed, Freud has been credited with an important role in setting the research agenda for contemporary cognitive psychology (e.g., Pribram and Gill 1976; Erdelyi 1985; Modell 2006; Westen, Weinberger, and Bradley 2007) and many aspects of cognitive science (e.g., Bilder and Lefever 1998; Smith 1999a; Wilson 2002). But the scientific standing of psychoanalysis and of its therapeutic claims has been severely compromised both by a lack of empirical support and its dependence on an outdated biology. Critics, in recognizing the particular cultural influences of fin de siècle Vienna on Freud's construal of emotional life, have leveled powerful arguments. They have portrayed him as a late Victorian thinker whose clinical observations and interpretations reflect the particulars of his time and place and not the timeless properties of personality that he sought to describe. However, as James Strachey whimsically observed about his own analysis with Freud in 1920, "As for what it's all about, I'm vaguer than ever; but.... I daresay there's SOMETHING to it" (quoted by Makari 2008, 342). I concur: Freud did get *something* right, something that remains an enduring contribution to the understanding of the human psyche, and I hope to clarify that *something* here, not by a scientific appraisal, but by a philosophical one. I will not argue that psychoanalysis constitutes a formal philosophy, but I will show that exploring Freud's project with the tools of philosophy offers important insights into psychoanalysis and from that vantage suggest its placement within its broadest intellectual and cultural contexts.[1]

Using the philosophical context in which Freud conceived his theory, this book reconstructs a "dialogue" with key philosophers. That exposition provides an important perspective on the foundations of psychoanalytic theory by analyzing key precepts—the basis of psychic cause; the philosophical standing of the unconscious; the role of rationality; the construction of the subject (i.e., an ego conceived without a "self"); and the ethical structure of self-awareness—as part of a larger philosophical debate. In this analysis, from its depiction of the unconscious to its formulation of mind, psychoanalysis is scrutinized as a philosophic topic. So, on my view, Abraham Kaplan's ironic comment, "Whatever else psychoanalysis has been called, nobody, I think, has accused it of being a philosophy" (1977, 75), requires redress.

Freud's Personae

To begin, one might well ask, *which* Freud? Several images beckon: The first originates in the late 1870s, grows through the mid-1890s, matures by 1910, and flourishes into the early 1920s. This Freud occupies himself with establishing a *science* of the mind based upon positivist precepts. The Freudian unconscious resides in the biological domain, he insisted, and the empiricism of psychoanalysis sought to capture its character scientifically.[2] Accordingly, *Professor* Freud claimed a place for his method and theory within the academy with the other biological sciences.

A complementary identity, the physician, emerges from the first. This second Freud reached beyond positivist biology to achieve his therapeutic goal, namely the rehabilitation of his patient. *Doctor* Freud, rather than assuming the stance of a disinterested observer, becomes an active participant in the process of healing. In this scenario, the radical positivist dichotomy of subject (analyst) and object (patient) collapses as a different dynamic develops between analyst and analysand. Both the emotional content of the "data" and the elements of subjective interpretation would raise theoretical and practical problems for Freud's "science."

A third persona emerges from these biomedical identities. Despite a steadfast commitment to certain scientific ideals, Freud melds into a more speculative theorist after 1913. Beginning with *Totem and Taboo* (1913b), he offered, over the next 25 years, frankly speculative accounts of the primordial family, the character of religion, the psychodynamics of historical figures, the nature of society, and the fate of civilization. Although this shift from individual psychology to various forms of social philosophy did not alter his basic bio-clinical orientation, these later cultural-historical writings were inspired by ambitions to extend his science of the mind to a wide array of humanistic concerns about the existential status of humans, the metaphysics governing their belief systems, the psychology of nations and civilizations, and perhaps most tellingly, the justification for the *kind* of inquiry he had promoted throughout his career. In this last instance, I am referring to the inquiry per se as the means to human freedom and the full potential of human industry. This humanistic Freud remained hidden in the deeper recesses of his personality and appeared once he regarded his scientific work as fundamentally completed. That the *humanist* Freud remained silent for so long reflects the complex political identity he tirelessly promoted and the demands of defending his new "science of the mind."

Yet he appreciated and, perhaps more telling, his readers responded to his wider concerns:

> My interest, after making a lifelong detour through the natural sciences, medicine, and psychotherapy, returned to the cultural problems which had fascinated me long before, when I was a youth scarcely old enough for thinking.... [T]he events of human history, the interactions between human nature, cultural development and the precipitates of primaeval experiences (the most prominent example of which is religion) ... [are] studies, which, though they originate in psychoanalysis, stretch far beyond it, [and] have perhaps awakened more public sympathy than psycho-analysis itself. (Freud 1935, 72)

Freud's enduring interests in what might be termed social or anthropological philosophy, and beneath these disciplines a supportive humanism, offer important clues towards understanding Freud's thinking and the intellectual framework in which to place his work.

In building his theory, Freud adopted, at least implicitly, a philosophy that supported both his science *and* his therapy. For his psychology, he employed a form of naturalism (oriented by evolutionary theories) constructed around a dynamic psychic will; for his therapy, he accepted a mind-body duality, which utilized a conception of reason independent of psychic (biological) forces. The first position reflected his identity as a neuroscientist; the second served his humanism; the former he celebrated; the latter remained subordinate, if not moot, during much of his career. My study moves from the first domain to the second, and in so doing, emphasizes the ethical strengths of psychoanalysis. I thereby seek to replace the endless discussions of Freud's epistemology with a description of psychoanalysis as a moral philosophy. By means of this recontextualization, Freud's project assumes its just standing as an enduring achievement of redefining Western consciousness in its full deployment: Who am I? and What am I to be?

The analysand's internal dialogue addresses no object, but instead becomes a voice of his or her own introspective articulation. In the process, "the self" disappears and only a subject remains, a voice unto itself in dialogue with itself. So the narrator reduces to an unnamed author, in which the commonsensical pronoun (he, she, I) suffices. This pronominal subject represents a general (and implicit) reference to personal identity, namely, a human agent immersed in human activities and concerns. Since that inner voice of self-consciousness is only alluded to and never developed, "the self"—the philosophical category developed throughout the modern period to identify this voice of feeling, consciousness, and rationality—ironically, does not appear in Freud's writings. So we might well ask, "*Who* is the subject?" Is the conscious ego "the self?" If so, to what degree does self-consciousness qualify to establish personal identity in light of the partiality of self-knowledge? And if the conscious ego is *the self*, how are the other elements of the mind placed within the constellation of individual identity? (This confusion has led to many imbroglios, such as legal responsibility for deviant behaviors, not to speak of commonsensical identifications of personhood.)

Freud has reflexivity follow its own course in the modality of free association, and then in a second stage those reflections become the subject of analysis guided by an autonomous rationality. (Note, I am using "reflectivity" in reference to an active introspection, while "reflexivity" denotes a more passive mode of self-consciousness.) Accordingly, the ego's faculty of reason requires (and assumes) degrees of freedom in making its observations and assessments, albeit limited by various psychic obstacles (resistances and defense mechanisms). Through the help of the analyst these barriers may be overcome. So despite an abiding skepticism, Freud nevertheless assumed the integrity and autonomy of ego's reason to conduct its own investigation. However, while the ego represents that faculty of reason, its power or authority is never established.

The nascent object-relations aspects of Freudian theory result from the unsure standing of the ego. Philosophically, that weakness is striking: *Philosophically* the "ego" does not equate with the "self."[3] Indeed, the agent of Freudian psychoanalytic interest remains the self-conscious ego, and the philosophical project of defining the self was never attempted. Instead, Freud dealt with a circumscribed agent, one whose voice of reason engaged in introspective analysis. And that faculty hinged upon a critical turn, one taken with no apparent deliberation (nor clearly articulated), namely, the autonomy of reason, which confers the ability both to (1) scrutinize the natural world and draw judgments about it, and (2) determine moral choice and take ethical action in conjunction with the supervision of the superego. Again, Freud did not specifically define his use of "autonomy," and the word itself only appears once in his entire opus (Kobrin 1993), yet this basic tenet lies embedded within psychoanalytic theory.[4]

Reason's instrumental role promotes the self-interests of the individual and the social collective in which she or he lives. The demands of controlling unconscious desires and at the same time mediating the fulfillment of those desires within the cultural context requires that the ego establish, and enact, an individualized system of value in which desires are weighed and judged on a spectrum wider than immediate pleasure. In the analytic setting, the ego must weigh the strictures of the superego against the drive for instinctual pleasures, and in the interpretative stage of analysis, revise understanding and personal choice. That process mixes ingredients from diverse psychic sources, and, in the end, some rational insight must be coupled to emotional recognition and resolution. While the affective dominion assumes dominance in identifying sources of neurotic thought and behavior, it is reason that finally must adjudicate and ultimately govern through its insight and rationalization. From a philosophical perspective (as opposed to clinical), this latter aspect of psychoanalysis is emphasized here in order to understand reason's dual roles, namely, not only enforcing ethical conduct but also establishing moral coordinates of behavior. Indeed, to recall the leading epigraph to this book, for Freud, reason is humankind's only hope.

By placing the unconscious in the *body*, and the knowing, deliberating ego in the *rational mind*, Freud understood Reason just as Kant had originally configured his own transcendental project: An autonomous rationality allows the mind to examine nature independent of natural cause; and the selfsame autonomy of reason confers on humans their sovereign free will, which in turn establishes their ethical standing, namely the ability to assume responsibility for their actions. This conception offered Freud's patients the option of exercising interpretative reason, coupled to affective recognition, to achieve control of their lives: Insight and catharsis (Laplanche and Pontalis 1973, 60–61) led (at least potentially) to freedom from the shackles of a despotic unreason. Exactly *how* (and whether) such clarity worked to achieve emotional liberation remains an unresolved claim, but putting aside the theoretical mechanisms and clinical data upon which most debate revolves, I endeavor to characterize the *philosophical* foundations of psychoanalysis and, in so doing, explain Freud's lasting contribution.

In broad outline, we begin with a description of Freud's struggle to establish psychic determinism and how that problem, formulated by his philosophical mentor, Brentano, haunted the development of psychoanalysis. After an extended examination of certain aspects of Freud's epistemology, we then probe the foundations of his moral inquiry as configured by Kantianism. That formulation establishes the basis for interpreting Freud's multifaceted characterization of human agency, again situated within the nineteenth-century philosophical tradition. This narrative exploits multiple perspectives, for no single, encompassing description suffices to capture the philosophical complexity of Freudianism. In some cases we have evidence that Freud was aware of the philosophical traditions in which he worked, and in other respects certain influences percolated down to him through secondary sources and influential mentors. From that composite, he took sides—rejecting certain philosophical positions and adopting others—in order to address various agendas. Accordingly, he drew from competing philosophies, mixed his science with a unique hermeneutics (Gill 1994; Brook 1995), and configured the human simultaneously in the biological and the moral domains. Based on these multiple perspectives, this book describes the philosophical heterodoxy of the theory, and more specifically, how it catches various elements of different philosophical schools and refracts them with its peculiar lens. In short, to portray psychoanalysis philosophically, we must draw from many reservoirs.

Upon this framework a conceptual scaffolding becomes available for placing the various components of psychoanalytic theory: the positivists provided the basic epistemological schema; metaphysically, Freud followed Kant's approach to the determinism–free will paradox, which lies at the heart of psychoanalysis; and with Hegel, Schopenhauer, Kierkegaard, and Nietzsche, Freud joined a great debate about the nature of human identity.[5] From that discussion, the ethics of psychoanalysis emerge, for the manner in which the agent is construed determines the character of the ethics associated with the subject (Tauber 2001; 2005). So while Freud cannot formally be placed among the philosophers, he nevertheless may profitably be regarded from their vantage in order to better understand his own undertaking, and perhaps more importantly, by considering him in that tradition, we enrich our own philosophical understanding of the matters he considered so profoundly. From this perspective, matters pertinent to psychoanalytic practice and clinical interpretations fall well beyond the borders of my inquiry:

1. Although psychoanalysis as "science" first framed, and then dominated, the debate about the status of the discipline, its truth claims, its therapeutic efficacy, and finally, its role as an intellectual enterprise (Decker 1977; Hook 1959), I consider that discussion, at least in its formal terms, moribund. While scientific knowledge serves Westerners as the basis of truth, when the debate was posed in these terms, psychoanalysis failed the standards of Freud's day (Decker 1977) and even more so the gauntlet of later critics (e.g., Grünbaum 1984; Eysenck 1985; Crews 1986; Holt 1989; Webster 1995; Macmillan 1997; Cioffi 1998a). Indeed, the scientific status of Freud's theory could not fairly articulate the critical importance of psychoanalysis for defining notions of personal identity and reconstructing that identity

along normative lines. My interpretation thus eschews further appraisals of Freud's scientific thinking, and, instead, we will consider other
modes of knowledge more appropriate to the task of characterizing
psychoanalysis.

2. I resist the pull of debating the merits of Freud's enterprise as a
psycho*therapy*. Although relief of suffering provides psychoanalysis
with an essential orientation, the efficacy of psychoanalysis as a *clinical* endeavor is not examined. For my purposes, understanding that the
clinical outcome of analysis assigns a telos to the investigation suffices.
Freud himself, towards the end of his career, had subordinated the clinical program by forthrightly aligning psychoanalysis with *psychology*,
leaving "medicine" (i.e., therapeutics) to lesser interest.[6] I see this shift
as part of Freud's trajectory towards his original humanist concerns,
and, aligned with this movement, I suggest he acknowledged misgivings that he had achieved the *scientific* results he had hoped to establish. Accepting the clinical limits of psychoanalysis, we are left with
what I believe is Freud's abiding contribution—the *humanist* project
he developed under the auspices of psychoanalysis. Accordingly, scant
attention is paid to his descriptions of the various psychic complexes
or to the standing of Freud's more narrow theoretical concerns. Instead, this study follows the broad outlines of Freud's own intellectual
biography, namely, the shift from a postulated science of the mind to a
humanist inquiry of the soul.

3. Because my discussion seeks to capture the cardinal philosophical
elements of psychoanalysis, the vicissitudes Freud's theory suffered at
the hands of his various followers (Brown 1964; Roazen 1975; Makari 2008) do not pertain to this study. Anna Freud had correctly concluded, even before her father died, that orthodox theory had been
replaced by various psychoanalytic schools, which must be considered
part of the ongoing process of creating a psychoanalytic psychology
and psychiatry (A. Freud 1967). I would not claim she advocated
ecumenical peace, but she did highlight what should have appeared
obvious to the most impassioned champion of one group or another,
namely that psychoanalysis by the 1920s, both theoretically and socially, had assumed diverse theoretical orientations, but nevertheless,
principles of therapy *built upon* the original foundations.[7] These later

disputes simply highlight the strength of Freud's influence, which must reside in the deepest structures of his thought. Thus, while I acknowledge the heterodoxy of psychoanalysis, which in turn reflects the diversity of interpretations of Freudianism, again, I am not concerned with endorsing or rejecting the particularities of Freud's clinical theory.

Kantian Themes

As summarized below, the first three chapters of this book deal with key aspects of Freud's epistemology and metaphysics, while the last three chapters explore the general outline of the ethics that underlie psychoanalysis. The middle chapter (chapter 4) then serves as the narrative's hinge to bridge the discussion of how Freud employed Kantian precepts to develop a philosophy of moral agency. Indeed, Kant, in striking ways, served as Freud's philosophical North Star. In elaborating psychoanalysis, Freud sought to establish a model built on psychic cause. He argued, on the one hand, that humans are subject to unconscious activities (framed within a biological conception), and, on the other hand, that the rational faculty of the ego permits, given proper support and articulation, the means of both understanding the deterministic forces of the unconscious and freeing the rational ego from their authority. The entire enterprise depends on an implicit notion of autonomy, whose exercise would free the analysand from the tyranny of unconsciousness in order to pursue the potential of human creativity and freedom.

Thus in the effort to liberate an ensnared psyche, psychoanalysis depends on an ego capable of separating itself from its own instinctual biology and thus radically distinguishing itself from the causation sequences described by objective analysis. This basic schema, of course, simplifies Freudian concepts of the ego and the unconscious as somehow radically dissociated, when in the later development of his theory, Freud posited a structure with considerable overlap. But in the analytic context, rational reconstruction of complex early experience generates understanding (and perhaps therapeutic results) only because of reason's autonomy. This conception of reason is lifted directly from Kant, and like Kant, Freud employed this rationality for both epistemological and moral ends. Epistemologically, the study of the (natural) unconscious domain of the mind followed a strategy indebted to Kant's conception of reason, namely a faculty independent of nature and thus able to study phenomena and generalize laws describing natural causes. And beyond this epistemological formulation, reason's autonomy represented the fundamental requirement for Kant's notion of moral responsibility. Accordingly, Freud relied on reason's autonomy to establish criteria of normative behaviors; more deeply, reason so configured offers the means for establishing psychological freedom from oppressive psychic drives.

I am not suggesting that Freud closely followed Kant to the extent of seeing the categorical imperative, the kingdom of ends, and the negation of self-interest as the content of some true moral system. Further, I am not arguing that Freud followed Kant in terms of the *content* of moral philosophy; for example, he did not subscribe to the renunciation of self-interest as the basis of morals at all. And perhaps most saliently, Freud did not derive "autonomy" from a conception of the self, the argument that because humans are rational and reason permits only one moral law, we are free because we dictate the one moral law to ourselves. However, while Freud did *not* follow key tenets of Kant's moral philosophy, he *did* adopt from Kant the broader framework in which the autonomy of reason is the basis for the personal struggle to establish a life deemed "free." In this sense, Freud radically reconfigured Kant's original formulation much along the lines Nietzsche pursued.

This interpretation fuses two distinct notions of autonomy. Nietzsche's moral scheme is typically taken to be almost perfectly opposed to that of Kant, inasmuch as they are presenting two opposing conceptions of morality. For Kant, the self-dictated law is one and universal; for Nietzsche, the transfiguration of values replaces the unitary with a radical pluralism, in which emerges a unique expression of one's own personal needs and requirements for "health" (Tauber and Podolsky 1999). On this axis, Freud closely aligns with Nietzsche in both the flexibility of the norms governing behavior and perhaps more importantly in the potential for self-determined choice on a spectrum of options. So for Freud and Nietzsche, autonomy has shifted from recognizing the rational and some universal moral order to a radical individualism, where autonomy enacts the characterization of human potential, a potential that would move biologically driven humans to a new moral order (Tauber 1995). What separates Nietzsche and Freud is the role of reason: Nietzsche celebrates the instincts, while Freud champions the reason that would control them. In that triangulation, I place Freud between Kant and Nietzsche.

In this general scheme, a complex duet is played out between Kant and Nietzsche, where psychoanalysis offers a promissory note: Take one's history in hand to command the effect of emotional traumas to declare a liberation and the forthright assertion of personal autonomy for a life of meaningful love and work. Here we hear most clearly the call of Nietzsche's Zarathustra, who demands that humans strive towards some as yet unrealized ideal. The notion that such a venture is feasible, that it is morally inspired, that it serves to actualize human potential, has carried forth the Romantic expression of individuality to become a credo of contemporary Western societies. Psychoanalysis, as a means of personal investigation, thereby becomes a tool for self-responsible choices directed towards that ideal. Outlining that effort and inspired by its possibilities, Freud legitimately becomes a vital author of contemporary ethics. Indeed, I will argue that dwelling on Freud's epistemological quandary displaces the more essential moral query he assigned himself.

From this vantage, I see Freud's science evolving into the humanist project mentioned above. Freud's thought thus coordinates two philosophical axes: The first concerns the establishment of a "scientific" phenomenology of the mind, which is basically reductive in character; the second "humanistic" vector, holistic and constructive, directs the interpretation towards certain humanistic ideals, whose values and purpose, while distinct from the scientific venture, directs psychoanalysis. In short, Freud transfigured his clinical insights into a mode of ethical inquiry guided by the hopes of human potential.

Freud the Ethicist

Of course the definition of individual freedom and the boundaries inside which choice might be taken constitute key questions of lingering interest in assessing psychoanalysis. Indeed, to what degree does psychoanalytic insight command the unconscious? Needless to remind readers, over this issue furious battles have been fought, but at the very least, for Freud, the ends of interpretation are emotional recognition and rational insight directed towards change. And this position decisively shifts the question from the epistemological domain to the moral. On this view, although psychoanalysis may fail to offer a Nietzschean liberation (cure) as Herbert Marcuse (1955) and Norman O. Brown (1959) prophesied, analysis promises at least to provide Spinozean insight, which in itself comprises an ethics. Beyond the analysis qua analysis, a revised understanding of one's personal history, behaviors, choices, maladjustments, conflicts, and neuroses allows some reconstructed understanding of one's personal identity, goals, and placement in the world. Here I am referring to certain commitments made towards some normative ideal. Indeed, Freud wrote quite explicitly on this normative structure: "*Analysis replaces repression by condemnation*" (Freud 1909b, 145), by which he meant that the ego asserts control on acting out desires or breaking constraints. That telos not only defines the trajectory of analysis, but establishes the *possibility* for a revised personhood. Through psychoanalysis, the burdens of early experience, namely the identification of the residua of lingering oppressive neuroses that distort personal potentials, are shed or reworked to allow a form of rebirth, an *autopoiesis*. The sheer audacity of the project divides unequivocally between those who declare "their heartfelt wish that Freud might never have been born" (Forrester 1997, 9) and others who believe that he deserves defense as "a great philosopher" (Cavell 2001) or "revolutionary" (Lear 1990, 3).

Freud's grandiose ambitions have been extensively listed and examined by his biographers, and suffice it to note a single famous anecdote:

> Freud clearly fancied himself an Oedipus, defeating the dark riddling voices of the subconscious. When, on his fiftieth birthday (1906), a number of his intimates presented him with a medallion engraved with a portrait of himself on the obverse, and a replica of Oedipus answering the Sphinx on the reverse, he turned pale. Next to the nude Oedipus, the following words from Sophocles' *Oedipus Tyrannos* were inscribed (line 1525): "Who divined the famed riddle and was a man most mighty." (Scully 1997, 230)[8]

Ernest Jones explained the "pale and agitated" reaction as due to Freud's belief that he had encountered

> a *revenant*, and so he had.... Freud disclosed that as a young student at the University of Vienna he used to stroll around the great arcaded court inspecting the busts of former famous professors of the institution. He then had the phantasy, not merely of seeing his own bust there in the future, which would not have been anything remarkable in an ambitious student, but of it actually being inscribed with the *identical* words he now saw on the medallion. (Jones 1953–57, 2:14)

Indeed, Freud attempted to create no less than an entire philosophy of history and culture. While he was roundly criticized for these speculative ventures, he felt fully justified, because he held that psychoanalysis had captured certain universal truths about human nature. Thus the science, which he himself recognized was not fully developed (e.g., Freud 1920, 60), nevertheless offered him a platform upon which to develop the theory well beyond its original intent. And, of course, he would not be inhibited.[9]

In acknowledging the limits of his scientific enterprise, Freud himself referred to his theory of the instincts (*Die Trieblehre*) as "our mythology" (1933, 95) and famously admitted to Einstein, "Does not every science come in the end to a kind of mythology like this? Cannot the same be said to-day of your Physics?" (Freud 1932, 211). This "codicil" refers not only to the provisional character of scientific theory (Fulgencio 2005), but also to a metaphysical boundary, a domain beyond human understanding, which he believed lies under all human knowledge. Again, Freud drew on a Romantic idea:

> The ultimate basis on which all our knowledge and science rest is the inexplicable. Therefore every explanation leads back to this by means of more or less intermediate stages, just as in the sea the plummet finds the bottom sometimes at a greater and sometimes at a lesser depth, yet everywhere it must ultimately reach this. This inexplicable something devolves on metaphysics. (Schopenhauer 1974b, 2:3)

In this sense, Freud thought he had plumbed the depths of the psyche and discerned the dynamics governing behavior, but only to a level that human reason permitted. The unique grammar and semantics he had devised were only "logical" inventions to describe that which had no logic. So in admitting the limits of psychoanalytic *science*, Freud devised a *mythology* to express the inexplicable.

Psychoanalysis leads Freud to the mythic hero, who knows his fate and still struggles against it with the use of two tools: reason and the imperative to *know*. Freud, like the ancient Greek tragedians, presented his drama of the human being on a mythic stage. The métier was "science," but the psychoanalytic "play" emerged from a creative amalgamation of fact and fancy; of history and memory; of knowledge and imagination to reenact an ancient myth about human nature. Analysands tell a tragic story: Humans, destined to know their past and having lived the fate of their experience, come, like Oedipus, to understand the true character and deeper meanings of that experience, and thus finally come to answer the fundamental question, Who am I? The analysand must take her place among several actors in her psychic drama, and while holding some sense of self-identity, she also must recognize that in the recesses of a distant childhood, others have impacted and molded her to behave defensively in a world, where even those who love and secure her have inflicted trauma and lasting wounds. Unable to change the course of one's life, the only recourse resides in *recognition* and *reconciliation,* and then ultimately, *responsibility* to take hold of one's nature (Lear 1990, 170–72; Sherman 1995; Reeder 2002). The analysand, as Oedipus, then follows the tragic course of self-knowledge, and in the full encounter with the past, understands the impact of her unique heritage that has cast the injured into the world. The dual message of psychoanalysis thus fulfills the tragic criteria of self-knowledge, acknowledgement, acceptance, and then transformation.

This passage of the hero marks a rite, a stage of maturation, presented in the language of advanced Western societies and yet resonating with the classical origins of our civilization. While following a clinical scenario, analytic insight and the accompanying emotional recognition reenacts a passage described by the ancients and reenacted in various modern contexts (Campbell 1949; Rank 2004; Rudnytsky 1987; Bowlby 2007). The "myth of psychoanalysis" is not a *fiction*, but rather a complex description of the psyche using allusions and metaphors coupled to an analytic.

In this sense, Freud created a new dramatic form—the dominant myth of the twentieth century—where the Oedipal story becomes universal, not so much as a story of psychosexual development, but as an expression of the more general plight of human existence.[10]

Psychoanalytic tenets continue to exert a profound influence on how we have come to understand personal agency, because whatever is discarded from the particulars of Freudian theory, the contours of his basic investigation remain intact and continue to guide contemporary conceptions of personal identity and the hope for individual growth and self-fulfillment. Building on the psychoanalytic schema, Freudianism has defined the general parameters by which these various aspects of personhood might be understood. He demanded forthright exposure and discussion of that which creates a disjunction between what we strive for and what we in fact *do* and *experience*. In this sense, Freud created a moral investigation of great power and influence, not in the classical sense of presenting a systematic procedure for determining ethical choices, but rather in asserting the basis for human action—a self-awareness, driven by an appreciation of counterforces—that choice beckons. More, choice arises from recognizing new opportunities. So, in acknowledging the pervasive influence of unconscious forces, understanding devolves into freedom. Introspection results in rewriting the personal narrative, and from this critical vantage I maintain that reflexive interpretation not only defines what psychoanalysis *is* and *how* it does whatever it does, but that the *process* of analysis itself is fundamentally an ethical venture as defined above. As a theory of interpretation, psychoanalysis offered philosophy an application, or a mode of "practical philosophy," that still awaits further development.

Given Freud's commitments to a biological conception of the psyche, the promise offered by psychoanalysis represents a remarkable synthesis of an outstanding tension. In this regard, Freud must be considered philosophically inspired; perhaps a "naturalized" philosopher, certainly a reluctant practitioner, but one who nevertheless followed a quest to better understand the evolution of culture, the character of human history, and the existential standing of human beings. On this reading, the promised result of psychoanalytic investigations resides in the humanistic realization of human potential—enacted beyond the domain of scientism.

Following the ancient ethical precept of "Know thyself," Freud held that insight per se is a moral achievement: self-reflection becomes a moral undertaking, because self-knowledge provides the perspective required for ethical deliberation. Freud's stew of epistemological ideas obscures this deeper ethical character of his theory and practice, and whether he succeeded or failed as a clinician does not alter the basic moral thrust of psychoanalytic theory.

Narrative Outline

The first three chapters consider key aspects of Freud's epistemology, the larger context of his positivist aspirations, and the limits of that approach as applied to psychoanalysis. Thus we begin with Freud's early years at the University of Vienna, where he studied philosophy under the tutelage of Brentano, the charismatic and highly influential forerunner of twentieth-century phenomenology and various schools of logic. Freud encountered Brentano at the exact moment his mentor sought to establish the philosophical basis of the new science of psychology as an empirical discipline. Brentano devoted considerable attention to various theories of the unconscious, only to reject each. In so doing, he presented the conceptual obstacles such theories faced, which Freud would later work to overcome.

Freud's attempt to establish a science of the mind begins with the philosophical challenge posed by Brentano, reviewed in chapter 1. Throughout Freud's long defense of his own work, Brentano's adamant rejection of an "unconscious" persisted as a lingering shadow to interrogate Freudian tenets, and, indeed, Brentano had set the legitimizing criteria and the conceptual template for Freud's own investigations and justifications (Brentano 1973, 107). I argue that Brentano's original objections continued to haunt Freud, and from that tension, Freud's later theory found its orientation, specifically, an argument built from cause. On this reading, Freud's claims for the scientific basis of psychoanalysis were framed in answer to Brentano. Inasmuch as Freud destroyed his early correspondence (Freud 1960, 141), we have only remnants of biographical data to support this interpretation.

The empirical basis of psychoanalysis has been understood in myriad ways, and chapter 2 defines two logical challenges: The first concerns the

Freudian syllogism for establishing the causal inference of the unconscious, which I maintain demonstrates a circular argument; the second restates Wittgenstein's cogent observation that reasons are not causes, at least not in the sense in which psychoanalytic explanations assert, and that Freud's causal logic conflates reasons and causes. These arguments are supported by Freud's own doubts expressed late in his career, where the adamancy of his scientific posture is mitigated by an open-minded acknowledgment that the discipline required a more robust development. More, I maintain that Freud, at the end of his career, acknowledged that he ultimately built his theory on an assumption, and by rigorous Brentanean criteria, he had failed to establish its scientific basis. These considerations then lead to the logical positivists and Karl Popper, who together would reject the entry of psychoanalysis into the halls of science. Exploring their position highlights not only the weaknesses of Freud's *scientific* endeavor, but points to another direction in which we might salvage his efforts and recognize his accomplishments.

Chapter 3 places Freud firmly within the most pertinent philosophical debates of his own period by comparing and contrasting his positivist commitments to the critiques offered by historicists (represented by Wilhelm Dilthey) and neo-Kantians (Friedrich Lange and Wilhelm Windelband). Together their respective philosophies offer, on the one hand, a powerful rejoinder to the positivist view of unmediated empiricism and, on the other hand, a spirited defense of the human sciences that must rely on other modalities of understanding. Indeed, late-nineteenth-century neo-Kantians were principally concerned with the limits of knowledge and the purging of metaphysics from their epistemologies. In this regard they joined ranks with positivists, but unlike them, they were highly suspicious of positivism's embrace of an uncritical empiricism and therefore more skeptical about the presumed ability to capture "the real" in any final fashion. Of these, Lange and Windelband (from different origins) set the agenda for those who rejected the incipient scientism generated by the technical successes of the positivist program. In opposing the positivists, they held that the restraints of the mind's inner structure and basic organization left the world-in-itself ultimately unknowable. Experience of that world was thus limited by the mediation of various categories of understanding that Kant originally described in the transcendental deduction developed in the *Critique of Pure Reason*. From that epistemological position, these neo-Kantians believed that "philosophy can identify the limits of knowledge ... [but] beyond these limits ... philosophy itself can no longer establish any substantive conclusions" (Windelband quoted by Bambach 1995, 81).

Freud rejected such skepticism and instead accepted the immediacy of experience and the objectivity of scientific observation, inasmuch as he sought, and then prescribed, a positivist approach to his own clinical-based description of the mind. That mode of investigation denied its own reliance on a weak fact/value distinction (that would eventually collapse in post–World War II critiques of the positivist position [Tauber 2009]) and certain metaphysical assumptions, which in several respects further weakens psychoanalytic theory. Following consideration of the epistemological arguments offered by the neo-Kantians, we are ready to return to Kant and configure Freud's theory from a Kantian perspective.

Of the various components of Kant's system, the one most relevant to this discussion focuses upon the fundamental dilemma of reconciling the determinism of the natural world (in this case, the influences of the unconscious) and the autonomy of reason, which bestows moral responsibility and free choice. And in parallel, the unresolved tension in psychoanalytic thinking arises from these competing visions of human nature, namely a biologically conceived organism subject to primitive drives and a rational faculty independent of those deterministic forces. To delineate Freud's own understanding of this problem, chapter 4 describes the conception of Kant's formulation of reason's autonomy and how Freud employed that schema for very different purposes.

On this Kantian view, psychoanalysis becomes an ethical inquiry, similarly based on reason's emancipation and the potential of freeing humans from what Kant called their "immaturity" (1996d), and which Freud described in clinical terms of dysfunctional defenses, neuroses, and repressions. At this point, we are in a position to expose the fundamental tension in psychoanalytic theory, a beguiling paradox in which natural cause and moral reason—determinism and freedom—are conjoined despite their apparent logical exclusion. Notwithstanding reason's standing, its authority remains disputed, even problematic, in the Freudian universe, because rationality is always in precarious balance with its counterpoise—the pervasive power of the arational. Analysis raises self-consciousness to a new level of complexity. Self-consciousness itself becomes acutely self-conscious in the encounter with the unconscious, which appears as radically enigmatic, even a stranger, to the (rational) ego. More, that primordial element behaves dangerously, not only as a result of its unpredictability, but also because its control is always in question, and so the unresolved challenge to Freudianism circles around the ability of reason to accomplish its assigned tasks. Given Freud's respect for the power of the unconscious, he might well have aligned himself with Hume's prescription of ethics as rationalized emotion and thereby discounted the ability of rational thought to distinguish subjective self-interest from more complex choices. When discussing the superego, a Humean dynamic is operative, but in the context discussed here—moral inquiry as a deliberate and enlightened pursuit—Freud sided with Kant.

This tension is further explored in chapter 5, where Freud's understanding of the biological character of human nature resides in a powerful critique of Kantianism. At one level, Freud simply accepts the biological basis of human agency, which appropriately follows the logic of his clinical and scientific training. Committed to the naturalism of the laboratory and hospital, Freud comfortably affiliated with the biomedical models of his era, and in the context of the *philosophical* understanding of this dimension of human nature, he closely aligned himself with the Nietzschean-Schopenhaurean line of post-Kantian philosophy. Clearly, Schopenhauer and Nietzsche complement Freud's own conception of the ego as biologically derived from, and subject to, primordial organic drives and instincts.

Schopenhauer contested Kant's conception of the noumenal self, and replaced that formulation with the notion of the self as divided by demands of "representation" and "will." However, just as Kant failed to reconcile the intersection of two kinds of reason, Schopenhauer failed to resolve the conundrum of dividing agency into two domains, and only with Nietzsche does the will alone triumph, with "representation" assuming a subordinate position. Putting aside the influence Nietzsche might have had on Freud, we must appreciate how their respective notions of the organic basis of human nature help explicate the grounding of psychoanalytic theory. Nietzsche's Will to Power places humans firmly in the domain of the biological, where vitality reduced to instinctual conflict resonates powerfully with Freud's own conception. For each of them, despite multiple layers of history, culture, and psychological denial of this instinctual realm, the psyche is best characterized from the perspective of animal origins, whose primitive markings Freud sought and interpreted.

The consequences of the instinctual orientation present a moral agent essentially individualized and independent, so when others appear in the psychic drama, they generally become contestants. However, while an atomistic ethos enacts much of Freud's and Nietzsche's respective conceptions of human striving, this aspect alone does not encompass Freud's moral project, which offered an ethical response to the dangers of unchecked human instincts. Bona fide self-awareness and reason coincides with the voice of analysis, whose strategic placement is a given as an "ego" constrained by rational self-awareness. Presumably, the ego's self-consciousness must be accounted for as the result of human evolutionary history (Wegner 2002), but Freud never interrogates its philosophical identity, and following the genealogy of his thought, he built upon an understanding of introspective self-reflection whose autonomous character is fraught with unresolved difficulties.

Chapter 6 explores Freud's complex use of reflexivity, whose history marks much of post-Kantian philosophy. Reflexivity, at least in the modern context, begins with Descartes and evolves into a particular dialogical mode with Hegel's dialectic. In the seventeenth century, "reflexivity" was coined as a new term for introspection and self-awareness. It thus served the instrumental function of combating skepticism by asserting a knowing self. In this Cartesian paradigm, introspection ends in self-identity. An alternate interpretation recognized that an infinite regress of reflexivity would render "the self" elusive, if not unknowable. Reflexivity in this latter mode was rediscovered by Hegel, who defined the self through the encounter with an Other: The introspective process ends when the self-contained individual confronts the Other and thereby articulates its own identity in that engagement. With this background, building on the complex interplay of the reflexivity theme, we will see the origins of Freud's own (undeveloped) object-relations psychology, and more deeply, the philosophical character of self-consciousness he employed.

As already mentioned, Freudian psychoanalytic explorations are organized with a "voice" pursuing its own subterranean workings, and in this sense, the ego (and only part of the ego) possesses a faculty seemingly independent of the mind's biological substratum. Freud thus based his science on a biological conception of human nature, but he characterized the interpretative faculty as a humanist. This basic unresolved tension, truly the paradox of a free willed-reason coupled to deterministic unconscious forces, demands address. Exploring the moral implications of this schema frames chapter 7, where we examine how, through various modes of human identification and interpretation, psychoanalysis presents a method by which the analysand attempts to redefine herself in hope of more effectively pursuing satisfying love and work. In this context, "moral" refers to the values that orient individual needs and motivations. Defined by the existential and psychological challenges of the analysand, Freud's criteria reflected underlying currents of Romantic and Enlightenment ideals, which in turn are based on a humanist vision of human potential. So beyond the character of human nature exposed by Freud's inquiry, the humanistic configuration of psychoanalysis as a therapy for a sick soul tilts his endeavor towards a tempered optimism.

Totally committed to the process of self-exploration, Freud's moral inquiry became his key philosophical expression. In this sense, we have come full circle: Freud's project as read through a humanist lens fulfills a complementary aspect of the scientific project, one inspired by his earliest interests. Viewed in this manner, the philosophical conundrum of self-consciousness—residing at the core of the issue of the self—shifts from a *problem* to a *solution*, for with the ongoing, ceaseless process of self-examination, the inquirer adopts a method to achieve the insight at the core of philosophical inquiry. Of course, the inquiry is never completed (e.g., Wittgenstein 1968, sec. 133, p. 51e), but Freud, the physician, declares his therapeutic intent based on the ongoing inquiry itself: For him, self-awareness becomes a vehicle to carry insight, which in turn begets liberation through an affective transaction conducted through the unconscious communication of analysand and analyst (Freud 1912a, 111). Acute self-reflectivity thus becomes a value, sui generis.

Note, as already mentioned, Freud takes this position facing an unresolved metaphysical quandary: From the scientific milieu in which he worked, psychoanalysis is based upon the causal chain of the unconscious, and from another domain he assigned freedom of choice through both emotional enactment and rational insight. So the analysand's conviction that she has free will and through understanding may achieve liberation from crippling unconscious forces opposes the fundamental commitment to a biological determinism from which Freud makes no attempt to escape. This determinism–free will paradox pits the two poles of psychoanalytic theory in fixed and irresolvable opposition. The concluding comments weigh these positions and find that in the calculus of Freud's thought, his humanism—the logic inherent in the hope of self-determination and heroic engagement—ultimately puts the entire psychoanalytic enterprise within the Enlightenment and Romantic ideals of human achievement and thus ultimately sides with freedom.

No doubt Freud was pessimistic, but I maintain that his pessimism was coupled to psychoanalytic cures and from those accomplishments he steadfastly proceeded to develop his theory, both practically and conceptually. The method rested on a complex configuration of rational insight and catharsis, which then leads to some degree of control of unconscious drives. This key presupposition of an emotional reenactment coupled to rationality's promise, presented as a given, I regard as a problem that reappears in different guises throughout Freud's opus. Chapter 4 presents the version of reason I see Freud lifting from Kant, and the following chapters refract that form of rationality: chapter 5 in juxtaposition to Schopenhauer and Nietzsche; chapter 6 in regards to the silent "self"; chapter 7 in the context of the moral interpretation I offer.

The précis of the story: Freud translated Kant's admonition that we strive for "maturity" (1996d) into a program that drew deeply from Western notions of personhood: autonomy coupled to emotional dependency; personal responsibility shackled to deterministic forces; self-consciousness aware of an elusive subterranean identity. Despite the inextricable linkage of these couplets, he remained committed (albeit cautiously, even skeptically) to the exercise of self-determination, perfectionism, and the power of reason, to seek (and perhaps achieve) self-fulfillment and some form of self-redemption. In formalizing our vague intuitions that we are not necessarily the identities we project (or even know), he radically altered Western notions of personal identity. A new self-conscious awareness was thus born, and because the full development of identity politics created by his insights have yet to be exhausted, Freud's philosophy—unsystematic, deliberately undeclared, and often ill-formed—commands abiding interest.

Chapter One _____

The Challenge (and Stigma) of Philosophy

> As for the biographers, let them worry, we have no desire
> to make it too easy for them. Each one of them will be
> right in his opinion of "The Development of the Hero,"
> and I am already looking forward to seeing them go astray.
> —Sigmund Freud, letter to Martha Bernays,
>   April 28, 1885 (1960, 141)

WHAT ARE THE PHILOSOPHICAL ANTECEDENTS of Freud's attempt to establish a science of the mind? As already briefly mentioned, during his early university days Freud explicitly rejected philosophy, because of its "speculative" character. He struggled with balancing the intellectual appeal of philosophy with the "certainty" he hoped to find in positivist science. That move heralded the series of clinical studies that would eventually emerge in the therapeutic system of psychoanalysis, a psychiatry he would consistently call a "science." Freud never abandoned his commitment to scientific knowledge and perhaps more importantly, scientific reason. As he wrote late in his life, "Our best hope for the future is that intellect—the scientific spirit, reason—may in the process of time establish a *dictatorship* in the mental life of man" (1933, 171; emphasis added). Yet the currency of the therapeutic encounter is emotional, and to objectify the subjective would be a daunting challenge. Nevertheless, Freud hoped to distance himself from the analysand to the extent that allowed a scrupulous assessment, and in that pose, he wore the mantle of clinician and scientist seeking an objective description of psychic events and behavior.[1] Putting aside the scientific status of Freud's work, the focus of my immediate concern rests on Freud's own attitude towards philosophy. Failing to recognize the assumptions of his own investigations, he segregated psychoanalysis from "philosophy" on the charge that philosophers equated mind with consciousness. Furthermore, they propounded unfounded speculations and assumed false conceits of comprehensiveness. Indeed, throughout Freud's early and late writings, psychoanalysis seemingly had no weltanschauung beyond that of science itself (e.g., Freud 1894, 1933, 158ff.), which, following a clinical empiricism, embraced positivist tenets. That philosophical structure largely defined the development and presentation of his "new science."

The stigma of philosophy never lifted, and even in Freud's most speculative essays, he maintained that his critical views of religion, social organization, the future of civilization, the character of art, and so on, were legitimate extrapolations of his clinical findings, and thus they assumed a different character than those methods or interpretations that could not claim some scientific basis for their respective approaches. Thus for Freud, psychoanalysis offered a positivist basis for understanding complex human behaviors and institutions and thereby distinguished itself from previous speculative philosophies. He donned the scientific cloak even when proselytizing. Of several disavowals, this one, from his *Autobiography*, succinctly states his argument:

> I should not like to create an impression that during this last period of my work I have turned my back upon patient observation and have abandoned myself entirely to speculation. I have on the contrary always remained in the closest touch with the analytic material and have never ceased working at detailed points of clinical or technical importance. Even when I have moved away from observation, I have carefully avoided any contact with philosophy proper. This avoidance has been greatly facilitated by constitutional incapacity. (1925a, 59)

However, this self-assessment is too simple, and thus incorrect. While he was not a philosopher, Freud knew philosophy and drew from that tradition as he built his theory, consciously or not.

Certainly, by 1913, when Freud began to shift his thinking about the ego's structure (e.g., 1914a; 1917a) and its relationships with others (1913b), his writings exhibited an altered character and eventually assumed a new identity under the guise of a "metapsychology." So while he continued to espouse positivist ideals for the science of psychoanalysis, he acknowledged that he had returned "after making a lifelong *détour* through the natural sciences, medicine, and psychotherapy ... to the cultural problems which had fascinated me long before, when I was a youth scarcely old enough for thinking" (Freud 1935 72). As explained below, Freud retreated from orthodox philosophy for science, but that abandonment was to a particular brand of philosophizing. "Philosophy" for him was represented by the lingering influence of idealism and more generally what Freud called "speculative" and "totalizing" philosophies. His aversion to philosophy's confusion and critical faults led him to focus on an epistemology more to his liking, which also meant forsaking his earlier humanistic ambitions. As he later explained, "In my youth I felt an overpowering need to understand something of the riddles of the world in which we live and perhaps even to contribute something to their solution" (1927a, 253). Most immediately that meant research in a physiology laboratory, but underlying that work, Freud held to a much broader agenda.[2]

Ambivalence marks Freud's relationship to philosophy. In a letter written to Wilhelm Fliess on New Year's Day, 1896, Freud admits to a powerful philosophical inclination:

> I see how, via the detour of medical practice, you are reaching your first ideal of understanding human beings as a physiologist, just as I most secretly nourish the hope of arriving, via these same paths, at my initial goal of philosophy. For that is what I wanted originally, when it was not yet at all clear to me to what end I was in the world. (1985, 159)

While the extent Freud held to his earliest desires, of course, cannot be resolved, one might fairly conclude that he went through several stages and seemed ever-conscious of the philosophical context of his thinking.

A duality complicates Freud's ambitions. Just as he mused about his philosophical interests, he composed the most positivist models of the mind. This scientific orientation is clearly demonstrated in his 1896 correspondence with Fliess, where he reported to his friend the schema of the *Project for a Scientific Psychology* ("Draft K" of the correspondence). There he revealed his commitment to neurophysiology as classically conceived. Although he called the project a "Christmas Fairy Tale" (1985, 162), Freud postulated a model of the mind where neuronal integration and organization was to lead to a physiological model of the mind and ultimately a psychopathological depiction of neuroses. This speculative attempt, despite its tentative postulates, represents a schema that would be followed throughout Freud's later development of psychoanalysis, a schema of energetics borrowed from physics and applied to the psyche (Glymour 1991, 44–85). Indeed, as Alasdair MacIntyre quipped, according to this model, the mind was "to take its place among the inhabitants of the 'billiard-ball' universe of Newtonian mechanics" (1958, 17).

Similar analogies drawn from mechanics and thermodynamics appear in other scientific models at the turn of the last century (e.g., Darwinism [Depew and Weber 1995]) as biologists and various social scientists sought disciplinary legitimacy in applying extended metaphors inspired by physics to their respective fields of study. How various aspects of Freudian theory reflected the general scientific culture and attitudes of his intellectual milieu have been well described (Kitcher 1992; Decker 1977), and more specifically, this notion of psychic forces defining complex behavior conveys the general tenor of Freud's scientific thinking.[3] From the earliest speculations and throughout his mature period, he remained passionately committed to a scientific model that would mirror physics, the paragon of the natural sciences. Freud was influenced, as were all physiologists by the 1880s, by the German reductionists, Brücke (his immediate mentor), and earlier proponents (Emil du Bois-Reymond and Hermann von Helmholtz), who sought to establish all biological phenomena on a common chemical-physical basis that would characterize organic phenomena on the basis of forces, analogous to what was established in the physical sciences (Galaty 1974; Moulines 1981).[4] The mechanical character of forces in opposition or at least in some kind of linkage underlay Freud's own conception of neurological function, which was then readily extended to his psychology (Sacks 2000).

Freud's view of what constitutes knowledge is readily understood given his research training and the context of his clinical investigations, but as he presents this physiological model to his confidant, he draws back and admits that despite the allure of this scientific hypothesis, it truly remains in service to another calling altogether, philosophy. Indeed, Freud's original intent had been a *philosophical* characterization of the mind, but as he himself admitted, in order to achieve this goal he detoured first into neurophysiology and then into psychiatry. This affectionate reference to philosophy in his letter to Fliess belies the many instances in Freud's *published* writings where he firmly established a distance between himself and philosophers and, more specifically, between psychoanalysis and philosophies of mind. How might we account for this division?

A simple explanation follows Freud's defense of psychoanalysis. Throughout his writings he sprinkled remarks directed to those detractors who claimed that psychoanalysis failed the scientific standards of the age. He thus had to establish that (1) psychoanalysis was objective (i.e., *scientific* in following a most austere objectivist truth doctrine) *and* (2) it was *not* philosophical. Simply, for Freud, if psychoanalysis was a science, it could not be tainted with philosophy. Considering his background in neurophysiology and his commitments to the ascendant positivism of the age, Freud's flirtation with a reductive model served an important orienting function for what was to become an altogether different approach to understanding psychopathology.

Freud struggled throughout his career to bridge the gap between his aspiration to create a science of the mind and his interpretative method. He believed that adherence to positivist principles would not only bolster the truth claims of psychoanalysis, but would also align this "new science" with the Machian hope that all knowledge might be unified under the single banner of science.[5] To illustrate this point, consider Freud's own assessment: Toward the end of his career, he again asserted the well-trodden antiphilosophy path:

> It is not permissible to declare that science is one field of human mental activity and that religion and philosophy are others, at least equal in value, and that science has no business to interfere with the other two: that they all have equal claim to be true and that everyone is at liberty to choose from which he will draw his convictions and in which he will place his belief. A view of this kind is regarded as particularly superior, tolerant, broad-minded and free from liberal prejudices. Unfortunately it is not tenable.... It is simply a fact that the *truth* cannot be tolerant, that it admits no compromises or limitations, that research regards every sphere of human activity as belonging to it and that it must be relentlessly critical if any other power tries to take over any part of it. (1933, 160; emphasis added)

This statement fairly summarizes Freud's philosophical commitments: truth is only scientific truth and thus intolerant of other truth claims.

Further, a latent scientism lurks here as Freud rails against those he identifies as pluralistic in their pursuit of truths derived by different methods. Finally, he condemns philosophy as arrogant in its systematic conceits: Philosophy might "behave like a science, and works in part by the same methods," but it is inferior because of "the illusion of being able to present a picture of the universe which is without gaps and is coherent, though one which is bound to collapse with every advance in knowledge" (1933, 160). Freud's diagnosis of philosophy's fatal weakness was "over-estimating the epistemological value of our logical operations and by accepting other sources of knowledge such as intuition" (1933, 160). He then brushes philosophy aside (it has such limited appeal), and then charges after religion (his true target), which shared with philosophy the defect of untenable totalizing explanations. Note that the assaults against philosophy also included evasive strategies: When tainted by suggestions of prior philosophical influences, such as Schopenhauer and Nietzsche, Freud claimed, "I was less concerned with the question of priority than with keeping my mind unembarrassed [by philosophy]" (1925a, 60). But Freud doth protest too much. Below we will trace the intellectual origins of his project and show that a philosophical challenge underlay his psychoanalytic project.[6]

Freud's Positivist Allegiance

At the University of Vienna during the early 1870s, Freud was deeply interested in philosophy and considered fulfilling a dual doctorate in zoology and philosophy (Freud 1990, 95). He supplemented his physiology courses, taught by Ernst Brücke, with an intense series of lectures delivered by Franz Brentano, whose commitments to empiricism, logic, and natural scientific ideals influenced Freud's later approach to psychology (Freud 1990, 94–105). Having entered the university in 1873 (finishing his medical studies 1881), Freud enrolled in six of Brentano's lecture courses from the winter of 1874 through the summer of 1876. These were the only nonmedical courses he took (Merlan 1949). Of note is that he visited Brentano outside of class, and it seems that some intellectual intimacies were shared. In Freud's account of his impressions of Brentano,

written in letters to his friend Eduard Silberstein (1990, 102–3), we detect
the seeds of the powerful influence of his teacher on the later construction
of psychoanalysis (Merlan 1949).

Brentano, as a pioneering phenomenologist, became an apostle of "inner perception," which Freud later was to take along his own distinctive
course. The full genealogical intellectual tributary is detailed below, and
suffice it to note here that Freud's detour into neurology arose, at least
in part, in the agreement with his philosophical mentor that philosophy
was "in absolute chaos" (Freud 1990, 102).[7] Brücke, a major exponent
of materialism and reductionism, more likely directly influenced Freud's
interests in models of the mind based on a physiology grounded in physics and chemistry. Eventually, Freud chose to side with the more certain
objectivist approach Brücke offered (Glymour 1991), that is, physiology. This early competition between philosophy and physiology would
be replayed in later years as Freud struggled between the demands of a
reductive science and an introspection that taxed the limits of science.
So, ironically, despite his dismissal of the philosophers' identification of
"mind" with "consciousness," Freud himself was forced to employ introspection and conscious deliberations, despite the all-too-evident stricture
imposed by such methods.

Regardless of these early influences, by Freud's third year of university
studies, the basic choice had been made: Like many of his generation, he
discarded idealism and endorsed positivism. After all, he was caught in
the turbulent philosophical currents of the time, which were dominated
by responses to the idealist inheritance that were for the most part rejecting of Hegel and his followers. So placing Freud philosophically is
complicated by the intellectual crosscurrents in which he worked, and
more specifically, the tension between a renewed positivism and a lingering idealism.[8]

Although Brentano disavowed affiliation to Kantianism (Freud 1990,
103–4; Smith 1997, 9–15), he actually distanced himself more specifically from Hegelianism. He thus joined two general intellectual currents
of the era: The first was a direct rejection of Absolute (Hegelian) Idealism, which spawned a newly developed phenomenology. First authored
by Brentano and then prominently developed by Edmund Husserl, introspection found its arch-philosophical proponents. The second major

philosophical movement born in the rejection of idealism might best be described as "radical analyticity." First grounded in logic and then philosophy of language, analytical philosophy would dispense with metaphysics, and instead language and logic would become philosophy's chief concern. Led by Gottlob Frege, Bertrand Russell, and G. E. Moore (Hylton 1990; Rockmore 2006), this latter movement, with an ascendant naturalism, would give birth to logical positivism (also referred to as the Vienna School). This complex history may be seen as a general realignment of philosophy and science, an adjustment that underpinned much that became evident in phenomenology, historicism, value theory, and logic.

However, for our purposes, the most direct development for Freud's philosophical undertaking was the evolution of "natural philosophy" into "science." Scientists, by the end of the nineteenth century, found themselves pursuing a course independent of their philosophy colleagues, one that increasingly accorded science the role of adjudicating truth claims and establishing knowledge (Schnädelbach 1984, 66–108). Science thus attained an intellectual autonomy, which when coupled with the drive of increasing technology and the growing institutional and social power of its professionalization, established a confident (and assertive) normative character to research and its products (Tauber 2009). Originating with August Comte in the 1820s, extended by Ernst Mach in the 1890s, and finally matured in the Vienna Circle in the 1920s, positivism dominated philosophy of science during the first half of the twentieth century, and thus set the standards for truth claims during Freud's professional life.

Freud's embrace of scientism (and positivism more specifically) followed the fashion of his time. By the end of the nineteenth century, the natural sciences, left to their own technical pursuits, ascended to great heights of technical mastery of nature. That success required a philosophy to account for an epistemology, which seemingly built from commonsensical notions of empirical knowledge. Positivist philosophy assumed its hegemonic hold on the scientific community, which began to refer to "scientists" instead of to "natural philosophers" after William Whewell's suggestion for a new designation in his *Philosophy of the Inductive Sciences* (1840, cxiii). Positivist triumphs led to romantic reactions, which took many forms, but suffice it to note here that a disenchanted universe posed the question of human's existential standing in a new way: How to place humans in relation to the nature they experienced. While the objective component of that problem was soon adopted by a new discipline, psychology, the various expressions directed at the deeper metaphysical challenge soon dominated discussion of the signification of science's findings. In other words, with objectivity given, the unresolved problem became *subjectivity*. And so, any attempt to employ science as an instrument for *unifying* reason would have moved against a strong positivist tide, which was firmly committed to its other concerns. Thus did Kant's separation of reason with each faculty directing itself to two disparate realms—the natural and the metaphysical-moral—assume new complexities (discussed below, chapter 4).

Those scientists who embraced this newly evolved positivist philosophy were, by and large, pleased to leave the problematic philosophical (defined as "metaphysical") questions behind them as they pursued their investigative projects. Freud chose to align himself with them, not only because of the appeal to methodological authority, but more deeply as a personal response to the crisis of modernity generally experienced at the turn of the twentieth century (Megill 1985). (To what extent he shed metaphysics we leave for later comment.) To seek new foundations and save rationality in the face of crushing obstacles comprised an intellectual mission dominant among German intelligentsia (Bambach 1995). Thus positivism, which seeks radically neutral and objective knowledge (by omitting to account for its own values and self-refuting assumptions), organized Freud's ever-present desire to legitimate psychoanalysis by linking its theories and the clinical data upon which they were based with those sciences that he thought had achieved a kind of objectivity he admired.[9]

Freud's "physics envy" belied his scientific aspirations, for he could not overcome the insurmountable normative structure of his enterprise. Scientific theories generally fall into two camps: Some are simply descriptive with no judgments about optimal or suboptimal states. Such theories, which characterize the natural sciences, for example, Newtonian mechanics or general relativity, are value-neutral (i.e., relative to human or subjective values) and thus nonnormative. Of course, they are *not* value-free, but rather judged and governed by their own hierarchy of values, for example objective, universal, coherent, parsimonious, "aesthetically elegant," or simple. Other kinds of theories embed different social or personal values in their descriptive structure that are necessarily derived from human experience, and, accordingly account for conditions on a *normative* spectrum of values. Physics is not evaluative in this way, because there is no value judgment on whether an eclipse of the moon, itself, is good or bad, better or worse (at least not in Western secular society). Needless to say, the effects on human life of such phenomena are valued, but the phenomena themselves, at least in their descriptions, are neutral and only elicit a normative judgment relative to how that phenomenon or theory affects human well-being. Despite Freud's ecumenical views, he still was guided by various normative notions. This orientation focused his investigational model, namely, an extrapolation from functional coordinates that allowed humans to flourish.

Following an account of human behavior reaching back into Enlightenment and Romantic traditions (Steiner 1995; Kirschner 1996), Freud placed self-reflection on a spectrum of ideal types or character structures. Deviation or failure to achieve these ideal types were diagnostic of "immaturity, neurotic illness, character disorder or the like" (Macklin 1973, 144). Moreover, they served as idealized goals for self-actualization in which normative inclinations and potentialities find their telos (Meissner 2003, 291). These analytic stories framed individual life histories to achieve certain ends. The teleological structure of psychoanalytic theory clearly oriented Freud's epistemology, directed his investigations, and defined his interpretation of the clinical data. Arising from physiology, function follows parameters of success and failure for prescribed goals, and with these basic coordinates, he placed psychic life on a clinical spectrum defined by (relatively) normal and pathological states. This endeavor rested on clinical judgment and application of norms that organized an understanding of psychic function and the psychotherapy directed at correcting its aberrancies.

Freud's positivist project built on the ideals of the physical sciences breaks apart on these normative shoals (Tauber 2005, chap. 1; Tauber 2009), for the neat division of *objective* facts and *subjective* values only admits the separation of certain kinds of facts from certain kinds of value. The interpretative nature of psychoanalysis disallowed such a simple prescription, although formally, Freud held to his earliest scientific principles. Embracing objectivity divorced from personal value to universalize his findings, Freud thereby sought to earn psychoanalysis scientific authority. However, a philosophy that had served a newly emerged scientific medicine so well—a view from nowhere, the absent perspective—is not only inappropriate for psychoanalysis, its aspirations are unattainable as well. Even allowing for the broadest tenets as holding some universal value—the general nature of unconscious drives and the determinism of early experience—these can only frame (in a most general way) the interpretation of the particularities of human experience. The analysis must be heavily influenced by nonobjective values, namely the goals established by analysand and analyst, the data admitted for interpretation, and of course, the interpretation itself. On this view, psychoanalytic findings, as in any clinical scenario (Tauber 1999; 2005), must adjust the brackets of objectivity to fit the peculiarities of the individual.

Yet Freud never abandoned his scientific criteria and guiding ideal. Indeed, the very definition of neurotic rests on a neurophysiological base, inasmuch as *neurosis* literally means "pathological state of the nerves" (Reeder 2008, 119), and given Freud's neurophysiological orientation, he effortlessly adopted that perspective in his study of "neurotic" behavior. That he sided with the scientist persona as opposed to the clinician is supported by many references, but perhaps most clearly stated in a late overview of psychoanalysis, where he wrote, "The future will probably attribute far greater importance to psychoanalysis as the *science* of the unconscious than as a therapeutic procedure" (1926b, 265; emphasis added). So for Freud, the therapeutic result was construed as a fortunate *product* of a successful analysis, but the scientific status of the analysis remained primary for him. Note that the verisimilitude of the analytic process was predicated on Freud's early therapeutic successes, so one might easily argue that the medical aspects were critical to assigning truth claims for his interpretations. Irrespective of these considerations, Freud in the end eschewed the therapeutic as subordinate to the scientific inquiry, or in other words, science trumped medicine, simply because of the better application of his positivist ideals.

If confronted, Freud, I believe, would have argued that his science formulated new categories of function, that is, scientific discoveries, which he viewed as fulfilling certain epistemological criteria. From his perspective, these fulfilled some positivist criteria of his truth claims. In other words, he would separate the epistemological project (by minimizing its normative content) from an underlying moral (subjective value-based) grounding. However, a basic problem cannot be escaped: When we consider the set of states he identified that must be opened and changed, for example, repression yielding to recognition, delusion replaced by insight, guilt yielding to freedom, he established the criteria of success for his *epistemology*, and in every instance—an evaluative judgment, an interpretative analysis, a standard of behavior—reflected a set of nonpositivist values applied to a clinical history that then was integrated into a psychoanalytic interpretation.

Positivism's appeal explains Freud's presentation of psychoanalysis, its methodologies, and more deeply its fundamental formulations. But he did not engage directly with the inherent philosophical tension that distinguishes normative and nonnormative science. Instead, he took his argument against a weaker opponent, the "philosophers." The general tenor of Freud's remarks about philosophy attempted to rebut the criticism that psychoanalysis offered little clinical evidence or scientific rationale for its practice and thus fashioned itself, willy-nilly, as a contemplative discipline. Specifically, Freud complained that "philosophers" (whom he does not identify, but must include Brentano, as discussed below) regard the mental as consciousness and ignore the unconscious, the true seat of the mind (1900, xxv). In 1925, Freud penned "The Resistances to Psycho-analysis," in which he forgives physicians (encumbered with their mechanical, materialist orientation) for misconstruing the authority of psychoanalysis, but to the philosophers he offers no respite. He accuses them of narrowly perceiving "mind" only in its conscious functions, and thus failing to recognize that "what is mental is in itself *unconscious* and that being conscious is only a *quality*, which may or may not accrue to a particular mental act" (1925b, 213–22; 216). Further, Freud simply asserts that because philosophers have no experience with hypnosis or dream analysis, they are locked into self-observation and thus, consciousness. Freud then laments that psychoanalysis resided in some middle position between medicine and philosophy, deriving no benefits from any kinship with either discipline on either flank. On a more general note, he complained that if not "philosophy," certainly "speculation" served as the condemnatory judgment, and to suffer indictment as practicing simple conjecture, or worse, moved psychoanalysis beyond a scientific argument to speculative opinion. (Early defenders of psychoanalysis would repeatedly attempt to distance themselves from their critics by following Freud's general strategy of placing psychoanalysis within the constellation of the descriptive sciences and clinical medicine.)

In sum, Freud's defense of his theory draws a distinction between the "science" of psychoanalysis and the "speculation" of philosophers. This polemical position, however, belies the complexity of the influences on psychoanalytic theory by ignoring the difficulties of drawing bridging concepts between Freud's own clinical empiricism and strong neuroscientific modeling, on the one hand, and on the other hand, the philosophical construction of a new discipline that heavily depended (albeit without acknowledgment) on the antecedents of previous characterizations of unconsciousness, for example, Hegel (Mills 2002), Schopenhauer, Eduard von Hartmann, and Nietzsche (Ellenberger 1970).

Walking a tightrope between science and speculation, Freud admitted that "in the works of my later years ... I have given free rein to the inclination, which I kept down so long, to speculation" (1925a, 57). In referring to *Beyond the Pleasure Principle* (1920) and *The Ego and the Id* (1923a), Freud uses "speculation" in the narrow theoretical confines of psychoanalysis proper, which actually begins with *Totem and Taboo* (1913b). These ventures placed him on a slippery speculative slope, so with *Future of an Illusion* (1927b), *Civilization and Its Discontents* (1930), and in his last work, *Moses and Monotheism* (1939), Freud gave free rein to broad psychocultural critiques, each of which is *highly* conjectural. What seems inconsistent, given his well-rehearsed denials, is that by his late career Freud freely admitted to such proclivities. After noting that his theoretical revisions to psychoanalytic theory had essentially ceased in the early 1920s with his "division of the mental personality into an ego, a super-ego and an id" (1923a), Freud went on to describe a "regressive development" (1935, 72):

> My interest, after making a life-long *détour* through the natural sciences, medicine, and psychotherapy, returned to the cultural problems which had fasci-

nated me long before, when I was a youth scarcely old enough for thinking.…
I perceived ever more clearly that the events of human history, the interactions
between human nature, cultural development and the precipitates of primaeval
experiences … are no more than a reflection of the dynamic conflicts between
ego, the id, and the super-ego, which psychoanalysis studies in the individual—
are the same process repeated upon a wider stage. (1935, 72)

Despite his earlier disdain for such speculation and the unorthodoxy of
his scientific program, Freud's indignation about the dismissal of his theory appears again and again (1913a, 178–79; 1916, 97–98; and 1923a,
14–15) as he sought to defend the critical, that is, scientific, character
of psychoanalysis (1901, 1–279; 259 and 1940b, 144–207; 158–59).
After all, "[We] venture … to transform metaphysics into metapsychology" (1901, 259).[10] Given the conviction that he had so conclusively
demonstrated the basic structure and dynamics that characterize human
thought and action, his frustration at the resistance to his ideas is self-
evident. Indeed, the rejections smacked of the denials a club might inflict
on a hopeful applicant, for his writings ironically have deep philosophical
commitments not only to philosophies of mind and language, albeit of
disputed character (e.g., Glymour 1991; Cavell 1993; Modell 1993), but
also to various philosophies of psychology; he coupled elements derived
from psychiatry and sexology to his own interpretations and modes of
study. Melding these ideas, Freud presented a unique and novel approach
to understanding personality, motivation, and moral identity. Simply to
deny "philosophy" ignores any insight into his theorizing offered by a
deeper examination of the complex conceptual scaffold that supports
psychoanalysis. To explore those reaches of Freud's venture, we begin
with his own appraisal.

Towards the end of his life, Freud wrote a short essay ("Post-script to a
Discussion on Lay Analysis," 1927a) concerning the relationship between
medicine and psychoanalysis, and he carefully drew a line to separate
"*scientific* analysis and its *applications*" (213). He acknowledged that
clinical challenges grounded the psychoanalytic encounter, but he regarded psychoanalysis as a branch of psychology, not medicine, and he
was concerned that "the therapy not destroy the science" (209; see intro-

duction, note 6). Among the various issues that brought this relationship to his attention, he commented that medical school hardly offered a suitable training for a psychoanalytic career, and instead he advised a very broad education in the humanities and social sciences. When commenting on his own career, Freud wrote:

> After forty-one years of medical activity, my self-knowledge tells me that I have never really been a doctor in the proper sense. I became a doctor through being compelled to deviate from my original purpose.... I have no knowledge of having had any craving in my childhood to succour suffering humanity. My innate sadistic disposition was not a very strong one, so that I had no need to develop this one of its derivatives. Nor did I ever play the "doctor game"; my infantile curiosity evidently chose other paths.... I scarcely think, however, that my lack of genuine medical temperament has done much damage to my patients. For it is not greatly to the advantage of patients if their physician's therapeutic interest has too marked an emotional emphasis. They are best helped if he carries out his task coolly and, so far as possible, with precision. (208–9)

(Note that the last admonition would suitably be addressed to a scientist.) Putting aside the issue of the clinical character of Freud's endeavor for now, consider the basic dichotomy he has identified: physician versus scientist. And for him "scientist" meant psychologist.

"Physician" held Freud to a therapeutic mission, one he obviously accepted, but that context did not fully fit his aims. As he writes further in this essay, the neurotic serves the science of psychoanalysis, because as in clinical medicine, the pathological more clearly defines the workings of the normal. Indeed, for Freud, psychopathology was a tool for deciphering the normal mind. Obviously his efforts included a therapeutic outcome, and the audience he addressed was putatively committed to psycho*therapy*, but the point Freud is making, an admission of a deeply personal nature, is that his *own* self-image, and more to the point, the true character of psychoanalysis, did not fall within the clinical domain so much as within the scientific. In some sense, his remark might be understood as an implicit admission that psycho*therapy* was not coincident with psycho*analysis*. For him, the therapeutic result was construed as a *product* of the analysis, and the analysis, its scientific status, was primary.

I have assumed … that psychoanalysis is not a specialized branch of medicine. I do not see how it is possible to dispute this. Psychoanalysis falls under the head of psychology; not of medical psychology in the old sense, nor of the psychology of morbid processes, but simply of psychology. It is certainly not the whole of psychology, but its substructure and perhaps even its entire foundation. The possibility of its application to medical purposes must not lead us astray…. It is argued that psychoanalysis was after all discovered by a physician in the course of his efforts to assist his patients. But that is clearly neither here nor there. (1927a, 252)

So what did Freud mean by "psychology" and, more generally, "science?" I have already cited Freud's own admissions about early interests, motivations, and persistent allegiances to philosophy, albeit he remained reluctant by any standard. And now I am highlighting his self-proclaimed identification with psychology, a human science, but a science nevertheless. Note that that identification was the last of several shifting identifications; for example, during the earlier *Project* era of the mid-1890s, Freud dismissed psychology for what he hoped was a more promising physiology (Decker 1977, 67–68), although his knowledge of psychology as a science in its own right (as advocated by Wundt, for example) was limited to Brentano and the clinical material he first encountered in France. Given these limitations, how are the designations Freud employed reconciled?

Perhaps Freud understood "science," particularly in relation to philosophy, in ways less apparent than a simple dichotomy he used in his writings. Science, as already mentioned, had only recently emerged from "natural philosophy" as a distinctive activity, and more saliently, even among those who continued to identify as philosophers did so as champions of science. I believe the key to unlocking what appears as a frozen opposition may be in Freud's earliest philosophical training, where "philosophy"—in its best sense—was taught as aspiring to a scientific ideal. Thus, I am applying one of Freud's principal lessons to himself: the child is the father of the man, and this genealogical analysis will show the lineage of Freud's own understanding, and begins by exploring the intellectual relationship Freud enjoyed with Brentano. On this reading, Brentano's mentorship offered the original framework in which Freud organized his own empirical studies, but furthermore would present Freud with a set of criteria by which to justify a theory of unconsciousness. That justification eventually formed the conceptual basis of psychoanalytic theory.

The Mentorship of Franz Brentano

Freud received an essential orientation from Brentano, who, during his first encounters with Freud in 1874, had just been appointed professor. From Brentano, a man undoubtedly charismatic and committed to a "fundamental reformation of philosophy" (quoted by Spiegelberg 1982, 28), Freud learned a style of philosophy that would recompense him for shifting from what he initially considered his true vocation to another. In that revised choice, Freud followed basic precepts of Brentano's teaching—from the general orientation of what constituted true philosophical reasoning to the more specific frame of reference his mentor provided for a new "psychology."

Brentano's particular views on the character of the mind, and "the unconscious" in particular, played into Freud's later deliberations. Indeed, the thesis expounded here is that Freud's theory of the psyche responds to Brentano's own criteria for establishing a science of the mind, which focused in large part on refuting notions of the unconscious and making "mind" synonymous with consciousness. In short, Freud remained Brentano's pupil, rejecting some of the philosopher's principal teachings and keeping others. On this reading, Freud pursued "science" as Brücke taught, but developed psychoanalysis as Brentano advocated for his own psychology, albeit with radically differing views of unconsciousness.[11]

From *Studies of Hysteria* (Breuer and Freud 1895) through his clinical middle period, Freud worked as a scientist and thought as a Brentano's student. Others have extensively commented on the Brentano-Freud relationship (e.g., Merlan 1945; 1949; Barclay 1959; 1964; Fancher 1977; McGrath 1986; Frampton 1991; Cohen 1998a; 1998b; 2000), and here I wish to focus specifically on how Brentano posed the question of unconsciousness, and then draw connections between that formulation and how Freud himself structured his own theory of psychodynamics.[12] My first thesis: Freud's thought was profoundly influenced by his first philosophi-

CHALLENGE OF PHILOSOPHY   **41**

cal mentor to the extent that he formulated his defense of psychoanalysis
as a rebuttal to Brentano's denial of an unconscious, and he did so on the
singular problem of psychic causation. To this matter we now turn.

Brentano's writings have enjoyed a surge of renewed interest as historians of the analytic philosophy movement have come to appreciate his
wide influence on the development of twentieth-century logic and philosophy of language in both the Anglo-American sector and the European
(Poli 1998a; Jacquette 2004a). He published little during his career, and
while his students prepared posthumous works, much dispute reigns over
the interpretations of his later positions. For our purposes, Brentano's
early writings, which dealt with his specific views on psychology, provide
a clear statement on how he construed philosophy, and a study of the
mind more particularly.

In 1874, coincident with the publication of Wilhelm Wundt's *Principles
of Physiological Psychology*,[13] Brentano issued *Psychology from an Empirical Point of View* (1973), which served as a manifesto for later phenomenologists. It declares the "irreducible distinctness of psychology's
subject matter" (Simons 1973, xiii) and attempts to make the discipline
independent of both philosophy and physiology (xvi). The title emphasizes
Brentano's key point: The empiricism he sought eschews metaphysical
speculation and replaces it with a peculiar experiential basis as its subject of inquiry. However, for him, "empirical" does not mean experimental (at least not as understood today), and unlike Wundt at Leipzig and
William James at Harvard, who, in 1879, each established his respective
laboratory for such investigation, Brentano confined himself to purely
introspective methods, or "introception" (Simons 1973, xvii). This metod
was to distinguish itself from a more subjective introspection, and in
this regard Brentano clearly sought to establish his psychology on a firm
empirical, that is, scientific basis. By gleaning scientific facts that were
subject to laws, Brentano, like neo-Kantians of the same period, sought a
human science subject to natural law. He thus showed the impressionable
young Freud that psychology, in this new configuration, must synthesize
evidence presented by inner report and objective observation. Following
these precepts, Freud would base his entire analytical investigation on the
integration of mental and physical states (McGrath 1986, 114ff.).

To categorize Brentano's philosophical project is difficult, because the distinctions between positivism and what can only be described as a Kantian orientation commingle at this stage of philosophy's evolution (discussed in chapter 3). Positivism clearly goes its own direction with the delineation of its program as a philosophy of language with the Vienna Circle in the 1920s, but in the last quarter of the nineteenth century, these distinctions are less apparent, and Brentano is caught in the crosscurrents of debate about the terms of dispute. He could not join the positivists, because of his steadfast adherence to metaphysics; he would not affiliate with the neo-Kantians; and while he was not counted among the phenomenologists (who appeared with Husserl around 1900), Brentano fits best as a proto-phenomenologist. Foregoing some final assignment, let us first focus on Brentano's general philosophical position.

Despite the claims of laboratory scientists and the experimental orientation of their research, Brentano maintained that what might have been called "philosophy" was still science. Indeed, he held that "the true method of philosophy is none other than that of the natural sciences" (the fourth habilitation thesis of 1866, quoted by Spiegelberg 1982, 31). He sought a renewal of philosophy by placing its discourse on an equal footing with the methods of the natural sciences, and to do so, he would create a psychology to achieve that status. From his perspective, psychology was not only the "crowning pinnacle" of the sciences, it was "destined to become the basis of society and of its noblest possessions, and, by this very fact, to become the basis of all scientific endeavor as well" (Brentano 1973, 3). After conceding that the psychology of his day was regarded "by the great mass of people with ... contempt" (3), he endeavored to clarify the fundamental concepts that would establish its foundations and thus unify the various approaches vying for dominance. And that base was to be found in empiricism, albeit radically different from the psychologism of his contemporaries (e.g., Gustav Theodor Fechner and Rudolph Lotze). He began his *Psychology* with a clear declaration:

> The title which I have given this work characterizes both its object and its method. My psychological standpoint is empirical; experience alone is my teacher. Yet I share with other thinkers the conviction that this is entirely compatible with a certain ideal point of view. (Brentano 1973, xxvii)

And that vantage was his own introspection, principally through the consideration of idealized types rather than detailed observation of concrete cases (Spiegelberg 1982, 33).

Brentano's psychology is divided into two genres, descriptive and genetic.[14] The former (the focus of our interest) is concerned with the basic problem of identifying the subject matter of psychology and the divisions of mental phenomena. This catalogue project asked,

> Are sensations, feelings, judgments, separate phenomena of equal rank? Here the prerequisites of any protocol description seem to be either missing or highly controversial. It thus appears that what descriptive psychology demands at the very outset ... is a peculiar intuitive examination of the phenomena for their primary properties, for their "natural affinities," and for their diversities. (Spiegelberg 1982, 35)

Brentano asserted that such an endeavor was logically prior to other sciences (like physics) and would yield a psychology that was autonomous from a natural science like physiology. In other words, Brentano's psychology would be organized by its own laws within its own domain and thus independent of concepts adopted from other sciences.

Reaching back to Aristotle, his philosophical lodestone, Brentano defines "psychology": "The word psychology means *science of the soul*" (1973, 3), and accordingly the "'soul' [is] the nature or ... the form, the first activity, the first actuality of a living being" (4). This proved too broad a definition, and thus Brentano cites how Aristotle himself delimited the scope of psychology and thereby offered a definition that fulfilled Brentano's own requirements:

> [Aristotle] dismisses the thought of investigating the organs that serve as intermediaries between a desire and the part of the body toward whose movement the desire is directed. For, he says, such an investigation is not the province of one who studies the soul, but of one who studies the body. (5)

Then Brentano brings the definition into its modern context, and, more to the point, within the borders of his own approach:

> In modern terminology, the word "soul" refers to the substantial bearer of presentations (*Vorstellungen*) and other activities which are based upon pre-

sentations and which, like presentations, are only conceivable through inner perception. Thus we usually call soul the substance which has sensations such as fantasy images, acts of memory, acts of hope or fear, desire or aversion. We, too, use the word "soul" in this sense.... So it appears that just as the natural sciences study the properties and laws of physical bodies, which are the objects of external perception, psychology is the science which studies the properties and laws of the soul, which we discover within ourselves directly by means of inner perception, and which we infer, by analogy, to exist in others. (5)

All the Brentanean elements are here: mind as "presentations"; an empiricism based on "inner perception"; a distinction between study of the physical/body domain (i.e., physiology); and a true psychology of *mental* activities. He recognizes that the mental is initiated in physical events, and consequently the psychologist will skirt the line separating the two disciplines, since it is "the task of the psychologist to ascertain the first mental phenomena which are aroused by physical stimulus, even if he cannot dispense with looking at physiological facts in so doing" (7). In short, Brentano would protect psychology from physiology and use descriptions of inner, private states to support a philosophy of the mind. (Note that "inner perception is not to be confused with inner observation of our mental states, since anything of that sort is impossible" [33].) As a science, that approach was short-lived (note its conspicuous absence from such magisterial histories of psychology as provided by Koch and Leary 1992); as a philosophy it enjoyed a more auspicious future in twentieth-century phenomenology.

For Brentano, natural science examines physical phenomena, and all phenomena are appearances, not Kantian things-in-themselves, and so Brentano builds his psychology on Kantian foundations:

We have no right ... to believe that the objects of so-called external perception really exist as they appear to us. Indeed, they demonstrably do not exist outside of us. In contrast to that which really and truly exists, they are mere phenomena.

What has been said about the objects of external perception does not, however, apply in the same way to objects of inner perception. In their case, no one has ever shown that someone who considers these phenomena to be true would thereby become involved in contradictions. On the contrary, of their existence we have that clear knowledge and complete certainty which is provided by im-

mediate insight. Consequently, no one can really doubt that a mental state
which he perceives in himself exists, and that it exists just as he perceives it.
Anyone who could push his doubt this far would reach a state of absolute
doubt, a skepticism which would certainly destroy itself, because it would have
destroyed any firm basis upon which it could endeavor to attack knowledge.

*Defining psychology as the science of mental phenomena in order to make
natural science and mental science resemble each other in this respect, then, has
no reasonable justification.* (Brentano 1973, 10; emphasis added)

Having secured the distinctiveness of mental phenomena and the access to them through inner perception, Brentano goes on to define the
basis of that discrimination through the *intentionality* of the mental. Accordingly, mental phenomena are those directed towards some object,
an inherent characteristic of thought (and one that physical phenomena
lack): "Obviously there is no act of thinking without an object that is
thought, nor a desire without an object that is desired" (89). Thus to differentiate mental and physical phenomena, Brentano used the doctrine of
intentionality with a very specific and novel meaning:

> Every psychical phenomenon is characterized by what the Scholastics of the
> Middle Ages called the intentional (or sometimes the mental) inexistence of an
> object, and what we shall like to call, although not quite unambiguously, the
> reference to a content, the directedness towards an object (which in this context
> is not to be understood as something real) or the immanent-object-quality.
> Every mental phenomenon includes something as object within itself, although
> they do not do so all in the same way. In the representation something is rep-
> resented, in the judgment something is acknowledged or rejected, in desiring it
> is desired, etc. This intentional inexistence is peculiar alone to psychical phe-
> nomena. No physical phenomenon shows anything like it. And thus we can
> define psychical phenomena by saying that they are such phenomena as contain
> objects in themselves by way of intentionality (*intentional*). (This translation
> combines Spiegelberg's [1982, 36–37] and the standard English translation
> [Brentano 1973, 88–89].)

Reference to an object is thus the key feature of the psychical: "No hearing without something heard, no believing without something believed,
no hoping without something hoped, no striving without something

striven for, no joy without something we feel joyous about, etc." (Spiegelberg 1982, 37). Intentional states are "of" or "about" something and occur in various modes—perception, memory, desire, belief, fear, and so on. The actual *object* of the mental state, of course, is not itself mental, but a representation of it, so the *content* of an intentional state is mental (an image, concept, idea, etc.). The actual object is then constructed from these contents, and a triad must be configured between intentional contents, intentional objects, and actual object (McIntosh 1986).[15]

"Intentionality" (at least at this stage of Brentano's thinking) thus defined and characterized the mental, and as its fundamental precept, all referents *became* referents according to their intentional characteristic.[16] Upon the critical distinction of physical and mental phenomena, Brentano's "phenomenology" (a term he later disavowed) was to be erected around the problem of how to distinguish mental phenomena from those objects in the world, and beyond the question of how to characterize them, how do such phenomena reveal the dynamics and structure of the mind?[17] The general transcendental character of the investigation seems self-evident (despite Brentano's complete rejection of Kant's synthetic a priori, not to speak of his metaphysics), and further (again like Kant), Brentano accepted that causes (whether physical or mental) may only be inferred as a psychological characteristic. This general perspective structured Brentano's own views of the unconscious, and in turn influenced Freud's own approach and eventual justification of psychoanalysis.

Brentano's philosophy has been the source of much debate (e.g., Jacquette 2004; Margolis 2004; McAlister 2004); however, Freud, disregarding (and likely unaware) of these concerns, would employ intentionality for his own purposes in at least five ways:

1. Brentano keenly schematized the mind-body duality and acknowledged its authenticity. Thus objects in the world exist in the mind only as intentional objects, and therefore

This very intentional existence is for the mind an effective [real] existence. Because the intentional existence is for the mind an effective existence, all psychic activity is directed toward these intentional creations with the dual aspect of relationship to the outward object and the inner needs of the self. (Barclay 1964, 18)

Note that in this version of Kantianism (further considered in chapters 3 and 4), Brentano eclipses a transcendental deduction and makes no effort to define some underlying structure—psychological or philosophical—in which he might ground intention. But Freud takes "intention" and develops a comprehensive theory around it. In this regard, he goes well beyond Brentano's ambitions.[18]

2. Brentano's concept of intentionality offered Freud a critical foundation in which psychoanalysis will find its own footing. The definition of psychism becomes

the mere intending of something, as meaning—without appealing to self-consciousness. But this as one writer has said, contains the whole of Freud's discovery "the psychical is defined as meaning, and this meaning is dynamic and historical."[19] Husserl and Freud are seen to be heirs of Brentano, who had both of them as students. (Ricoeur 1970, 379)

On this reading, the conscious component of intention (so important to Brentano) is pushed aside for a deeper psychic intention, namely, that which froths forth from the reaches of the unconscious mind. There intention exists as psychic drives or biological forces, and when integrated with the intention of consciousness, the mind becomes unified. Accordingly, intention goes all the way down, and thus Freud created a theory in which multiple layers of intention exhibit themselves for interpretation.

3. More particularly, Freud's formulation of psychic investment or cathexis (*Besetzung*) is directly taken from Brentano, inasmuch as psychoanalytic theory regards desires (libidinal and aggressive), perception, memory, and belief in the same way "intentional state" was originally defined (McGrath 1986, 436).

4. Intention assumes a central role in the metapsychology papers "On Narcissism" (1914a), "Instincts and Their Vicissitudes" (1915b), and "Mourning and Melancholia" (1917a), where Freud constructed the ego as an object of psychic investment (McGrath 1986). In the first case, narcissism is defined as "the libidinal investment of the ego," where one might love oneself (past or present), what one might like to become (future), or what was once part of oneself. This latter formulation serves as the central motive of "Mourning and Melancholia": Despair arises when "reality testing has shown that the loved object no

longer exists, and it proceeds to demand that all libido shall be with-
drawn from its attachment to that object" (Freud 1917a, 244). When
mourning is complete, the ego is freed as it reinvests libido elsewhere.
And again in "Instincts," the person as both subject and person as object (of sexual instincts) is drawn.

5. Finally, intention constitutes an ethical dimension in the sense that
for Freud, "the trick to psychoanalysis is that the origin of meaning is
sought in the seeker, in the source of the question" (Egginton 2007,
10), which refers not only to the hidden or disguised forms of intention
(understanding), but also to how psychoanalytic insight depends upon
(and revolves about) "meaning"—meaning in the particular domain
of some emotional significance for the analysand (Breuer and Freud
1895; Freud 1910a). Structuring each of these domains, we find the
ethical intent of the inquiry itself, one developed by the rational, reflective subject, as offering the framework for the analysis qua analysis.
(This last theme is developed in later chapters.) Thus the key Brentanean construct would assume varied and distinctive roles in psychoanalytic theory, which will reappear in Freud's own psychology. However,
a critical difference emerged from their differing views about unconsciousness, a matter that deserves careful scrutiny.

Brentano and the Unconscious

Most generally, intention brings the mental into the conscious arena, and
as discussed below, for Brentano this distinction is critical, inasmuch as
he deliberately discounted the notion of the unconscious. And so finally
we come to a direct link with Freud's later project: What is the status of
the unconscious? Recall that Freud took courses from Brentano from
1874 through 1876; he twice visited Brentano in his private apartment
in 1875; Brentano's *Psychology* was published in 1874. That the position
Brentano elaborates in his treatise served as the template for his discussions with Freud seems highly likely, and thus a careful examination of
that work provides the basic position Brentano would have advocated in
his discussions with Freud.

Brentano explicitly dealt with the unconscious in two sections of his
Psychology: In the shorter (and less developed) of two excursions (1973,

54–64), he contests two theses of Henry Maudsley (1835–1918), a pioneering English psychiatrist, who advocated positivist principles for a science of the mind. In his *Physiology and Pathology of the Mind* (1867), Maudsley asserted that (1) psychology should be based on physiology, and (2) the most essential aspects of thinking are unconscious. Brentano resisted both theses. He dispenses with the "other minds problem" (which provoked Maudsley's original retreat into the unconscious) as well-trodden and essentially irrelevant, and focused instead on the status of the notion of unconscious mental activity as subject to scientific scrutiny.

Brentano approached the question of the unconscious by first presenting Maudsley's position in *Physiology and Pathology* (1867): "*Material conditions are the basis of consciousness* ... of which physiology alone can give an account" (Brentano 1973, 56). Further, the brain has "*a vegetative life*" (organic metabolism, physiological processes) "without our being conscious of it"; ergo, "*Mental life does not necessarily involve mental activity*" (Brentano 1973, 56). These observations lead Maudsley to observe that "the greatest part of the mind's life is inactive," by which he meant that "*mental activity does not necessarily involve consciousness*" (Brentano 1973, 57), and, most saliently, "'*the most important part of mental action*, the essential process on which thinking depends, is *unconscious mental ... activity*'" (Brentano 1973, 58, quoting Maudsley 1867, 20). Thus, in the end, only physiology of the unconscious mind has any promise of defining mental life, because consciousness only represents a residua. Yet, alas, physiology has no handle on deciphering the problem.

In uncoupling Maudsley's position, Brentano first observed that psychological considerations underlie the argument; namely, it is psychological insight that has pointed Maudsley in the direction of unconscious causes and effects, a tradition traced to Aristotle and Leibniz. But more importantly, the very notion of an unconscious seemed untenable to Brentano: First, all mental activity, as such, is reportable and thus available to consciousness. Indeed, it made no sense to Brentano to speak about the mental other than as conscious thought, speech, and reasoning. Those faculties, after all, *are* the mental. (Recall, this confinement to consciousness as *the* mind provoked Freud's consistent distaste for what he called "philosophy.") And second, while humans might strive for some ultimate governing laws of the mental in physiological research, this does not in any way confirm Maudsley's appraisal of unconsciousness; indeed, it cannot attain a scientific status because his conception cannot be proved or disproved. That position, according to Brentano, immediately disqualified Maudsley's approach: if a hypothesis cannot be tested, it cannot qualify as science.

In sum, Maudsley had asserted "physiology" over "psychology," but admitted that in 1866 (the time of his critique) physiology had no ability to describe this dimension of the psyche and that "there are really no grounds for expecting a positive [objectivist] science of the mind at present" (Brentano 1973, 55, quoting Maudsley 1867, 28). Brentano, committed to formulating a vigorous psychology, dismissed the dichotomous selection and claimed instead that the question at hand was not choosing between physiology and psychology, but rather "Science—to be or not to be" (1973, 56). Of course, Brentano was engaged in building a new science, one in which physiology has been subordinated to introspection, and more to Brentano's primary position, how could the self-referential character of mental activity even be subject to physiological examination as Maudsley construed it? On all accounts then, Maudsley goaded a strenuous Brentanean defense, but one that only offered a foretaste of Brentano's most cogent and important argument.

Brentano's second discussion of the unconscious (found in Book II of his *Psychology*) is his most extended. In the chapter "Inner Consciousness" (1973, 101ff.), he directly faced the matter by asking "whether there are any mental phenomena which are not objects of consciousness. All mental phenomena are states of consciousness; but are all mental phenomena conscious, or might there also be unconscious mental acts?" (102). After listing a host of philosophers from Aquinas to Eduard von Hartmann, as well as a slew of contemporary psychologists, who acknowledged a realm of unconscious mental processing, Brentano begins his critique with the observation that all had failed at establishing the character and function of "unconsciousness." Nevertheless he observed that proponents had argued on the basis of indirect evidence, which Brentano discards as too fallible.

In 1868, von Hartmann (1931) characterized unconsciousness as "heterogeneous" as compared to conscious thought, and Brentano goes to some length to reject those claims (1973, 107–11).[20] Brentano also cited Maudsley about the provocations of dreams: "Let anyone take careful note of his dreams, he will find that many of the seemingly unfamiliar things with which his mind is then occupied, and which appear to be new and strange productions, are traceable to the unconscious appropriations of the day" (112, citing Maudsley 1867, 16). Other examples abound, and the point seems self-evident that Brentano comprehensively knew the literature about unconsciousness, but he actively searched for logical reasons to discard claims of inclusion in a psychology based on empiricism. Brentano thus made a metaphysical commitment, and whether that commitment was to method or logic, he was steadfast in his opposition. Simply, given the rich history of those who explored the unconscious (Ellenberger 1970) and its foundational role in idealist philosophies (Jacob 1992), he must be regarded as holding an unwavering view of the mind that would *only* account for conscious thought and perception, and the rest was to be explained away.

Freud began in a different place and sought to answer a different set of questions. As a physician, he explored the origins of abnormal behaviors, and in that undertaking, conscious thought could not be reconciled with manifest phenomena. In recognizing that even normal psychic life revealed unconscious experience and "thought," a novel conception of the mind emerged. However, in making his own case, Freud would have to deal with Brentano's criteria, which were presented as three strategies that might establish the status of unconsciousness. Each of these would be critical to Freud's own project (Brentano 1973, 105):

1. Identifying a *cause* that does not appear in consciousness (e.g., learning a language or riding a bicycle)

2. Perceiving *effects* from unconscious mental phenomena (e.g., the collective experience of listening to music derived from myriad bits of sound)

3. Establishing whether mental phenomena are simply below the *threshold* of consciousness, yet nevertheless might be discerned if sought(the coughing of a neighbor may be "ignored" if one is absorbed in a task)[21]

The key issue linking these three explorations is *causation*, and in that light, Brentano set three fundamental criteria by which cause might be established: (1) the factual status of the putative unconscious fact (effecting unconscious cause); (2) a constancy of the cause-effect relationship (with no other complicating consequences); and (3) a requirement that "unconscious mental phenomena, to which the hypothesis appeals, do not contradict, in their succession or in their other characteristics, the recognized laws of conscious mental phenomena" (1973, 106–7).

Thus for Brentano, the problem of establishing the epistemological status of the unconscious rests, first, on direct evidence, which in turn rests on his stringent requirement that "experience" must confirm the existence of an unconscious faculty like any other object, "For it is self-evident and *necessarily* the case that there can be no unconscious ideas in the domain of our *experience*" (Brentano 1973, 105; emphasis added). Such a criterion is perfectly consistent with his own philosophical position, in which the "unconscious" is, at least, inconsistent with his primary premise that (conscious) *experience* characterizes the mental and the *mental* in turn is intentional, so a mental act is that which is directed towards an *object within itself*, and accompanying that direction is an awareness of that intention, that is, consciousness.

But beyond the evidentiary constraint, Brentano demands that the laws governing mental functions conform, or at least not contradict, natural laws established by conscious thought. This caveat opens the door for establishing unconscious mental events if

> their succession and other characteristics ... reveal themselves in their effects, just as the laws of the external world, the laws of inertia, the laws of gravitation, etc., manifest themselves in the sensations which are their effects. So it is particularly necessary that the origin of the mental phenomena assumed to exist despite the absence of consciousness should not be considered to be something utterly and entirely inconceivable itself. (1973, 107)

Brentano made clear that he was willing to acknowledge multiple causative routes, even overdetermination, if evidence could be adduced for such causation. The question always comes back to the empirical support. This Brentano thought was lacking, and he focused most of his attention of the remaining discussion on refuting the evidentiary claims made by advocates of unconsciousness. Basically, what they argued as evidence or reasonable inference, Brentano rejected. Note that the kind of evidence Brentano demanded was not available. Indeed, Freud's own project begins at this juncture.

So beyond espousing a causative line, Brentano joined his reductionist colleagues in the broader demand of applying universal laws to all natural phenomena, which, of course, includes the mental. This naturalism is crucial for Freud's own pursuits, inasmuch as he too, as a neurophysiologist, originally set for himself the same scientific standards guiding his own agenda. Further, by adopting positivist objectivist principles for his methodology, Freud sought a unified domain of natural law that could be applied to an "entity" that remained hidden from direct observation. Indeed, following the *effects*, as Brentano had suggested, would prove a viable strategy in Freud's hands. Despite Brentano's dissatisfaction with the evidence to date, Freud hoped to provide the causative cascade his mentor demanded for a science of the mind. At least that was his intention. But in the end, even with Freud's analysis, "causation" would not be understood as Brentano had conceived, which proved to be an enduring imbroglio for psychoanalytic theory. The next chapter explores this matter in detail.

Chapter Two

Distinguishing Reasons and Causes

> It is true that philosophy has repeatedly dealt with the problem
> of the unconscious, but with few exceptions, philosophers have
> taken up one or other of the two following positions. Either their
> unconscious has been something mystical, something intangible
> and indemonstrable, whose relation to the mind has remained
> obscure, or they have identified the mental with the conscious
> and have proceeded to infer from this definition that what is
> unconscious cannot be mental or a subject for psychology.
> These opinions must be put down to the fact that philosophers
> have formed their judgment on the unconscious without being
> acquainted with the phenomena of unconscious mental activity,
> and therefore without any suspicion of how far unconscious
> phenomena resemble conscious ones or of the respects in which
> they differ from them.
> —Sigmund Freud (1913b, 178)

IN ESTABLISHING THEIR RESPECTIVE PSYCHOLOGIES, Brentano and Freud
presented radically opposed philosophies of mind: Brentano assigned
the unconscious to metaphysics, while Freud claimed to have studied
the unconscious as an object of scientific scrutiny. The key element in
their divergent views hinged on the notion of psychic causality. Brentano
set the criteria that Freud later would attempt to fulfill in his own theory,
and in this sense Freud remained committed to Brentano's original philosophical project, one guided by empiricism and strict observational standards. That Freud failed to fulfill Brentano's challenge is illustrated here
by an analysis of Freud's circular argument for unconscious causation,
which he ironically constructed upon Brentanean precepts. In a subtle,
undeclared admission late in his career, Freud finally acknowledged that
psychoanalysis was built on an assumption, and by rigorous scientific
criteria psychoanalytic theory failed the positivist standards originally

claimed. Summaries of critiques by Wittgenstein and Popper highlight not only the weaknesses of Freud's scientific endeavor, but point to another direction in which psychoanalysis effectively follows a hermeneutical strategy (Gill 1994; Brook 1995). Recognizing the strengths of that interpretative orientation not only justifies Freud's own project, but also explains its logical basis.

Competing Philosophies, Competing Conclusions

The fundamental question, or at least one of the basic issues with which Brentano dealt, centered on the "unity-of-mind problem." Instead of a schema that would invoke partitioned segments of the mental, like Freud's id, ego, and superego, Brentano went to great lengths to keep the mind fully cohesive as a singular whole. Notably, in the second book of his *Psychology*, in a chapter entitled "On the Unity of Consciousness" (155ff.), he pointedly identifies the issue and reiterates that while there are primary and secondary objects of intentionality, cohesiveness reigns:

> Our investigation has shown that wherever there is mental activity there is a certain multiplicity and complexity. Even in the simplest mental state a double object is immanently present. At least one of these objects is conscious in more than one way.... But this lack of simplicity was not a lack of unity. The consciousness of the primary object and the consciousness of the secondary object are not each a distinct phenomenon but two aspects of one and the same unitary phenomenon; nor did the fact that the secondary object enters into our consciousness in various ways eliminate the unity of consciousness. We interpreted them, and had to interpret them, as parts of a unified real being. (1973, 155)

We need not delve further into Brentano's project to appreciate how the integration of "primary" and "secondary" objects allowed him to postulate a unified mental apparatus, which in turn permitted him to remain within the epistemological constraints of introspection. The underlying philosophical telos of this endeavor resided in his effort to establish a new science, and that approach only allowed him to pursue "objects" within the reach of direct observation. The benefit of that restriction was to direct philosophy away from speculation into a novel critical arena. He thus sought to create a means to accommodate the standards of the natural sciences, whose tools (when appropriately applied) presumably presented evidence that was objective and, by the standards of the times, "real." In sum, Brentano sought for philosophy an avenue out of skepticism, away from speculation, and into a newly defined scientific niche. Freud followed, but his pursuits yielded a very different picture of psychology.

Freud's investigations *were* empirical in the service of establishing a cascade of cause, just as Brentano demanded. Beginning with *Studies in Hysteria*, Freud cites (in its opening passages) the argument for effective causes (Breuer and Freud 1895); continues with an explicit account of manifest translations in the *Interpretation of Dreams* (Freud 1900); further develops his theory in the analysis of parapraxes (e.g., slips of the tongue) and "errors" of everyday life (Freud 1901) and jokes (Freud 1905a); and later provides his most explicit defense of detected effects (e.g., "The Unconscious" [Freud 1915a, 167]) and threshold effects (e.g., hypnosis [Freud 1912b]). Brentano seems to be sitting on Freud's shoulder, whispering cautionary caveats. Indeed, in "A Note on the Unconscious in Psychoanalysis" (1912b), Freud specifically addresses what he identifies as "philosophical" objections, which I infer are veiled references to his teacher. Indeed, the defense against each of Brentano's stipulations is, quite simply, to list all of Freud's case studies, for each of the issues raised by Brentano in his own *Psychology* is answered in one form or another throughout Freud's writings—from the *Interpretation of Dreams* (1900), to his summary *Introductory Lectures* (1915–17), to the final *Outline* (1940b). In short, Freud consistently and doggedly argued for his interpretation of the psyche's structure around the validity of establishing causal connections between unconsciousness and manifest behavior and conscious thought. In so doing, he hoped to directly respond to Brentano's challenge.

Freud would argue for a causative pathway built with forces bubbling to the surface of consciousness from some mysterious unconscious source of mental activity. Although the *Project* of 1895 is rife with Newtonian dynamics and mechanical balances, these speculations are, at best, metaphorical approximations of a still uncharted "force field." Nevertheless, the general notion of psychic forces following some mechanical model of pressure control and release may be found underlying Freud's later theorizing. Precise psychic dynamics were never stipulated, certainly not in any form that approached mental "laws." Instead, Freud perceived a system of conduits from the deep reservoir of unconscious drives, memories, and traumas, to gain "release" in dreams, jokes, slips of the tongue, and expression through various neuroses. Putting aside the specifics of this Newtonian model, Freud maintained that the unconscious was not governed by the same logic of cause and effect established in common experience. Based on his clinico-pathological case studies, he maintained that the unconscious had its own laws, which would give rise to a vast array of behaviors (given the peculiarities of individual defenses and repressions), and more to the point, if mental causation fulfilled the strict criteria Brentano had set for cause-and-effect relationships, then Freud's own discovery would have been made long before his own psychoanalytic investigations. For Freud, looking at conscious behavior and mentation as the full domain of the mental could not capture the full dimension of psychic life, and precisely because Brentano focused exclusively on consciousness, he missed the dynamic structure of the psyche.

A cautionary note about Freud's philosophy of science must be made here. As a positivist, Freud distinguished empirical findings from speculative theorizing. His "metapsychological" speculations demarcate his empirical reports and conclusions, which he regarded as comprising a clinical science, even a "natural science" (Freud 1940b, 158), from the theoretical models and conjectures in which he placed these clinical findings. After all, Freud understood that the various models of the mind he proposed could only offer an orientation for his clinical observations. From his early writings, these frameworks were formulated as hypotheses (for example, a "psychic apparatus"), which he described as "theoretical fictions" (1900, 603) that he might employ to further the larger agenda:

> We are justified, in my view, in giving free rein to our speculations, so long as we retain the coolness of our judgment and do not mistake the scaffolding for the building. And since at our first approach to something unknown all that we need is the assistance of provisional ideas, I shall give preference in the first instance to hypotheses of the crudest and most concrete description. (1900, 536)

According to Freud, such constructions were required to help establish the laws psychoanalysis sought to discover (1940b, 158; Fulgencio 2005), and he maintained that such theorizing followed the same basic procedures employed by natural scientists, who used similar approximations to link together their findings into some coherent model useful to order phenomena otherwise uncoordinated (Freud 1940b, 159).

So, on the one hand Freud carefully relied upon "facts" to ground his observations, and on the other hand he circumspectly differentiated facts from constructs (like the libido), which he acknowledged as just that—constructions, models, hypotheses, proto-theoretical heuristics. With his science split between an objective empiricism and speculative components, he felt confident that he might rest his case on observations and leave the theory or organizing principles to sort themselves in various ways:

> For these ideas are not the foundation of science, upon which everything rests: the foundation is observation alone. They are not the bottom but the top of the whole structure, and they can be replaced and discarded without damaging it. The same thing is happening in our day in the science of physics, the basic notions of which as regards matter, centres of force, attraction, etc., are scarcely less debatable than the corresponding notions in psycho-analysis. (Freud 1914a, 77)

Yet the facts and the theory could not be separated, and despite Freud's guarded comments, the philosophical integrity of his enterprise quickly became suspect (Decker 1977). The objective basis of Freud's case reports has been subject to continued debate (e.g., Bernheimer and Kahane 1990; Skues 2009), and it seems reasonable to conclude—given our sensitivity to the constructive character of social knowledge (e.g., Fleck 1979; Latour 1993; Jasanoff 1995; Knorr Cetina 1999)—that the analytic exercise extends "all the way down," namely, "the facts of the case" cannot reside outside the interpretive framework in which they reside (Zammito 2004). On this view, despite positivist protestations, psychoanalysis cannot escape cultural bias, one that extends over the entire therapeutic spectrum—from the categorization and expression of emotional mental illness to the more common dis-ease of modern life (Canguilhem 1989; Kleinman 1988; Shorter 1992); from the scientific positions then in vogue (Kitcher 1992) to the naïve positivism that underlay that science (Tauber 2009).

This fact/theory problem (already noted by Goethe at the end of the eighteenth century [Goethe 1988a]; Tauber 1993) is a nodal point for our critique, which in brief rests on discerning the circularity of Freud's argument: In building his case for psychoanalysis, Freud followed the dominant tenets of laboratory investigations. Trained as a research scientist, he was well aware of the positivist criticism that would be applied to the theoretical foundations he had placed under his reports. His defense rested upon a trusted empiricism, one, however, that could hardly support his theoretical construction. Lacking the critical distance from which his psychological examination might be evaluated, Freud elevated his observations to a sacrosanct neutral, objective status. However, failing to appreciate the value-laden, theory-dependent character of his clinical "facts" (Tauber 2005; 2009, chap. 2), Freud committed a basic logical error: the notion, for example, of a slip of the tongue (a clinical fact as it were) became such a "fact" as a *result* of the theory that made it so. In other words, the parapraxis itself (the fact of the matter) is *defined* as a manifestation of unconscious cause and, indeed, can only be a "slip of the tongue" within the psychoanalytic theory from which such phenomena are explained. This circularity plagues Freud's account of the unconscious, and as detailed below, the key issue of psychic causation cannot be proven by his approach.

That Freud drew parallels between the natural sciences and psychoanalysis reveals a sensitivity to the philosophical problems he faced, for in differentiating fact and theory, Freud sought a science of the mind that would fulfill positivist tenets. As we tease apart the various strands of psychoanalytic logic, the heart of these philosophical concerns lies open—the crucial challenge of establishing psychic cause. Accomplishing that task, of course, remained a formidable undertaking, and as we will demonstrate, despite Freud's own acute awareness of the issues at hand, he nevertheless failed to accomplish his self-assigned scientific goals. That failure strikes at the core of the philosophical standing of psychoanalysis, and from the rubble of its collapsed pretensions, another understanding beckons. First, the dismantling.

Did Freud Meet Brentano's Challenge?

Did Freud meet Brentano's standard of psychic causation? To answer this question let us consider (almost at random) the short article Freud prepared for the thirteenth edition of the *Encyclopedia Britannica* (1926b). It was written after all of his major theories of the mind's structure had been presented, and in this mature summation he depicts psychodynamics and the psyche's structure from three points of view (a well-traversed format): the dynamic, the economic, and the topographical.[1]

> From the first of these standpoints, the dynamic one, psychoanalysis derives all mental processes (apart from the reception of external stimuli) from the interplay of forces, which assist or inhibit one another, combine with one another, enter into compromises with one another, etc. (265)

This conception mirrors Freud's earliest model (Freud 1955, 295–397; Pribram and Gill 1976), which depends on relating neuronal "force," "counterforce," "energy transfer," "resistance," "discharge," "inertia" to describe a closed system of interacting neurons that must have appeared even to him as fanciful. These electrochemical events were hypothetically linked to the flow of sexual energy, and ultimately the model offered an explanation of neurosis through mechanisms of imbalanced energy. Freud was contemplating a kind of economics of nervous force, whose putative imbalance or disturbance might explain psychopathology. (As discussed in chapter 5, Freud drew on his understanding of Darwinism in support of this thesis.) He reiterated the schema in *The Interpretation of Dreams* (1900, 598–99), in which the economy of psychic energy followed a similar pattern of release and balance, and again in the review of his "metapsychological" formulations, where Freud described "a psychical process in its dynamic, topographical, and economic aspects" (1915a, 181). In its final articulation (Freud 1920, 7–61), "two great destinies of energy" account for "the entirety of the psychical process down to the minutest increment" (Boothby 2001, 5) to ultimately define human psychology in terms of clashing forces of unification (Eros) and disintegration (death) locked in entropic battle (Freud 1920; Phillips 2000, 75ff.).

Theoretical speculation leads to the suspicion that there are two fundamental instincts which lie concealed behind the manifest ego-instincts and object-instincts: namely (a) Eros, the instinct which strives for ever closer union, and (b) the instinct of destruction, which leads toward the dissolution of what is living. In psychoanalysis the manifestation of the force of Eros is given the name "libido." (Freud 1926b, 265)[2]

The economic or quantitative aspects of drives were accounted for in a psychical calculus of directional and additive forces; dynamic regulation was accomplished by defenses, which protect against the overaccumulation of psychical forces:

Pleasure-Pain Principle.—From the economic standpoint psychoanalysis supposes that the mental representations of the instincts have a cathexis of definite quantities of energy, and that it is the purpose of the mental apparatus to hinder any damming-up of these energies and to keep as low as possible the total amount of the excitations to which it is subject. The course of mental processes is automatically regulated by the "pleasure-pain principle"; and pain is thus in some way related to an increase of excitation and pleasure to a decrease. In the course of development the original pleasure principle undergoes a modification with reference to the external world, giving place to the "reality-principle," whereby the mental apparatus learns to postpone the pleasure of satisfaction and to tolerate temporarily feelings of pain. (Freud 1926b, 265–66)

Again, the conceptual difference between *Beyond the Pleasure Principle* (1920) and the *Project* (1895) resides in a rheostat Freud has placed on the psychic energies, a psychic "apparatus" to regulate the flow of energies, which display themselves psychodynamically along an axis of pleasure and pain.

The topographical representation of ego, id, and superego metaphorically places the psychoanalytic stratification of the mind in separate spatial domains in which these psychic forces vie:

Topographically, psychoanalysis regards the mental apparatus as a composite instrument, and endeavours to determine at what points in it the various mental processes take place. According to the most recent psychoanalytic views, the mental apparatus is composed of an "id," which is the reservoir of the instinctive impulses, of an "ego," which is the most superficial portion of the id and one which is modified by the influence of the external world, and of a "superego," which develops out of the id, dominates the ego and represents the inhibitions of instinct characteristic of man. Further, the property of consciousness has a topographical reference; for processes in the id are entirely unconscious, while consciousness is the function of the ego's outermost layer, which is concerned with the perception of the external world. (Freud 1926b, 266)

Note that Brentano's unity-of-consciousness picture of mental life has been replaced with a "composite instrument." A hierarchy, a stratification simulates biological organization of the brain, where the "vegetative" functions are found buried in the lower reaches (e.g., the medulla), while the highest cognitive functions are found in the superficial co tex. This crude analogy actually depicts Freud's topographical picture quite well, and it is not far-fetched to suggest that the metaphors of higher-better, lower-worse (Lakoff and Johnson 1980) orient this configuration of lower instincts and the higher reaches of conscious mediating abilities.

Freud cannot escape the biology of his earlier training, as he writes,

All of these forces are originally in the nature of instincts; that is to say, they have an organic origin. They are characterised by possessing an immense (somatic) persistence and reserve of power ("repetition-compulsion"); and they are represented mentally as images or ideas with an affective charge ("cathexis"). (Freud 1926b, 265)

He has reduced consciousness to the mere tip of an iceberg of swirling organic forces, whose release is predetermined. The choice psychoanalysis offers is partial control of their expression as modulated by affective recognition, rational insight, and moral censorship, or alternatively, perversity if the instincts are allowed their free release. In contrast to Brentano, whose notion of mind was essentially that of consciousness, Freud presents the unconscious as the dominant faculty of mind, and what humans know of their own psyche points to a hidden reservoir barely appreciated. Indeed, we are strangers to ourselves.

The article ends with Freud's very brief explanation of why psychoanalysis had met with hostility: from medicine, because it stressed "psychical factors" to explain disease; from the wider culture, a "disinclination" to assign critical importance to sexuality (childhood and adult); and "from the philosophical point of view, in its *assuming as an underly-*

ing postulate the concept of unconscious mental activity" (1926b, 269; emphasis added).[3] In the *New Introductory Lectures on Psycho-analysis*, published a few years later, Freud explains that "assumption" refers to the *inference* of a causative source of certain psychic phenomena:

> The oldest and best meaning of the word "unconscious" is the descriptive one; we call "unconscious" any mental process the existence of which we are obliged to assume—because, for instance, we infer it in some way from its effects—but of which we are not directly aware.... If we want to be more accurate, we should modify the statement by saying that we call a process "unconscious" when we have to assume that it was active *at a certain time*, although *at that time* we knew nothing about it. (1933, 70)

Following Brentano's prescription, the inference from effects is not enough, because cause has not been established. (The original German *erraten* [1933, 77], here translated as "infer," more typically is translated as "guess" or "divine.") Inference is only that, indirect postulation of cause. And from there, assumption follows. Freud acknowledged this problem, but sought to rectify it with additional support for his basic thesis:

> So far we should have learnt nothing, and not even earned the right to introduce the notion of the unconscious into psychology. But now we come across a new fact which we can already observe in the case of errors. We find that, in order to explain a slip of the tongue, for instance, we are obliged to assume that an intention to say something particular thing had formed itself in the mind of the person who made the slip. We can infer it with certainty from the occurrence of the speech-disturbance, but it was not able to obtain speech expression; it was, that is to say unconscious. (Freud 1933, 70)

(What is here translated as "infer" is, in the original German, *erschließen* [1933, 77], which has more diverse meanings: open, unlock; make accessible, disclose; conclude, infer, and most saliently, deduce.)

Freud's logic schematizes as follows:

1. A slip of the tongue is an "error" in consciousness (fact).
2. Such an "error" is a mental act (premise).

The fact of the case is uncontested, but that the slip of the tongue is a "mental error" is already a judgment with certain consequences (i.e.,

mental acts have intentionality; see number 3 below). Indeed, the error is
a premise in Freud's argument since he has classified all such observations
as "mental acts."

3. A mental act is intentional (definition, a Brentanean precept that Freud
   describes as an "assumption").
4. The mental error is unintentional to consciousness (restatement of
   number 1), but intentional in unconsciousness (second premise, i.e., not
   derived).

Before Freud can assign intentionality to a mental act in the unconscious, he must establish the unconscious, so the premise is actually
dual: premise$_a$, *there is an unconscious*; premise$_b$, like conscious mental acts, intentionality characterizes unconscious mentality. Freud thus
allows unconscious intentionality, which is a radical deviation from a
Brentanean definition of the mental, although Freud borrows from its
basic conceptualization.

5. Therefore, the error must be an unconscious mental act (deductive
   conclusion).

There is no logical progression here. Freud has already embedded the
idea of an "unconscious mental act" in his earlier premise about unconscious intentionality (step number 4). The last step, again, is not derived
from the above, but restates the initial inference about unconsciousness.
He admits as much when he writes to explain the parapraxis, namely,
one is "obliged to *assume* that an intention" has been formed. Finally, he
concludes that

6. Such acts arise from an unconscious source, the unconscious (inductive
   conclusion from assembly of many similar inferences).

Again, the very unconscious he sought to prove is already assumed, and a
collection of case examples based on the same logic does not change the
logical status of the unconscious as he derived it.

Let us review and unpack this argument: At one level, Freud simply seeks to incorporate such errors as errors of the *mind*, but more directly he keeps intentionality, because he still requires *cause*. Indeed, intention is essential to Freud's theory, for it serves as the key to unlocking

these kinds of mental error. Freud takes the line that if the slip of the tongue is apparently unintentional, but still mental, then it *is* unintentional in a behavioristic understanding of consciousness. So for Freud, in contrast to Brentano, the assignment of unintentionality does not mean that the behavior is not mental, only that it is not *conscious*. And because the error remains a mental act for Freud, it must be an *unconscious* one. Finally, Freud argues that a vast array of data show a similar mental structure. But if a logical error has been committed, then all of the examples lie fallow.

Brentano had dismissed such arguments half a century earlier in the presentation of his own psychology, and, indeed, despite Freud's assurance that the inference is *certain*, he must realize that an inference is only a process of reasoning from a premise to a conclusion. The logical structure shows instead that he has drawn his inference from a premise that already contains the conclusion: although the mental error is unintentional to consciousness, it retains its intentional character in an unconscious source. What Freud hopes to derive along a causal chain of reasoning from empirical data is in fact an inference drawn directly from his *definitions* of the mental (constituted by conscious and unconscious activities), which he has not established. In short, the reasoning is utterly circular and the entire argument collapses, at least as Brentano would have undoubtedly concluded.

If Freud is not using a deductive logic, what type of reasoning has he displayed? Formally, Freud invokes "inference to the best explanation" (Lipton 1991), not a syllogistic proof.[4] However, a more comprehensive approach in understanding Freud's method must account for the reconstruction of the unconscious as a widely interpretative venture with a particular telos. The analyst reconstructs the intention of the speaker by either having her agree that the postulated intention is recognizable, or at least plausible (then the error emerges from a more superficial unconscious source, "the preconscious"), or if no such reconstruction presents itself, the intention is regarded as buried and therefore must be excavated from the depths of the unconscious proper (Freud 1937a). Indeed, depth psychology is designed for such explorations, and in its narrative reconstructions, the "intention" then is established. Of course, the entire interpretation hangs together as a whole; one piece supports the others, and so a hermeneutic circle must be established. Here we come to the fork in the road for understanding Freud's enterprise.

Generally speaking, hermeneutics is a theory of the rules that preside over an exegesis. As applied to the human sciences, literary criticism, theology, and philosophy, hermeneutics serves as a nexus for discussions of philosophies of meaning, but that approach makes no appeal to a *scientific* stratagem for establishing the linkages the psychoanalyst seeks: "Causation" resting on interpretation is a sequence; however, the items in that sequence are linked not by some law of causality constitutive to the elements themselves, but by the "integrity" of the whole, in this case the interpretative whole. Thus the connections are provided by the overall structure of a narrative or interpretation, which places one element in juxtaposition to another by an imposed schema—the integrity of the whole, whose "glue" is the purpose, message, or general function of the matter. In other words, some overriding meaning or telos coordinates the parts so that the elements support the whole, and the whole, in turn, defines those constituents and their relationship to each other.

In the attempt to establish psychic cause, Freud has offered an *interpretation*. An interpretation, while failing to establish causality, *does* offer an explanation, albeit one constructed within its own definitions and guided by its own inner logic (as described above). The overall structure of that interpretation is framed by "meanings," and these interpretative elements—the parts, if you will—then are assembled to compose larger meanings through a more comprehensive interpretation, and so on. Simply, the psychological narrative becomes a product of a hermeneutical strategy, where cause is embedded in the constructed schema as a product of a larger interpretative enterprise.

A second criterion, the empirical one, demands that causality be tested within boundary conditions established for the experiment. This issue, precipitated by Popper's falsification stipulation, has had a rich literature. Suffice it to note here, perhaps too simply, that Freud's conception of psychic determinism cannot fit the scientific criteria demand by Popper (nor for that matter, Brentano) (Popper 1959; 1963; Bouveresse 1995, 83–96). Because Freud cannot provide such evidence, he failed to establish psychoanalysis as a demonstrable *scientific* theory. He never explained (or justified) why his orthodox therapy was superior to other forms of introspective psychotherapy. Indeed, after a century of practice, psychoanalysts have still to demonstrate conclusively that psychoanalysis fulfills its own therapeutic promise. This judgment summarizes many devastating critiques, from hostile (e.g., Grünbaum 1984, Eysenck 1985; Crews 1986; Hobson 1988; Kitcher 1992; Webster 1995; Macmillan 1997, Cioffi 1998a) and even sympathetic while critical (e.g., Farrell 1981; Holt 1989; Parisi 1989) critics, and so we are left with a certain irony in Freud's own pronouncement found in the opening line of his final *Outline of Psycho-analysis*: "Psycho-analysis makes a basic assumption, the discussion of which is reserved to philosophical thought but the justification for which lies in its results" (1940b, 144).

This basic tension, arising between a scientific explanation and a hermeneutical interpretation, resides at the foundations of psychoanalysis and has been recognized by many. Stan Draenos succinctly states the conflict, one embedded deeply in Freud's bivalent approach:

> A contradiction runs through Freud's writings like a fault line. It arises from the fact that psychoanalysis presents itself as knowledge of two different kinds. On the one hand, psychoanalysis takes the form of an understanding of mind obtained through the disclosure of hidden meanings in dreams and neurotic symptoms. On the other, psychoanalysis takes the form of an explanation of mind secured in the elucidation of the mechanisms and systematic relation of a "mental apparatus."
>
> To bring these two forms of knowledge together within one science is like trying to square a circle. For they carry with them visions of mind that are fundamentally at odds. In seeking to understand mind through interpretation of meaning, Freud takes the mental as a property of a subject and his inner life. In seeking to explain mind as a mechanism, he places mental phenomena among the natural objects of the external world. Mind as meaning and mind as mechanism, however, lie on opposite sides of a great divide first enunciated by Descartes's famous dualism, in the distinction between *res cogitans* and *res extensa*, consciousness and matter, subject and object. (1982, 7)

Freud, of course, straddled the line.

The unconscious as some entity fails the criteria of identification, and as Alasdair MacIntyre observed, the unconscious in fact must be regarded as an "activity," which appropriates terms more aptly applied to a neurophysiological conception of psychic function. Indeed, MacIntyre makes the significant point that Freud repeatedly went back and forth between mental and physiological descriptions and in the process confused the two categories as either symmetrical or at least freely interchangeable. MacIntyre charges, not unfairly, that

> Freud preserved the view of the mind as a piece of machinery and merely wrote up in psychological terms what had been originally intended as neurological theory.... What Freud in fact does is to bring a scheme of explanation derived from neurology to the phenomena which his psychological studies had forced on his attention. (1958, 22–23)

MacIntyre observes that Freud himself, at some level, understood the inner tension of the connection he attempted to make:

> The fact is that local diagnosis and electrical reactions lead nowhere in the study of hysteria, whereas the detailed description of mental processes such as we are accustomed to find in the works of imaginative writers enable me, with the use of a few psychological formulas, to obtain at least some kind of insight into the course of that affection. (Freud 1955, 160–61; quoted by MacIntyre 1958, 44)

Without this distinction, category errors flourished and inconsistencies developed.

MacIntyre regards the basis of these errors as originating in the language of psychoanalysis. Freud uses "unconscious" in several grammatical modes: as a noun, "*the* unconscious," as well as descriptively, that is, "unconscious" as an adjective or adverb. In the first case, he invents a new term in which he has to prescribe a meaning and a use, which he does by building from a Cartesian formulation of the mind as separate and distinct. This domain is inhabited by ideas, but instead of *consciousness* equated with "mind," Freud builds a complex topographical structure, in which the unconscious dominates. In this construction, "unconscious" is used as an adjective for describing actions, dreams, emotions that were hitherto unrecognized, and he "introduces the unconscious as a noun not to describe, but to explain" (MacIntyre 1958, 45). MacIntyre maintains that this basic Cartesian understanding of the mind, namely, a "space" in which entities we call "ideas" exist, was transmitted directly by Brentano to Freud (37, 46).[5] The principle question then becomes, given Freud's Cartesian assumptions, how does the unconscious as an *explanatory concept* cash out from that basic formulation? The argument presented below builds upon Wittgenstein's influential argument about Freud's conflation of reasons and causes, an issue that assumes centrality in Freud's own preoccupation with Brentano's challenge.

Wittgenstein's Critique

Wittgenstein's comments on Freud divide between a general indictment (Freud's "whole way of thinking wants combating" [Rhees 1967, 50]) and a more specific criticism of psychoanalytic logic, in which Freud's "abominable mess" arose from confusing reasons with causes (Moore 1993, 107–8). First, we will consider the logical question, while the more general metaphysical issue is postponed to the next section. The critique of Freud's logic hinges on the distinction Wittgenstein made between causes as descriptions of natural phenomena following an ordered sequence and displaying that order as defined by rules or natural laws, in contrast to the interpretations offered to explain virtually everything else. That "everything" includes ethics, aesthetics, religion, and, of course, psychoanalysis. This distinction is key to Wittgenstein's approach, and it was built from a complex philosophy of language, which must serve only as the background to the discussion below.

Wittgenstein obviously believed that psychoanalysis offered something important.[6] How to characterize that importance remains somewhat problematic, because he made little more than offhand observations to students and colleagues, and to the extent that he wrote in his journals, those comments appear as interjections in a much larger project.[7] Fundamentally, according to G. E. Moore, Wittgenstein believed that Freud's work exemplified "philosophical mistakes" (Moore 1993, 107), and in particular, the lack of clarity of distinguishing a fact from a hypothesis marked the Freudian argument. To make his case, Wittgenstein focused on the difference between establishing causes and offering reasons to explain psychic phenomena. In discussing *Jokes and Their Relation to the Unconscious* (1905a), Wittgenstein observed that

> Freud encouraged a confusion between getting to know the *cause* of your laughter and getting to know the *reason* why you laugh, because what he says sounds as if it were science, when in fact it is only a "wonderful representation [performance]." This last point he also expressed by saying "It is all excellent similes, e.g. the comparison of a dream to a rebus." (Moore 1993, 107)

Much requires unpacking here.

For Wittgenstein, the key issue concerned the nature of knowledge, and (as already mentioned) by this he meant scientific knowledge, as opposed to interpretation. For him, scientific discovery entailed hypotheses, which might be tested and if true, effective in predicting phenomena. From such studies, rules (laws) might be derived. Psychoanalysis, however, possessed no such rules, that is, none even analogous "to the rules which will tell you what are the causes of stomachache" (Moore 1993, 107). Instead, Freud "had genius and therefore might sometimes by psycho-analysis find the *reason* of a certain dream" (107). In this last regard, psychoanalysis closely aligns with aesthetics, and indeed, Wittgenstein called Freud's investigation of jokes an "aesthetic investigation" (107). (This allusion to aesthetics is discussed below.) Wittgenstein challenged the assumption that all jokes (and by extrapolation any unconscious manifestation) shared some common psychic denominator, that is, covert mechanisms of psychic release. While successful analysis depends on the analysand agreeing with an explanation offered by the analyst (or discovered by the patient), such a process simply cannot pose as science: "There is nothing analogous to this in Physics; and that what a patient agrees to can't be a *hypothesis* as to the *cause* of his laughter, but only that so-and-so was the *reason* why he laughed" (108).[8]

Wittgenstein observed, as many others, that analysis never finds a resting place, a position of some finality that determines the "correctness" of interpretation, either that of the analysand or the analyst. The "right" analysis "does not seem to be a matter of evidence" (Wittgenstein 1958, 42), nor for that matter, do interpretations of dreams as wish fulfillments fulfill the criteria of proof. Establishment of cause simply does not apply to the psychoanalytic discovery.[9] For Wittgenstein, analysis is *speculation*

(1958, 43, 44), which is a particularly noxious condemnation considering Freud's own aversion to speculative reasoning. Accordingly, the success of psychoanalysis resides in its ability to offer an alternative life interpretation, one that provides new paths for behaving and thinking. While giving up one way of thinking and adopting another may be beneficial, Wittgenstein asks, does that process reveal the *workings* of the mind? "Can we say we have laid bare the essential nature of mind?" (45). The Freudian evidence only attests to the effectiveness of the analyst to help reconfigure the analysand's life story, or in other words, to create a new "myth" (51).[10]

For Wittgenstein, instead of providing a positive science of motivation, psychoanalysis offers a hermeneutics, which is most akin to an aesthetic interpretation, both as procedure and as experience.[11] The analysis is not invalidated; the "inspiration," as he calls it, remains a crucial personal experience, but it does not qualify as something holding a scientific status, and thus a form of epistemic *knowledge*. The validity of the interpretation must stand on its own ground and make its own distinctive truth claims, as an "aesthetic" procedure, which must be judged on its own merits. How to judge an interpretation of psychic phenomena then corresponds to an adjudication that must occur as an interpretation undertaken with its own rules (as discussed above).

This Wittgensteinian point concerns how psychoanalysis should be conceived as a "language game," a "game" that has its own rules and whose correspondents understand an entire grammar of speaking. Beyond the lexicon, the grammar includes an array of assumptions, conventions, and history that confers insularity and provides coherence for those committed to its enterprise. As such, Freudianism is first, and foremost, a cultural *practice*, and that practice cannot masquerade as a science simply because the rules radically differ. Wittgenstein sourly complains about the game qua game: "My super-ego might say of my ego: 'It is raining, and the ego believes so,' and might go on 'So I shall probably take an umbrella with me.' And now how does this game go on?" (1980b, 1:130e). For Wittgenstein, the "game" of cause is one defined by scientific practice that fulfills the criterion of some regularity, a "cause-effect" relationship that is typically characterized by a law or at least a rule. Once a cause is established, *ceteris paribus*, an expected effect results. Wittgenstein insists that Freud cannot twist reasons into causes by claiming a scientific analysis, simply because no interpretation of the sort provided by psychoanalysis conforms to the kind of objectivity and verification characterizing investigations in the natural sciences.

When Freud grumbled that Pierre Janet seemingly regarded the unconscious "a makeshift, '*une façon de parler*,'—that he had meant nothing real by it" (Freud 1916–17, 257), he foreshadowed Wittgenstein's far more devastating critique, which

> regarded the "hypothesis" of the unconscious as really no more than a manner of speaking which creates more philosophical difficulties than the scientific ones it claims to resolve.... What Wittgenstein refuses to acknowledge in psychoanalysis ... is nothing less than its ontology. (Bouveresse 1995, xvii)

Wittgenstein thereby rejected the grounding that Freud postulated for psychoanalysis: Again, causes reside in the domain of scientific proof and objective knowledge—knowledge available to all; reasons provide an interpretative framework in which to understand human experience—an individualized understanding peculiar to the singular perspective of the agent. And that perspective derives not only from an individual's past experience, but also from the analysand's future motives and goals.

So instead of engaging psychoanalytic theory as a *theory* as understood in the natural sciences, Wittgenstein accepts the telos of analysis in its humane terms as a mode of interpretation that comprehends one's life in some ordered fashion, in which meaning is created, articulated, and understood. And here we find another source of Wittgenstein's dismay at assigning reasons as a category of cause:

> The explanation by reasons belongs to the category of teleological explanation, which "consists in making phenomena teleologically intelligible rather than predictable from knowledge of their efficient causes." (Bouveresse 1995, 77; quoting von Wright 1971, 8)[12]

In the end, "Wittgenstein objects that discovering a determining cause and agreeing to the existence of a reason or a motive constitute two very different things. And they continue to be different, even when it is allowed that a reason can also be a cause" (Bouveresse 1995, 82).

Despite challenging the underlying logic and aspirations to give psychoanalysis scientific standing, Wittgenstein valued Freud's accomplishments as an *ethical* project: "In a way having oneself psychoanalysed is like eating from the tree of knowledge. The knowledge acquired sets us (new) ethical problems; but contributes nothing to their solution" (Wittgenstein 1980a, 34). However, Wittgenstein's focus on Freud's methods absolved him from discussing the ethical import of psychic analysis, and this, of course, was completely consistent with the steadfast commitment to eschew *philosophical* comment on topics inaccessible to logical and linguistic analysis. So the matter rested, with little more said on the moral aspects of psychoanalysis, but as discussed in later chapters, recognizing Freud's inquiry as thoroughly ethical offers a rich understanding of what psychoanalysis *does* and to what it is committed.

Freud and the Later Positivists

To place Freud within the larger philosophical context immediately prior to the powerful shifts initiated by Wittgenstein and Heidegger, respectively, let us pause for a moment and gaze at some aspects of the extraordinarily varied and interesting intellectual landscape that Freud might have surveyed between 1910 and 1925. During that period, each of the principal parties—historicists, neo-Kantians, and positivists—were seeking foundations upon which to build their respective philosophical systems, albeit with very different goals: The historicists rightly claimed the constitutive role of culture and history, but they could not repel the charges of relativism. The neo-Kantians were left with the same imbroglio of configuring the mind in nature that had perplexed Kant a century earlier, so they set themselves the task of *understanding* the metaphysics grounding knowledge. But the high tide of neo-Kantianism had crashed into the wall of a resurgent positivism, which had reached back to an empirical tradition that would subtract "mind" altogether and leave the assembly of "perceptions" as both necessary and sufficient to build knowledge; in the process they would seek to *eliminate* metaphysics. (The Nietzscheans had eclipsed the search for philosophical foundations altogether, and for the purposes of this discussion we postpone their appearance on the Freudian stage until chapter 5.) This triangle serves as the manifold in which I will situate Freud the epistemologist: He aligned himself with positivists, although he would be unceremoniously discharged from their assembly; he seemed to have been essentially ignorant of the historicist program, and to the extent he knew their agenda, he would be disinclined to engage the issues; and with the neo-Kantians, he might have found himself in productive dialogue to clarify (and strengthen) his own project. That relationship will be examined in the next chapter; here we consider the positivist program and its significance for Freudianism.

By the 1920s, positivists had switched the terms of engagement from essentially a Lockean empiricism to a new domain of logical analysis: With logical positivism (also known as the Vienna Circle), *language* became the arena in which to examine science's philosophy. These positivists maintained that scientific method is the only source of knowledge, and that a *statement* is meaningful only if it is "scientific," that is, empirically verifiable. (For our purposes we will ignore the differences between "logical" and "empirical" positivists.)[13] We return to Wittgenstein, who, despite his disavowal of the Vienna Circle, must be credited with setting positivism on a different philosophical track, one that keenly identified the conceits of Freud's psychoanalytic *science*.

Wittgenstein, the "early" Wittgenstein, lurks as the shadow figure in this history. In *Tractatus Logico-Philosophicus* (1998), he presented a "picture" theory of language that allowed for the legitimacy of certain propositions based on their factuality, and for the rest—ethics, metaphysics, aesthetics—he advised that we must remain "silent." Throughout his writings, he drew distinctions between "facts" as derived from objective methods as opposed to other kinds of experience—emotional, supernatural, ethical—in which personal (and thus unverifiable) belief confers a radically different status to certainty. And because language and thought are inseparable for Wittgenstein, much of "thought" would remain inarticulate; further, the status of private thought was highly problematic.

Wittgenstein regarded philosophy as failing to find solutions to traditional metaphysical problems, because their articulation could not fulfill *logical* criteria. He did not deny their presence as human challenges, but he rejected *philosophical* solutions to such questions. Accordingly, the narratives woven around the classic philosophical issues—moral action, aesthetic judgment, personal identity, and so on—were, for him, simply misconceived if some kind of *logical* formulation was expected. In Wittgenstein's terminology, questions of this kind are "nonsense," because they are bereft of final adjudication, or any hope of one. In contrast, such a question as "Is it raining?" demands a meaningful response: "Yes, it is raining" or "No, it is not raining." His approach bequeathed a philosophy of language that restricts the province of logic to logic; of knowledge (in a empirical positivist fashion) to science; and of ethics to metaphysics, where philosophy's analytical tools are inapplicable. Accordingly, he sought to comprehend the locks and chains in which language ensnares human understanding and the problems we pose for one another as products of false application of logic. Language thus becomes a system for solving problems, and from another vantage, philosophical problems are characteristically confusions bestowed by language itself, or as Wittgenstein famously noted, "Philosophical problems arise when language goes on holiday" (1968, 19e), which orients analysis as coincident to, and embedded in, the analysis of language. Accordingly, the aim of linguistic analysis is to solve philosophical problems, or in the words of Wittgenstein, "to shew the fly the way out of the fly-bottle" (1968, 103e).[14]

In this vein, Wittgenstein distinguished scientific knowledge from "nonsense," but nonsense—that which made life humane and significant—was hardly disparaged on its own account. He was driven to show how philosophy had failed to make this fundamental distinction and thus compromised its own efforts to distinguish epistemology from metaphysics, aesthetics, and ethics, and thereby embroil itself in pseudo-problems, that is, issues that were not subject to philosophical inquiry. In sum, Wittgenstein's philosophy was based on dissolving philosophical imbroglios as matters of confused thought and language. So, distinguishing scientific questions from others and breaking the conceits of certain philosophical questions became his primary concerns. And as discussed, psychoanalysis served as a ready target.

Wittgenstein's most profound attack on Freudianism was directed at the metaphysical character of the theory. Indeed, the long discussions of distinguishing reason and causes are only examples of Wittgenstein's general approach. So when he lamented that Freud's "whole way of thinking wants combating" (Rhees 1967, 50), he was referring to Freud's "mythology" as a metaphysics, namely, an attempt to discover the real that underlies phenomena (Edwards 2004). On this reading, Wittgenstein becomes an "antiphilosopher" inasmuch as he opposes Western metaphysics, which begins with Platonic forms, extends through Kant's noumenon/phenomenon distinction, and goes beyond to Nietzsche (Heidegger 1979). For Wittgenstein, metaphysical inquiry is directed at, first, recognizing the determinate structure of the world as a presentation to humans as only a specific instance of a general, underlying reality that is *hidden*, and, second, defining the world in acknowledgment of that mystery of Being through *explanations*. Wittgenstein argued that instead of seeking hidden reality that gives order to the world, philosophy should discern how language functions to present the world, and in this sense, language *is* reality. Wittgenstein thus opposed any form of metaphysics not only because of the limitations of language and logic to discern such a hidden reality, but in a positive fashion of limiting philosophy to the role of deriving *clarity* by an examination of language itself, which must suffice to present reality to us (Edwards 2004, 127–35). "Philosophy simply puts everything before us, and neither explains nor deduces anything.—Since everything lies open to view there is nothing to explain. For what is hidden, for example, is of no interest to us" (Wittgenstein 1968, sec. 126, p. 50e). Of course, to accept this position is to dismiss Freud's entire corpus as metaphysics, and for that matter all the philosophy in which we might situate him is similarly discarded as misdirected and incoherent. Such was the effect of Wittgenstein's radical critique of Western philosophy.

Beyond taking note of the implications of this antiphilosophical orientation, at least in the terms discussed here, the philosophical discourse of Freud's contemporaries still provides a fecund interpretative context in which to situate psychoanalysis. So, without further following the Wittgensteinian tack, note that much of the criticism directed at Freud by the logical positivists and the neo-Kantians (considered in the next chapter) argued that psychoanalysis was, at heart, metaphysics, just as Wittgenstein observed. Wittgenstein's positivist followers similarly discarded metaphysics as meaningless and thus suitably ignored and endeavored to ground science in language, which they had hoped would follow logical analysis. These efforts failed (as Wittgenstein might have predicted given his suspicions), and into the new opening, a spectrum of options ranging over varieties of naturalism, pragmatism, constructivism, and relativism have made their respective claims (Zammito 2004; Tauber 2009). The positivists discredited metaphysics altogether, whereas Wittgenstein simply argued that metaphysics, aesthetics, and ethics essentially lay outside of philosophical discourse. This is not to say that such questions are meaningless, but rather that different kinds of discourse are required to entertain the problems they pose. In the misunderstanding of the *Tractatus*, the Vienna Circle espoused an analytic philosophy, which would extend Wittgenstein's general position to ends he would disallow, and while flirting with the group in its early stages, he eventually divorced himself from their deliberations (Monk 1991; see especially 287–88).

Twentieth-century positivism begins with this antimetaphysical program, most explicitly and clearly espoused by Ernst Mach, who dedicated himself to the elimination of metaphysics and the unification of various disciplines under the banner of common methodologies and precepts based on the natural sciences (Cohen 1970a). He was drawn to psychology by his doctrine (and hope) that all scientific propositions might be formulated in terms of perceptions. Standing in opposition to Brentano's implicitly holistic conception of consciousness, both in how he viewed intentional objects and the nature of its function and structure, Mach argued for the primacy, in fact the exclusivity, of perceptions, a view based on strict empiricist doctrine. He thus pursued Comte's original agenda through advocacy of a radical empiricism and an accompanying objectivism. So while both Mach and Brentano embraced empiricism, Brentano legitimized consciousness as *mental* phenomena, whereas Mach sought to reduce such phenomena to physical characterization. This "genetic psychology" putatively would take its place among the natural sciences, addressing the same sorts of questions about mental phenomena that other sciences pose about physical phenomena (Mach 1914; McAlister 1982, 13). Mach reasoned that an objective understanding of the knowing perceiver would fulfill the ultimate goal of establishing the unification of science, from psychology to physiology to chemistry to physics (Cohen 1970b).

Philip Frank, a leader of the Vienna Circle, acknowledged Mach's important contributions to later developments in the positivism program, both in Mach's opposition to metaphysics and through his staunch defense of an austere scientific program, one based on an objective empiricism: "Whether it be a proposition of physics, biology, or psychology, it can only be proved or refuted by comparison with observation" (Frank 1961, 90). More, he interpreted Mach's scientific program as one based on scientific *statements*: "Mach never maintained that our world consisted of complexes of perceptions, but that every scientific proposition was a statement about complexes of perceptions" (90). And here, in the move to eliminate the knowing agent and the possibility of metaphysical prejudice, science would now be conceived as a system of logical statements (albeit based on empirical observation), a system unto itself whose logic and consistency would be regarded as a mirror to nature. Such a constellation of autonomous scientific propositions that would constitute the scientific enterprise brought positivism to its apogee.

According to Wittgensteinian precepts and Machian definitions of legitimate scientific statements, the Viennese positivists adopted the analysis and critique of language as the focus of their philosophy of science. To get to science, they pursued both a "negative" program and a "positive" one. The first dispenses with "nonscience" (a major focus of concern) by establishing a linguistic conception of analytic truth that would provide an account of the nonempirical character of logico-mathematical knowledge. Without appeal to metaphysical principles or abstract entities (like concepts or ideas), the positivists attempted to establish the a priori status of logic and mathematics compatible with a radical empiricism by showing the truth of these propositions through logical analysis. This then became the "positive" program, an effort to discern the logical structure of truth statements and apply them to an epistemology that would afford true knowledge. They did so by building on the analytic-synthetic distinction by arguing that because metaphysics, ethics, aesthetics, and theology did not fit into either the analytic or synthetic categories, their respective claims were made on the basis of a misuse of *language*.[15]

Having putatively secured logic and mathematics, and having pushed metaphysics aside, positivist philosophy was then freed to do epistemology in the same analytical *linguistic* manner, and so philosophy in this tradition became the analysis and clarification of meaning with the use of logic and scientific method; concomitantly, metaphysics *tout court* was rejected, since statements alluding to some transcendental reality could not be verified.[16] Thus the lynchpin of the positivist critique became "verification," whose application to psychoanalysis would prove devastating.

Verification, the key to cognitive significance, rested on mutually exclusive criteria: logical and factual. Thus meaningful statements were either analytic—independent of empirical considerations and reliant on language alone (as Willard Van Orman Quine wrote, "grounded in meanings independently of matters of fact" [1980, 20])—or synthetic (assertions that were verified or falsified by empirical procedures, or again Quine, "grounded in fact" [20]). This analytic-synthetic distinction provided the philosophical foundation for the demarcations the positivists attempted to employ—theory/observation, discovery/verification, fact/value. Freud's theory failed each of these criteria for a scientific endeavor, yet in an unexpected display of generosity, some logical positivists generally were unwilling to summarily dismiss Freud's attempts to decipher the unconscious (e.g., Feigl 1958, 394, 436; Frank 1977). No such respite appeared with Karl Popper's dismissal of psychoanalysis, which proved to have a wide influence.

Popper, who, never affiliated with the positivists and, for all of his differences with the Vienna Circle, embraced the demarcation of science and pseudo-science as central to his own philosophy of science. However, he moved against the "verification" program and offered instead his famous falsification criterion (Popper 1959; 1963). Disputing the putative confirmations offered by criteria of verification, Popper held to a deep skepticism and projected that doubt as the basis of scientific investigation and theory construction. According to Popper, if a theory could not be falsified, it could hardly count as scientific. He came to this view by following Hume's thesis that inductive generalization was *logically* invalid; that is, no collection of particular observations will verify a general statement.

Accordingly, scientific theories cannot be verified by any amount of observational evidence (a point Quine later took further in his underdetermination thesis [Tauber 2009, chap. 3]). Given the challenge of induction as a rational principle, Popper argued that the rationality of science rested on the logical principle of *modus tollens* (If A, then B; not B, therefore not-A). He thus regarded the fallibility of scientific knowledge as the crux of scientific truth claims, and in the ongoing critical activity of the laboratory, he emphasized how scientific evolution progresses on the backs of refuting evidence. In his famous configuration of "conjectures" and "refutations," a hypothesis leads to an observation, which in its ability to falsify the original hypothesis generates a new conjecture. Popper argued that science proceeded best with the formulation of the most falsifiable hypothesis, preferably a simple conjecture with abundant empirical content, and then the search for negative evidence begins. Once refuted, a new hypothesis initiates the process again, and so on. Such a test was easily applied to Marx's dialectical materialism and Freud's psychoanalytic theories, each of which failed his criteria for science, because neither could be falsified (Popper 1963, 34–37).[17] For our present purposes, the important philosophical point is that for Popper, hypotheses followed one another in some kind of cascade pattern, where observations falsify one hypothesis, which is then replaced with new hypotheses in a stepwise fashion.

Later developments in philosophy of science were to dethrone Popper and the Vienna Circle, but certainly during the 1930s, either the positivists' verification demands or Popper's falsification standard left psychoanalysis outside the pale of those committed to understanding science philosophically and protecting the laboratory from invasion by pretenders. For them, psychoanalysis was at best a mysterious, yet potentially effective, therapy; a metaphysical construction; and at worst a simple myth. Freud would not have to wait for Popper to brand his efforts as scientifically untenable, for his own peers were most happy to do so without the encouragement of philosophers (Decker 1977).

Freud's Own Assessment

In light of the above discussion, Freud's comment that psychoanalysis must assume *"as an underlying postulate* the concept of unconscious mental activity" in the *Britannica* article is an astonishing admission. After a lifetime of assembling clinical evidence, framing that evidence into various models, applying those models to complex historical and cultural scenarios, and fighting with detractors in all guises (even within his own movement), Freud now, towards the end of his life, tips his hat and admits that a *philosophical* elephant has, since the beginning, resided in his celebrated chambers, and furthermore, it had hitherto been ignored. He lamely gestures to the tentative status of the theory:

> It must not be supposed that these very general ideas [referencing depth psychology described above] are presuppositions upon which the work of psychoanalysis depends. On the contrary, they are its latest conclusions and are in every respect open to revision. Psychoanalysis is founded securely upon the observation of the facts of mental life; and for that very reason its theoretical superstructure is still incomplete and subject to constant alteration. (1926b, 266)

Freud thus reiterates the distinction between his empirical observations and the interpretations he attaches to them (Fulgencio 2005) and restates a basic precept of the scientific creed: Following the best scientific principles, facts remain inviolate, but how they are situated within a theory is always open to question. That is a reasonable posture to take, where Freud remains suitably circumspect and ever mindful of the dynamic quality of a vibrant field of inquiry, and so he bows his head modestly to the judgment of history and the future developments of psychoanalysis. But perhaps that interpretation is too obvious? Is there, hidden in this short aside, a veiled insecurity?

A more intriguing hypothesis is that Freud knew he had *failed*. As he wrote in *Beyond the Pleasure Principle*,

> It may be asked whether and how far I myself am convinced of the truth of the hypotheses that have been set out in these pages. My answer would be that *I am not convinced myself* and that I do not seek to persuade other people to believe in them. Or, more precisely, that *I do not know how far I believe them*. (1920, 59; emphasis added)

Whether Freud is here referring strictly to the metapsychological argument or to the more basic underlying theory upon which it is based remains ambiguous. And even putting aside the disingenuous denial of polemic intent, Freud's tentativeness seems apparent, and one wonders what shifted the bravado of his earlier defenses to such an admission. I suggest that he was aware that by this point he could not fulfill Brentano's criteria for establishing the unconscious as some separate entity or faculty of the mind. By inferential reasoning, he was convinced, but convictions are not easily translated into proof. Admitting to an assumption, he concedes that the basic postulate is not grounded. He found empirical support, but cause was not established as he had originally hoped. Indeed, at the end of *Beyond the Pleasure Principle,* Freud suggests that biology might "blow away the whole of our *artificial* structure of hypotheses" (1920, 60; emphasis added), and he still presents his thoughts because they "deserve consideration" (60).

Note that Freud does not directly admit to a failure, but rather takes refuge in the ongoing success of the movement he founded. However, that is a sociological description of the triumph of his theory, not the validation of psychoanalysis on the basis of the scientific standards he sought to apply to his investigations. In short, his dismissal of philosophy in earlier pronouncements here is replaced with an oblique reference to his *"assuming as an underlying postulate"* to establish the legitimacy of psychoanalysis. The concept of the unconscious has thereby been transfigured from an empirically based entity or activity or force to an abstract *idea.*

I am not suggesting that Freud at any point relinquished the basic claims of his theory, namely its sexual orientation, its topographical and economic stratifications of the mind, or the veracity of its fundamental interpretations. Most importantly, in recognizing that psychoanalytic theory must be open to revision, the core idea of an active and operative unconscious mind affecting conscious life was held sacrosanct. How that would be substantiated Freud left to posterity. In this regard, he was hardly modest or conciliatory, despite the reduction of the *science* of psychoanalysis to a compelling *inference.*

Nevertheless, Freud's abiding insight remains essentially intact. Physicalist accounts, still in the twenty-first century, have a most tenuous hold on "the mind," and the causation so eagerly sought by Brentano and all those neuroscientists who followed in his wake has yet to be established. Nevertheless, irrespective of the causal lines that remain to be drawn, that unconscious processes occur has become a truism. But for Freud, unconscious processes inferred an entity, *an unconscious,* and that has proven to be highly problematic, inasmuch as the topography he postulated seems now only a convenient mapping, hardly qualifying as bona fide designations or entities of the mind. At best, they represent convenient ways of cataloguing various mind functions.

We need not condemn Freud's construction in the particularities of its conception to acknowledge that by focusing on unconscious processes, he identified a nexus of psychic activity that profoundly affects conscious life. The evidence evinced by current cognitive science conclusively demonstrates that general insight (e.g., Wilson 2002). Conscious thought in its various articulations arises from deeper emotional phenomena and unconscious perceptions, and to restrict discussion to conscious thought ultimately distorts thought itself. Of the many rebuttals Freud offered to his detractors, the following from his late *Autobiography* seems most appropriate:

> Psycho-analysis regarded everything mental as being in the first instance unconscious; the further quality of "consciousness" might also be present, or again it might be absent. This of course provoked a denial from the philosophers, for whom "consciousness" and "mental" were identical, and who protested that they could not conceive of such an absurdity as the "unconscious mental." There was no help for it, however, and this idiosyncrasy of the philosophers could only be disregarded with a shrug. Experience (gained from pathological material, of which the philosophers were ignorant) of the frequency and power of the impulses of which one knew nothing directly, and whose existence had to be *inferred* like some fact in the external world, left no alternative open. It could be pointed out, incidentally, that this was only treating one's own mental life as one had always treated other people's. One did not hesitate to ascribe mental processes to other people, although one had no immediate consciousness of them and could only infer them from their words and actions. But what held good for other people must be applicable to oneself.... The further question as to the ultimate nature of this unconscious is no more sensible or profitable than the older one as to the nature of the conscious. (1925a, 31–32; emphasis added)

Specifying the "philosophers" not only focused his wit, but claimed an alliance with a more insightful general consensus. That unconscious mental functions exist had already attained an accepted status among the intelligentsia in fin de siècle Europe (Decker 1977), despite most psychiatrists' disdain and that of those philosophers whose dogged denial raised Freud's ire. Whether an "unconscious" occupied a region of the mind, and what such an unconscious *did* and what it *signified* for conscious thought and behavior comprised outstanding questions. Few ventured forth to engage such seemingly imponderable issues. Freud did, and within the context of his time and the locale of his own interests he created a system of analysis by which to explore his intuitions.

After all of the critiques are weighed and justly considered, we are left with the widespread success of Freud's theory, at least in terms of its impact on Western cultures. Indeed, it is difficult to overestimate his influence despite the hostility and notoriety in the general public that was provoked by the dominant role of sexuality (infantile and adult) in his schema. If impolitic sexuality had been subordinated in his writings, the more general biological mechanisms he invoked would also have proved inadequate to account for psychic life beyond those few persons whom that schema seemed to fit. And as discussed above, the philosophical pretenses of the theory suffered even more disdain. Yet, again, psychoanalysis possesses an enduring *something*. So, putting aside the positivist critique (which has suffered its own ignoble demise), when Freud acknowledged that the unconscious rests on an assumption, that does not mean his project *failed*. Indeed, if we accept that the scientific credentials had not been satisfactorily demonstrated, his lasting achievement must lie elsewhere. To identify that elsewhere, we turn to other contemporaries of his who wrestled with the same epistemological and metaphysical issues that haunted his own project. In that search, a more fruitful discussion might have ensued with the neo-Kantians, who would have identified psychoanalytic descriptions of the unconscious as a metaphysical inquiry in terms that might have allowed for fruitful debate, as opposed to outright dismissal.

Chapter Three

Storms over Königsberg

> The fish in the pond ... can swim only in the water,
> not in the earth; but yet it may strike its head against the
> ground and sides. So, too, we might with the notion of cause
> survey the whole realm of experience and find that beyond it
> lies a sphere which to our knowledge is absolutely inaccessible.
> —Friedrich Lange, *History of Materialism* (1950,
>   book 2, second section, 216)

FREUD'S EFFORT TO ESTABLISH PSYCHIC CAUSE WAS, of course, part of
a larger psychology. Yet despite sustained defensive efforts, his science
would suffer unremitting attacks. The charges are now well rehearsed:
Objective criteria could not be established, and prediction remained elusive. No one would deny that Freud was engaged in an empiricist project, but that would not necessarily yield a successful *scientific* product.
The earliest criticisms, by and large, revolved around the specific claims
of Freud's construction. Among sexologists and psychiatrists, the debate
(and rejection) generally followed the contours of the respective disciplines (Decker 1977). The second level of dispute concerned the status
of psychoanalysis fulfilling positivist standards. Given the interpretative
character of psychoanalysis (the transference phenomena, the emotional
nature of introspection, the frailty of memory, and the criteria of therapeutic success), how ironic to base psychoanalysis on positivist precepts
by which an objectivist science demands absolute division of subject and
object. Despite such strictures, Freud nevertheless believed his technique
could overcome the subjectivity of analyst-analysand interpretations of
human behavior. Seemingly he discounted the emotional influence of
analytic judgment and the "character" of the analyst as important elements in the dialectic exchange constitutive of psychoanalytic practice
(Kite 2008). These weaknesses of psychoanalytic theory have been exhaustively discussed, and in many respects represent a superficial observation: psychoanalysis fails positivist criteria. A more interesting ques-

tion concerns the philosophical standing of psychoanalysis as a human science, and as an interpretative project, how might it be characterized? So putting aside the applicability of positivist tenets to Freud's thinking, here we will consider how the attacks on positivism itself affects our understanding of the philosophy undergirding psychoanalysis.

A deeper problem confronted Freud than either answering the rejections of clinicians or repelling the dismissals by those who would disparage his scientific aspirations: Psychoanalysis was caught in a philosophical vortex that enveloped all of the human sciences. Whether the debates occurred in anthropology, psychology, or sociology, the theme was the same: How might the human sciences organize themselves upon the same positivist principles Comte had originally suggested? Indeed, what constituted a human science dominated fin de siècle academic debate: (1) defining the scientific credentials of psychology, and the philosophical response in phenomenology (Spiegelberg 1982); (2) discarding a lingering Hegelianism in the face of a new analytic approach to metaphysics (Hylton 1990); and (3) resolving (perhaps displacing) claims of Kantian epistemology (and science more specifically) in the face of these other developments (Willey 1978; Friedman and Nordmann 2006). Freud was caught in the riptide of this philosophical crisis. From one direction, his science was highly suspect, and despite valiant efforts to establish the unconscious as suitable for scientific study, he would play a defensive role throughout his life. In reconstructing a hypothetical debate between Freud and the key critics working in his most generative period, it seems reasonable, even allowing for his acquaintance with these interlocutors, to assume that he would have been blinded even to the possibility of an alternative interpretation of his enterprise given his materialist commitments and the functional mind-brain dualism in which he worked. Nevertheless, we will proceed with an imagined discussion, for Freud's psychoanalytic theory intersected with the same epistemological problems debated by philosophers from various schools of thought, who were linked by their rejection of the positivist program. So putting aside the specific critiques about the empirical standing of associative phenomena or the criteria for assigning pervasive effects of childhood sexuality, a more fundamental philosophical crisis faced Freud as argument swirled about the standing of the human sciences, namely the criteria of study

and the objectives sought. In presenting that history, the deeper philosophical weaknesses of psychoanalysis will be highlighted.

Let us set the intellectual stage: During Freud's key formative period,
debate raged about the very character of knowledge and the cognitive
nature of the knowing agent based on a scientific epistemology. A general
consensus among many nonscientists held that philosophy grounded on
a Cartesian notion of *res cogitans*, replete with certainty and autonomy,
had lost its standing. With Nietzsche's multi-perspectivism, the single perspective of a stationary (and authoritative) *cogito* was challenged; and
more broadly, scientism, with its demands on empirical knowledge at
the expense of other kinds of experience, restricted philosophical inquiry
within unacceptable limits (Bambach 1995; Megill 1985). So the German
philosophical debate focused precisely on those items the positivists were
most adamant to protect: the standing and basis of truth and objectivity
as understood within a universal framework.

Upon this platform, several competing orientations opposed the positivist philosophy, which was regarded by sociologists and other dissent-
ing philosophers as too narrow to incorporate science within an analysis of culture. For these critics, the knowing subject was inextricably
immersed in its history, language, and society, and thus some absolute
objectivity simply could not be attained. The attack divided into distinct camps. The neo-Kantians (the major focus of this chapter) not only
sought dominance over the resurgent positivists, but took on hermeneutists and humanistic historicists, as well as the rising Nietzscheans
and the declining rear-guard Hegelians. While the neo-Kantians were
critical of Kant, they would follow his method and end with notions of
reality closely aligned to the formulation he had originally proposed,
namely, a product of the melding of nature and mind. Reality is not just
"out there," but rather emerges as a synthesis of human cognitive capacities, and in this sense the neo-Kantians were somewhat allied with the
historicists, but rejected them because of the implicit relativism in their
historical calculus.[1] In such a construction (discussed in detail below),
values of various kinds must be invoked, and thus the ideal contours of
"objectivity" would be widened and yield to a philosophical pursuit of
value, writ large (a project specifically promoted by Wilhelm Windelband [1919; 1980, 169–85]).

Note that for all of these philosophical combatants, the issue was not science per se, for after all, in the German context the argument concerned the character of science appropriate to various objects or topics of study. Implicit and assumed, "truth" emerged within a scientific discourse, so the question, more pointedly, revolved around the very notion of what sort of knowledge about humans is possible (Smith 1997; 2007). In response to these challenges, neo-Kantians, like Windelband and Heinrich Rickert (1962), who rejected the most austere positivism, still sought a proper "scientific" approach to the crisis in philosophy: Rejecting philosophy as a Hegelian science of metaphysics, they proposed a science of knowledge, which would unify the natural and human sciences, and in that attempt, they offered formalizations that mimicked the systematization of their positivist opponents (Bambach 1995; Könke 1991). On this view, the neo-Kantians occupied a middle position that sought some unification of the natural and human sciences as they were arrayed between the Nietzscheans on one end of the skeptical spectrum and positivists on the other. Historicists, like Wilhelm Dilthey (1833–1911), represented another middle position, one that deeply influenced the human sciences in particular (Decker 1977; Schnädelbach 1984). We begin with an outline of Dilthey's position and its relevance to Freud's own approach, which will be followed with consideration of how neo-Kantians would refract psychoanalytic theory.

The Search for a Philosophy of the Human Sciences

Although Freud did not specifically debate whether psychology was a natural, as opposed to a human, science, he enthusiastically embraced a naturalism lodged in the biology of his period (Sulloway 1979; Kitcher 1992). Freud's contemporary Dilthey, who self-consciously considered the conceptual challenges facing the newly emerging human sciences, adopted a more circumspect stance. Dilthey's approach exposes much of what Freud did *not* consider in seeking to establish a science devoted to human behavior. While their aspirations were similar, Dilthey demurred from the scientism marking Freud's own efforts and instead offered a more nuanced description of the quandary, one that sought a more expansive stage than positivism on which to pursue a scientific agenda. To highlight that which Freud ignored or misconstrued, we briefly review Dilthey's position.

Dilthey's classic division of the human and natural sciences on the axis of explanation (*erklären*) and understanding (*verstehen*) was directed at establishing the bona fides for the human sciences by both differentiating them from the natural sciences and at the same time recognizing their shared epistemological claims for objectivity (Dilthey 1988, e.g., 98; 1976, e.g., 218; Rickman 1976, 11–20). Accordingly, the scientist treats nature as an object of inquiry and explains forces and functions through discernment of causal laws. The physicist or biologist observes his object from the outside and remains alien to it. In contrast, the scholar of the human sciences requires interpretation and discernment of meaning to understand her object of study. The science of interpretation, hermeneutics, thus is distinguished from the methodology and aims of the natural sciences by fully embracing a personal perspective. However, this admission of a specified perspective does not suggest that validity, even objectivity are unattainable.[2] As Dilthey wrote,

> The human studies are distinguished from the sciences of nature first of all in that the latter have for their objects facts which are presented to consciousness as from outside, as phenomena and given in isolation, while the objects of the former are given originaliter [*sic*] from within as real and as a living continuum [*Zusammenhang*]. As a consequence there exists a system of nature for the physical and natural sciences only thanks to inferential arguments which supplement the data of experience by means of a combination of hypotheses. In the human studies, to the contrary, the nexus of psychic life constitutes originally a primitive and fundamental datum. We *explain* nature, we *understand* psychic life. (Dilthey 1977, 27; emphasis added)

Dilthey built from the Kantian notion of *Verstand* as an intellectual faculty for scientific explanation of natural processes, thus allowing humans to relate to natural phenomena without providing insight into that underlying reality. Psychic experience, in contrast, was direct.

In his epistemological and psychological writings, Dilthey joined the diverse attempts to reconcile the demands of formulating a philosophy that adjudicated the claims of Hegelians and neo-Kantians (e.g., Rickert and Windelband), psychologists and phenomenologists (Husserl especially), positivists and neoromanticists to establish the legitimate standards, in the face of a growing scientism, for objectivity applied to the arts, history, psychology, and sociology. (Note, "objectivity" is interchangeable here with "true," "valid," "legitimate," and their variants.) He aligned himself with the tradition beginning with Giambattista Vico in claiming that we can truly know only what we ourselves have brought forth, and thus humans have a kind of access to psychological, social, and historical reality that is impossible to achieve in the study of nature. Thus he joined those pitched against the claims of a domineering positivism in a world that obviously could not be reduced to the strict demands of a naturalized, dehumanized science (Zaner and Heiges 1977, 6).

While I discuss the neo-Kantians in detail below, here we should consider the other major contemporaneous description of reason's application to the natural and human domains offered by Wilhelm Windelband (1848–1915). Postponing a discussion of neo-Kantian concerns, suffice it to observe that Windelband shared with Dilthey the need to differentiate, and legitimate, the logic of the human sciences. Windelband did so by differentiating "idiographic" from "nomothetic" reason. The first, applied to human sciences, refers to a case-based understanding, while the latter refers to explanations based on natural laws. As he explained,

> Empirical sciences either seek the general in the form of the law of nature or the particular in the form of the historically defined structure. On the one hand, they are concerned with the form which invariably remains constant. On the other hand, they are concerned with the unique, immanently defined content of the real event. The former disciplines are nomological sciences. The latter disciplines are sciences of process or sciences of the event. The sciences of process are concerned with what was once the case. If I may be permitted to introduce some technical terms, scientific thought is *nomothetic* in the former case and *idiographic* in the latter case. (Windelband 1980, 175)

Then Windelband makes the critical point that would focus Freud's own interest:

> Should we retain the customary expressions, then it can be said that the dichotomy at stake here concerns the distinction between the natural and the

historical disciplines. However, we must bear in mind that, in the methodological sense of the dichotomy, psychology falls unambiguously within the domain of the natural sciences. (175)

Freud believed he had fulfilled the criteria that would place psychology in Windelband's schema, namely, ostensible general (or scientific) laws of behavior. However, Windelband himself introduced an important caveat, one that would no doubt focus the debate about Freud's methods and conclusions:

> We should also bear in mind that this methodological dichotomy classifies only modes of investigation, not the contents of knowledge itself. It is possible—and it is in fact the case—that the same subjects can be the object of both a nomothetic and an idiographic investigation. This is related to the fact that, in a certain respect, the distinction between the invariable and the unique is relative. (175–76)

That two kinds of understanding are at work in the human and natural domains seems self-evident to those opposing the orthodoxy of scientism, but how might that difference be understood and legitimated? In the idiographic case, *meaning* ultimately determines the basis of judgment. Indeed, integrated and cohesive knowledge must be ordered by some mediating function, and in such disciplines as history and psychoanalysis, an overall interpretative conception guides the inquiry and interpretation.

While Windelband placed the science of psychology in the nomothetic sphere, he would not concede that physiology and psychic process might capture the measure of human value. As we will discuss in detail below, *value*, for Windelband, served as the nexus of his counterattack against positivism. For him, the worlds of "fact" and "value" simply existed in separate domains, and in an ironic sense, this separation, whose division was celebrated and employed for radically different means by the positivists, also served Windelband's larger philosophical aims of preserving human judgment in the older Kantian sense. In *Introduction to Philosophy*, Windelband explicitly defined the difference between the natural and human sciences as reflecting an irreconcilable metaphysical division. Indeed, the basic positivist tenet of seeking some unified understanding of the world becomes a misconceived aspiration:

The world of values and the world of reality, the provinces of "ought" and "must," are not foreign to each other. They are in mutual relation everywhere. But they are certainly not the same thing. There is a rent in the fabric of reality.... We cannot get over the contradiction.... From the very nature of the case this final problem is insoluble. It is the sacred mystery. (1921, 357–58)

From a more general point of view, the differentiations Dilthey and Windelband made in their respective descriptions of different kinds of knowledge offer a taxonomy of the sciences. Each resisted placing the sciences under the same form of philosophical logic, that is, positivism, for then the human sciences would be regarded as also-rans. However, in making these distinctions, a crisis emerged: "As historical questions were transformed into questions of truth, value, certitude, verifiability, and objectivity, historians left to philosophers the task of securing epistemological foundations" (Bambach 1995, 59). As discussed below, Windelband sought to demonstrate that truth was not merely a logical condition, but a universal value as well; indeed, logic was hardly the province of science and mathematics alone, but was also integral, albeit in different form, to human history, culture, and anthropology (Bambach 1995, 61). And most importantly, while "truth" would hold center stage, and while "fact" would serve as the currency of truth functions, for Windelband, "value" trumps "fact." This complex matter (reserved for the last section of this chapter) deserves careful scrutiny, for it is the lynchpin securing psychoanalysis its place in the debate. Indeed, Freud might have found Windelband an ally of sorts, albeit the terms of defense would be radically altered.

In conclusion, Windelband and Dilthey focused the concurrent demands for historical "understanding" (which encompasses the domain of hermeneutics)[3] and scientific "explanation" to comprehend the human world, and, most saliently, their inherent conflict. The resulting turmoil, which enveloped modernist philosophy, tracks directly back to Kant's formulation of reason and its consequences. The apparently irreconcilable demands of historical and scientific consciousness, despite Kant's best efforts, left modernists again to seek philosophical foundations and coherence. Note that Dilthey still held to the basic modernist intuition that foundations and unification were required:

The coherence of all knowledge from which all efforts at foundation must proceed stretches beyond the thought of separate persons and contains the inner necessity of a scientific conclusion.... How this coherence arises—this coherence of the totality of knowledge—that is what we must search for; it offers the basic foundations for a true theory of knowledge.... There is no perspective without an objective order. This is the fact which is finally the guarantee for the objective and real validity for our knowledge. ("Nachlass" quoted by Bambach 1995, 177)

Windelband readily recognized the impossibility of such unification, as did Dilthey, who in failing to find a synthesis acknowledged the inherent contradiction of a historicist (humanist) position claiming *scientific* objectivity.[4] Protagonists in this debate over human versus natural science aligned themselves across several other divides. Freud found himself, albeit without acknowledging his position, in both frames of thought. The early Freud assumed a staunch positivist stance in seeking a science of the mind along positivist principles (e.g., Freud 1955); the later Freud placed meaning in the fulcrum of interpretative analysis and thus might well have found an alliance with Dilthey (Freud 1910; 1933). Given the fundamental issues that enveloped his theory and practice, Freud could have profitably entered debates with the neo-Kantians, who struck at an even deeper stratum in their attack on the prevalent positivist philosophy of science, one that had been inspired, like Dilthey's attempts, to find a new synthesis. Next we consider the neo-Kantian perspective and reflect on how (in silent dialogue) it illuminates Freud's own efforts.

Neo-Kantianism and the Question of the Real

Given the profound influence of Kant on nineteenth-century German philosophy, Kantianism is detected in virtually all movements, whether as expositions of his transcendentalism or as reactions opposing him through Hegelianism and its variants. Indeed, Kant had set the agenda: "For some he was the philosopher of empirical science; for others the enemy of dogmatic metaphysics; and for still others, the rescuer of morality and religion from skepticism" (Willey 1978, 131). Of course, neo-Kantians saw themselves as his direct heirs, but they too could hardly decide on which aspect of his philosophy to emphasize, nor, for that matter, the most important facets. That being said, while neo-Kantianism divides between the Marburg School and the Southwestern (or Baden) School,[5] the disputants were joined in the common purpose of examining the foundations of knowledge and arguing for the implications of understanding the limits imposed by the mind on knowledge's application. Simply, the neo-Kantians may fairly be regarded as all falling under the rubric of defining an epistemology whose value structure would broaden human *knowledge* beyond the positivist restrictions.

The movement began as a new philosophical discipline, *Erkenntnistheorie* (or modern theory of epistemology), which, during the 1820s and 1830s, arose in response to a waning Hegelianism and doubts about the possibility of objective knowledge. Friedrich Trendelenburg, dissatisfied with the current formulations of the relationship of philosophy and science, revisited this critical Kantian concern during the 1840s, and in his own explorations founded what became neo-Kantianism (Könke 1991, 11ff.). The neo-Kantians are collected only with some difficulty, inasmuch as the choice of their philosophical interests spread across all philosophical disciplines, and their interpretation of Kant also diverged widely (Schnädelbach 1984, 105). They fiercely debated the possibility and nature of transcendental knowledge, idealist versus materialist interpretations of Kant, the nature of values, the basis of ethics, and the character of the human mind.

Psychologism became a central issue in the attempt to decipher—some would say, to misconstrue—the nature of the mind and the knowing subject in Kantian philosophy (a problem that has continued in current debate [e.g., Zoeller 1993, 445–66]). Whether they were supportive of psychophysiological readings of Kant's first *Critique* (e.g., Eduard Zeller and Friedrich Lange), or hostile to such interpretations in favor of more logically oriented readings (e.g., Windelband), late-nineteenth-century neo-Kantians were determined to "prevent the subordination of consciousness to undifferentiated experience" (Willey 1978, 108). Despite radical differences, each delivered a refraction of Kant's epistemological and ethical philosophies, founded on a particular understanding of the transcendental determinates of experience. The most influential assigned consciousness a unifying role in relation to experience, just as they had bestowed such a role on philosophy in relation to the sciences. This single feature, the centrality of consciousness, would determine Freud's own rejection of any affiliation with the neo-Kantian approach. Nevertheless he might have gained significant insight from the debates about the character of mind that emerged among this group. Further, the status of "reason" applied to the new discipline of psychology would have received a full hearing, one that would have placed Freud's own approach in a more critical context. Finally, he might have been more circumscribed in his positivist aspirations if he more fully recognized the basis of the confrontation with the positivists over the issue of "reality," namely, how is *the real* known?

Freud had studied Kant, and even without a sophisticated understanding he appreciated the basic Kantian precepts: To comprehend the natural world and the moral domain required, respectively, "pure" (or theoretical) and "practical" reason. Pure reason applied to the understanding, the Kantian faculty that spontaneously systematizes and organizes those cognitive functions by which humans address and then glean knowledge of the natural world. Such knowledge is derived from appearances—the cognitive product or the phenomenon that humans perceive. The noumenon, the thing-in-itself, cannot be known, indeed, it cannot be observed, only "thought." Given the success of human cognition in navigating the world and discerning its workings, Kant remained confident that the categories of understanding, those cognitive faculties by which reason ordered the plenum of experience, were, in some fundamental way, synchronized to natural happenings. (Those sympathetic to this point of view would later argue that these abilities were developed through Darwinian evolutionary mechanisms.) In short, Kant's schema of pure reason made the natural world intelligible, and thus susceptible to scientific investigation.

The second kind of thought, "practical" reason, dealt with the moral realm by operating analogously to the workings of pure reason: Each type of reason was autonomous and thus capable of following its own dictates; each operated with its own particular modes of knowing; and each corresponded to some order—natural or moral. Thus reason's products included discovery of laws, that is, natural laws through pure reason, as well as the prescriptions of a categorical imperative discerned by practical reason. The consequence of this division was, from Kant's perspective, a way to save religious belief. But what he in fact did (for those so inclined) was to legitimatize one way of knowing as "real" in a particular sense, and the other as "less real" in that same sense. Accordingly, science could claim a special standing, and it was this ethos of authenticity of the real that appealed so powerfully to Freud and the intellectual society he inhabited (Decker 1977; Schnädelbach 1984).

The neo-Kantians, following Kant, assumed an "antirealist" position, which starkly contrasted with the positivist's metaphysical realism, although their differences were not explicitly presented in these terms.[6] Building upon the Kantian noumenal and phenomenal division, and the crucial role of cognitive structures in perceiving the world, these antirealists invoke Kant's first *Critique*: If the mind is *constitutive* of any knowledge of nature, then a cognitive construction of reality must occur. Kantian knowledge derives from "pure reason," whose categories in which we think—substance, causality, and so on—determine the "is-ness" of our perceptions (phenomenon), rather than the thing in itself (noumenon). Kant's antirealism did not deny that there is an *an sich* (in itself), only that we can have no direct (unmediated) knowledge of it. We are restricted to knowing the world by our cognitive faculties, whose structure permits only a particular refraction. "What the things may be in themselves I do not know, and also do not need to know" (Kant 1998, 375 [B333]).

According to the antirealist, the manner of perceiving the world and acting in it depends on the particular character (viz. biology) of the human mind, *and* on the world's existing for us (i.e., can be known) as defined by those faculties of knowing. Consequently, the picture offered by science at any moment in history is a product of the mind *and* nature, and more, the mind does not manufacture the world, but rather, "The mind and the world jointly make up the mind and the world" (Putnam 1981, xi). The picture created is neither final nor absolute. Indeed, reality itself is only what human cognition *knows*, or might know, and this gives post-Kantians the wedge to break up the positivist ideal of objectivity and the corresponding reality so described. Note, however, that the argument is not over *reality*, for almost all agree that electrons exist, but rather on *how* we know and whether the mode of knowing determines what *is*.[7]

The neo-Kantians basically committed themselves to this general understanding that nature, *with* mind, constitutes reality. In contrast to realist positivists, by and large, the neo-Kantians would define truth *epistemically*, namely truth derived from the best application of human cognitive functions. The *concepts* assigned to those truth statements comprise the constructivist domain, for the standing of *truth* (final, contingent, deflationist, whatever) constitutes the ongoing practice (or problem) of science (Lynch 1998; 2001; Armour-Garb and Beall 2005; Tauber 2009). So, in accepting the "certified results of science," as antirealists, the neo-Kantians would add certain methodological strictures and caveats to the Kantain core position, thus qualifying truth claims, while the realist-positivist would proclaim that the scientific picture is *really* true. In the end, each rests with some confidence that "truth" has a best approximation. The difference lies in *how* truth is grounded.[8]

On this platform, the neo-Kantians recast Kant's epistemological project by negotiating "a middle course between the extremes of absolute idealism and naturalism while incorporating features of both" (Willey 1978, 81). Skeptical of positivist assumptions developed from Lockean empiricism, they sought to understand how thought captures the empirical world, so, following Kant, they argued about the conditions that effectively established such perception and understanding. This orientation focused their epistemological project, but some neo-Kantians specifically opposed the claims of an ascendant positivism, not only on epistemological grounds, but also on metaphysical ones. Optimism, fueled by the rapid progress of science, that metaphysical questions would be set aside by naturalistic explanation left skeptics uneasy with the derivative products of such a materialistic orientation. Specifically, a purely materialist conception of the world would undermine freedom and, along with it, morality and religion (Könke 1991, 89–90). Kant seemed to offer a suitable solution to this challenge, as his critical method paved the way toward conceptualizing the mind as aware of its own limits regarding metaphysical questions, even if those limits were constantly changing because of scientific progress. Freud might well have found inspiration from such "centrist" philosophers if he had cast his philosophical net more widely, and in that discussion the question of the metaphysics of psychoanalysis would have been directly confronted. To construct such a debate, let us consider the framework offered by Friedrich Albert Lange (1828–1875).

Response to Materialism

Lange offered a "psycho-physiological" reading of Kant, which served as a skeptical reminder of positivism's conceits and warned of a misplaced scientism. That philosophical position might well have interested Freud as he grappled with establishing a theory of the psyche. The challenge of describing something that cannot, by its very nature, be directly examined, presented Freud with a classic scientific problem: The unconscious, which he so carefully described from clinical data, exists in a "space" from which various behaviors emerged for scrutiny. These phenomena, like all phenomena, demand assignment on the spectrum of "the real," and to discern unconscious processes through psychoanalysis is analogous "to the perception of the external world by means of the sense organs" (Freud 1915a, 171). But more deeply, how would "mind" be configured in a materialistic universe? Freud's philosophy of mind does not directly confront this question other than in a late admission that his theory could not connect brain states to various mental functions (Freud 1940b, 144–45). For Freud, ironically, the mind has no *philosophical* standing. Perhaps a better grasp of this issue might have clarified his thinking and certainly revealed many of his own assumptions. In those deliberations, he would have joined a rigorous debate concerning the relationship of mind and matter.

One of the major disputes in philosophy of science during the last half of the nineteenth century concerned the standing of materialism. The argument originated with the attempt by materialists (notably Karl Vogt, Ludwig Büchner, and Jacob Moleschott) to extend the assumptions of the natural sciences to a metaphysical position: Accordingly, all that exists is matter or is entirely dependent on matter. Putting aside the precise meaning of the doctrine, profound quandaries are posed: What exactly constitutes matter? What are its properties? How are the space and time in which matter extends dependent on it? And, most pressing for the neo-Kantians, what is the relationship between matter and the consciousness perceiving it?

Among those most articulate in framing the issue was Lange, who, on the basis of his major work, *The History of Materialism and the Critique of Its Contemporary Significance* (first published in 1866), enjoined a renewed Kantianism along the lines described above. He was heavily influenced by Hermann von Helmholtz, who had opposed the materialists on metaphysical grounds, indeed, discharging their metaphysical claims altogether, and argued that science had provided staunch empirical support for the Kantian position. For Helmholtz those findings were limited to the scientific sphere, that is, what possessed empirical support, and no wider domain (Moulines 1981). Holding firmly to scientific investigations, the "wider domain" referred to metaphysical assertions, which, aside from questions ranging from religion to ontology, would include claims for the character of "mind" (and "consciousness," in particular).[9] According to Helmholtz, studies of perception empirically confirmed what Kant had taken as a priori requirements for knowledge:

> The result of [scientific] examination, as at present understood, is that the organs of sense do indeed give us information about external effects produced on them, but convey those effects to our consciousness in a totally different form, so that the character of a sensuous perception depends not so much on the properties of the object perceived as on those of the organ by which we receive the information. (Helmholtz 1995, 13, quoted by Hussain 2005, 7)

Despite his enthusiasm, Helmholtz recognized that the route from sensory perception to consciousness could not simply be traced through nerve transmission (Hussain 2005, 7), so to account for the mind's organization and the basis of consciousness, Helmholtz followed the Kantian representative model of the mind, one that would be elaborated by later neo-Kantians (e.g., Ernst Cassirer [see above chap. 2, note 13]):

> Perhaps the relation between our senses and the external world may be best enunciated as follows: our sensations are for us only symbols of the objects of the external world, and correspond to them only in some such way as written characters or articulate words to the things they denote. They give us, it is true, information respecting the properties of things without us, but no better information than we give a blind man about colour by verbal descriptions. (Helmholtz 1995, 14, quoted by Hussain 2005, 8)

Building from his reductionist foundations (see above chap. 1, note 4), Helmholtz moved from sensations to external reality by inference, and thus he would not discard idealism for materialism, since he regarded both interpretations as *metaphysical hypotheses*. Returning to Kant again raised the realism/antirealism question by asking whether the natural sciences offered a picture of reality in itself. Helmholtz sided with Kant: "accepting the success of empirical methodology and materialistic explanations did not entail accepting a materialist ontology or epistemology" (Hussain 2005, 8). On this platform, Lange presented his own philosophy.

Lange's *History of Materialism* (1950) endorsed Helmholtz's own caution, and while Lange acknowledged the power of materialistic explanation *within* science, that position could hardly suffice for a fundamental epistemology, and even less, an ontology. As a neo-Kantian, Lange was dedicated to the cause of the natural sciences, and like Helmholtz, he regarded the new science of perception as support for Kantianism, where the "real" becomes a product of perception and the mind's organization of that data.[10] Given the mediating function of human cognitive faculties, Lange was concerned with the physiological distortion of the "real" world, concluding that even apparently simple sensations are, in fact, products of complex collective perceptions. While acknowledging that such mind functions may eventually be dissected into their physiological components (book 2, first section, 211; third section, 202ff.), Lange did not judge such advances capable of changing the fundamental Kantian insight that the world as perceived is simply the world as perceived. In other words, the mind constructs the world according to its capacities, and whatever scientific understanding might be achieved, the basic conceptual and perceptual restrictions remain, where the "world" becomes a mirror of the mind because of human psychology (book 2, third section, 221).

However, Lange was not simply restating Kantian principles, in which the deduction of transcendental categories provided objective knowledge about the world, for according to him, even if "the idea of cause is rooted in our [cognitive] organization," we must realize that "for this very reason it has unlimited validity in the sphere of experience, but beyond it absolutely has no meaning" (book 2, first section, 212). And here we come to the crux of Lange's movement away from Kant; namely, despite any possible contributions to the understanding of experience obtained by physiological study, nothing about the *ground* of experience might be ventured. In other words, psychology could not venture beyond the limits of its own science into the ontology of experience. Thus Lange regarded all metaphysics "as a kind of madness possessing only an aesthetic and subjective justification" (cited by Könke 1991, 151), and he would not be beguiled by the conceits of scientism.[11] For Lange, the notion of "objective reality" functions only as a vague reminder that there must be *something* real that forms the initial stuff of phenomena, although we can never allow ourselves to speculate on the nature of such phantoms.[12] In short, for Lange, a transcendental organization of ideas "remains ... just as unknown to us as the things that act upon it" (book 2, third section, 219) and thereby he configured Kantianism for a materialist setting.

Lange could not, according to his own skepticism, suggest any truths about the ground of experience, and in this light we appreciate Lange as a "Kantian"—a Kantian who is even more skeptical than Kant himself. For Lange, the original Kantian question of the possibility of experience remains *the* question of philosophy, and not even Kant's own notion of apriority is a satisfactory vehicle for discerning the issue at hand. Beneath Lange's epistemic conception of materialism, then, is a primary concern with the question of experience. He believed that even in the notion of "'mental' organization [humans see] only the transcendental side of the phenomenal physical organization" (book 2, third section, 205 n. 60); all explanations of the unity or even the possibility of experience, both physical and mental, are undermined by a fundamental skepticism based in the infinitely regressive nature of thought.[13]

In summary, while disputing the metaphysical claims of the materialists, Lange nevertheless fell perilously close to falling "under the spell of empirical science" (Willey 1978, 88) and "stood ... much closer to a form of naturalism than ... to the neo-idealism of other Neo-Kantians" (Könke 1991, 163). On this reading, Lange may well be regarded as an important "bifurcation" in the diverging paths of late-nineteenth-century Kantian idealism and the various naturalistic philosophies adopted by later positivists: He represents a case example of a philosopher inspired by Kantian idealism and caught in the cross-currents created by materialists' advocacy for science. He walked a tightrope strung between his enthusiasm for the new experimental psychology, which promised to put the "mind" in focus as an object of scientific inquiry, and wariness towards a scientism that seemed ever present in the wake of the explosive growth of scientific knowledge. Lange clearly identified the issues at stake and appropriately cautioned against establishing some metaphysical basis for the truth claims made in the name of science. His skepticism and challenge to the warrants made in the name of materialism and the positivism that supported it would have presented Freud with a powerful challenge.

Lange and Freud

Lange's epistemology obviously goes hand in hand with his psychology, and in *The History of Materialism* he wrote at length about his interest in "scientific psychology" (Lange 1950, book 2, third section, chap. 3), namely, a psychology that was based not on theories, but rather on the mechanistic interplay of psychic forces. This orientation echoes Freud's own formulation (present from his earliest analogies to mechanics [Freud 1955] to the mature theory of the "dynamic" and "economic" structure of the psyche [Freud 1915a; 1923a]). Other parallels with Freud are found in their respective interests in association psychology (Lange 1950, book 2 , third section, 189), the artifice of memory (book 2, third section, 185), and musings over the psychology of dream states (book 2, third section, 191–92). Although we hear preludes to what will become dominant themes in Freud's own project, Lange would have been highly skeptical of psychoanalysis. Despite introducing issues exhaustively addressed by Freud, Lange does not pursue psychological questions because he argued that they, like metaphysics, (1) ignore the basic Kantian problem of how experience is possible (book 2, third section, 188), (2) indulge in "self- observation," which he believed to be fraught with epistemological fallacies (book 2, third section, 169), and (3) are inclined toward "*self-delusions*" (book 2, third section, 193; emphasis added). Indeed, Lange could easily have posed as Freud's nemesis, despite Lange's attack on Brentano's dismissal of unconscious mind functions.[14]

The first objection might be dismissed inasmuch as Lange served philosophy, while Freud addressed psychology, and so their respective agendas were quite different. The second objection however, is more difficult to release. Freud accepted the legitimacy of introspective psychologies, which in the late nineteenth century enjoyed wide appeal. From James to Wundt, from Brentano to Husserl, psychologists and philosophers joined in this program, and Lange found himself in the minority opposition. So while Lange and Freud might have concurred that "it is quite impossible to draw a fixed line between internal and external observations" (Lange 1950, book 2, third section, 172), this tenet led Lange to depart from psychology, whereas for Freud, it became the nexus of psychoanalysis.

In turning to the final objection of "self-delusion," Lange raised the specter of metaphysical error. He saw how unwary scientists become enmeshed in the grips of a metaphysical picture and accepted metaphysical categories without recognizing that such structures framed their epistemology and gave them a false positivist depiction of the world. Lange was intent on puncturing those conceits, and he would have undoubtedly been dubious of Freud's positivist efforts. Lange (endorsing Helmholtz) "resolves the activity of the senses into a kind of inference" (Lange 1950, book 2, third section, 228), and mechanism becomes "only a necessary occurring *picture* of an unknown state of things" (229; emphasis added). Although he focused on sensory perception, the same general principles apply to higher orders of conceptual thinking, and on that basis, the apparatus of conscious rationality is even more subject to the limitations he has delineated for immediate sensory processing:

> The senses give us, as Helmholtz says, *effects* of things, not faithful pictures let alone the things themselves. To these mere effects however belong also the senses themselves, together with the brain and the supposed molecular movements in it. We must therefore recognise the existence of a transcendent world order, whether this depends on "things-in-themselves," or whether—since even the "thing in itself" is but a last application of our intuitive thought—it depends on mere relations, which exhibit themselves in various minds as various kinds and stages of the sensible, without its being at all conceivable what an adequate appearance of the absolute in a cognizing mind would be. (Lange 1950, book 2, third section, 230)

And the conclusion is then quite apparent: "The Idealist can, and must in fact, in natural science everywhere apply the same conceptions and methods as the Materialist; but what to the latter is definitive truth is to the Idealist only the necessary result of our organisation" (Lange 1950, book 2, fourth section, 324). In other words, an objective posture, an Archimedean point that might give the positivist appraisal anything more than a *picture* determined by the mental apparatus applied, does not exist.

Freud connived to walk on both sides of the street: On the one hand, he followed an idealist course in exploring the unconscious and applying transcendental principles for its decipherment (Bergo 2004), and on the other hand, he professed a positivist confidence in establishing laws of the unconscious through empirical methods that seemingly ignored its transcendental commitments. The unconscious scrutinized as a natural object thus presented itself as both a biological entity suitable for positivist examination and a deduction from some transcendental requirement for establishing cause in the psyche realm. In the former guise, according to Lange's position, Freud paradoxically remains a metaphysician (a characterization already discussed in another context in chapter 2).

This bivalency would plague psychoanalysis throughout its development and offer critics ample opportunity to attack its weak flank, the putative scientific theory. By insisting on making psychoanalysis an objective science, Freud betrayed the more fundamental commitment to the deductive understanding of the unconscious. That inconsistency would leave psychoanalysis open to scathing criticism, for instead of claiming the approach as a method of *interpretation* through inferences and narrative constructions, limited by constraints easily identified and embracing a circumscribed skepticism, Freud sought to establish psychoanalysis as a means to decipher psychic cause—a positivist science of the mind—and thereby lost the support of those who understood the philosophical errors he committed.

So how might we situate Lange vis-à-vis the Freudian approach? Lange died in 1875, well before Freud began his descriptive psychology, but let us postulate how he might have reacted: On the one hand, Lange would have accepted the representational nature of the psychoanalytic process and fully endorsed those transcendental deductive strategies to capture mind function. In this sense, he might well have appreciated Freud's own efforts to determine the "categories of understanding" that both organized and presented the unconscious to scrutiny, and in that sense he might well have appreciated the hermeneutic power of the method. On the other hand, Lange would have been dismissive of Freud's own metaphysical position, namely, that the "mind" can be depicted as comprising various components—ego, superego, and most startling, the id. Perhaps Freud might have conceded that the experience of dreams and their analysis afforded a view analogous to "perceptions," but to then postulate a metaphysical entity, the unconscious, would be to slip into the same error Lange detected with the materialist position. Indeed, he would argue that Freud was in this sense a materialist, and in his espousal of positivist epistemological conceits, the error was completely consistent with their mistakes. (Freud's *Project for a Scientific Psychology* [1955] offers the clearest illustration of his materialistic commitments.) On these terms, Lange would certainly have joined the critical chorus offering a voice of caution to Freud's positivist stance and would have provided philosophical reasons to pause and reconsider the philosophical assumptions grounding psychoanalysis.

In sum, Lange would surely have considered Freud a metaphysician under the terms described here, and, accordingly, the philosophical foundations of psychoanalysis rested upon a shaky manifold. In acknowledging those weak supports Lange would have highlighted the epistemological limits of such investigations. Freud, however, in building his psychology failed to appreciate the deeper questions about the nature of experience and the standing of introspective methods. This extension of Kantian epistemology would have disjointed Freud's own efforts, and in that criticism we see what psychoanalytic theory would forego in order to maintain its own analytic commitments.

Windelband and Freud

A second neo-Kantian line of criticism appeared with Windelband's attack on positivism through a distinctive strategy, one that placed him close to Lange in their shared assessment of the metaphysical issues lying at the heart of the search for scientific truth. As a neo-Kantian, Windelband recognized that the limits of pure reason (directed at the natural world) espoused by Kant could not support science's epistemology and that another element, "value," not only defined knowledge (its basis and application), but also conferred a necessary telos for reason's direction in the pursuit of any epistemological enterprise.

Windelband's understanding of the place of value in epistemology introduced a challenge to positivist ideals, since he was dissatisfied with the philosophical grounding of objectivity. The aspiration of positivists to lead the human sciences to the naturalistic ideal required a value system that would order the respective inquiries. Positivism's approach depended on a dichotomy between facts and values, the objective and subjective ways of knowing, respectively (Putnam 2002). Long before the current post-Kuhnian views of the value structure of science achieved wide acceptance (Tauber 2009), Windelband would ask, What is the relationship of facts and values? What is the standing of "facts," and how are they qualified? Where did "value," specifically in reference to the human sciences, find its philosophical place? The ability to define or maintain a system of values to support the notions of a radically objective science (Tauber 2009) rested upon the fact/value distinction (traditionally strung on an objective/subjective axis), but the basic division could not be maintained, because facts assume their meaning through a much wider constellation of values than the particular objectivist values positivists embraced. Indeed, facts attain their standing through the values that structure the very acquisition of data, and another array of values determine their significance and meaning. On this view, the dichotomy of "facts" (products of a stark objectivity) and "values" (typically construed as subjective) collapses in analytic practice. (This line of criticism proved important, since the collapse of the fact/value distinction became the fulcrum of positivism's fall in the last half of the twentieth century.)

Freud, in following the positivist line, based psychoanalysis on a notion of objectivity that he believed modeled the natural sciences, and in that orientation, he made no allowance for assessing how psychoanalytic theory assumes its own values, and how those values directed his epistemology.[15] While Freud recognized that personal and cultural conditions and values played a critical causal role in the development of neuroses (e.g., 1913a), he failed to account for how these same influences played upon the analyst's objectivity. He would seek a psychic reality, and that reality, indeed, a positivist-inspired reality, was to conform to objective standards of the day (Decker 1977). Freud was so confident of the scientific status of his approach that he maintained that philosophy would be "unable to avoid taking the psycho-analytic contributions to psychology fully into account" (Freud 1913a, 178), and furthermore, psychoanalytic theory might be applied to philosophy itself to reveal "the subjective and individual motives behind philosophical theories which have ostensibly sprung from impartial logical work, and can draw a critic's attention to the weak spots in the system" (179).[16] How ironic that he failed to recognize the basic cultural dependence of his own interpretations (e.g., Bernheimer and Kahane 1990), not to speak of his reliance on certain now debunked views of fin de siècle social sciences (Kitcher 1992). However, the quaintness of those pictures of the social and natural worlds as viewed from our own era is not the point; the Freudian philosophical commitments focus our interest. Windelband offered an important point of view to dissect this matter.

Windelband's critique pointed to the very heart of positivism's conceits: Where did "value," specifically in reference to the human sciences, find its epistemological status? Windelband traced this fundamental question concerning the character of science and more generally, knowledge, to Kant's division of reason, and from that bifurcation, he attempted to delineate the justified claims of each domain and their respective relationship to each other. His philosophical inquiry (described below) sought to identify a "bridge" of value that would confer a philosophically sound understanding of objectivity. In the Kantian context, he remained unconcerned with the objective reality conferred by individual contributing factors of experience, and instead, he emphasized the uniting relationship between mind and matter, experience and history, which characterized human life. Accordingly, Kant's method "implies the undeniable fact that our thought is on all sides pressed irresistibly beyond our actual experience of empirical reality" (Windelband 1921, 46) to establish coherence of the world and the possibility of attaining objective knowledge.

In this regard Windelband shared much with the Marburg neo-Kantians, but unlike Lange, philosophy was "no longer a problem of the origin of knowledge, but of its validity" (Windelband 1921, 182). Furthermore, even though Windelband's philosophy was driven by a belief in the necessity of a unity of reality, he, like Lange, held an abiding skepticism that he might *know* such a reality (Windelband 1961, 80). At the same time, Windelband hoped to rescue objectivity from severe skepticism by recognizing its role in the sciences (human and natural) and in moral action. Thus we see a philosophical intuition at work: Despite holding to an antirealist position, objectivity is not only an aspiration, but also a working value.[17]

According to Windelband, philosophy's inquiry, while guided by an assumption that it might discover a system of values universally valid, had failed, and thus the investigation must proceed with new provisions in place of a discarded framework. In seeking an epistemology by which to capture *all* science, Windelband asked, How might a universal value be construed and what epistemological function would it fulfill?[18] That he failed to accomplish his philosophical goal is less important than his keen identification of the false dichotomy of "facts" and "values." Windelband offered a challenge the positivists could not admit: If objectivity emerged in a historical process that reflected various epistemological strategies, which in the end gave no final adjudication and certainly did not capture all objects of interest in the human sciences, then what might a universal value be? The positivists embraced objectivity and the autonomous standing of facts based on a commonsensical empiricism, and that was the end of the matter for them, more or less.[19]

Freud might have benefited from discussion with Windelband on these matters, but instead he was satisfied to assume the coherence of the world; he disregarded the philosophical problem of the mind-world division; and most immediately, he adopted a well-demarcated subject-object division, assigning certain values to the analyst, others to the analysand, each person in the dyad operating within a normative structure derived from a biomedical model (Tauber 2005). In short, Freud adopted a laboratory scenario, and in doing so, he lost the distinctive value structure of the human sciences that Dilthey and Windelband were seeking, albeit in very different ways. (Dilthey understood that the human sciences required their own interpretative criteria, and Windelband sought to uncover the metaphysical assumptions underlying objectivity.) Freud would resist each, and by refusing to yield his positivist ground, his tunnel vision would expose the Achilles' heel of psychoanalysis: In arguing for the *scientific* basis of his theory, Freud focused on the criteria of his claims as the product of a positivist-inspired investigation, when all the while he was applying an interpretative strategy to deal with the subjectivity of the analysand. The conundrum stands unaddressed.

Freud made no allowance for assessing how psychoanalysis assumes its own values or how the theory deviates from standards of objectivity applied in the natural sciences. Given the privacy of memory and emotion, no tests analogous to those used to define physical phenomena availed Freud, such as other modes of verification that would confer objectivity, that is, consensus from several points of view. Considering that all measurements result from negotiations between the analysand and analyst, verification offered by different perspectives cannot be achieved. The analysand's story may be "true," but more deeply, it has been conceived and carried forth as an explanation of behavior, language, or dreams; an exploration of memory; a probe of motive, and so on. Such interpretations, which obviously have certain "objective" foundations, ultimately can only reflect the personal history and personality of private experience. Truth claims, then, must rely solely on what is accepted, again by the psychoanalytic dyad, as a coherent, integrated story fashioned by an overarching idea or theme. That conception assumes the contours of personal identity.

Windelband's position may now be highlighted in juxtaposition to Freud: Where Freud understood his scientific data as bridging the mind-brain division, Windelband would see as a fundamental error. Namely, Freud failed to recognize the basic philosophical challenge posed by psychoanalysis: All formulations of the relationships between the material and the psychical, including "the realm of the unconscious ... are *metaphysical* problems" (Windelband 1921, 164–65; emphasis added). Lange had maintained a similar position, but unlike Lange, Windelband believed that "metaphysics is ... a critical inquiry into the logical forms of the real" (1921, 203). Accordingly, explicating metaphysics would offer the basis for identifying normative values that transcend experience. The goal of metaphysics for Windelband, then, was critically to seek identifying patterns, uniting values, and delineate underlying themes in which humans experience a coherent reality. Indeed, if Freud had reframed his theory in this Windelband-inspired format, he would have cast psychoanalysis as a *human science* with its own legitimacy based on precepts distinctive to its own purposes. Is it too much to suggest that the metaphysics that formed Windelband's central problem would have offered Freud a philosophical avenue to address that which he perilously ignored?

Windelband's comments on the unconscious, in particular, offer us an immediate link between them and provide a clear statement of their differences. Speculating on some bridge between mind and physics, that is, some psychic function that interrupts "the purely mechanical-physical process" (Windelband 1921, 162), Windelband opined,

> Since there is a psychological basis for the assumption of an intermediate realm [between psychic and physical] of the unconscious, it may be, with proper caution, extended to the provinces of natural philosophy and metaphysics. If ... [we are compelled] to assume conditions which we cannot satisfactorily regard as physical, yet they are not, as far as our knowledge goes, conscious processes, we seem to be justified in supposing that they are unconscious purposive powers ... but we must be quite clear that in either case the unconscious is only a name for something that is *assumed* on the analogy of the psychic, without anybody being able to say, apart from this analogous feature, what it really is—in fact, only a name for an unsolved problem. The causal-mechanical thought of science must always endeavor to find a way out of this difficulty, and it therefore rejects the vital force of all such hypotheses. (Windelband 1921, 147–48; emphasis added)

But what if the "causal-mechanical thought of science" could be employed to study the unconscious itself? Given Windelband's belief that the "agnosticistic thing-in-itself is merely a dark chamber into which people cast their unsolved problems without obtaining any light whatever on them" (1921, 195), what would he say to Freud's notion of the unconscious as an object suitable for scientific study? Windelband explicitly attributed primal instincts and drives toward immediate pleasure to unconscious motivating factors (210–12), and asserted that even "Kant lent a certain sanction to this view when ... he expressed the opinion that pleasure and displeasure are related to the purposiveness or nonpurposiveness of their objects" (210–11), but there his psychology ends. We will not find Windelband in dialogue with Freud on this matter. However, if the discussion probes the deeper philosophical issues underlying their respective interests, an important parallel appears.

Let us consider Windelband's primary philosophical concern, the search for an elusive, if not absent, ideal of objective value. He did not provide a reason for his assumption of the existence of objective values, but consistent with his Kantianism, he assumed such values as a product of, or coincident with, human autonomy (Bambach 1995, 79). Accordingly, Kant's moral theory framed the very basis of knowing: A value system must preserve autonomy, which in turn grounds both the epistemological project and the ethical. So we come to the heart of the paradox that would also appear in Freud's own endeavor, namely the imbroglio of free will and moral responsibility working within a naturalistic universe governed by physical cause. Specifically, how does free rational inquiry intersect with the arational unconscious and putatively not only achieve insight into the workings of that psychic source of behavior, but also control it? Windelband joined this discussion through his own positioning of "value" in an epistemology that would bridge this division, a synthesis that he thought offered the only way to approach "the great problem of the psycho-physical connection as ... an incomprehensible causality of dissimilar things" (1921, 155).

Previously, the Cartesian problem of how to connect the mind and substance had been approached by neo-Kantians as a formal investigation of the mechanism of the transcendental deduction. But Windelband did not concern himself with the formal conditions of thought, for as Lange had also maintained, "There is never any ontological ground on which to divide experience into 'inner' and 'outer'" (Bambach 1995, 72). Instead, Windelband posited a third term, "value," as the connection between the mental and the physical. Thus he sought to meld experience in its epistemological modality within a subjective context—value—in which experience is mediated to become coherent knowledge (1921, 184; 1961, 72). While Windelband would regard the search for objective value as a metaphysical issue, I would argue that "value," in itself, must be understood within a human context. Indeed, Windelband himself acknowledged the cultural context and historical evolution of value in precisely these terms. Order takes the form of the

> double aspect of all logical laws: on the one hand they are rules for the empirical consciousness, according to which all thinking which has truth for its aim

should be carried on; on the other hand they have their inner and independent significance and being, quite independent of the actual happening of ideational processes, which are or are not in accordance with them. We may call the latter their *value-in-themselves*, the former their *value-for-us*. (Windelband 1961, 24)

If we refer back to the earlier discussion of Windelband's distinction between nomothetic and idiographic modes of knowing, in the latter case, *meaning* ultimately determines the basis of judgment, and meaning, of course, is contingent on personal values and interpretation. And here we find the respective roads of Windelband and Freud crossing, for if

the empirical sciences, led by Psychology, have developed [processes] in order to describe and causally explain ... phenomena [and] the sciences exhibit the historical forms of human knowledge, [then] it is in or by them, in their historical sequence, that logical thought has progressively sought to determine the nature, the meaning and the value of knowledge and of science. (Windelband 1961, 5–6)

It must therefore be possible to "demonstrate the existence of ... ["ontologically objective norms of thinking, willing, and feeling"] ... from psychological data" (Picard 1920, 177). Freud would certainly agree, but as a scientist, he, unlike Windelband, posited specific norms based on specific empirical data.

In short, Windelband attempted to transcend inquiries into the linkage of mind and nature by focusing on a supposedly normative relationship between the two, that is, a "bridge" of value that linked the two domains. And like Kant, he built his philosophy on the freedom of reason, where "autonomy" is understood as *consciousness* of a norm and deliberate choice (Picard 1920, 158).[20] Of course, Windelband's conception of norms as primarily logical principles reflects his interpretation of Kant's categorical imperative, and so, in that sense, he is utterly divorced from Freudianism. Freud would argue (if asked) that Windelband made a fundamental error in assuming that (1) the moral law (as value) is universal, and (2) that humans are independent of the so-called "tendencies of the will" (an argument discussed in chapters 4 and 5). This is a particularly important point: For Freud, the categorical imperative has been transmuted into the superego, and the authority of that faculty remains problematic.

If we put aside the source of moral will, Windelband and Freud shared the fundamental Kantian *approach,* which regarded the freedom of reason as the means of inquiry, where an astute epistemology must be employed to clear the ground for free thinking if one is to liberate one's rational faculties and fulfill a moral potential. The difference with Freud is not in the freedom of reason and the potential for insight, but rather the very conception of moral responsibility, again a matter fully explored in later chapters. Suffice it to observe here that Freud (unknowingly) shared Windelband's primary concerns, namely, the search for a correspondence between the psychic and the physical, and between the moral and the natural. This fundamental, unresolved question, as Windelband understood, results from Kant's splitting of reason (Neiman 1994):

> A psychic causality of meanings, values, and purposes, and parallel with it a physical causality of position and direction, with their various forms of motion; and the two supposed to correspond at every step! That is the strangest adventure we were ever asked to believe. (Windelband 1921, 164)

Given the imbroglio of how to understand "the common causality of the dissimilar in the action of body on soul and soul on body ... we find ourselves compelled to assume unconscious states which are not physical, yet are not in the proper sense of the word of a psychic character [i.e., consciousness]" (164). On this point, Windelband finally comes face to face with Freud:

> In modern thought this [assuming unconscious states] has had the peculiar result of interpolating a third realm, the realm of the unconscious, between the realms of *cogitatio* and *extensio*, into which the Cartesian school distributed reality. However, the fact that all the arguments in favour of this intermediate realm are derived from psychology and its attempts to explain conscious phenomena necessarily implies that this unconscious must be more closely related to the psychic world than to the physical. The hypothesis of psycho-physical parallelism therefore combines the unconscious and the conscious in a unity which is independent of the physical world. All these problems, in fine, are metaphysical problems, and the difficulties which were experienced by the par-

allelism that was based upon the older metaphysics merely show that the ultimate solution depends upon the question how far human knowledge can be confident of passing beyond the two kinds of experience, the external and the internal, and attaining the nature of reality. (165)

Freud accepted the challenge; Windelband remained skeptical precisely because of the metaphysical nature of the problem.

Windelband readily applied this skepticism to other metaphysical realms and dogmatic approaches, for like Lange, he believed that every ethical or metaphysical explanation of the objective link between reality and experience can be dismissed for epistemological reasons. For him, then, the unconscious suffers an even higher degree of obscurity than conscious thought, and here the respective paths of Freud and Windelband decisively diverged. For Windelband, "Philosophy is concerned only with the question where we must, in all circumstances, seek the *reason* for this change of the sensuous into the suprasensuous" (1921, 324; emphasis added). And, further,

> is the world really as purposive, as harmonious, beautiful, and perfect as it ought to be in order to sustain the burden of the teleological argument? Kant took these premises for granted, but ... both ... the purposive and the purposeless ... are found everywhere ... [W]hat is the relation of what ought to be to what is? Of the world of timelessly valid values to the world of things and temporal events? That is the final problem. (351)

Indeed, the challenge of establishing some link between the moral and epistemological domains may fairly be regarded as Kant's lingering central problem, and Windelband is only one of many who argued about the extent Kant had "solved" the quandary and where a better solution might lie. In that tradition, Windelband denied Kant a resting place; Freud did not explicitly recognize the problem and assumed a metaphysics that would allow his epistemology to be guided by some simpler (perhaps naïve) criteria of truth devoid of moral (value) factors. As for the moral domain, it rested within its own boundaries. From the psychoanalytic perspective, actions were ordered by an imposed superego tempered by emotional demands, personal goals and rational insight, and there the matter might have stood: Morals are products configured by family, history, and culture; religion is an illusion to quell psychic disruptions; personal ethics derive from childhood experiences and the mechanisms that dealt with them, successfully and less so.

Alas, neither psychic reality nor Freud's own greater philosophical project may be so easily characterized. Instead, psychoanalysis restates the quandaries bequeathed from Kant's splitting of reason, and just as Windelband recognized that the gulf separating the moral and natural domains might be bridged by reason's autonomy, so too would Freud implicitly employ this same notion of freedom upon which to erect his own method. On this view, psychoanalysis, utilizing an epistemology far removed from its positivist origins, finally emerges as an ethical project, one that begins with Kant's notion of human freedom. So, to decipher the deeper reaches of Freud's thought, we must go further back in philosophy's history, "back to Kant," in order to understand how Freud based psychoanalysis on Kantian precepts.

In the next chapter, I will argue that the theoretical link between the foundations of Freudian psychoanalysis and Kantian idealism is their shared understanding of reason's autonomy. The central paradox of accounting for this independent capacity of the mind, which permits the individual to navigate the world freely, haunts each of their respective pursuits. Kant's method sought to delineate the boundaries of freedom (and therefore the moral) by challenging the immediate "truth" of our experiences. Freud attempted to liberate the individual by controlling the causal chain of instinctual drives by rational understanding and free choice. Both used reason's autonomy to fulfill their respective agendas, and from that shared position, Kant protected metaphysics, while Freud saved humans from his own conception of the Darwinian animal. On this reading, Freud might be considered a neo-Kantian, albeit a most idiosyncratic member of that most eclectic group of philosophers.

Chapter Four.

The Paradox of Freedom

> Causality in accordance with laws of nature is not the only
> one from which all the appearances of the world can be
> derived. It is also necessary to assume another causality
> through freedom in order to explain them.
> —Immanuel Kant (1998, 484)

FREUD'S DISAVOWALS ABOUT PHILOSOPHY do not absolve him from complex philosophical debts: Indeed, Freud (and later commentators) have failed to explain how the origins of psychoanalytical theory began with a positivistic investment without recognizing a dual epistemological commitment. Simply, Freud engaged positivism because he believed it generally equated with empiricism, which he valued, and he rejected "philosophy," and, more specifically, Kantianism, because of the associated "transcendental" qualities of its epistemology. But the relationship between Freud and Kant is not so simple.

We find Freud on both sides of the divide. His philosophical commitments were split between aspirations for a positivistic science of the mind (originating in his neuroscience investigations) and an interpretative strategy that rested upon Kant's argument about the transcendental relation of mind and nature. Here we will explore how Kantian philosophy, rather than obstructing Freud's project, offered him a conception of reason required for psychoanalysis to function both as an interpretative method and a therapy. Basically, Freud divided the mind between the unconscious grounded in the biological and thus subject to some natural causation, and a rational faculty, which lodges itself in consciousness and exists independent of natural cause. The critical distinction resides in Freud's acceptance, as a *psychologist*, of a functional mind-body dualism, and in the higher functions of the mind, he places the repository of interpretative reason. This is basically a Kantian construction, whereby reason assumes an independent character that allows for a detached scrutiny of the natural world.

Beyond this epistemological partitioning, Freud further followed Kant in assigning the scrutinizing ability of a rational self-consciousness the basis of choice and moral reckoning. Consequently, the epistemology leads to a moral philosophy. Freud's debt to Kant thus centers on the dialectical interplay of each domain with the other, and in the end a "moral-epistemology" emerges. To explicate this interpretation, we begin with summarizing Kant's philosophy of mind.

Freud's Understanding of Kant

References to Kant's *Critique of Pure Reason* are sprinkled throughout Freud's writings. Indeed, Freud knew Kant well enough to dispute certain basic Kantian precepts (Freud 1920, 28) and Kantian arguments (Freud 1990, 110–11), or draw on detailed Kantian insights (Freud 1905, 12). (The English *Standard Edition* lists 19 instances where Freud invoked Kant [Guttman 1984].) In an unusual nod to Kant, Freud wrote in 1915,

> In psycho-analysis there is no choice for us to assert that mental processes are themselves unconscious, and to liken the perception of them by means of consciousness to the perception of the external world by means of the sense organs. We can even hope to gain fresh knowledge from the comparison. The psycho-analytic assumption of unconscious mental activity appears to us ... as an extension of the corrections undertaken by Kant of our views on external perception. Just as Kant warned us not to overlook the fact that our perceptions are subjectively conditioned and must not be regarded as identical with what is perceived though unknowable, so psycho-analysis warns us not to equate perceptions by means of consciousness with the unconscious mental processes which are their object. (1915a, 171)

Similar comments appear in *The Interpretation of Dreams* (Freud 1900, 615–17), but reference to Kant is not made there, rather only to a general analogy between the sense organs and conscious thought processes.

Freud saw some connection between Kant's noumenal self and the psychoanalytic unconscious. Neither can be directly perceived, and instead each must be interpreted by emerging phenomena. Clues provided by dreams, slips of the tongue, jokes, neurotic behaviors, and so forth, then serve psychoanalysis with the desiderata of the unconscious, and while the unconscious cannot be directly observed, like a noumenon we may infer its existence as refracted through psychoanalytic techniques analogous to Kantian categories of understanding. And like Kant's apperception of the ego, the unconscious seems to have a "unity"—an integrity of its own, and drives, which follow their own telos and exhibit their own distinctive character. One might argue that this primitive "id" becomes the object of inquiry as some elusive entity perhaps not so different from the noumenon of the natural world. (A detailed discussion of Kant's understanding of selfhood is postponed to chapter 5, where his formulation serves as the foundation for later critiques and thereby situates Freud's own conception of personal identity.)

In private conversations, Freud mused on whether his own categories of understanding the mind (the analysis of repressions in particular) related to Kant's transcendental philosophy. In several informal discussions with Ludwig Binswanger these issues were aired (also discussed in this context by Bergo [2004]). In 1910, Binswanger reported that Freud entertained that his version of the unconscious was close to Kant's noumenon:

> He thought just as Kant postulated the thing in itself behind the phenomenal world, so he himself postulated the unconscious behind the conscious[ness] that is accessible to our experience, but that can never be directly experienced. (Binswanger 1957, 8)

Freud's gesture to "barebones transcendentalism" (Bergo 2004, 342) and Kant's "thing in itself" arose again in 1913 during a discussion between Freud, Binswanger, and Paul Häberlin:

> Freud asked [Häberlin] whether Kant's thing in itself was not identical with the unconscious. [Häberlin] denied this, laughing, and suggested that the two notions were on entirely different levels. (Binswanger 1957, 9)

No further comment is made, other than Häberlin's (as well as Binswanger's) dismissal of the idea, but as already cited, Freud in 1915 seemed still attached to some parallel between his own thinking about the unconscious and the Kantian noumenal/phenonal construction. He held on to this echo until the very end.

In the posthumously published *Outline of Psycho-analysis* (1940b), Freud reiterated his earlier conviction and presented the "psychical apparatus" as a noumenon:

> In our science as in the others the problem is the same: behind the attributes (qualities) of the object under examination which are presented directly to our perception, we have to discover something else which is more independent of the particular receptive capacity of our sense organs and which approximates more closely to what may be supposed to be the real state of affairs. *We have no hope of being able to reach the latter itself*, since it is evident that everything new that we have inferred must nevertheless be translated back into the language of our perceptions, from which it is simply impossible for us to free ourselves. But herein lies the vary nature and limitation of our science.... *Reality will always remain "unknowable."* (196; emphasis added)

The Kantian position could not be more explicitly formulated. Freud goes on to draw parallels between psychoanalysis and physics, since he regarded each discipline as following the same basic scientific strategy: perceptive abilities are constantly improved; sense perceptions permit connections and dependent relations to be made, which are "somehow reliably or reproduced or reflected in our internal" thought; "understanding" follows that in turn permits prediction and control (196). He concludes his primer on scientific method with another parallel to physics:

> We have discovered technical methods of filling up the gaps in the phenomena of our consciousness, and we make use of those methods just as a physicist makes use of experiment. In this manner we infer a number of processes which are themselves "unknowable" and interpolate them in those that are conscious to us. (196–97)

Here we see Freud adopting the Kantian modification of empiricism: namely, to draw the causative linkage between phenomena, the observer must infer by *rational* means that, or how, event A causes event B. So by analogy, whereas the physicist employs experiment in which boundary conditions are limited and defined to establish causal connections, the psychoanalyst must "interpolate" the relations between two psychic events. Despite the obvious differences in the degrees of freedom characterizing each system, the "scientific" method is the same: Just as a physicist must posit the character and placement of an enigmatic particle based on observable phenomena, so must the psychoanalyst infer the character and expression of the psychical apparatus, whose public character appears as the expression of an unobservable unconscious.

Putting aside the irreconcilable differences between an experimental system and the psychoanalytic couch, the impossibility of controlling the boundary conditions of an analysis, and the vastly different interpretative criteria, the striking character of Freud's epistemology is the persistence of applying his notion of a Kantian noumenon to the problems of deciphering unconsciousness. Of course he made that linkage with the intent of legitimating psychoanalytic methods as a form of science. After all, given the example of the microscope, are not invisible organisms brought into view with the appropriate machine that enhances human perception? And does not the uncertainty of quantum mechanical "particles" not require intermediate inferential cognitive steps analogous to those employed by the psychoanalyst? Each must trace, through a series of deductions, concealed entities and processes. However, the "invisibility" metaphor only holds in part, for the issue does not revolve around the elusive nature of an unseen object, but rather the character of that object and the manner in which the conjectures about it are made.

Strictly, the Kantian noumenon is empty of content and resides outside nature, postulated but ever mysterious "in itself." The Freudian unconscious hardly fulfills that criterion, and here we come to an interesting confusion: In his clinical investigations, Freud remained unhesitant in pursuing the unconscious as a *natural* biological entity. He followed the scientific logic drawn from physics (e.g., electric effects) and from biology (e.g., variation within species), in which phenomena are witnessed and then accounted for by measuring forces—electromagnetism and natural selection, respectively. As in these natural sciences, Freud attempted to apply the same basic strategy to uncovering the underlying psychic forces by tracing observations back to their underlying causes.[1] As already discussed, establishing cause became the arch-principle of his project, and he repeatedly proclaimed the success of those investigations. Putting aside the question of whether he actually established cause, clearly the Kantian debt is not found in parallels between the unconscious and the noumenon. So the question is raised, why did Freud even entertain such a notion?

If Freud had deep doubts about the psychoanalytic project as fulfilling the criteria Brentano had established for him, then such a "philosophical parapraxis" may have some significance. In another private conversation, Freud made a fascinating comment precisely on this point. In 1910, Binswanger observed,

> Freud had a genuinely philosophical vein, *even though he was not aware of it.*... On one occasion, [Freud stated] ... that "the unconscious is metaphysic, we simply posit it as real." (Binswanger 1957, 8).

Binswanger challenged Freud, who quickly backpeddled and opined that "the proper term [for the unconscious] was not 'metaphysic' ... but metaconscious" (8). This correction might be interpreted as a parapraxis. If Freud suffered insecurities as a result of admitting the unattainable criteria set by Brentano, then this slip of the tongue might be an important clue to hidden fears.

Beyond the issue of the noumenal character of the Freudian unconscious, other aspects of Kant's philosophy Freud adopted require comment, namely the representationalism of psychoanalytic theory. For Freud, as for Kant, "It is not the thing itself, but a representation of it, that is being interpreted" (Rieff 1959, 105). This is hardly noteworthy in and of itself, inasmuch as the ether of "representation" permeated post-Kantian thought by the end of the nineteenth century. Nevertheless, we must note that for Freud, "the object of either conscious or unconscious mental processes is not the world itself but a *mental representation* of it, outer world or inner as the case may be" (Cavell 1993, 14). This assignment places Freud within the tradition of Anglo-American philosophers of language, where psychoanalysis becomes the relationship between words and the world they describe. From this perspective, Freud embraces an "internalist view according to which the role of language [consciousness] is to give expression to 'ideas' that are prior to and logically independent of it, ideas that are entirely subjective and internal" (Cavell 1993, 47): Through "interposition [of word-presentations] internal thought-processes are made into perceptions" (Freud 1923a, 23).

Thus representationalism appears at the foundations of psychoanalysis, where psychic experiences are represented with a new vocabulary and grammar; the objective reality of our judgments arises from a merging of conscious perceptions mediated by psychic "categories of understanding," and their synthesis in a consciousness capable of self-reflection offered psychoanalysis its basis of study.

Despite Freud's admitted agnosticism about the neurological basis of consciousness,[2] the question was critical to his model of the mind. Indeed, placing consciousness in a general *neurophysiological* schema of the mind oriented Freud's entire conceptual understanding of the psyche. To the extent he considered the nature of consciousness as a neuroscientist, he followed Helmholtz's theories of perception (Makari 1994). Accordingly, Freud characterized consciousness as a "sense organ for the perception of psychical qualities" (1900, 615). That orientation was elaborated in the 1895 *Project for a Scientific Psychology* (Freud 1955), which may be interpreted as a "connectionist" theory of the mind (Churchland 1991; Smith 1999a; 1999b). In such a schema, simple processors are arranged in an interconnected network. Freud postulated three such functional systems: (1) perceptual input; (2) cognitive processing; and (3) consciousness-generating. According to this model, all conscious items are ultimately sensations or associated with sensations and thoughts enter consciousness by "parasitizing sensation" (Smith 1999a, 417). So for Freud, the presentation of the unconscious to the conscious sensory faculty (albeit through complex pathways) comprised a metaphorical extension of the brain's general perceptive qualities (Natsoulas 1984; 1985). In the later topographical, dynamic, and economic conceptions, he utilized this basic organizational configuration to describe the ebb and flow of the incessant processing of neurophysiological events. And, as discussed above, perception for Freud followed a representational model, where proposition-like structures are processed much as language.[3]

This propositionally structured philosophy of mind derives most directly from Kant, who configured knowledge acquisition of the world (and thought) not through some direct empirical conduit, but rather through cognitive faculties. This antirealist position (see chap. 3, note 6) imposes a far-reaching metaphysical commitment (see the critiques in chapter 3), which fundamentally provided Freud with the philosophical tool to extract himself from the chains of Brentano's definition of the mental solely as consciousness. Albeit with different assignments, consciousness became the lynchpin of their respective psychologies.

> Psychological reflection informs us only that [there] are causes, unknown in themselves, which influence the rise of subsequent mental phenomena, as well as that they are in themselves unknown effects of previous mental phenomena. In either case psychological reflection can prove in isolated instances *that* they exist; but it can never in any way give us knowledge of *what* they are. (Brentano 1973, 60)

Freud denied this basic Brentanean tenet, and to the extent he successfully plumbed the depths of these "causes," Freud invoked a philosophy that permitted a process of inferential reasoning that would lead him back from "observed" conscious effects to their unconscious sources. After all, if the underlying reality of mental life exists in domains inaccessible to direct observation, then "sensations" or representations must serve as the desiderata that a conscious faculty might utilize. So while Freud wrote little about the nature of consciousness, we must appreciate the infrastructure of his thought: the entire psychoanalytic edifice rested upon a version of Kant's philosophy of mind.

In *The Ego and the Id* (1923a), Freud drew a bead on the crucial philosophical issue of defining mind and went to some length to describe, as he had many times previously, the repressed character of the unconscious, the transitory nature of consciousness, the latency of preconsciousness, and most beguiling, the utterly different logic employed by the unconscious relative to conscious thought. And most importantly, the unconscious *is* the mind, and psychoanalysis is the means of revealing its true character.

Because consciousness establishes conditions that preclude direct "observation" of the unconscious and, correspondingly, because the unconscious has no "language" (as normally construed) and functions with a "logic" alien to conscious thought, a new method is required for its discernment. The primary point, the foundation of the entire enterprise, rests on accepting that *the unconscious cannot be directly known*, inasmuch as it follows its own "laws" of cause and temporality.[4] Indeed, to *know* the unconscious in order to ultimately control it (and concomitantly free humankind from repression), another faculty, "reason," must be invoked. And reason's capacity to fulfill that role rests on an astonishing claim, one that truly indebts Freud to Kant. At the end of his 1915 acknowledgment to Kant (quoted above), Freud writes,

> Like the physical, the psychical is not necessarily in reality what it appears to us to be. We shall be glad to learn, however, that *the correction of internal perception will turn out not to offer such great difficulties as the correction of external perception*—that internal objects are less unknowable than the external world. (1915a, 171; emphasis added)

Thus, according to Freud, the tyranny of the despotic unconscious would be broken by reason's autonomy, by its ability to free itself from disguised and hidden psychic forces to discern deterministic causes of overt behaviors and thoughts that hitherto were inaccessible. So for Freud, the insight offered by emotional catharsis conjoined to analysis may result in some form of psychological release.

If we move beyond the immediate therapeutic implications of Freud's project to the larger philosophical construction of the ego, reason assumes special standing. In service to an ego driven by its quest for release from unconscious strictures, psychoanalytic insight, achieved by transference and rational interpretation, turns the analysand from a heteronomous state (controlled by unconscious forces) to an autonomous one. The person thus becomes a *moral* agent, who might discern psychic reality and then act responsibly, with new choices and means of control. On this view, to be human in a healthy (normal) sense is to accept moral responsibility as formulated by the Kantian ideal. As discussed below, this notion of moral agency adopts certain criteria of autonomy and free will, of which the most critical are the ability to (1) rationally self-reflect, (2) act freely and for understandable (rational) reasons, and (3) in a broad sense, be the originator of choices and actions. This Kantian scenario is enacted on the couch by self-reflection, rational interpretation, the freeing from internalized psychic influences, and the authorship of a reconceived autobiography. Achieving this independent authority, moral choice becomes fulfillment of self-defined goals and liberation from psychic control. The battle waged to achieve a new form of moral agency follows the flag of

self-determination. Thus psychoanalysis, which begins as an epistemological method, in the end serves an ethical enterprise.

Divided Reason

Although split by a cautious confidence and a despondent resignation,
Freud tirelessly promoted psychoanalysis as reason's best tool, an idea
lifted directly from Kant's conception of autonomy (Schneewind 1998),
which follows a complex philosophical development of reason's character. Kant's "criticism of reason" concerns the conditions and limits of
human cognition.[5] For Kant, the place of reason, the role of emotions, the
intuitions of the spiritual domain, and the ability to understand human
psychology each require a model of the mind that would account for their
respective claims to different forms of knowledge. For instance, on what
basis could knowledge of the natural world or the moral universe be
conceived as legitimate and unified? What schema might tie together the
natural world of cause and effect with the moral universe of an agent's
exercise of free will? What is the relationship between scientific thinking
as objective knowledge and, opposed to it, subjective ways of knowing?'

Kant attempted to mend these various divisions by first separating reason into two modalities, one that dealt with the natural world and the
other to navigate the moral. Although dealing with different domains,
reason still functioned as a whole, and Kant posited a faculty of judgment
that brought unity to thought. By drawing that synthesis, he provided a
rationale—and outlined the ability—for individuals to connect the theoretical (i.e., natural) and practical (i.e., moral) aspects of human reason
(Kant 1987). His formulation provided a model by which the natural sciences, anthropology, psychology, ethics, aesthetic judgment, and religious
belief might coexist, secure in their own domains.

A deeper complexity underlies Kantian reason: If the noumenal reality can only be refracted by reason's own laws, if the real is a synthesis of mind and nature, if the very self that knows the world is itself
a noumenon, what could reason's own foundations be? Kant's answer:
"Reason operates according to laws that it gives to itself" (Neiman 1994,
91). In other words, reason is independent of the natural world of appear-

ances and causation. And paradoxically, self-consciousness itself (like the unconscious) is phenomenally inaccessible, at least in any direct sense.

Further parallels appear: Kant meticulously derived reason's "laws," which include the unrequited search for the unconditioned (the ground or foundation of the world) (Neiman 1994, 86). Simply, reason becomes "the capacity to act according to purposes" (88), which is comprised by the search for its own grounding. Further, by seeking "its own reflection in nature" (88), reason structures reality according to a human perspective, not as the world *really* is in any final sense, but only in reason's own terms. In other words, human minds are "the lawgivers" to nature.

> Reason, in order to be taught by nature, must approach nature with its principles in one hand, according to which alone the agreement among appearances can count as laws, and, in the other hand, the experiments thought out in accordance with these principles—yet in order to be instructed by nature not like a pupil, who has recited to him whatever the teacher wants to say, but like an appointed judge who compels witnesses to answer questions he puts to them. (Kant 1998, 109)

Thus the "concepts of the understanding give order to experience; the principles of reason are the standard by which it is judged" (Neiman 1994, 6).

Indeed, reason has "complete spontaneity [to] make its own order according to ideas, to which it fits the empirical conditions and according to which it even declares actions to be necessary that yet have not occurred and perhaps will not occur" (Kant 1998, 541 [A548/B576]). Kant goes on to describe how reason possesses its own ordering principles (542 [A550/B578]), and thereby distinguishes itself from the world that it examines. Further, unlike certain human behaviors that have an obvious empirical content and thus deterministic causality, reason possesses no temporality (or what we perceive as natural causality) "and thus the dynamical law of nature, which determines the temporal sequence according to rules, cannot be applied to it" (543 [A553/B581]).

Thus to fulfill its function, reason must be free of experience, and, on this view, the ability to survey the world and make judgments depends on reason's independence of that world. Reason, accordingly, resides outside the natural domain, free and autonomous, to order nature through scientific insight and regulate human behavior through rational moral discourse.[6] This allows creative judgment in science and freedom of choice in the social (ethical) domain. Thus the autonomy of both theoretical and practical reason serves as the bedrock of Kant's entire philosophy, enabling the synthesis and apprehension of the natural world and the discernment of the moral universe. Here, finally, we can join the two paths Freud followed from his earliest university studies: In pursuing science, Freud was committed to defining the deterministic causation of natural phenomena, and when studying unconsciousness, he applied this same principle to follow instinctual drives. Irrespective of the overdetermination (multiple causes) of psychic phenomena and the inaccessibility of the unconscious, which "has no organization, produces no collective will ... [nor] logical laws of thought" (Freud 1933, 73) (above all, the law of contradiction), psychoanalysis—*as a science*—would discover the dark workings of the unconscious mind by establishing through retrospective reconstruction a causal chain of mental events. Thus psychoanalysis, following the basic premise that effects have causes, evolved to discern the "strict determination of mental events" (Freud 1923b, 238) and expose "the illusion of Free Will" (Freud 1919a, 236).

However, as previously discussed (chapter 2), the backward reconstruction of a *putative* causal chain by construing *reasons* does not qualify as establishing *cause*. Freud, through a complex convolution, extrapolated neurophysiology to psychology, and thereby aspired to establish *mechanisms* of disease. In configuring psychoanalysis as a scientific discipline, he simply ignored the gapping chasm between the causal mechanistic laws of the natural domain, which defined his idea of scientific explanation, and the interpretative reconstructions he devised to explain mental phenomena. In short, Freud applied what he thought were *scientific* causal links, because he believed he was dealing with *natural* phenomena that could be discerned through spectacles devised for physics and biology, when in fact he supplied *reasons* that were derived from inferences and interpretations of *mental* phenomena that had no explanatory power in the natural sense he wished to apply.[7] Simply, he mistook two different ontologies as the same and in the process applied the same epistemologies when different strategies were required. In a sense, he ignored one of Kant's cardinal tenets: two kinds of reason were required to address the *physical* and the *metaphysical*, and as explored in the previous chapter, Freud failed to recognize the metaphysical character of the unconscious and thus made a fundamental category error in his analysis of the psyche.

If Freud had succeeded in making the unconscious a natural object suitable for scientific study, then his naturalization of the mind would be credible. The position taken here, albeit in debt to the vast critical literature, accepts that he failed. On that view, the "mind" and "the ego" and "the unconscious" serve as placeholders for the corresponding targets of scientific scrutiny. On this account, the unconscious, then, is a metaphysical construction whose definition has served useful purposes, but it cannot be confused with the brain functions from which its behavior emerges. This hardly denies its reality, but that reality is configured in a universe that excludes natural objects and forces. Kant, and in a different voice, Wittgenstein, considered each domain as separate and distinct, so the character of knowledge and the reason employed to achieve its ends were also distinguished. In this vein, Freud's triumph rests on the successful application of "practical" reason, when ironically he thought he was employing "pure" reason. That misassignment accounts for Freud's error (or Whitehead's term, "misplaced concreteness," to characterize this general mistake [1925]), which nevertheless yielded success. Ironically then, whereas Freud thought he was doing science, he in fact was conducting a highly novel, creative, and fecund interpretation of how humans think, conduct their lives, exhibit character, and create personal identity. Simply, he conducted a moral investigation, one that remains a steadfast testimony to his insights. An outline of that achievement follows, and we will return to consider this aspect of his work again in other chapters framed by different contexts.

The Psychoanalytic Ego

Schematically in the last formulation, the rational ego (with its own laws, logic, and language) and the arational id function with differing causalities through their respective operations and goals. As the id strives for its own aggrandizement, the ego, with its countervailing rationality, attempts to restrict it. Functionally then, the ego mediates reality as it responds to the libidinal drives of the id as well as the restrictive demands of the superego and thus is "threatened by three kinds of danger" (Freud 1933, 77).

> The poor ego ... serves three severe masters and does what it can to bring their claims and demands into harmony with one another. These claims are always divergent and often seem incompatible. No wonder that the ego so often fails in its task. Its three tyrannical masters are the external world, the super-ego, and the id. When we follow the ego's efforts to satisfy them simultaneously—or rather to obey them simultaneously—we cannot feel any regret at having personified this ego and having set it up as a separate organism. (77)

Psychoanalysis would empower the ego's rational faculty by penetrating the unconscious to discern its functions through rational inquiry. Simplistically, this schema structures Freud's notion of psychodynamics, and while no neat partition exists in Freud's mature presentation, where the ego is divided between conscious and unconscious components (1933, 78), for this discussion suffice it to leave rationality (for better and for worse) insulated within the conscious faculty of the ego, or as Freud wrote, "The ego stands for reason" (1933, 76). Indeed, this repository (which Freud called a "separate organism") is the crucial arena in which psychoanalysis ultimately achieves its own goals: Reason "understands" and then putatively better restrains the unconscious drives that inhibit or prevent goals and behaviors established by the rational faculty. More, "Freud designated as the ego that authority which decides which contents are repressed from consciousness" (Tugendhat 1986, 130), and thus the ego must be the target of psychoanalytic intervention.

Despite confident assertions, Freud's program functions in ambiguity: Given that the self-conscious, rational ego functions autonomously, what grounds that function and by what authority does reason achieve its adjudicating role? *What*, indeed, is this ego, this agent, this me or he or she? And more to the point, the philosophical character of reason and its active personification were also left nebulous, and possibly incoherent, throughout its various characterizations (dating from the early 1890s to the topographical definition described in the *Ego and the Id* [1923a]). In short, the ego's ontological character, the *Ich*, swings between the Cartesian indubitable self and the Kantian noumenon, which is fundamentally unknowable given its complex conscious/unconscious structure (Laplanche and Pontalis 1973, 130–43). So, *what* is this rational faculty enlisted into the deliberations of consciousness? These questions are, of course, central to a critical assessment of psychoanalysis, but Freud himself offered little guidance, largely because this issue eclipsed his interests. Simply, he took *reason* as a given, and just as a carpenter uses a hammer, so Freud applied reason to construct, and deconstruct, the psyche.

In Freud's mature writings, the ego became a complex composite of conscious and unconscious domains, with the latter in dynamic intercourse with the id and superego. Indeed, the ego as part of the mental triad increasingly attracted his attention as he pondered the mystery of a rational faculty surveying and judging other domains of the mind. He explained this ability in almost an offhand gesture in his 1933 lecture, "The Dissection of the Psychical Personality:"

> We wish to make the ego the matter of our enquiry, our very own ego. But is that possible? After all, the ego is in its very essence a subject; how can it be made into an object? Well, there is no doubt that it can be. The ego can take itself as an object, can treat itself like other objects, can observe itself, criticize itself, and do Heaven knows what with itself. (1933, 58)

Freud might have then further developed this Kantian construction, but he did not, and instead he observed how consciousness becomes self-consciousness:

> In this, one part of the ego is splitting itself over against the rest. So the ego can be split; it splits itself during a number of its functions—temporarily at least. Its parts can come together again afterwards. That is not exactly a novelty, though it may be putting an unusual emphasis on what is generally known. (1933, 58)

Agreed, and in this wave of the hand, Freud skirts the philosophical status of consciousness and the rational faculties upon which his entire enterprise rests.[8] Of course he was in good company.

Some have argued that Kant held an incoherent theory of self-consciousness as understood on the subject-object model (the so-called reflection model, whereby reflection is analyzed by a two-termed relation between the subject of consciousness and the object of consciousness), because this theory presupposes the self-conscious awareness it attempts to explain; others dispute that Kant even held that position, and instead maintain that a subject-object structure does appropriately apply to an understanding of self-knowledge, which of course is a different problem altogether (Tugendhat 1986, 55–60, 133–43; Keller 1998, 103–5, 252 nn. 19, 20). This issue becomes particularly pertinent in later formulations (e.g., Hegel and Kierkegaard). Be that as it may, Freud offered nothing to this discussion. Self-consciousness, and more particularly the faculties of reason, is simply given, and here at the interface of his clinical descriptions and philosophy, we see the limits of Freud's epistemology, which we have already discussed in different contexts.

We will again consider other aspects of Freud's epistemology, but for now, based on the issues raised here, one must conclude that Freud's views on self-consciousness remain stuck in an unsophisticated folk psychology. Yet he does fulfill a remarkable philosophical role as a moral philosopher. In building the case for that claim, we return to further consider his debts to Kant.[9]

Whither Freud and Kant?

As already discussed, Freud himself remained conspicuously silent about any philosophical allegiance beyond "science," so he did not present his notion of the unconscious in explicit Kantian terms, nor did he explore the relationship of language and thought, which was to dominate post-Wittgenstein philosophy (Cavell 1993; Gomez 2005, 9–15, 103–6) and Lacanian psychoanalysis (Boothby 2001). More, he actively rejected attempts permitting psychoanalysis to claim legitimacy independent of that paragon of knowledge of his era, science. In short, as Freud regarded philosophy, he could not consider psychoanalysis *philosophically*. Instead, he was engaged with clinical conditions that required empirical methods, which he identified as "science" (as opposed to "philosophy"). His psychical hypotheses aped physical principles (see the discussion of Draft K in chapter 1), and, while understanding that science had its own philosophical structure, he uncritically and exclusively accepted the positivist mode, leaving other constructions aside.

However, in other respects Freud's implicit acceptance of Kant's formulation offers a rich philosophical soil in which to plant psychoanalysis. The theme we will now explore concerns how Freud's philosophy arises from the deepest reaches of his humanistic interests and commitments. In a complex duet, I maintain that (1) even without a sophisticated understanding, Freud appreciated the basic Kantian precepts, and (2) Freud shared with Kant a vision of human beings as committed to a moral venture. I base this interpretation on reading Freud as a modernist, who conceived psychoanalysis fulfilling the quest of moral responsibility. So on this general Kantian view, psychoanalysis becomes an ethical inquiry, similarly based on reason's emancipation and the potential of freeing humans from what Kant called their "immaturity" (1996a), and which Freud described in clinical terms of dysfunctional defenses, neuroses, and repressions. To justify this claim, we will follow several lines of argument, and here we begin with an outline of Kant's notion of human freedom and morality.

Kant may fairly be credited with the invention of individual autonomy (Schneewind 1992, 309–41; 1998). His clearest exposition is found in the famous response to the question, "What is Enlightenment?" to which he answered, "*Enlightenment is mankind's exit from its self-incurred immaturity*" or as he further extolled, "Have the courage to use your *own* understanding" (1996d, 58–64). He goes on to celebrate the virtues of an independent mind guided by rationality, moral forthrightness, and above all, a vision of personal freedom that captures these moral and epistemological virtues. Note that the entire enterprise rests on the notion of reason as fully autonomous (O'Neill 1992). Freud similarly understood humans as capable of achieving freedom by breaking the shackles of repressive defenses and disarming unrecognized unconscious drives. Putting aside the degrees of freedom potentially achieved through psychoanalysis, that possibility was predicated on a view of an autonomous rationality, which in turn makes humans *metaphysically* free and *morally* responsible. Psychoanalysis, based on this capacity, offered two arch-lessons: The first teaching concerned the *opportunity* to discern hidden psychic forces, and in that understanding stymie their pernicious effects on human conduct. Reason, in the form of enlightened rationality, thus serves as the vehicle of personal liberation, specifically by uncoupling the determinism of early experiences and allowing reasoned choice. Such reason could only function if it achieved some degree of independence from a dominating "a-reason," and thus Freud integrated Kant's basic formulation of reason with a new method of inquiry.

In an instrumental sense, reason becomes the tool by which humans become moral in each context—Kantian and Freudian. Indeed, the very possibility of self-discovery and moral choice must be predicated on notions of freedom, and thereby the two endeavors powerfully resonate, even as they occupy differing domains of discourse. So despite the deterministic character of the Freudian universe, he, like Spinoza before him, understood that personal insight and understanding constituted the basic freedom humans possess, and more, their defining characteristic. The second lesson entailed a moral mandate: In the successful scenario, psychoanalysis putatively allows *exercise* of choice, which ultimately frees humans to pursue a mental life cast in some normative framework. Putting aside the problematic definition of "normal" (explored in chapter 7), *normative* suggests perfectionism, which directs the ethical enterprise. In other words, psychoanalysis becomes an exercise of moral behavior formulated in terms of some clinical insight. Based on "an ethic of honesty," knowing authentically (i.e., a knowing that is psychically informed) becomes a "primary ethical act" (Rieff 1959, 322). Self-consciousness then becomes "a task" of reflective discovery, of self-awareness (Ricoeur 1970, 45). The task has a teleological structure—the moral command to "know thyself."

However, as Freud showed so dramatically, "knowing" through self-consciousness may be totally inadequate to the challenge, and in this analytic scenario, self-consciousness itself becomes a problem,

> for our capacity to turn our attention on to our mental activities is also a capacity to distance ourselves from them, and to call them into question.... The reflective mind cannot settle for perception and desire, not just as such. It needs a *reason*. (Korsgaard 1996, 13)

And reason serves the moral, inasmuch as we are constantly judging actions, relationships, and choices. Accordingly, this process of self-discovery leads from alienation (because "I do not at first possess what I am" [Ricoeur 1970, 45]) to the freedom of self-identity, self-knowledge, and self-understanding. In grasping "the Ego in its effort to exist, in its desire to be" (Ricoeur 1970, 46), this ethic moves the fundamental moral question from "What ought I *do?* to "What should I *be?*" To that end, Freud's method of discovery, which began as a therapy for severely ill patients (obsessive compulsives, hysterics, the war traumatized, and even psychotics), has over the course of the past century also evolved into a broadly applicable existential psychology which has enrolled analysands with minimal dysfunctional neuroses.

In shifting from those afflicted with serious psychiatric disease to individuals suffering from unhappiness and maladjustments, psychoanalysis enacts an ethics of self-appraisal with the coupled goal of self-improvement. The entire enterprise rests on reason's autonomy and the capacity to exercise freedom of choice and thereby assume ethical responsibility (Sherman 1995). Psychoanalysis thus becomes a moral philosophy of investigation underwriting an ethics of personal identity. Note that the moral agent on this reading is centered on reason, not the superego. Obviously, for Freud, the two represented two entirely different modalities to express the ethical, one as a liberator, the other as part of a potentially despotic unconscious. In the topographical model, the superego is the repository of moral consciousness, "an agency ... in the ego which confronts the rest of the ego in an observing, criticizing and prohibiting sense" (Freud 1939, 116). In this last articulation, Freud described the superego as "the successor and representative of the parents (and educators) who superintended the actions of the individual in his first years of life; it perpetuates their function almost without change" (117); as formed by the "inhibiting forces in the outer world, [the superego] becomes internalized" (116) and thus a potential source of neurosis. Derived from childhood experience and explicit training (or conditioning), a moral imperative becomes a policing of individual desire and behavior that may or may not be consonant with benefit to the individual. Freud succinctly described these dynamics as follows:

> This super-ego can confront the ego and treat it like an object; and often treats it very harshly. It is important for the ego to remain on good terms with the super-ego as with the id. Estrangements between the ego and super-ego are of great significance in mental life ... [T]he super-ego is the vehicle of the phenom-

enon we call conscience. Mental life very much depends on the super-ego's being normally developed—that is, on its having become sufficiently impersonal. And that is precisely what it is not in neurotics.... Their super-ego still confronts their ego as a strict father confronts a child; and their morality operates in a primitive fashion in that the ego gets itself punished by the super-ego. Illness is employed as an instrument for this "self-punishment," and neurotics have to behave as though they were governed by a sense of guilt which, in order to be satisfied, needs to be punished by illness. (1926a, 223)

Even in the nonneurotic case, the superego's chief function "remains the limitation of satisfactions" (Freud 1940b, 148). For Freud, the individual always remains his focus, and more particularly, individual welfare, and thus the restrictions imposed on the pleasure principle through the super-ego faculty always require a mediation, sometimes successful, sometimes not. Thus psychoanalysis, through its faculty of reasoned analysis, would free the ego, not only from the instinctual drives of the id, but also from the neuroses imposed by a despotic superego.

Recognizing those limits, the "science" of psychotherapy putatively offered rational humans insight into those dynamics, which as a therapy would, at best, afford strategies (through self-awareness) to achieve some state of emotional independence from a tyrannical unconscious. He offered "transference" as the vehicle for such emancipation, and without going further into those dynamics, suffice it to note that Freud sought to find a synthesis between the role of rational understanding and emotional recognition of early trauma to achieve "cure" of the patient through psychoanalysis.

So now we must confront the most ironic of Freud's debts to Kant: While free will might be an illusion, its assumption serves as the very basis of the therapeutic enterprise. After all, introspection and reasoned examination depend on some disjunction between an "unreasoned" id and a rational ego. Indeed, analysis as an exercise of reason over nature not only serves Freud's *scientific* ambitions, but also draws upon the Kantian construction of reason as constitutive of *moral* inquiry. Free will, the ability to make decisions independent of deterministic cause, is for the modernist the bedrock of moral responsibility and choice. Indeed, Freud devised psychoanalysis as a means for liberating the ill neurotic by exposing the workings of the id, as in the famous adage, "Where id was, there ego shall be" (1933, 80). He meant, quite specifically, that by "making conscious what is unconscious, lifting the repressions, filling gaps in the memory" (1933, 435) the ego would be strengthened "to achieve a progressive conquest of the id" (1923a, 56) and thereby attain relief of unconscious forces.

Freud, in building a case for the moral will, allows reason various degrees of freedom in determining the ethical framework in which choices must be made (presumably in service to a reality principle in which the individual will find greater happiness, or at least less conflict). To put it simply, I am referring to the psychoanalytic process itself, whereby insight and perspective emerge from a new appraisal of personal identity (and moral agency more generally). Reason thus functions as an arbiter of ethical choice, and here we see Freud implicitly accepting the Kantian prescription of moral agency as residing in some autonomous authority of self-responsibility based on reason's autonomy: "The power to judge autonomously—that is freely (according to principles of thought in general)—is called reason" (Kant 1996a, 255 [7:27]).

Three cardinal characteristics form Kant's depiction of reason: (1) the antecedent standards of reason are unknown and unknowable; (2) reason is like a currency—ideas must be exchanged, justifications must be accepted, options and choices must be understood, and actions must be explained; and (3) most importantly for Freud's own project,

> Reason must subject itself to critique in all its undertakings, and cannot restrict the freedom of critique through any prohibition without damaging itself and drawing upon itself a disadvantageous suspicion. Now there may be nothing so important because of its utility, nothing so holy, that it may be exempted from the searching review and inspection, which knows no respect for persons. The very existence of reason depends upon this freedom. (Kant 1998, 643 [A738/B766])

In this famous quote, Kant encapsulates the Enlightenment project: Reason is the medium of both morals and action, but it has no final dictatorial authority and is thus always subject to criticism. In what Adam Seligman calls "modernity's wager" (2000), Kant presents the gambit to liberate the modern individual from external social and religious norms by supplementing them with the rational self as its own moral authority. However, humans cannot appeal to some final rational authority, or even rationality itself, to discover the foundations of morality. In this scheme, (1) *reason* becomes the vehicle of moral discourse; (2) moral agents, persons, discover and act according to principled autonomy;[10] (3) the will that might discover a universalized moral imperative has no prior antecedent or given moral code; and (4) the exchange of reasons generated by autonomous individuals creates a community's rationality that may be freely understood and then chosen. So on this view, Kant dispensed with all sovereignty, including reason's own claims, established the basis for self-governance as the basic characteristic of ways of thinking and willing, and in so doing, created a moral "space" in which external authority was replaced with individual responsibility and communal normative standards. He thereby set the foundations for later conceptions of moral agency.

While Freud adopted the underlying premise of Kantian freedom, he departed from Kant's philosophical path by assuming a naturalistic stance. Unlike Kant, who sought to recognize and act according to a universal categorical imperative, Freud assigned the placement and character of value (and choice) within the individual's own psychical apparatus. He provided the means by which value and morality were formed and incorporated into the psyche, and he presented a dynamic psychology that accounted for the interplay of values in individual behaviors. In this sense, Freud rejected the universal, pristine idealism of Kant's moral law, and he would decipher the moral domain, not as constituted by some metaphysical moral order, but rather one composed of chaotic drives and desires of a psyche striving for its own self-fulfillment and pleasure. As unruly emotions clash with the reality principle, moral choice must be made, and so one dimension of psychoanalytic theory's ethical structure conceives of an ego monitor, whose character declares itself the mediator between the reality principle and self-aggrandizing inner drives. That ego function itself is subject to both superego demands and a socially imposed conscience, and so a universal moral imperative has been replaced by a radically conditional moral culture. Freud thus replaced Kant's precept with a *relative* conception of the right, one that arose from the contingency of culture, the vicissitudes of history, and most importantly, the constitution and demands of psychic drives and needs.

Insofar as Freud devised psychoanalysis to break the causal chain of instinctual drives so they might come under the rational control (as opposed to repression) of the ego, and thus free choice—as opposed to psychological determinism[11]—might be achieved, a gap opened before him: Reasons are not causes; retrospective reconstructions are not causal; interpretation follows its own ways, and the basis of clinical efficacy would seek no firmer grounds than reference to insight. Indeed, Freud never explained, beyond the procedures of disclosure and analysis, how the leap from one domain (natural causation) to the other (moral freedom) might be accomplished. Note that this unresolved tension appears in various formats during this period, and one can hardly fault him for failing to meld this metaphysical breach. However, in that admission we must recognize that Freud left a huge conceptual gap (uncharitably, a contradiction) that has vexed commentators, who, despite extensive d bate, have failed to reconcile this inner fault line of psychoanalysis (e.g., Meisner 2003, 53–112). In this vein, how the subsequent twentieth-century fate of psychoanalysis intertwines with the uses and rejections of Kantianism (Hanna 2001; Guyer 2006) deserves renewed attention.

Freud, while pausing to acknowledge Kant, did not see his own project in the Kantian tradition, not only because he regarded that course of philosophy as hopelessly speculative and contemplative, but more deeply because it was based in idealism. So, identifying himself as a scientist, Freud could not abide placement with the unnamed philosophers, whom he regarded as following an outmoded school of thought. Those philosophers whom he confronted approached the mind with a different set of tools, none of which was empiricist, and thus failed to engage him on grounds of his own choosing. And because Kant was simply off limits, and because Freud committed himself so doggedly to his scientific project, he failed to acknowledge and explicitly develop psychoanalysis as a moral enterprise, a designation that best captures the character of psychoanalysis.

The Paradox

While Freud regarded the ego in various theoretical formulations as embodied (the last being a mixture of conscious and unconscious faculties [Freud 1923a]) and thus subject to scientific scrutiny, on my reading, the full *philosophical* thrust of Freud's formulation points to the ego as a *moral* agent. Indeed, when Freud addresses the analysand as a *person*, he does so as one committed to a certain kind of inquiry, which itself constitutes an ethical undertaking in various ways: a scrutiny of behavior within a normative framework; a relentless self-assessment; a telos of individual perfection. And as discussed, this endeavor rests upon a conception of reason's autonomy, which ultimately determines how the knowing subject discerns the world and herself. This epistemological independence also allows the subject, as a *moral* agent, to act with varying degrees of freedom in opposition to the determinism of unconscious forces.[12] The full expansion of this claim must await later discussions, and here I only wish to emphasize how Freud's epistemology services his moral project.

Reason's autonomy determines the ground from which the knowing subject discerns the world (in this case, the psychoanalytic process), and this epistemological independence also allows the subject, as a *moral* agent, to act with varying degrees of freedom in the natural world (which includes the unconscious). Such parallels consequently go beyond the epistemological frameworks in which Kant and Freud worked, for they each began with an epistemology and ended with a moral philosophy. In these regards, the Freudian and Kantian systems of thought begin at the same place, follow the same general course, and share a deep philosophical kinship: an ethics of freedom that must be based on reason's independence and the capacity to judge itself. Freud erected that position against a competing notion of agency, namely one construed as organic and primitive, that is, ultimately instinctual. Acknowledging the authority of that essentially biological view complements the Kantian moral portrait he saw as juxtaposed against it. For indeed, Kant, and Spinoza before him, recognized that humans must make ethical choices within a naturalistic construct. Below (chapter 5), we will explore Freud's understanding of a naturalistic moral construction on the foundations shared by psychoanalysis and Kantian idealism, which each posit an understanding of the freedom of reason as a prerequisite for moral agency. Indeed, unpacking (and reconciling) this duality is, on my view, the central philosophical challenge of Freud's theory.

This problem was eloquently stated at the end of Kant's *Second Critique*, where he famously mused on the mystery of reason's ability to bridge the moral and natural domains:

> Two things fill the mind with ever new and increasing admiration and reverence,.... *the starry heavens above me and the moral law within me*. I do not need to search for them and seek them as though they were veiled in obscurity or in the transcendent region beyond my horizon; I see them before me and connect them immediately with the consciousness of my own existence. (1996c, 269)

And so Kant accepted the immediate reality of both aspects of human nature, and even though freedom appears to contradict nature, one must think of oneself in both modalities (both free and subject to nature's laws), not only because they coexist in the immediacy of human thought, but because they are

> *necessarily united* in the same subject; for otherwise no ground could be given why we should burden reason with an idea [freedom] which, though it may without contradiction be united with another that is well established, yet entangles us in a business that brings reason into difficult straits in its theoretical use. (Kant 1996b, 102)

This paradox—the dual characteristic of the human being as a creature of the organic world and yet one who exercises free choice independent of natural causation—is thus resolved on the basis of reason's standing and the arch-precept of human freedom leading to moral responsibility. The entire Kantian philosophical edifice hangs together on these intimate linkages, and while Freud does not address the issue head-on, he basically accepts this construction and, with it, assumptions supportive to his own agenda.

If both Kant and Freud reject the idea that there is a direct correspondence between the mind and the world, then how do they believe the individual can act freely in a world to which he has no immediate connection? Is not the individual inescapably bound up in his world of representations, which themselves are psychically determined? As both focus on the interface between the world of representations and events in the "real" world, they must account for an independent capacity of the mind—reason—that permits the individual to navigate the world freely, that is, to allow for moral responsibility. Kant's method sought to delineate clearly the boundaries of freedom (and therefore the moral) by challenging the supposed "truth" of the vast majority of our experiences. Similarly, Freud sought to liberate the individual by breaking the causal chain of instinctual drives and containing them through rational control and free choice.

Two "tectonic" plates constantly shift in Freud's theory: One, associated with science, commits to naturalism—naturalistic explanations governed by naturalistic cause. This issue of *cause* served as the organizing theme of my "Brentano chapters," inasmuch as Freud's mentor had established the key thematic challenge to a science of the unconscious that oriented Freud's own approach, for better and for worse. That matter rested on inferences drawn from various conscious manifestations, for example, dreams and parapraxes. Clearly, Freud's entire scientific edifice was built on a deterministic metaphysics drawn from these data. However, Freud noted, early in the formulation period, a complication of a "strictly and frankly deterministic" (Gay 1988, 119) philosophy of mind:

> Many people, as is well known, contest the assumption of complete psychical determinism by appealing to a special feeling of conviction that there is a free will. This *feeling of conviction* exists; and it does not give way before a belief in determinism. Like every normal feeling it must have something to warrant it. But so far as I can observe, it does not manifest itself in the great and important decisions of the will: on these occasions the feeling that we have is rather one of psychical compulsion, and we are glad to invoke it on our behalf ("Here I stand: I can do no other" [Martin Luther's declaration at the Diet of Worms]). On the other hand, it is precisely with regard to the unimportant, indifferent decisions that we would like to claim that we could just well have acted otherwise: that we have acted of our free—and unmotivated—will. According to our analyses it is not necessary to dispute the right to the *feeling of conviction* of having free will. If the distinction between conscious and unconscious motivation is taken into account, *our feeling of conviction* informs us that conscious

motivation does not extend to all our motor decisions.... But what is thus left free by the one side receives its motivation from the other side, from the unconscious; and in this way determination in the psychical sphere is still carried out without any gap. (Freud 1901, 253–54; emphasis added)

This passage from *Psychopathology of Everyday Life* is the clearest expression of Freud's own understanding of this issue in terms of the hesitant believer. In later writings he was less patient. For example, addressing his reader in the *Introductory Lectures*, Freud admonishes any resistance quite severely: "You nourish the illusion of there being such a thing as psychical freedom, and you will not give it up. I am sorry to say I disagree with you categorically over this" (1916, 49), and later, "You nourish a deeply rooted faith in undetermined psychical events and in free will, but that is quite unscientific and must yield to the demand of a determinism whose rule extends over mental life. I beg you to respect it as a fact.... I am not opposing one faith with another. It can be proved" (106). Was this in part a rhetorical flourish? After all, in other places he was more circumspect, in that he "cherished a high *opinion* of the strictness with which mental processes are determined" (1910a, 29; emphasis added) or that psychoanalytic technique is based upon the "strong *belief* in the strict determinism of mental events" (1923b, 238; emphasis added). (Such wording reminds one of Freud's use of *assumption* in other contexts discussing the causal chain from the unconscious [see chapter 2].) In these more cautious statements in which "belief" and "opinion" are employed, Freud seems to have left the door ajar for the entry of choice. What squeezes in?

Connected to the hold of the unconscious and the determinism it exercises is a medical motif very much in ascendancy in fin de siècle Europe. The identification of infectious diseases and the first successful therapies against them, the elucidation of basic genetics and the causal basis of inherited disease, the decipherment of the body with x-rays and laboratory tests of bodily fluids, each testify to the power and enthusiasm with which a new medical science took hold on the imagination of Westerners. As a *physician*, Freud entered that cultural ethos with his own prescription: the unconscious is the source of emotional malady; the therapy is interpretation. In that simple schema, he melded a natural causal cascade of psychic events with an autonomous reason applied to the coupling of emotional recognition and release, analytic insight, and finally, some degree of emotional modulation and control. So, given the centrality of psychic determinism in Freud's thinking, a meta-rule also operates in opposition, for the other massive foundation of Freud's thought rests on freedom of the will, where reason's autonomy allows the rational ego to examine and then master the unconscious.

The larger vision includes an emancipation of sorts. Freud held that psychoanalysis "does not set out to make pathological reactions impossible, but to give the patient's ego *freedom* to decide one way or the other" (1923a, 50). Thus, because psychoanalysis depends on reasoned analysis, which demands, as Kant so clearly argued, some version of self-governing reason (one independent from the natural world governed by natural cause), Freud consequently held onto two fundamentally opposed metaphysical positions—humans are determined; humans are free—and because of their divergent vectors, Freud, like Kant, split the mind's faculties.

Kant developed two forms of reason in order to save metaphysics and more immediately, human autonomy and its product, moral responsibility. Freud similarly allowed for divided psychic faculties to account for his interpretative method and to fulfill humane therapeutic goals. Whereas Kant explicitly faced the determinism paradox and committed his philosophy to respond to its demands, Freud simply acknowledged that he would assign reason a particular role in his psychotherapy, and that was the ostensible end of the matter. After all, nowhere in Freud's science of the mind does he address the "source" of reason, or in another vernacular, he ignores any attempt to establish the *identity* of the person who lies upon his couch or the consciousness that constitutes the commonsensical pronominal agent (matters discussed in later chapters). He simply avoids the issue of selfhood and the place of consciousness altogether. So, in the same vein, Freud omits any attempt at grounding the notion of ego choice beyond the implicit promise of psychoanalytic insight and the freedom afforded with its attainment. Because Freud eschewed resolving, or even considering, the determinism–free will tension, he quite correctly disassociated himself from the philosophical enterprise that would deal with this problem.

But the basic philosophical question of freedom of will is hardly re-solved by simply citing the meta-structure of psychoanalysis as a thera-peutic pursuit, especially in the face of Freud's repeated denials of the exercise of psychic choice. If reason and consciousness are not ground-ed in some notion of personhood or biology, then on what basis can Freud just implicitly invoke analysis as a form of liberation? He does not specifically address the challenge; indeed, he does not even acknowledge it beyond his well-known late pessimistic musings about the promise of analytic success (e.g., 1937b), or for that matter, civilization itself (1930). So if psychoanalytic theory has a glaring conceptual weakness, it resides in this unaddressed (and, of course, unresolved) imbroglio of the determinism–free will paradox.

The underlying tectonic plates collide because one of them, the deter-minism exerted by unconscious psychical forces—constituted by natural-istic causation—*opposes* the other, free will, which Freud categorically refers to again and again as an illusion (e.g., 1919a, 236). Yet he still provides a promissory note: analysis, through the exercise of interpreta-tion (itself, assumed freely evinced), and free choice may liberate. Thus the very structure of Freudian psychoanalysis sits on a deep fault line, namely, the paradox of *inferred* psychic determinism and the governing *conviction* of choice and liberation. The former position is detailed in every facet of Freud's theoretical and clinical writings; the latter is left largely silent, yet governing. But in the end, as evidenced by the psycho-analytic enterprise itself, Freud opts for human reason, heroic struggle, and assertion of human potential. He does that within the humanistic context, leaving the stark determinism of his science to the side as he steadfastly pursued human freedom and self-fulfillment.

In conclusion, Freud's indebtedness to Kantianism does not make him a Kantian, for he joined certain Kantian ideas with those derived from a deep appreciation of the biological character of human emotions. In this latter respect, Freud must be regarded a Darwinian, closely aligned to Nietzsche, whose philosophy begins not in some dialogical *response* to Kant, but in *reaction* against him.[13] Indeed, autonomous individualism, associated with a liberated self, freed from political, religious, and social bonds, is a distinctly post-Kantian modification attached during the ro-mantic era (Tauber 2001; 2005). "Autonomy" for Freud does not share any allegiance with Kant's specific notions of the categorical imperative and the negation of self-interest as the content of some true moral system. Further, Freud did not derive "autonomy" from a conception of the self (i.e., humans are rational and reason permits only one moral law; therefore we are free because we dictate the one moral law to ourselves). Freud employed "autonomy" to achieve a different moral vision, one more closely aligned to Nietzsche's (and Emerson's before him [Stack 1992]), namely, the potential to achieve some undefined perfected state in the expression of a re-conceived individualism. Beyond the specific construction of reason's autonomy as a prerequisite of scientific inquiry and the adoption of reason's independence of unconscious psychic forces, Freud employed autonomy in this romantic sense, one that had been adopted by Nietzsche and other late-nineteenth-century thinkers who would reinvent the aspirations for personal potential, that is, the struggle to establish a life deemed "free."

In the next chapter, we will examine how philosophers following Kant reconfigured "autonomy," not only by realizing moral choice and accepting moral responsibility (Kant's undertaking), but by adding that humankind might also perfect itself according to its own dictates. At this juncture, we witness an important transition in the evolution of moral philosophy, which carries Freud far from Enlightenment ideals and aligns him with Nietzsche, where Kantian reason is balanced against a biological construction, and morality thereby shifts from enacting some universal moral order to adopting a radical individualism. However, for Freud no simple identifications will suffice, and as we further probe the philosophical structure of psychoanalysis, we will continue to appreciate the multi-focal character of Freud's philosophical commitments.

Chapter Five

The Odd Triangle

KANT, NIETZSCHE, AND FREUD

> A consciousness of one's own self and a consciousness of
> other things, are in truth given to us immediately, and the
> two are given in such a fundamentally different way that
> no other difference compares with this. About *himself*
> everyone knows directly, about everything else only very
> indirectly. This is the fact and the problem.
> —Arthur Schopenhauer (1969, 2:192)

FROM AUGUSTINE TO OUR OWN ERA, introspection is inextricable from
"self-consciousness," which in turn is integral to and, in some sense, coincident with various understandings of selfhood. Simply, self-consciousness
is enacted through self-reflexivity, and in this process of self-awareness,
identity emerges. But the word "reflexivity" has a more circumscribed
history. Reflexivity appears as a paradigm of understanding the self during the early modern period, coincident with the preoccupation with op-
tics and the birth of a new physics of light. "Reflexivity" was first applied
to cognitive introspection, in referring to "thought as bending back upon
itself," in the 1640s, when theologians, philosophers, and poets embarked
on their respective introspective inquiries only to "stop" at some point to
redirect consciousness into the world.

The modern "self" emerged formally in philosophy with Descartes's
conclusive *cogito ergo sum*, which established that mental states formed
the basis of self-identity. The Cartesian understanding of the self provides a defense against epistemological skepticism, for the very existence of reality depended on the recognition and bona fide character
of a "knowing" agent. In the splendid solitude of his self-exploration,
Descartes dispelled doubt by self-inquiry and made self-consciousness
the sine qua non of selfhood. His "thinking thing" was indeed a think-

ing *thing*—for him. This identification of "a self," an ego that might know the world, served as the foundation of his philosophy and that of all those who followed or contested that formulation. For example, Descartes's basic notion of a core self was bolstered by the divergent philosophies of Locke and Leibniz; for each, "reflection" as perception of oneself, or attention to what is "in us," organized much of their respective epistemologies. In other words, no matter how they differed from the Cartesian system, each depended on a singular definition of a knowing entity.

This conceptual tradition continued well into the twentieth century through philosophy's phenomenological pursuits and psychology's introspective explorations, for example, Wundt, James, Brentano, and, of course, Freud. And if philosophical schools have victories, the basic Cartesian model still powerfully dominates folk beliefs about selfhood. Common sense asserts that reflexivity reveals an inner self-identity, an entity that navigates the world and experiences emotions and its environment as a bounded subject. In short, I am a self; you are a self; the social world is composed of selves. Accordingly, by probing personal thought, impressions, and feelings through reflexive self-inspection, one may sense a private ego, which, while elusive, remains sufficient to capture some inner essence of who we are. In short, self-consciousness per se grounds and thus satisfies the commonsensical criteria for selfhood, which, in the context of self-responsible, considered choices and actions, identifies moral agency as well. After all, if self-consciousness becomes the basis of personhood, and thus we know the mind as distinct from the world, that very distinction makes our self-chosen action in the world radically our own. In this sense, the commonplace sense of free will arises from the Cartesian metaphysics of selfhood, where a "mind" decides its course in the world in all respects. The psychology that was to follow in the wake of this mind-body construction charts the evolution of the philosophy of psychology, and Freud too was subject to Descartes's fundamental bifurcation: the unconscious psyche, depicted in its original physiology as forces and instincts of brain-states (the body) (Freud 1955), is contrasted with the rational, contemplative, interpretative ego, which represents the Cartesian mind that the analyst addresses and that the analysand recognizes as his own person.

Yet when critically probed in the mid-seventeenth century, the self was nowhere to be found. For Hume, only passing perceptions, bundled and psychologically cohered, sufficed for defining a self, and thus he crippled the Cartesian formulation. And if "a self" did not exist, what is the personal agent we refer to as "the self" or "the ego" that mediates knowledge and morality? Kant concurred that the ego as an entity could neither be observed nor known. Instead, the self was the subject of experience and a presupposition of all representations. "Anything ascribed to the 'I' is ipso facto a predicate or object of the I, not the I itself" (Inwood 1992, 121). So Kant, albeit from a different perspective and for different reasons, could not locate the self. For him, the reflexivity of self-consciousness was essentially no different than the ego's survey of the world at large. So when the ego was observed as an object, Kant treated it as he would any natural object. And here we must begin to unpack Freud's own formulation based in this tradition.

The Transcendental Apperception of the Ego

Kant took the "pure subject" of Descartes and Locke—and the somewhat ambiguous posture of Rousseau—and showed that the self was capable of knowing itself only because it could also know the world as an object (Keller 1998; Allison 2004). Experience qua experience is structured according to a priori categories of understanding. These included the principles that every event has a cause and that objects have substance and exist in space and time. As a priori, these principles cannot be established empirically. Knowledge arises from the synthesis of concept and experience, and as it is "transcendental," that is, nonobservable as a process, and therefore it must be presupposed (Longuenesse 2006). Synthetic a priori knowledge is possible because, according to Kantian tenets, humans can infer how experience must conform to the categories of understanding. Kant's understanding of the synthetic a priori depends on the synthesis of concept and experience. We can have such knowledge of reality only as "phenomena"—as objects of empirical enquiry; phenomena are discoverable; they enter into relationship with us. This was a crucial refutation of those rationalists who attempted to describe reality as apprehended by the pure intellect, and it represents the foundation of establishing the reality of the phenomenal world—the world of appearance. To apprehend this reality, a subject is required.

In direct response to Hume, the transcendental argument moves from the nature of experience back to understanding the subject of experience; that is, it arrives at a view of what we must be like in order to have experience as we do. Thus, the observing subject is defined by inference: The self is observed as the external world is known, even as ultimate reality remains elusive. The noumenon, whether subject or object, is an existent; though in itself an unknowable, it is an inferred reality that reason must postulate. Transcending experience and all rational knowledge, reason must assume the existence of noumena as the source for all science and philosophy (Guyer 1992; Allison 2004; Longuenesse 2006). Accordingly, humans never directly know natural objects, since human cognition is restricted by its own modalities and categories of understanding. And because we know the world only through these cognitive faculties, the world, the thing-in-itself, remains in effect hidden behind the strictures of our perceptions, their organization, and finally their interpretation. What we know of the world is then a distillation of these functions to generate phenomena. A phenomenal object is known through sensory experience organized by the categories of understanding, and reflects an amalgam of "mind" and "nature."

Because the shape of reality is partly formed by the mediation of the observer, the things in themselves are insurmountably a translation or an interpretation. The self thus emerges, since in the idea of a thought, every mental content embeds the notion of a subject that has an immediate and intuitive unity. Kant refers to this unity as the transcendental unity of apperception (Kitcher 2006). "Apperception" in this sense means "self-consciousness" (the inner, fundamental, *unified* sense of consciousness that precedes the content of our perceptions) and "transcendental" indicates that the unity of the self is known as the presupposition of all (self)-knowledge. In certifying the conditions for knowing, more generally, Kant posited functions that *order* experience and make it meaningful—intuitions of space and time and the categories of understanding, for example, quantity, quality, and relation. In Kant's scheme, the self is an "original unity" whose mental state are not adjuncts but properties. Identity is then corollary to the first-person presupposition that the self exists as an object (Keller 1998). Thus introspection, organized in the same way humans perceive the world, could yield no "entity," and, instead, Kant left the matter with postulated transcendental conditions for self-consciousness.

So for Kant, reflexivity could not discern the subject-in-itself, and, the self, like any other thing-in-itself could only be "known" by the same a priori categories of pure reason that determine knowledge of the world (Kant 1998, 230–34). This formulation describes "a self" that is left undeclared beyond defining those conditions:

> The consciousness of oneself in accordance with the determinations of our state in internal perception is merely empirical, forever variable; it can provide no standing or abiding self in this stream of inner appearances, and is customarily called *inner sense or empirical apperception*. That which should *necessarily* be represented as numerically identical cannot be thought of as such through empirical data. There must be a condition that precedes all experience and makes the latter itself possible, which should make such a transcendental presupposition valid. (Kant 1998, 232 [A107])[1]

The transcendental unity of apperception is of crucial importance to Kantian idealism; moreover, it has far-reaching implications as the foundation or starting point of all later philosophical treatments of the self. At issue is the unity of the self, not only as an object, but more crucially as a subject, not something that simply can be known, but as a willing, feeling, knowing agent. Kant uses the principle of transcendental apperception in justifying synthetic a priori knowledge and the unity of thinking and of self-consciousness in general. It thus serves as the supreme or original principle of all human experience:

> No knowledge can take place in us, no conjunction or unity of one kind of knowledge with another, without that unity of consciousness which precedes all data of intuition, and without reference to which no representation of objects is possible. This pure, original, and unchangeable consciousness I shall call *transcendental apperception*. (Kant 1966, A107, p. 105)

There are three claims (or features) for this faculty: identity, unity, and self-consciousness.[2] The subject must be identical through time, for without such identity, the ability to recall and maintain continuity would fail.

KANT, NIETZSCHE, AND FREUD

The basis of unity refers to the requirement of an active subject to unify its experience. This ability in turn rests upon the third feature, that of self-consciousness, which refers to the capacity to reflect on its own unity and identity: "That is, as the word 'apperception' already indicates, Kant is arguing that self-consciousness is . . . a condition of experience" (Pippin 1989, 19). Thus, Kant argues for an active and self-aware self, and this is pivotal: The self must reflect upon itself to *attain* its autonomy: "Being *in* a subjective state . . . does not count as having an experience *of* and so being aware of that state unless I apply a certain determinant concept. . . and judge that I am in such a state, something I must *do* and be able to know that I am doing" (Pippin 1989, 19).[3]

Thus reflexivity does not discern the subject-in-itself, and the self, like any other natural object, could only be observed by the same a priori categories of pure reason that determine knowledge of the world (Kant 1998, 230–34).[4] As a result, having dispensed with defining an *entity*, Kant presents only the necessary conditions of knowing, and the transcendental apperception of the ego refers to a metaphysical category. Indeed, precisely because of Kant's own careful avoidance of arguing for, or postulating against, any first-order understanding of metaphysics, self-identity—the subject qua subject—must be left unaddressed. For Kant, reflexivity is a remnant of the basic organization of the human mind: Humans observe their own thoughts and emotions just as they observe the world, but just as they are limited in their knowledge of the exterior reality, so are they restricted in knowing themselves. Indeed, "the self" might then be regarded as the silent doppelgänger that follows humans throughout life (O'Donnell 2004).

Freud drew on this formulation, but only as part of a composite. He coupled an idealistic-inspired conception of moral agency with a biological formulation developed from his deep commitment to a Darwinian characterization of human nature. In the discussion below, we will follow this construction from Kant to Schopenhauer and then to Nietzsche. Further, Hegelianism drove a particular rejection of Kant towards an understanding of selfhood (and more particularly, self-consciousness) that employed a reflexive arc construing reflectivity as constitutive to self-identification. Finally, Freud shared with Kierkegaard what might be called a "process-oriented" understanding of personal identity, according to which the notion of "the self" as an internal speaker or interlocutor is described as a retreating recursive reflexivity. The telos of that agent follows another trajectory, one again coupled to a biological grounding—an ongoing pursuit of self-realization (Nietzsche). Perhaps recognizing the elusive character of "the self," Freud built his own configuration of the introspective subject, one that embraced Kantian autonomy, exercised Nietzschean self-responsibility, acknowledged Kierkegaardian reflexivity, and pursued Spinozean self-knowledge. Drawing upon each of these schema, my interpretation of Freud's ideas about personhood appears as a mosaic in which each of these general characteristics contributes to a composite of guiding psychoanalytic tenets about personal identity. We begin with Schopenhauer's critique of transcendental idealism.

From Schopenhauerian "Will" to Freudian "Unconscious"

As we have discussed, the *Critique of Pure Reason* raised the general epistemological problem of the impossibility of knowing directly the thing-in-itself, since the noumenon bears no direct logical or experiential relation to the phenomenal world, which is the sole object of understanding. But the world *is* phenomenal and therefore potentially objectively known, that is, real and discernible to a knowing subject. However, for one case Kant allows immediacy of knowledge, namely, knowledge of ourselves. Such knowledge is uniquely practical and is available in the immediacy of the body and as an exercise of human autonomy. Accordingly, direct knowledge of the body radically differs from any other mode or object of apprehension. By allowing knowledge of the transcendental self as *practical* knowledge, some of Kant's critical successors remarked, he had explored the reaches of subjectivity, rather than established the foundations of true objectivity. When he referred to "our" experience or mind, the question is whether the "our" is to be regarded in a general sense (i.e., of human beings conceived impartially) or in the specific idealist sense in which "our" refers to the abstract subject (the "I" that is engaged in the intellectual construction of the world). "This ambiguity is crucial, since, depending on its interpretation, we seem drawn either towards an impersonal metaphysics, or towards a highly solipsistic epistemology" (Scruton 1982, 161).

This philosophical ambiguity introduced by Kant plagued nineteenth-century philosophy. One of the earliest critiques, and the single most important response to his epistemologically based concept of the self, was offered by Schopenhauer, who recognized that Kant had not established the basis of this inner sense. In his magnum opus, *The World as Will and Representation* (1969), Schopenhauer attempted to incorporate both an idealist conception of the subject as the nonworldly origin of objective experience and an embodied conception of the subject as an organic part of nature. Herein lies an intractable tension, in which the self arises within the world and yet somehow peers *at* nature from an external and detached perspective. The attempt to describe the nature of the self and its relation to the world follows these two disparate axes, namely, (1) a separate self that while still in its world, *represents* it from its own particular point of view, and (2) the noncognitive in-the-world character of the self, which partakes in the universal Will, the characteristic naturalistic force that bestows intentionality on the human organism. Schopenhauer thus established a conception that would prefigure much of the post-Kantian discussion of what constitutes personal identity.

The question whether knowledge of the world in itself is possible rests at the heart of the matter, and thus the profound problem of post-Kantian skepticism is laid open. Schopenhauer attempted to resolve this paradox by asserting that the subject and the object are both part of a universal Will. In other words, he posited an ontology common to both, which binds the self and the world it knows through some basic natural force. So for Schopenhauer, the word "Will" should convey the universality of "force" that extends from the drive of life to the most basic physical forces, each of which is an expression of an underlying ontological movement or drive (Simmel 1991 42; 44; Magee 1983, 142; Tauber 1994, 239–46). Accordingly, the Will underlies the world in its entirety and manifests itself in the multiplicities of all things known in experience, and in that move Schopenhauer attempted to expose the origin, development, and manifestation of all drives, which were all relegated to a primary Will.

Underneath the epistemological issues of how knowledge, perception, and objectivity are possible, lies the metaphysical substratum of the Will. So from the Kantian perspective, Schopenhauer equates the will with the "thing-in-itself" (and "phenomenon" becomes "representation")

(Schopenhauer 1974b, 1:268), and then he builds his notion of human psychology: "The will exists in itself, even in so far as it appears in the individual. Thus it constitutes the individual's primary and fundamental willing and is independent of all knowledge because it precedes this" (2:227). Since the will exists only for itself, knowing is a secondary and mediated function.[5]

We should note that there is a deep issue at stake between Kant and Schopenhauer. Where Kant had established the axiom of the phenomenality of the world (i.e., all that can be known are phenomena, not the thing-in-itself), Schopenhauer came to an opposing position: The world as appearance is unreal, and reality must be sought beyond it: "Kant senses reality as a category which produces experience, whereas Schopenhauer, who thirsts for the metaphysical absolute, senses reality in opposition to experience" (Simmel 1991, 20). That reality is the Will, and the effort to know the Will is to distill consciousness, that is, to know ourselves, which fundamentally is the body. And here we find the genesis of Nietzsche's own biologicism.

Beyond this organic formulation, Schopenhauer's construction highlights how Freud's own conception philosophically differs from Kant's. The entire framework of the Kantian conception of the subject of knowledge is called into doubt, because Kant's transcendental ego did not provide an explanation of how that-which-knows is at the same time a part of the knowable world of objects. Kantian epistemology becomes explicable, according to Schopenhauer, only as a secondary, epiphenomenal outgrowth of organism as Will: it is in willing, not knowing, that our essence lies (Janaway 1989, 350). To put the matter simply, Kant's pure a priori "I" contains no account of its instantiation by empirical beings.

Schopenhauer placed the subject in its world by articulating an organicism that promoted the naturalism that was to penetrate into virtually all areas of fin de siècle European thought. He thus initiated a shift in comprehending human nature, which gained momentum with Darwinism and culminates in Nietzsche. These intersecting ideas offer a critical orientation for orienting psychoanalytic theory, which is complicated by Freud's denial of being directly influenced by Schopenhauer (a strategy adopted also to deflect the influence of Nietzsche) (Freud 1914c, 15; 1925a, 59–60). Those claims are difficult to reconcile with Freud's own early (1900, 36, 66, 90) and later citations (e.g., 1913b, 87), which reveal detailed appreciation of Schopenhauer's notions of dreams and repression. Irrespective of the specifics of influence, Schopenhauer's philosophy elucidates Freud's theory of psychic drives and identity in two domains: a general orientation to a post-Kantian notion of reality that had various expressions among the later neo-Kantians (discussed in chapter 3), and more specifically through a novel dynamic psychological model, again derived from a critique of Kant as described above. This deeper impact on the psychoanalytic formulation of the psyche's topography and dynamic character of the mind filtered through to Freud by way of his psychiatric training and the tutelage of Theodor Meynert (1833–1892), who was a devotee of Schopenhauer. So to appreciate the Schopenhauerian elements in Freud's theory, this intellectual lineage must be tracked.

Freud's basic orientation derives in large measure from Meynert, who was a close friend of Brentano's and served as Freud's supervisor when the young scientist left Brücke's laboratory to practice medicine (McGrath 1986, 140–49). In 1883, after becoming a junior physician and rotating through various clinical departments, Freud was appointed to Meynert's Institute of Cerebral Anatomy, where he continued to conduct research on brain anatomy and soon thereafter on the clinical effects of cocaine (Ellenberger 1970, 474–77). Freud and Meynert developed a mutually respectful friendship, and Freud cites him in *Interpretation of Dreams* as "the Great Meynert, in whose footsteps I had trodden with such deep veneration" (Freud 1900, 437). At least during that stage of his career, Freud could acknowledge that his mentor's psychological model had deeply influenced him, and in turn, Meynert acknowledged his own debt to Schopenhauer, more specifically the late work, *Parerga and Parilipomena* (Schopenhauer 1974b; McGrath 1986, 144–47). The specific issue pertained to the dynamic psychological model that had developed from Schopenhauer's critique of Kant.

As has been mentioned, Schopenhauer begins with a basic division of Will and representation, and this division then is projected into a schema of the mind. Schopenhauer clearly posits unconsciousness (ascribed to its natural domain) and further describes the unstable relationship between unconscious and conscious thought. Similar to Meynert's own views half a century later, Schopenhauer opined, "Consciousness is the mere surface of our mind, and of this as of the globe, we do not know the interior, only the crust" (1969, 2:136). Seeing humans as subject to unknown inner forces that play havoc with rational actions and desires, he portrayed that inner dimension foreign to human inspection and control in an anatomic configuration. He left the matter at this stage, acknowledging the dynamic complexity of the psyche, its mysterious ways churning beyond human comprehension or control.

Meynert would follow this line of reasoning in application to his own anatomical studies, when, in conceiving a theory of the mind, the investigator transposed the anatomic model into a psychology. He maintained that the relationship between the brain and consciousness involved the interaction of a primary and secondary ego—a material brain (the primary ego) and a mental faculty (the secondary ego). In development, the secondary ego (the intellect, self-consciousness, and other higher functions) emerges from the primary state, which constitutes bodily feelings and instincts. These basic forces encounter the world and are either reinforced or denied, and those reactions are then presumably internalized and used to form the secondary ego. Such added elements from the environment thus take primary drives and channel them into various behaviors through two modalities—aggressive and defensive. A hierarchy of control (supported by phylogeny)—cortex over deeper brain structures—operates in Meynert's schema, so Schopenhauer's dichotomy of Will and representation, accompanied by an anatomical distinction, transmutes into Meynert's primary and secondary egos, and then into Freud's id and ego.

Much of Freud's theory echoes Schopenhauer's formulation, namely, a conscious ego that strives to make sense of its world and at the same time expresses the will that stems from unconscious drives. Schopenhauer readily acknowledged the interplay of the different aspects of rational consciousness as a product of unconscious drives, of the will of striving. In short, he placed humans firmly in the nature of organic creatures, whose actions and knowledge emanate from a primal Will. On this view, the Schopenhauerian Will is the direct precursor of Freud's id. What Freud described as the conflicted character of the psyche, Schopenhauer famously identified as *pessimism*, a pessimism arising from the inescapable torment inflicted by powerful and unfulfilled desires. This emotional dimension applied to the metaphysical construction represents a crucial addition. Of course, Freud distinguished psychoanalysis as a means to control and to rationalize the unconscious and to objectify its function. In that attempt to liberate humans from its powerful influence, if not dominance, he swapped a promising new psychic physics for a pessimistic metaphysics.

Another aspect of Schopenhauer's philosophical system highly relevant to our discussion pertains to how Schopenhauer framed the determinism/ freedom paradox we have previously considered in the Kantian context. Given that Freud and Schopenhauer each held to the radical determinism of the unconscious (sic. Will), how could free will be exercised? Schopenhauer, both in *Will and Representation* and in *Prize Essay on the Freedom of the Will*, differentiated freedom of action—there is none, that is, "Everything that happens . . . happens necessarily" (1999, 54)—and freedom of being, which he affirms: "Every being without exception *acts* with strict necessity, but *exists* and what it is by virtue of its *freedom*" (1969, 2:320–21).

To unravel this apparently contradictory position, let us begin with Schopenhauer's early work, *The Fourfold Root of the Principle of Sufficient Reason* (1974a), where he responded to Leibniz's tenet developed in the *Monadology* (1714), that no fact or truth lacks a sufficient reason (or cause). For Schopenhauer, that assertion is correct, but only as the result of the conditions of representing phenomena. Human reason represents the world, and it does so in four fundamental connections that arise in subject-object relations. Schopenhauer places the general root of the principle of sufficient reason in the subject-object distinction itself (which, of course, builds on Kant's own formulation), and then he develops his argument upon a structure whereby different kinds of objects require different kinds of reasoning: (1) material things: cause and effect; (2) abstract concepts: logic; (3) mathematical and geometrical constructions: reference to numbers and spaces; and (4) motivating forces: intentions, or what he called moral reasoning. These four different kinds of objects for which we can seek explanations thus require four independent explanatory paths (which do not intermingle or cross over), and, more to the point, the connections between the subject and object—no matter the object's type—are deterministic. Reason in its various modalities deciphers those relationships.

The freedom/determinism paradox is resolved by Schopenhauer's metaphysical construction of the primacy of the Will: Simply, the Will as the ontological foundation for all being is, by definition, free of causation. While events in the phenomenal world are determined, the Will, not subject to any forces or other conditions, freely pursues its own path. Phenomena are not *caused* by the Will (inasmuch as the will is their grounding), but become subject to causation as actions *in* the world. Humans are also governed by causal relationships as they act in the world, but since their existence is an expression of the Will (i.e., as free *existants)*, they are also free. And so Schopenhauer erected a *metaphysical* structure in which the transcendental conditions of action are grounded in the Will, while the principle of sufficient reason holds in the phenomenal world, making freedom and determinism compatible.

According to Askay and Farquhar (2006, 136ff.), Freud heavily borrowed from this metaphysical construction: (1) The unconscious, like the Will, is not subject to cause, and thus free; (2) humans, as *existants*, are free, and thereby Reason, the instantiation of the human, is free; and (3) all psychic actions are motivated by the unconscious/Will, but this is not the same as *caused* as described above. While the first two characteristics may have informed Freud's thinking, the third is problematic. To accept this parallel between Freud and Schopenhauer, we must regard the unconscious as providing the underlying transcendental *conditions* necessary for psychic phenomena and nothing more. That view of unconsciousness distorts Freud's understanding, which placed the id firmly within the biological world, where cause may not follow the laws of reason as normally construed. However, that placement does not eliminate the "logic" of unconscious forces, which simply cannot be characterized by rational criteria. In short, the psychoanalytic unconscious may resonate with the Will, but Freud would hardly accept a metaphysical description when he sought a scientific one.[6]

Although profoundly indebted to Schopenhauer, Freud abandoned the attempt to characterize the *metaphysical* structure of the mind. Indeed, Freud thought that he had disengaged psychoanalysis from metaphysics by creating a *science* of "the will." Others would pick up Schopenhauer's enterprise more directly, such as Eduard von Hartmann and later Nietzsche, each of whom appropriated Schopenhauer's Will for their own purposes. Renewed contact with those mysterious forces of instinctual nature was a key element of Nietzsche's early admiration (Nietzsche 1983), for he similarly understood humans as subject to incessant instinctual drives, whose apparent inhumane nature characterized the unharnessed Will. In reinvoking this primary element (this "will to life," in a transfigured role as "will to power"), he built upon Schopenhauer's refutation of rationality as the deep-seated and basic human characteristic. Each regarded reason as essentially an accident, at best a tool in the hands of the Will, and each dethroned rationality, replacing it with the primal Will (albeit formulated in different ways). Fundamentally both philosophers shared the view that the Will is not posited against, but resides outside, rationality. Freud would agree, but he maintained that reason in the guise of the ego's rationality might control that will for the ego's own purposes.

How do these various matters coalesce around notions of selfhood that lie at the philosophical base of the knowing subject? Epistemologically, Schopenhauer believed that the subject could become a passive mirror of the world, overcoming the subject-dependent forms of organization to become a pure subject-of-knowing (*Erkennen*). Accordingly, the empirical self has vanished in Schopenhauer's system, and the only sense of selfhood is an awareness of the self as a striving being, a self-aware willing entity. Spanning the continuum from rational thinking to unconscious action, the willing organism is physiologically based and teleologically organized. The Will in this instantiation is thus embodied and expressed as the need to propagate and prolong life. Freud would later formulate this drive into the various instincts, again unknown in any first-order way; they exert their effects independently of rational or conscious control. And again, like Schopenhauer, the border between "the ego" and the "Will" (or the unconscious) varies with self-consciousness (and analysis).

And most importantly, Freud, in adopting this basic orientation, also suffers Schopenhauer's inconsistent twofold construction of the self. On the one hand, the knowing subject is dependent upon forms of representation of the mind that are the result of some biologically based organization (ordinary empirical knowledge), and on the other hand, the pure epistemological subject mirrors the essence of nature, perceiving in an expanded fashion a reality independent of the forms representative of mind, that is, beyond normal categories of perception. Yet humans transcend ordinary experience, which allows for the appreciation of self-knowledge. How phenomena are known, and the perspective of reason, of autonomy, of self-consciousness, however, is not explained. Conceptual understanding keeps us removed from what Emerson called the "core self" (Tauber 2003), and Schopenhauer left personal identity as grounded in the Will alone, basically uncharacterized.

Hume had recognized that when we search within for that perceiving subject so readily assigned as *selfhood*, we find ourselves encountering the various objects of consciousness—passing thoughts, images, feelings, and so on—but never any entity separate from these contents. Consciousness is always *of* something; it always has an object, and the perceiving subject can never be encountered as such. "What is the 'I' that contemplates 'my consciousness of x,' and to what does 'my' in the latter phrase refer? Whatever it is, it is systematically elusive—we never grasp it" (Magee 1983, 107). The perceiver is that which is perceived, or as Hume said, the self is but a bundle of perceptions. Schopenhauer's analysis, although radically different, concludes in close agreement to Hume: The perceiving self is nowhere to be found in the world of experience.[7] The Schopenhauerian metaphysical self exists as the sustainer of the world but cannot itself enter the world, so, as with Hume, "subjects and objects are able to exist at all only as correlates of each other, [and] more to the point.... their *structures* are correlative" (Magee 1983, 107).

Kantian thought demanded the unity of the subject. Perception, knowledge, objectivity reside in a consciousness; they belong to an author of actions and purposes. Schopenhauer modified that presentation by recognizing that a self, described solely in philosophical terms, is inadequate: The psychological source of identity must be explored. And Nietzsche, despite all the differences, followed a parallel path, albeit highly critical.

So while for Schopenhauer the self is a pure nonobject, abstracted from all specific objects, states, or activities, Nietzsche argued that this was only a singular interpretation serving particular ends (Janaway 1989, 351). He attacked the very notion of a Cartesian "I think" as the explicit conduit of Schopenhauer's subject, that is, as reflective will. According to Nietzsche, "thinking," as epistemologists conceive it, simply does not occur: it is a fiction, arrived at by selecting the element from the process and eliminat-

KANT, NIETZSCHE, AND FREUD

ing all the rest, an artificial arrangement for the purpose of intelligibility. And in an even more direct challenge to Schopenhauer, Nietzsche argued: "One must not look for phenomenalism in the wrong place…. [N]othing is so much deception as this inner world which we observe with the famous 'inner sense'" (Nietzsche 1967, 264). Freud, of course, would develop this observation into an entire theory of the psyche, but instead of discarding attempts to fathom the "will" (the unconscious), Freud would pursue understanding its workings. Nietzsche took a more skeptical path by discarding the "I" that thinks (not to mention "rational thinking"), a radical position diametrically opposed to Freud's own championing of reason.[8] In the next section, we will examine how similar biological models of human nature coupled to differing understanding of reason's function lead to competing conceptions of moral agency. So while both Freud and Nietzsche built upon Schopenhauer's organic formulation of human being, their respective philosophies followed divergent trajectories, with protean consequences for Western identity politics and moral philosophy.[9]

Nietzsche and Freud

A major challenge to Kant's moral program developed with the ascendancy of naturalism in the nineteenth century. One tributary begins with Schopenhauer, who pushed self-consciousness away from some radically autonomous posture to lodge instead in the "Will." As already discussed, according to Schopenhauer's conception of the Will, knowledge of the world stems from physiological structure and function. Because such ability serves the primacy of the Will as embodied survivorship, the explanatory power of this body-based self over abstract formulations had an enormous influence on later nineteenth-century thought. Anticipating Nietzsche, Schopenhauer argued that empirical knowledge arises from, and is dictated by, the needs of the organism. He thus attempted to base Kant's unity of apperception in an organic substratum, that is, bodily striving.

Nietzsche diverged from Schopenhauer's vision of the Will with crucial implications for understanding human nature and the moral structure of human intention. The first difference lies in the role of perspective.

Nietzsche rejected the possibility of the pure knowing subject and saw the multiplicities of perspectives as integral to the *nature* of knowing: "There is only perspective seeing, only a perspective 'knowing';. . . . the *more* eyes, different eyes, we can use to observe one thing, the more complete. . . . our objectivity" (1967, 119). Never a mere mirror of the world as in Schopenhauer's formulation, rather the subject always achieves a partial reflection of the world limited by the perspectival nature of its own drives and interpretations. Recognizing the singularity and partiality of a particular vision epistemologically provides the knowing agent with an ironic global view. From this position Nietzsche attacked Schopenhauer's basic foundation of the pure self, where the world is the undistorted object of the subject's awareness. *All* is perspective and construction: the world, the self, and reason itself, whose own assumed autonomy is ultimately reduced to the will's striving. Reason as the rational has thus been transfigured into an unknowing tool for the instincts.

Nietzsche's own biologicism served as the conceptual foundation and organizing principle of his entire philosophy (Tauber 1994b). Indebted to a particular Darwinian vision of the organism, his Will to Power manifests itself as a disharmonious medley of competing instincts in constant inner strife.[10] This view of the organism—ever-changing and self-defining—strives for self-actualization in ceaseless competition with the environment and other individuals. The body not only provides the unifying element, the body *is* the self: "your body and its great reason: that does not say 'I,' but does 'I'" (Nietzsche 1959, 146). Nietzsche's philosophy is thus thoroughly permeated by (or tethered to) a biological formulation, one based on a raw "tooth and claw" Darwinism overlaid with a preoccupation with health and disease (Tauber and Podolsky 1999). Freud would adopt a similar biological orientation, one grounded, as Nietzsche's, in a Darwinian theory of human behavior, but organized around a different "therapeutic" perspective.

Freud's invocation of a biological construction for understanding the unconscious and his indebtedness to Darwinism has been exhaustively explored (e.g., Sulloway 1979; Ritvo 1990; Babitch 1999). Freud adapted basic Darwinian precepts in several respects: instinct theory; struggle and conflict as framing the mental paradigm; historical truth (the past as key to understanding the present); psychosexual stages (derived from phylogeny of sex) and (more specifically) the biogenetic law (Haeckel), further contaminated by a "psycho-Lamarckianism" (Sulloway 1992, 238–76), where as a result of prehistoric events, neurosis becomes a "cultural acquisition" (Freud 1987, 19). Indeed Freud's Darwinism includes a strong Lamarckian tendency inasmuch as he postulated that psychosocial traumas occurring during the early history of humankind are reenacted in various formats in the individual (e.g., Freud 1913b; 1939; 1987).

Freud followed the general acceptance of the evolutionary character of human civilization, the popular conception that ontogeny recapitulates phylogeny (e.g., "the individual's mental development repeats the course of human development in abbreviated form" [Freud 1910b, 97; Gould 1977, 155–62], a parallel he notes in other places as well [e.g., 1913b; 1919b, 260; 1987]). And in neurophysiological terms concerning the economy of the emotions, Freud invoked Darwin's own understanding of emotional expression, "namely, the overflow of excitation," which framed his earliest theorizing (Breuer and Freud 1895, p 91; Freud 1955), a view held in his mature works as well (e.g., 1926c, 133, 141). In addition, Freud co-opted Darwin's notion of adaptation, where the theme of anxiety fulfilling the biological function of reacting to danger, dominated his theorizing (1926c). As Freud recounted in his *Autobiography*, "The theories of Darwin, which were then [early 1870s] of topical interest, strongly attracted me, for they held out hopes for an extraordinary advance in our understanding of the world" (1925a, 8). That influence, so profoundly pervading the culture of the period (Kitcher 1992), remained a fixture of Freud's thinking throughout his life, from his first elective university course as a medical student in 1873 (enrolling in Professor Carl Claus's course, General Biology and Darwinism) to the late expression of instinctual conflict in *Civilization and Its Discontents* (1930) and Lamarckian inheritance of a primal drama in *Moses and Monotheism* (1939).

Despite the importance of Freud's linking evolutionary thought to psychoanalytic theory, the Lamarckian speculations, namely, the reconstruction of family conflict and its reenactment, have been generally condemned to "never pass from the realm of the fantastic to the realm of the real" (Parisi 1989, 487). Nevertheless, a psychology lodged in the instinctual domain is hardly radical, and today as testified by the vast literature in sociobiology and evolutionary psychology, efforts to trace communal behavior and moral agency to earlier primate behavior is hardly innovative (e.g., Sober and Wilson 1998; Joyce 2007), albeit contested (e.g., Buller 2006). However, describing the biology of complex behaviors is not our subject, for we are concerned with how Freud's commitment to placing the psyche in its archaic biological substrata becomes transformed by a ruling reason. To do so, we contrast Nietzsche's construction that minimizes the role of rationality in understanding agency (rational "higher" faculties are subordinated to the demands of the "lower" instincts), which in turn reflects a deep skepticism of reason, and Kantian reason in particular. Indeed, these views irreparably separate him from Freud.[11] Below, their complex intellectual relationship is summarized around two related issues: on the one hand, Freud afforded reason an autonomy that Nietzsche denied, and on the other hand, Freud formulated the psyche much as Nietzsche did by adopting an organic perspective and thereby committed himself to a Darwinian *biology*—a biological *science* of understanding. In short, whereas Nietzsche would celebrate the Will, Freud would endeavor to control it. Let us proceed by triangulating psychoanalytic theory with Nietzsche at one vertex and Kant at another.

The Instincts

In psychoanalysis, Man the Neurotic (the fundamental state of civilized human beings) arises from mental conflict. So for both Freud and Nietzsche, instincts in conflict characterize psychic life and remain, despite any and all interventions, irresolvable. Freud's pessimism may be traced back to this fundamental construction, where the opposition of reality and pleasure, life and death, libido and repression, presents the analysand as both subject to his or her instinctual psychic life and forever in conflict with it. Nietzsche, although agreeing in a conflict model of illness, works within a monolithic instinctual system—the Will to Power. Releasing its potential satisfies the requirements for health by placing liberated humans in harmony with their inner nature; Freud sees only perpetual conflict, and from this position the key challenge to psychoanalysis appears: How might the ego better deal with the demands of the unconscious?

From the beginning of Freud's theorizing in the *Project* of 1895, he sought to describe psychic dynamic forces, which, while changing in detail, was never abandoned. Assuming different characterizations throughout his career—from describing the sexual instincts in the life of the infant (Freud 1905b) to the final theoretical life-death dichotomy of Eros and Thanatos (Freud 1920; 1923a; Brown 1959; Ricoeur 1970)—Freud portrayed psychic life in terms of the effects of the ever-present instincts in the subterranean reaches of the mind.[12] These he described as making "somatic demands upon the mind" and "the ultimate cause of all activity" (1940b, 148). Regarding the "truth of the hypothesis," Freud later assumed a circumspect position (1920, 59) which reflected his suspicion that the neurosciences had not advanced sufficiently to justify his own claims about psychic function, whether the issue was the topography he proposed (1915a, 175) or the understanding of instincts that grounded his entire approach. Indeed, Freud's concerns became a later focus of severe criticism of his entire theory and the practice upon which psychoanalysis relies (Holt 1989, 127–40; Kitcher 1992, 155–83).

Freud's final attempts at devising a theory of the drives resulted in what has been aptly called a "metaphysics" (Brown 1959, 82), one in which psychoanalysis appears "in its most opaque and most unsympathetic form" (Brown 1959, 77; see above chap. 2, note 2). After all, Freud questioned his own formulation as offering a scientific foundation for psychoanalysis, and while he hoped to make the instincts more intelligible, he lamented, "The theory of the instincts is so to say our mythology. Instincts are mythical entities, magnificent in their indefiniteness. In our work we can never for a moment disregard them, yet we are never sure that we are seeing them clearly" (1933, 95).[13] This assessment, written near the end of his life, reflects the tortuous emendations Freud made to his descriptions of the instinctual structure of the psyche. While he never abandoned a dualistic structure of instinctual forces, these became increasingly abstract as he sought to accommodate clinical findings that did not fit neatly into one model or another.

Despite his own misgivings, Freud would defend his theoretical constructions as the first tentative attempts to devise a science of the mind. And, indeed, his key principle remained unchanged: A deep appreciation of the organic character of the human psyche as expressed by a duality of instinctual demands that encompassed all of psychic life. In the last presentation, on the one hand, Erotic instincts were sublimated into the inventions and discoveries of creative culture, and on the other hand, the death instincts were ultimately inimical to the flourishing of culture and destructive to civilization (Freud 1930). The fusion or redirection of these dual forces, at best in precarious balance, might result in destructive behavior or oceanic union.

In contrast to this understanding, Nietzsche offered a monolithic version of instincts. For him, to understand human psychology was to comprehend a singular vector of instinctual drives and behavior as the Will to Power,[14] and from this naturalistic position, he argued that humans *are* the body, the instincts, the unconscious. The areas where Nietzsche regarded ascendant human behavior, for example creative work, art, aesthetic experience, are but manifestations of the Will to Power. Freud's notion of sublimation based in a clinical context closely approximates this idea. For both, human endeavors, no matter how developed—aesthetics, ethics, logic, epistemology—remain firmly linked to their biological roots, that is, the Will to Power (Nietzsche 1967a, 173, 271, 289, 538) or in sublimation (Freud 1910b; Laplanche and Pontalis 1973, 431).[15]

However, they differed at a more fundamental level: Although Freud also conceived of a psyche in constant strife—the id, ego, and superego in conflict—Nietzsche would be dissatisfied with such a stratification, for a separation or hierarchy he thought dulls the dynamics of vying forces. But more importantly, Nietzsche would not empower the rational ego to rationalize (control) the lower drives. For Nietzsche, the individual *is* primordial will (or the erotic in Freudian terms) expressed by different affects, passions, behavior, intellects, but each a manifestation of a single individualizing force, groping for power. The most immediate sense, then, of personal identity, according to Zarathustra's acclamation, is the visceral body maximizing its erotic potential (Nietzsche 1959a, 146).[16]

Irrespective of the utility and success of their marshalling for the good of society, the instincts were also basic to Freud's conception of the mind, and putting aside the complex swing of his theory, the biology remained foundational. Further, the organic and the rational compartments were separate and distinct. But a hierarchy characterized this duality: Only through reason might potentially destructive elements be understood and thereby controlled. Freud pointed to an Enlightenment ideal where reason emancipates the tyranny of the instinctual body, in some ideal sense, so for him, reason's autonomy not only allowed for *understanding* the deterministic nature of moral responses, but also potentially made such insight a tool for a rational ego to *control* desire.

However, a complex equation is at work in Freud's view of rationality, because (like Nietzsche), he remained skeptical about the ability of rational thought to curb the emotions. Not only did Freud hold doubts about reason's ability to patrol and control the unconscious, he also was well aware of the lure of rationalized self-interest. His skepticism has philosophical antecedents in Hume's moral philosophy, which famously argued that ethics was but the rationalized outcome of emotional determinants, and the values guiding moral choices had similar origins. For Hume, reason was a derivative function to arbitrate a more fundamental human characteristic, the emotions, or in the vernacular of the day, the "passions." Hume reconfigured the relative roles of reason and emotion; reason was only a tool for deliberation and hardly could suffice as the source of moral choice and motivation. He maintained that preferences or desires cannot be motivated by reason alone, and that reason can only help direct human choices (Lindley 1986, 30). From this perspective, goals are determined by a complicated array of psychological and cultural factors, of which rational order may play only a small part. In what has become a famous hyperbole, Hume asserted, "Tis not contrary to reason to prefer the destruction of the whole world to the scratching of my finger" (1978, 416). In short, skeptical of reason's hegemony, Hume substituted a dual structure: the emotional dimension in which the "sentiments" fix the agent's ultimate ends; reason is left to determine the best way of achieving those goals.[17]

The Humean position asserts that moral action derives from a deeper sense of obligation or choice than that dictated by reason alone, and consequently, criticism of Hume's position generally dwells on the unsure footing of "proper deliberation" that determines whether the suppositions underlying reason's exercise are true or false. To act with false suppositions destroys the entire enterprise, and thus how to assure that reason's grounding is firm has remained a crucial sticking point (Brandt

1979; Parfit 1984). How is all relevant information assured access, and perhaps more to the point, how do preferences necessarily follow ideal rational deliberations? The entire rational inquiry is beset with a host of underlying suppositions and forces—cultural, historical, and personal— so that "ideal deliberation" cannot attain neutrality and complete closure. In short, rationality is context-dependent and value-ridden, which is not to say that humans do not act rationally, but, at the same time, to act morally requires more than just rationality.[18]

This construction resonates with Freud's notion of the superego (Freud 1923a, 28ff.; 1930, 123ff.), where individual morality remains subject to deterministic forces at play through the superego and choice is again either denied or severely compromised from aspirations to full autonomy and reasoned deliberation—not only from "below" but also from "above." Nevertheless, despite sharing Nietzsche's understanding of the power of instinctual life, and the prominent role of the superego, in the end, concerning the general role of reason, Freud sides with Kant, as testified by the enactment of psycho*analysis* itself. Freud, as a "neo-Kantian," regarded autonomy as that which made humans human, namely, rational and autonomous; Nietzsche, in contrast, portrayed humans in their full potential freed from a confining rationality. Because Nietzsche dismissed reasoned, dispassionate analysis, he would regard Freud's project as doomed by a rationalizing fantasy. Indeed, Nietzsche's radical biologicism, serving as a basic ontology for human agency, delegated reason to a subversion of the Will to Power that thereby represses full human potential. Unlike the duality Freud posits of a rational ego controlling an arational unconscious, Nietzsche acknowledged the unconscious as constitutive to human being and, furthermore, celebrated it. Thus Nietzsche and Freud differed in their employment of the instincts for their respective projects. Simply, while Freud would control instinctual drives through reason, Nietzsche would free them from a constricting rationality. So while both recognized the underlying character of civilized human behavior as some expression of a converted biological substratum, one would liberate those forces, while the other viewed them with profound suspicion and even dread. One saw the instinctual conflict as coincident with health, the other as the source of pathology; one championed the release of instinctual forces, the other their rational control.

The Moral Structure of the Will

Nietzsche, as Kant before him, created his philosophy with the goal of establishing a basis for human freedom. The biological conception of human nature served a descriptive function in Nietzsche's thought, in which he portrayed human vitality and creativity as fully expressed for human flourishing only in the free exercise of the Will. On this view, Nietzsche transformed the Will to Power from blind biological force to the foundation of human freedom and ultimately the creative basis of self-determination in human action (e.g., 1967a, 36, 366, 367). Thus, placing humans in nature goes well beyond identifying their instinctual character, and we misconstrue Nietzsche's genealogy of morals if his philosophy is naturalized (as a Hobbsian, for example). While much of his ranting was directed towards a negative appraisal of Western ethics, described in terms of enslavement to an imposed morality, Nietzsche did so to clear the ground for an argument for individual independence. Such autonomy includes the responsibility of establishing freely chosen moral coordinates and then acting accordingly. Thus individual choice, both in prescription and in action, defined his vision of the moral. Ironically, then, he adopted the same orientation argued by Kant, namely, a radical autonomy, but obligation has shifted from satisfying a rational act to answering a biological imperative (which is both vital and creative).

In asserting individual autonomy as both the means and basis for fulfilling human potential, Nietzsche proclaimed, perhaps more clearly than any of his nineteenth-century forerunners, the sanctity of human choice. Indeed, grounding individual action in a biology of human nature marks a significant change in conceptualizing human identity, and "autonomy" thereby assumes a new definition, one quite different from that formulated by Kant. Freud accepted the possibility of individual freedom, but that freedom was viewed much more narrowly. The individual is subject not only to the determinism of the unconscious, namely, the tyranny of the ever-present instincts, but to past experience and the injunction of a moral conduct impressed on the impressionable person. For Freud, freedom resides elsewhere.

This difference points to an important divergence in the underlying metaphysics governing the respective conceptions of human agency

presented by Nietzsche and Freud. Both saw civilized humans as dam-
aged, and more, each regarded the problems of civilization as resulting
in nihilism and neurosis, respectively (Brown 1959, 82–84): Nietzsche
regarded the suppression of a vitalizing natural Will as the cause of
sickness and a distortion of life, and Freud saw the consequences of repression as symptoms of illness (Tauber and Podolsky 1999). However,
while both concur that the revolt from nature results in sickness, for
Nietzsche a return to nature offers health; for Freud, no such option
exists, and instead he sought a more effective means to deal with the
perpetual conflict of reason and Will. From these differing positions,
divergent ethics emerged.

Nietzsche developed the Will to Power in multifarious ways. Controversy irrepressibly persists in the dispute over what is philosophy, poetics,
metaphor, or psychology, but little doubt exists that he utilized biology
to provide the language from which to critique nihilism and establish
his new ethics. His celebrated transvaluation (*Umwertung*) of values
originates with identifying what is "good" (the biological extension) and
what is "bad" (the Will's weakening or corruption by inferior competing forces) as organic manifestations. Thus the expression of the Will,
whether viewed from an evolutionary or physiological perspective, leads
to a vision of man governed by laws inviolate and uncontaminated by
anthropocentric or moral distortions, which not only disguise and distort
human's true nature, but hamper the achievement of life's purpose—developing, overcoming, becoming—through the Will to Power (Tauber
1994b, 249–61). This process, which Nietzsche sees throughout organic
nature, he termed "self-overcoming" (*Selbstüberwindung*) ("And life itself confided this secret to me: Behold, I am *that which must always overcome itself*" (1959d, 225]), and it is personified in the *Übermensch*. To
the extent this dynamic is integral to the individual, whether organism,
species, civilization, or morality, the law applies at each level of social or
biological function (Nietzsche 1967c, 161).

The ascendancy of power in the ethical domain (a Platonic erotic ascent of sorts) forms the basis of Nietzsche's morality. Just as an organism
might achieve some self-sustaining goal by volitional action governed by
self-control mechanisms, so too might humans follow an analogous path
to realize moral self-mastery. So in the larger context of Nietzsche's cri-

tique of culture, the antidote to nihilism becomes the endeavor of directing the Will to achieve a self-determined ethics. Accordingly, the higher the self-control, the greater the moral attainment. The individual thereby asserts her identity—freedom—in assuming responsibility for *Selbstüberwindung*, and in that pursuit, health is achieved, both psychologically and morally (Nietzsche 1959a, 542; Tauber and Podolsky 1999). Succinctly stated, "For what is freedom? That one has the will to assume responsibility for oneself" (Nietzsche 1959a, 542), and thus Nietzsche proclaimed the ethical integrity of individual choice and responsibility.

Nietzsche's unique contribution and importance does not reside so much in the celebration of the unconscious, nor even in its elucidation, as in his demand that instead of following moral precepts given by some authority or tradition, individuals first determine and then assume moral responsibility for themselves (1959a, 542). Human nature is fundamentally a striving, a form of perfectionism derived from an organic force of being, and a moral imperative follows in the same vein: Just as individuals pursue their self-prescribed vital paths as organic creatures, so would that biological vitality determine the veracity of the ethics that governed that behavior. That he provided no ethical direction for such striving in the social universe is one of his great failings,[19] but like Freud, self-awareness becomes the first step toward moral responsibility (Sherman 1995). In this endeavor they are inextricably linked.

On the potential of human freedom, Freud and Nietzsche join hands, albeit embracing different strategies: The very possibility of achieving some moral standing above or beyond the restrictions of the deterministic biology that grounds human behavior represents the ethical mission they both accept as fundamental to human being. However, they differ in the philosophical structure by which such an end is reached. Freud invoked rationality, placed in some undesignated, insular province of the mind, where reasoned interpretation served as the tool for cutting the chains of biological determinism. Nietzsche conceived human freedom not by splitting the mind between the drives and reason, but by using the selfsame biological drives as a vehicle to fulfill the potential of human creativity. In dispensing with the mind-body duality altogether, he built his system on a monolithic notion of the organic, in which the mind becomes just another expression of the body. In this schema, the organic

Will is directed towards some self-chosen moral telos. In other words, the inescapable Will transfigures into the moral domain, and in that expression a new vision of human nature emerges, in which the Will forms the very basis of personal identity and self-determined morality (Nietzsche 1967a, 356; 1966, 203).

In sum, for both Freud and Nietzsche, biological forces not only influence, but more fundamentally drive, human endeavors of all types. The Will or the unconscious, accordingly, resides at the very core of human being and forms the foundation of the person: Just as Freud would describe the unconscious as the psychic wellspring of human behavior, Nietzsche assigned the Will to Power the source of human identity. Freud then adds a second component, reason. Unlike Nietzsche, who constructed a schema by which an ethics might be formulated, Freud provided no such basis for the same basic portrait of human free will. The strategies differed, but Nietzsche and Freud shared the same aspiration: Marshal the potentially destructive elements of human nature by liberating the psyche through recognizing the vibrancy of human instinctual life, and from that understanding, achieve freedom from the despotism of repression (Nietzsche) or unbridled unconscious desire and the neurotic products of its repression (Freud). They, however, differed over the role of reason: For Nietzsche, the tyranny of reason was a faculty falsely invested with a power it could not support or justify, and for Freud, the demands of the id would be stymied through exercise of freed reason to subdue a force whose steadfast hold on human behavior must be challenged and then effectively channeled in love and productive work. However, Freud did not describe reason's agency, and leading from this ambiguity, he failed to define the elusive character of his moral actor.

When the ethical domain expands to include the communal collective, Freud and Nietzsche remain preoccupied with the individual at the expense of the social, and in line with their parallel construal of human nature, each sees conflict as inherent in human relationships. For Freud, the dynamics of psychoanalysis are oriented by conflict with others—past and present. The primordial parental domination of children, the Oedipal struggle, the precarious balance of Eros fending off Thanatos, each point to a Nietzschean preoccupation with struggle, however, in the Freudian view, not as a sign of health, but rather as the source of neurosis. Only later, with the development of "object" or "relational psychology" (discussed in the next chapter) and the social criticism evoked by psychoanalysis (e.g., Herbert Marcuse [1955]) would attempts appear to redirect Freudian theory explicitly towards a *constructive* social ethics. Freud himself, however, remained conspicuously silent in explicitly developing an ethics that would convert the instinctual drives towards building a social ethics. Indeed, for Freud, the imposition of social mores designed to inhibit and control sexuality, more often than not, directly precipitates neurotic behaviors. Of course, Freud cannot condone the free release of the pleasure principle or the exercise of unrestricted instincts (considering the dire consequences of patricide and the like), but in his preoccupation with the *problem* of the social, psychoanalysis finds itself seeking means to accommodate the demands of others in order to cope with their various impositions. This similarity grows from Freud's kindred understanding of the human animal, one that is locked in Darwinian struggle. For our purposes, the issue is the kind of ethics such an orientation demanded—in a word, individualistic. Indeed, psychoanalysis directs itself towards an understanding of the hidden instinctual drives and their disguised manifestations of neurotic *individuals*.

To conclude, in the Freudian universe, acknowledging the primacy of emotional recognition that lies at the base of the analytic experience, reason offers the necessary insight to accommodate analytic comprehension, and from insight, liberation becomes attainable. On that view, reason serves as a diagnostic and therapeutic tool as a consequence of its autonomy to scrutinize the unconscious. The understanding attained then frees the ego from the deterministic causality that drives instinctual pursuit of pleasure, on the one hand, and loosens the grip of an onerous and stultifying superego, on the other hand. So in the psychoanalytic scenario, the couplet of instinctual biology and despotic justice remain in one domain, and a rational ego scrutinizes and controls each in the service of some idealized basis of behavior. In this schema, Freud resides between Kant and Nietzsche: Human beings are obviously biological creatures subject to biological drives and instincts; what makes them *human* is their capacity to reason in the employ of some goal, and in the more specific arena of the ethical, some ideal. And here Freud's moral project begins.

Chapter Six

Who Is the Subject?

> For as long as philosophy has existed ... it has been
> concerned with the relation between self-reflection and
> freedom. Yet it has never been clear what self-reflection is,
> or what freedom is, or why the former should make any
> contribution to the latter.
> —Jonathan Lear (1990, 183)

FREUD'S THINKING ABOUT THE EGO combines several formulations, which begin with early modernist principles. In some sense, he draws an alliance with Descartes's meditation, "I am a thinking thing," as the "true" center of his identity. Indeed, the modernist endeavor to define personal identity begins by recognizing that the self cannot be derived, but instead, the Cartesian *cogitans*—the end point of the skeptic's query—serves as the starting point of self-consciousness.[1] Accordingly, to the extent that "identity" has a definition in the Freudian universe, it must be that which can be identified; that is, the conscious ego examines and hopefully controls the unconscious forces that remain hidden from normal scrutiny (Laplanche and Pontalis 1973, 130ff.). Functioning within a sector of the mind, a designated arena of psychic activity of a particular type, the rational ego (although in his later writings [e.g., 1933], "the ego" has no such singular property and combines elements of consciousness and unconsciousness) has the unique property of following "rational" and "logical" rules. That faculty, of course, was only part of a more general functional apparatus that serves as the mediator between the unconscious components of the mind and the world.

This ego derived from psychoanalytic theory possesses topographical characteristics and thus is situated in a "location" of the mind. And locality implies "borders." Even in the context of the "economic" configuration, the notion of the ego as some entity, albeit understood as exhibiting highly dynamic psychic activities, remains dominant. Of course, such a simple description distorts and thus misrepresents Freud's thinking about consciousness, the ego, and the array of issues related to them. To better address these relationships and governing notions of personal identity, we must consider a brief overview of *the self* as a philosophical problem, which draws, at least in this discussion, from three primary sources: Descartes, Kant, and Hegel.

As discussed in chapter 5, Kant left the reflexive project as a remnant of the basic organization of the human mind: Humans observe the world and observe thoughts and emotions, but just as we are limited in our knowledge of the exterior reality, so are we restricted in knowing ourselves. Accordingly, the self is an artifact of the knowing faculty. From this perspective, the transcendental ego occupies a default position resulting from Kant's novel metaphysics. But if another metaphysics takes hold, as it powerfully did in German Idealism, a very different philosophical construction appears, one that built on the recursive character of reflexivity. In fact, this altogether different formulation was already available at the same time Descartes wrote his *Meditations*. Instead of a terminated introspection ending in an entity with boundaries, one at least, Henry Jeanes (an obscure English minister, 1611–62), appreciated the infinite regress encoded in reflexivity and thus the problematic status of "the self": 'Then the mind in its reflexive workings can proceed in infinitum' (Jeanes 1656, 42; quoted by *Oxford English Dictionary*, vol. Q, 1971, 345). This latter sense of self-consciousness as an infinite regress presents an interesting dilemma: if reflexivity has no end, where, or what is "the self" (or what Descartes called a "thinking thing")? Jeanes's prescient insight only reached its acme in the mid-nineteenth century, when the notion of an entity constituting identity was eventually challenged on the grounds he originally suggested.

Simply, two constructions vied for dominance: self-reflection yields an entity, a core self (Cartesian); alternatively, self-reflection yields no such entity, and reflexivity becomes constitutive of another form of identity, one that has no prescribed borders and is better depicted as a function or a process. The first is identified with Descartes; the second most prominently with Hegel and Kierkegaard (Tauber 2006). Freud drew from both philosophical lines: from Descartes, the reductionist mode of analysis, a mechanistic model of

designated parts in motion, and most prominently, the inner perspectival view of the mind with all of its attendant metaphysical baggage (as
discussed in chap. 5). From Hegel, Freud adopted modes of dynamic
processes, evolutionary development, and a new set of dialectical rules
of logic (negation, condensation, displacement) quite at variance with
Cartesian order (Rendon 1986). And most profoundly, Freud combined,
sometimes with inconsistent consequences, an individualistic, atomistic notion of personal identity with one based on relational constructs.
Hegel's general relational formulation markedly inflects in Kierkegaard's
reflexive notion of selfhood, which took the Kantian mystery of self-consciousness and made it the acknowledged nexus of personal identity. This
turn from the *other* to an acute *self*-consciousness highlights the paradox
characterizing Freud's own conception of self-identity and introspection,
and while Freud apparently did not read Kierkegaard, important parallels are found in their respective notions of self-consciousness. Below we
will briefly review the history and construction of this reflexive notion
of personal identity in contrast to the older understanding, to set the
foundations for understanding Freud's moral agent as drawn from two
philosophical traditions of personal identity. In the previous chapter, the
ego, an entity—self-contained and autonomous—led to certain moral
characteristics, and now we will examine the ego conceived as a reflexive process, which will lead to another refraction of the moral personality. The latter characterization begins most directly with Georg Wilhelm
Friedrich Hegel.

The Relational Self

With Hegel, personal identity arises in a reflective construction, one established in confrontation with an Other, and in that confrontation an
ethics is forged. Since identity is established in that dialectic interaction,
reflexivity assumes an entirely different character from that argued by
Kant. Hegel's moral nexus demands a social dimension of intercourse,
and (as discussed in the previous chapter) Freud, in this context, closely
affiliates with Nietzsche, whose concerns are with establishing and protecting the individual.[2] Indeed, a Hegelian notion of agency discounts
the autonomy of persons construed as atomistic, but disputes the very

legitimacy of an individualistic understanding. However, in another dimension, Freud does build on the reflexive arc elaborated by Hegel and further developed most radically by Kierkegaard (Thulstrop 1980; Stewart 2003; Tauber 2006). This bivalent vision of the ego is also complicated by different Freudian constructions: In the early instinctual phase of psychoanalytic theory, an autonomous, Nietzschean model is implicitly applied, whereas in the later metapsychological period, Freud not only explicitly introduces object relations, but the ego itself is split by a reflexive mechanism (most evident in the papers on narcissism [1914a] and melancholia [1917a]). Thus review of the Hegelian formulation suggests the complex philosophical underpinnings of Freud's theory, which will be developed in due course.

Most narratives describing the philosophy of selfhood place Hegel at a conceptual hinge, where reflexivity assumes new directions. In his own attempt to present the ontological conditions of the subject's action and knowledge of the world, he clearly and effectively disputed Kant (and his early critics [Hegel 1977]) and thereby set the agenda for those who followed him (Löwith 1991).[3] Structured by the metaphysics of German Idealism, Hegel pursued the implications of reflexivity as *constitutive* to self-identity. Instead of reflexivity serving an instrumental function or regarded as an artifact, in his reconfiguration, reflexivity effectively shifts from observing an entity (Descartes) or describing the conditions of knowing (Kant), to constituting a process of identity *formation*. With this shift from an atomistic identity to what would become self-identity as a product of relation, self-consciousness is turned outwards into the world, where the means of interactions becomes the grounding of moral intercourse. In short, the self defines itself in relationship, and in that fundamental shift, not only does selfhood find a different course in its ongoing definitional quest, but moral philosophy shifts along with that new description (Tauber 2005).

The Hegelian construction actualized personal identity in self-conscious encounter with another, and thus pushed past "reflexivity" to "synthesis." In a famous scene of the *Phenomenology of Spirit* (1999), Hegel presents a primal encounter of two men, who engage in mortal struggle. One prevails and becomes Master, and the other, Slave. Only in the consciousness of the Other does identity emerge, and in this sense, introspective reflexivity fails to identify selfhood, indeed, it does not exist prior to the Other.[4] The self is only known as self-conscious difference, as the "not-I"—the "'I' that has its otherness within itself" (Hegel 1999, 30). This recognition is integral to Hegel's metaphysics, as the self-conscious ego both recognizes its own identity and concomitantly the *Geist* of which it is part.[5] Self-identity thus becomes inseparable from that of *Geist*'s own course, which includes the fate of the human collective. Here Hegel makes his social move, integrating the history of the individual, the commune, and *Geist* into an integrated whole. Persons achieve their individuality only as participants in social institutions, which Hegel regarded as the embodiment of freedom (Neuhouser 2000, 44–47). The point I wish to emphasize here is the social character of selfhood: The self is inseparable from the other, and from the whole. The contrast to Kant's own preoccupation with autonomy could not be more stark.[6]

A useful way of placing Hegel in the tradition of defining the self builds upon Charles Taylor's critical point that "the self" responds to the question, Who am I? which requires answers totally dependent on cultural or moral contexts (Taylor 1989). This is the dimension largely missing from Freud's concerns, but appear later in the object-relations psychologies that converge with a philosophy of selfhood emerging from the Hegelian tradition (discussed below). If persons are conceived in relation to others, assuming particular identities in those relationships, then a definition of selfhood rests on a social construction. This formulation challenges the subject viewed as an entity, an object that might stand alone. This atomistic notion of selfhood—one that has been described as "punctual" or "detached" (Taylor 1989)—dominated modernism, having arisen from two tributaries: (1) the agent of moral philosophy in post-Reformation England, whose political self-responsibility was radically asserted,[7] and (2) the scientific actor who would scrutinize the world, and himself, apart from any constitutive concerns. However, the self's "only constitutive property is self-awareness. This is the self Hume set out to find and, predictably, failed to find" (Taylor 1989, 50), for this identity, defined over time as some psychological continuity, is a construction that simply fails to fulfill the essential criteria of an entity, which must have objective status, standing independent of any description or interpretation and be captured in explicit description (Taylor 1989, 34–35). Most importantly, an object may be understood without reference to its surroundings or contingent circumstances.

Despite the difficulties of conceiving the self as an object or entity, this Cartesian-Lockean understanding of personal identity has held its course, supported by positivism in the nineteenth century and various individualist notions of autonomy in the twentieth. However, Hegel's version of selfhood offered an alternative, inasmuch as identity framed within human categories of personal and social action of value and meaning, demand that selves establish their identities by fulfilling the social criteria of agency. In the myriad roles persons play in their multitude of relationships, these guidelines must be flexible, as personality, experience, history, intelligence, and particular demands each contribute to how choices are made and enacted. Indeed, such choices create the personifications that refer to individual identities. On this view, *self* describes social and personal acts conducted by a moral agent.

The Nietzschean and Hegelian notions have been outlined, and suffice it to note here that Freud's early atomistic conception of personal identity by and large bypasses the Hegelian construction and instead reaches deeply back into the modern period to Descartes and most directly, to John Locke. Locke reified the mind and adopted a disengaged individualism, where in the course of positivism's ascent, the self in some sense "disappears." Freud drew on this conception, for the Lockean self amply fulfilled positivist criteria for achieving a radical objectivity, where the presence of the observing eye was to be expunged altogether. Taylor describes such a faculty as an "extensionless" self, a presence that cannot be localized or "found," but whose "power to fix things as objects" attests to its function (1989, 172). This power reposes in consciousness, a theme traced to Hume (and later to William James and the phenomenologists [Tauber 1994a, 207–15, 215–29]). However, the self simply cannot be reduced to some single psychological construction of continuity, not only because self-consciousness cannot be captured or defined, but more fundamentally because, as Hume himself realized, this was only a psychological conceit, a vague awareness of an identity function held together by psychological reflection (Hume 1978, 300–301). Accordingly, the "self" serves useful linguistic and psychological functions, but it has no basis that could be defined by any analytical criteria. And when Kant attacked the problem, recognizing the unique intimacy of self-consciousness, he conceded Hume's basic tenet: The self could not be *known*; only the conditions of knowing might be deduced.

Variations on these themes of selfhood emerged from the Kantian and Hegelian positions during the nineteenth century, because, in some sense, each had failed: Introspection could not end in any self-definition (Kant), nor could the logic of synthesis preserve individually based moral parameters for personhood (Hegel). Perhaps another strategy for another endeavor was required. Reflexivity lingered, but it took on new meanings and followed different logics as Romantic philosophers continued to struggle to answer Kant's basic challenges, namely, (1) how to synthesize experience fractured by different rationalities (e.g. positivist, moral, aesthetic, or spiritual subjectivity), and (2) how to understand moral choice (freedom) (Allison 1990; 2004; Schneewind 1998). Those pursuing responses to the first question replaced defining "a self" with the wider effort of mending the fracture of experience. In recognizing the limits of a self-consciousness that ultimately separated the self from the world, they sought strategies by which to place the self *in* the world in response to Schiller's challenge: "How are we to restore the unity of human nature ... ?" (Schiller 1993, 121; Beiser 2005; Tauber 2001; 2009).[8] The second question led to a focus on individualism, where autonomy and freedom (as centered on individual responsibility and potential) displaced a more integrative configuration of selfhood. This "cultural tilt" towards political, economic, and social independence has myriad sources, and as many explanations, but in that array at least one feature stands out: reflexivity assumed new intensity as it probed different dimensions.

The "Age of the I" (or more formally, "It is said to be the age of the first person singular" [Emerson 1963, 70]) was marked by a keen self-reflection on consciousness, moral agency, and the demands of a newly evolving positivism as configured by new demands for individual choice and independence.[9] The parameters by which such self-governance might be achieved, and the strictures placed upon achieving that goal, led to a renewed interest in defining selfhood—its characteristics, its boundaries, its potentials. In that inquiry, self-consciousness itself became an object of inquiry, as it served as one means of defining the self in its multiple modes—social, psychological, moral, historical, and so on. Indeed, by midcentury, each domain of personhood demanded reflexivity—the reiterations that would describe and evaluate the evolving relation between the subject and his natural, social, and divine worlds through self-conscious reflection (Tauber 2001).

The Cartesian tradition had subordinated an interactive, integrated self constituted by relationships, because the architecture of the self in the early modern period was based on the ego's independence—both as an objective observer of the world (to do science) and as a self-governing citizen (to participate in liberal democracy). The Romantic era made new demands on the self's constitution. Offering an admittedly oversimplified history, we might point to the early nineteenth century, when the autonomous self, with a new sense of individuality, found itself alone in the world and acutely aware of often conflicted relationships with God, society, and nature.[10] In some instances a celebration of those relations is evident, and in other cases we witness the troubled angst of alienation; in either orientation, a new self-consciousness characterized the age. Psychoanalysis grew in that rich soil (Kirschner 1996).

Let us summarize two key points concerning the self-reflexive subject: First, for this discussion, self-consciousness is the beginning of ethical conduct, as self-awareness and self-responsibility are inextricably intertwined (Sherman 1995). To achieve insight, of course, Freud relied on analysis—both at an unconscious affective level (Freud 1912a) and through rational interpretation, ostensibly guided by an enlightened analyst. Despite Freud's own ambivalence about the role of reason and the power of unconscious motivation, he still remained committed to a modernist conception of reason that bestows freedom. Self-evidently, as discussed in chapter 4, the entire psychoanalytic project rests upon the quiet authority of reason to understand and thus better to control the unconscious. After all, *interpretation* is key to his method. Moreover, autonomy reigns in the Freudian universe as an ethical *ideal*, and despite the obvious encumbrances to reason's rule, psychoanalysis commits to that faculty as the means of liberating the ensnared analysand. Thus Freud's method of self-appraisal (albeit in partnership with the analyst) makes him a "disciple" of Kant, inasmuch as a rationally based self-consciousness became *constitutive* to Freud's moral vision.

Second, while the Hegelian reflexive investigations each point towards an Other and a resultant social ethic (identity evolving dialectically with others), for Freud, self-consciousness remains ego-centric and constitutes a moral activity in and of itself. These differing approaches obviously reflect different concerns: Freud, engaged in a *psychological* project, sought to understand the structure of the mind and its functioning, while Hegel and his followers employed self-consciousness and introspection as a means towards establishing the *philosophical* conditions of personal identity. From the Hegelian position self-consciousness moved from an end in itself to another venture, that is, serving religious, social, or metaphysical agendas of establishing identities within various constructs.

Freud was not concerned with establishing the basis of personal identity beyond an implicit understanding of moral agency: The ego remains within the confines of its own self-identification, while the Hegelian dialectic pushes the self into the world (natural and metaphysical). In other words, Freudian self-consciousness becomes an ongoing project, not in relation to an other, but in relation to oneself. Notwithstanding that Freud does not speak of a relation of oneself to oneself (discussed in chapter 4), and thus leaves the ego ironically uncharacterized, turning reflexivity (passive) into reflectivity (active) becomes integral to the ways in which moral choices are made and enacted. These constitute the process of establishing an individual moral identity. In this sense, for Freud, self-consciousness is an "accomplishment," inasmuch as what is brought to consciousness from unconscious and preconscious sources represents an active process, and ultimately the success of psychoanalysis depends on self-awareness in various contexts (traumatic memory, social interactions, self-appraisals, etc.) (Tugendhat 1986, 127, citing Martin Bartels). Indeed, Freud's underlying premise that emotional recognition and rational insight lead to personal freedom makes self-consciousness the therapeutic means towards psychological and existential health. And more, to the extent Freud defines a self, it is the activity of self-consciousness—inspired by memory, led by reason, and directed towards liberation.

Eloquently described by Søren Kierkegaard in the opening lines of *Sickness unto Death*, self-reflection *is* the self:

The self is a relation that relates itself to itself or is the relation's relating itself to itself in the relation; the self is not the relation but is the relation relating itself to itself. A human being is a synthesis of the infinite and the finite, of the temporal and the eternal, of freedom and of necessity, in short, a synthesis. A synthesis is a relation between two. Considered in this way, man is still not a self.... Such a relation that relates itself to itself, a self, must either have established itself or have been established by another. If the relation that relates itself to itself has been established by another, then the relation is indeed the third, but this relation, the third, is yet again a relation and relates itself to that which established the entire relation. The human being is such a derived, established, relation, a relation that relates itself to itself, and in relating itself to itself relates itself to another. (1980, 13–14)[11]

Thus the recursive reflective self becomes an ongoing, synthetic exercise— a self-consciousness that has no bounds, and one that is ever-present.

Kierkegaard's depiction of selfhood suggests interesting parallels with Freud's project. First, what ends ceaseless introspection? In one sense, if reflexivity is constitutive to human consciousness, then there is no end. And when the question is considered within a larger framework, namely analysis itself, Freud understood that analysis never finally ends, that the process of self-discovery and further insight continues indefinitely (Freud 1937b). Because of the perpetual character of self-analysis, no fixed identity ever emerges, and the self-reflective *process* itself thus becomes constitutive to the ego's nature, namely one who seeks one's own character. Indeed, the very elusiveness of the inquiry of "the self" becomes the sine qua non of selfhood, and in that self-reflection an ethical personality (agent) emerges. So while "cure" designated completion, and many of Freud's cases end precisely at the point of conflict resolution, the larger analytic process as a form of self-discovery and understanding is ceaseless, as self-awareness is coincident with self-consciousness.

Second, Kierkegaard set the groundwork for existentialism's precept of self-responsibility and moral agency based on the fulfillment of some singular choice. Standing at the metaphysical chasm, with his celebrated absurd leap (see note 11), he invited the exercise of choice, however configured. He thus also championed moral self-responsibility, and from that orientation the Hegelian project was turned from its integrative aspirations to one committed to an existentialist examination of oneself. In this context, psychoanalysis parallels Kierkegaard's construction: For both Freud and Kierkegaard, *reflexion* became reflective and thus an *appraisal*. From the appraisal, decisions of personal choice and action are made.

To conclude, in turning to a more self-conscious awareness of identity, the reflexive arc assumed a more active *reflective* modality. To "reflect" connotes pondering, questioning and constructing ways of thinking about personal identity and moral agency.[12] Such an invigorated role in defining selfhood thus shifted attention from addressing epistemological skepticism to probing the configuration of the moral universe, namely the relation of the self with its world—natural and spiritual, public and personal. Since the formulation of selfhood leads to particular notions of moral agency (Tauber 2005, 85–123), we do well to ask, *who* is this agent, or perhaps more specifically, how does Freud configure personal identity? To this matter we now turn.

The Problematic Self

How might we characterize the nuanced Freudian understandings of personal identity and self-consciousness that lie at the heart of psychoanalysis? When philosophically construed, the self concept falls within three domains or definitional dimensions (Seigel 2005, 1–44): the physical or biological; the relational; and the reflective. Nietzsche champions the first; Hegel, the second; Kierkegaard, the third. And of course, within each category, much debate ensues about the character of each of these basic formulations. While we have employed this schema here, another approach also beckons, namely, the differences of "active" versus "passive" understandings of selfhood. As already noted, "reflexive" refers to a kind of passive self-reflection akin to a mirror, while "reflective" refers to an active, intentional self-awareness. The latter is associated with rationality and consciousness, which bear on the individual's relation to herself and the world (Seigel 2005, 12). In the psychoanalytic context, both active and passive modalities present themselves: interpretative analysis is obviously active, while the process of recollection through associative procedures falls within a passive mode. Both belong to the subject, but the respective voices appear differently. From these distinctions, apparent synonyms "subject," "identity," "person," "self," take on differing meanings depending on the context in which they are employed. "Self" refers to that which is mine (e.g., self-analysis, self-confident) in a passive, possessive sense, and also to that which distinguishes me from others as a particular being. But *self* may also serve as a placeholder for other active categories: moral agent; political entity; embodied individual. So the vocabulary that captures the spectrum of sameness and difference framing personal identity possesses many shades of meaning and participates in various kinds of descriptions and discourses. Contextual placement obviously ultimately denotes meaning, and no steadfast semantic rule applies.

The range of understandings in which to consider the status of "the self" in the Freudian context assumes even further complication by its peculiar lexical absence in his writings,[13] and, more generally, dispute arises because conceptions of personal identity shift through Freud's development of psychoanalysis (Holt 1989, 220ff.).[14] Most commentators simply accept "the self" as a Freudian category without critical note or justification (e.g., Thalberg 1982); others see the problem of the self as central to psychoanalysis and attempt to place that category in the Freudian universe (e.g., Cavell 2006); some have critically addressed the philosophical "confusions" of the Freudian "self" and still maintain its usefulness (e.g., Dilman 1984).[15] Adding further difficulty (at least for English readers) pertains to the basic translation of *ich* or *das Ich* with differing connotations.[16] Putting aside each of these matters, we may still conclude that based on the *use* of language, it seems that the "self" concept as articulated in the philosophical literature remained outside Freud's purview and perhaps even irrelevant to his project. He freely uses *Ich* (ego) as opposed to *Selbst* (self), and of course, the Freudian ego is never equated with "the self."

This issue of clarifying Freud's notion of personal identity is important for our purposes to the extent that it helps illuminate his notions of moral agency (considered in the next chapter). In that regard, it appears that Freud's theory did not depend on defining a notion of *selfhood*, per se. Furthermore, if he had sought such a construction from philosophers, he would have been offered little guidance. As previously discussed, by the nineteenth century, the idea of "the self" as *entity* followed two paths: In the positivist tradition, the self as observing scientist (a paragon of sorts) served as a pivotal point for organizing (and eventually evaluating) data. In this regard, the older Cartesian-Lockean conception held. However, the notion of the self as some entity had already been rendered vulnerable by Hume, and after Hegel, this formulation had been largely eclipsed in the philosophical literatures. As described above, reflexivity, whether following the Hegelian structure (ending with an object) or the Kierkegaardian (no object, just the reflexive faculty itself), moves the notion from some static, object status to an ongoing process. Never steadfast or finite, human self-consciousness, reason, and reflection each refract the character of that which conducts the inquiry. Neither Hegel nor Kierkegaard established the basis for such activity, but simply acknowledged its constitutive properties: Humans reflect as they seek meanings, and that is "simply" what they *do*. Beyond such phenomenological observations, what else can be *said*?

The implications of the reflexive position for ethics will be discussed in due course, but for now suffice it to note that even the staunch naturalist must face a dilemma in the context of this understanding. For instance, Nietzsche's formulation of an organism possessing intentionality or biological will hardly sufficed for his own self-conscious pursuits. Indeed, given his mistrust of reason, Nietzsche thought this naturalistic description of selfhood leaves further philosophical discourse on the consciousness of reflection as hopelessly muddled and metaphysical:

> Science—this has been hitherto a way of putting an end to the complete confusion in which things exist, by hypotheses that "explain" everything—so it has come from the intellect's dislike of chaos.—This same dislike seizes me when I consider myself: I should like to form an image of the inner world, too, by means of some schema, and thus triumph over intellectual confusion.... [But] I know that I know nothing of myself. (1883–88, no. 594)

While Nietzsche probed the issue of personal identity, he left the primordial self, the Will, as resolutely foreign and unknowable to conscious thought and understanding, while Freud, of course, adopted a radically different stance: The ego not only might interpret the unconscious, it could, through analytic insight, control unconscious forces as it navigated the social environment.

Freud's description of ego function attempts to capture the precarious balance the ego must achieve between the demands of the unconscious psyche and social reality, between inner desire and external necessity. To use Freud's famous simile, the ego is like a rider on horseback who must control the animal (1923a, 25), and that control may either employ neurotic mechanisms (in the pathological state) or rational insight (in the therapeutic scenario). While Anna Freud (1967) and later ego psychologists would emphasize the rational elements of ego control, such a capacity certainly lies implicit in Freudian theory from its earliest expressions. So with this basic construct, let us consider the language Freud used at face value.

The psychoanalytic scenario establishes a disjunction within the subject himself—the analytic faculty instantiates the commonsense notion of the person (the analysand), while the inner drives of the id represent something separate, distant, and foreign to that knowing agent. And we are left to ask, who is this knower, this "he who must find the courage" (Freud 1914b, 152) to pursue self-knowledge? When Freud explained to the Rat Man that "he ought logically to consider *himself* as in no way responsible for any of these [vindictive and cowardly] traits in his character (1909a, 185; emphasis added), *who* is this "himself" to which Freud refers? Of course there is no singular agent or entity, and Freud himself left ambiguous how the conscious ego brings the unconscious into thought, into reflection (Reeder 2002, 53ff.). And more to the point we are considering, psychoanalysis replaces the Cartesian *res cogitans* or Lockean punctual self (Taylor 1989) with an ongoing Kierkegaardian reflexivity, a self-conscious *process* of interpreting—no more and no less. That activity, at least in the construal of Freud's theory and practice, becomes a meaning-seeking activity, endowed with its own intentions, which, in its pursuits, not only makes choices—distinguishing good and bad, better and worse—but finds meaning in those choices. Personal significance serves to focus judgment's function, an arbitration of experience to create human reality. Of course, the search for meaning is never-ending, for there is no set goal. Instead, the inquiry itself is the raison d'être. In the end, psychoanalysis becomes a means of learning a new way of interpreting or narrating one's own story, and then with varying degrees of success, living one's life in reconciliation with that knowledge. So when we might ask, *Who* is this agent of inquiry?, Freud offers a deafening silence: Ich is simply me, a self-reflexive, self-conscious, interpreting *person*.

Throughout the clinical context, pronominal language reflects the perspectival distance occasioned by the physician scrutinizing his patient. In this analytic encounter, the patient simply recounts clinical data—stories, dreams, memories, slips of language, and so on—so at one level, the analysand appears phenomenologically as a voice, whose reflections, feelings, behaviors, choices, stories, and so forth, articulate agency. So in a first-order fashion, psychoanalysis structures a phenomenology of self-consciousness, namely, experience and self-reflections. These comprise what we *are*, for the reconstructed narrative offers *nothing else to be*.

The next move is something else—an analysis in which a perspective is required to make some judgment about significance and meaning. Those hermeneutics are, of course, complex: On the one hand, Freud, following Nietzschean themes, centered the psyche in the unconscious domain, which phylogenetically and existentially exists as the center of a primordial animal agency; and on the other hand, the conscious ego, fitted with rationality and social awareness, is assigned the task of presenting to the world, and itself, the agency of action and deliberation. And when the superego is added, the ego, in a profound sense, is "formed" by its demands and strictures, to become the source of conscience, self-observation, and the formation of a mature, ethical ego (Freud 1923a, 36–38).[17] Of course, each domain—conscious ego, superego, and id—comprises the person, and thus personal identity from the psychoanalytic perspective must be constructed from the basic structure of the psyche, namely some composite of the psyche's centers of activity—ego, superego, and id. While each component contributes to personhood, Freud clearly aligned psychoanalysis with the rational ego, the repository of self-consciousness and moral agency. In directing attention to the ego on the couch—the analysand—he sought to empower the interpretative faculty against the unconscious id and superego. After all, the *me* is *my* inner voice, the articulation of *my* thoughts, *my* intentions, *my* reason, *my* desires, and *my* memories. What else can I *be*? In terms of the definitions discussed above, this possessive sense of mind and character appropriately designates this "me-ness" as *selfhood*, which is an important designation, for beyond these epistemological considerations, an implicit sense of self-responsibility accompanies this assignment. If, after all, I am a "me"—and "me" connotes mine—then I assume a certain accountability that differentiates me from some neutral "person" or characterized "identity." So "me" not only refers to a different degree of intimacy with this identification, but also a sense of responsibility for this creature who walks among other like bodies and minds. The germ of moral agency thus lies in wait in this construction, a matter we will explore in later sections.

However, a perplexing problem remains, one that has vexed philosophers who have grappled with the self question:

> I should like to ask, *who* is the subject of the unconscious—if it is a subject.... Who is the dreamer? ... Who is the subject of fantasy? ... Who is the subject of desire? ... Who makes a transference onto the analyst? ... But the very formulation of these questions already suggests that the identity of the unconscious is multiple, rigorously speaking unnameable, *unverifiable*. This may be so quite simply because of a very general law making the unconscious "itself": identity, as such, is not susceptible to identification; *it does not identify itself....* That is why, rather than being seen as a detective story question, the question "who?" has to be seen as naïve ... it asks the impossible.... To say who I am—who thinks, who wishes, who fantasizes in me—is no longer in my power. That question draws me immediately beyond myself, beyond my representations, toward a point—we shall name it, the "point of otherness"—where I am another, the other who gives me my identity. (Borch-Jacobsen 1988, 8–9)

Accordingly, the Freudian analysand assumes a dual identity: On the one hand, the *subject* as "other" to itself, as a stranger to itself, presents itself in various primary manifestations, which are then subjected to psychoanalytic interpretation. The ego apprehends the secondary manifestations as representations of this domain. Psychic experience, memory, and behavior are distilled, translated, and articulated (albeit filtered by various defense mechanisms) from the unconscious reservoir and placed within consciousness (and reason) for analysis. So, in the mature theory, three individuals lie on the couch: a "stranger"—personified as the id; the "voice"—the unmediated expression of experience; and finally, "me" (the "you" from the analyst's perspective)—the observing, interpreting, feeling, knowing person. Let us consider each in turn.

In terms of personal identity, the id must be regarded, at best, as a component of a complex composite constituting the person. As a biological component it attains no more intimacy than a body part, just as the workings of my finger are suitable for scientific investigation, so that as part of the hand its structure and nerve innovation give me knowledge *of* that body part. Unless it is incapacitated, the finger holds little direct interest and may even be construed as somehow foreign to my own inner self, albeit a cherished appendage, if you will. Indeed, because my finger has the unique standing of being *my* finger, it becomes an object of some wonder when I consider its participation in some complex activity, for instance playing the piano. The anatomic part then presents a relationship to me that is at the same time unqualifiedly *mine* and yet distinct from me in terms of my own self-consciousness. In other words, I can look at my finger and see it as a finger, somehow separate yet part of me, the self-conscious me. In a similar way, but even more radically, the id, and the unconscious more generally, may be so characterized. The id's identity always remains strange, fundamentally alien to the knowing agent.

The second individual on the couch, the unself-conscious voice of experience, knows no perspective, and surfeit of the analytic vantage, it experiences the manifestations of the unconscious in the same "lived" way I might walk in a room and seat myself: I do not reflect upon each element that constitutes my walking and sitting. I just do it. This "voice" partially fulfills the criteria of selfhood inasmuch as this is the presentation that articulates the person in social intercourse and the "object" of self-reflection. In terms of the unconscious exhibiting itself, for instance in a dream state, I similarly just dream. No "distance" exists between the subject and her voice: there is no Archimedean point by which a vantage might be gained to survey the "my-ness" of my dream, of my voice, or of my memory. In this posture, there is no capacity of representing that other (the id) to my self-conscious ego, simply because I am *not* self-conscious in this nonreflective state. In this modality, Freud deciphers the subject qua subject, not in some static subject-object relation, but rather as a subject in action; in emotion; in behavior. In this sense, the analysand exists *first* as the subject of experience, an articulation of the subjective private voice, a voice that makes no attempt to reflect, only express. On the basis of free association, this voice becomes the conduit to the psyche and provides the material for the self-conscious ego, the personification of the *unreflecting* analysand. The analyst aids and abets the expressive process by becoming an "alter ego," and at this juncture the third figure on the couch appears.

As a "derivative" product—one created by a self-consciousness directed towards a particular form of analysis—the subject becomes a *rational, interpretative* analysand and is thereby ultimately trained by the analyst to create or discover a self-reflective identity. In a partnership with the analyst, the analysand's rational faculty is interjected, and in this move of scrutiny they turn the "voice" into a subject who observes an "other," the unconscious. However, as Mikkel Borch-Jacobsen observed (quoted above), the subject as object can no longer be "identified." In other words, this objectification splits the subject, one part scrutinizing the other, that is, examining an *other*, which Freud called the id, the "it." Analysis does not reveal "a self." Instead, identity appears fractionated—part scrutinizer, part scrutinized.

In short, Freud functions with dual modes of engagement: First, as a phenomenologist he focuses on experience (captured by free-associative monologues, dreams, parapraxes, and such), and just as the speaking subject in the associative posture makes no allusion to an identity, neither does the analyst. Experience, memory, and the voice of associations are "bracketed," and such phenomenological expression suffices to capture what had hitherto been the "problem" of personal identity (Askay and Farquhar 2006). The self as such disappears, and experience alone becomes the subject of interest. Second, as the analyst objectifies various components of the psychic apparatus, no attempt at constructing a totalizing composite is made, so again the self never appears as such. Relationships between the id, ego, and superego are charted, but in no instance does a totality emerge. So to the extent that Freud may be assigned to a philosophical school, consider him a phenomenologist gathering "data" in which a totalizing conceptual self is not required.

One final comment: If psychoanalysis is *"the science of the unconscious mind"* (Freud 1923b, 252), then one might fairly conclude that the notion of a *self* was beyond that inquiry, in large part because the notion of selfhood is inseparable from self-consciousness. In turn, consciousness serves to decipher the unconscious in the psychoanalytic scenario, and to the extent Freud deals with consciousness as a theoretical construct, it thus falls into two general categories of interest. First, at the level of discourse where data emerges and analysis begins, consciousness remains problematic in terms of the veracity of its conjured memory, the legitimacy of its associations, and the rational conclusions of its interpretations, a critique famously associated with Sartre (1956) and more recently Frederick Crews in the infamous "memory wars" (1995). Second, when consciousness is placed in juxtaposition to unconsciousness, Freud must situate each component in the larger schema of the neurophysiological mind (see chapter 4). In this latter context much is at stake, because at the heart of psychoanalytic theory, consciousness must be accounted for in relation to the unconscious components of the psyche if the ego, as mediator, is to function with the power of all of its capacities. A theoretical flank has thus been exposed: if psychoanalysis is, indeed, *the science of the unconscious mind," what* is consciousness, and for that matter, what is the relationship of reason to the general category of consciousness, and more specifically, how is self-consciousness conceived? These questions found little consideration as issues that required Freud's direct attention, for in the analytic encounter, "There is no need to discuss what is to be called conscious: it is removed from all doubt" (1933, 70). For him, consciousness, and more saliently, self-conscious insight, were constitutive to psychoanalysis; in regards to reason, as we have discussed, Freud was satisfied with its instrumental use, and as with the issue of self-consciousness, further discernment apparently was not necessary for his theoretical purposes.

Conclusion

Let us summarize and conclude: Since Freud makes no serious attempt to unify the various compartments of the psyche (allowing the topographical and economic formulations to provide the framework for ego functions), he is not committed to a *self*—some totality of personal identity—and thus he remained satisfied with a commonsensical, assumed notion of personhood. Taking this position, he directed his attention to another construction, his patient, who is addressed by the ordinary "you," "he," or "she," and who must translate private experience into a public (i.e.,

accessible) reflection. In deciphering the manifestations of the unconscious, the id appears as some alien creature, one that must be accounted
for and controlled. Indeed, analyst and analysand organize a conspiracy
to deal with this unwelcomed doppelgänger. From that starting point,
the analysand generates an autobiography built through an imaginative
reconstruction of memory and thereby comes to a revised comprehension
of a lived life and possibly a reconfiguration of personal identity.

For Freud, the analysand is framed by the therapeutic context. Inasmuch as relief of emotional suffering and attainment of psychic insight organized his efforts, he required no other telos for psychoanalysis, nor did he require a particular construct of personal identity. He
remained satisfied with the full realization of an *assumed* agency endowed
with certain characteristics: The ego qua ego—potentially rational, self-
conscious, and, to varying degrees, autonomous—always served as his
organizing point. Indeed, that was enough. After all, the Western philosophical heritage has exhibited various kinds of failure when probing the
ontological basis of selfhood, so Freud might fairly be excused for simply
dispensing with the problem, at least as classically presented. He just used
the commonsensical notion of personal identity, and that ends the matter. But philosophically this omitted elaboration is striking, for the basis
of Freud's conception of the mind thus remains a fractured entity, whose
integration becomes an unsolved challenge.

In some respects Freud's understanding presciently presented a view
that would contribute to postmodern conceptions of selfhood, whose
origins date at least to the mid-nineteenth century. As romanticism initiated its own exploration of identity, the self soon lost its boundaries.
Eventually the very question of an entity that might be designated "the
self" became highly problematic, and the authenticity of such an entity
challenged. Ironically, the Romantic deconstruction of the subjective self
generated by new claims for objectivity were complemented by an increasingly unsteady foundation for subjectivism originating from within
its own quarter. So what began in the high Romantic period as a trial of
self-examination culminated in discovering either a "stranger" at the seat
of the human soul (e.g., Emerson [Tauber 2003]) or an alienating, endless
self-centered self-consciousness (Tauber 2001, 203–29). Later commentators exposed a misplaced confidence in any such *entity* as a self, and,

instead, they shifted the vector of inquiry to another course. This line argued that the search for the self either was endless (and thus futile), empty (and consequently divorced from personal experience), radically indeterminate (and thereby rendered irrelevant), or, as in the Freudian case, essentially unnecessary and thus a misconceived category. Accordingly, as an artifact of social and historical contingencies, the unity of the self is at best a deceptive construction, a remnant of an older and discarded metaphysics.[18] Assaults on humanism (in the sense Freud espoused) similarly suffered ignoble dismissal (see Ruti 2006 for review and a poststructuralist defense). Further, autonomy and individualism, those crucial characteristics of the Romantic self, are thereby rendered impotent as the self as entity deconstructs in the postmodern world (Tauber 1994a, 201ff.).

Despite invocation by postmodernists (Mackenzie and Stoljar 2000), Freud finds no ready home in that camp inasmuch as he relies on key modernist precepts: In asserting the rational faculty of the ego and claiming autonomy that would lead to the individual's perfection, Freud implicitly embraced the Cartesian "thinking thing" understanding of selfhood, and furthermore (as discussed in chapters 4 and 5) he cannot be separated from the Kantian formulation, which leads to the basic functional psychoanalytic interpretative apparatus. So while he refrained from defining personal agency with explicit coordinates or foundations, and more directly exhibited how we are strangers to ourselves, Freudian psychoanalysis nevertheless serves an ego that through guided interpretations effectively enlists autonomous reason to achieve rational self-responsibility. In this sense, an unenlightened ego transmutes to an identity in which *self-identification* becomes a set point for therapeutic success.

So we conclude that although a *latent* conception of selfhood ultimately orders the narrative story that emerges in analysis, such an implicit identity never appears as a governing status in Freud's writings. The analysand is not construed beyond the ordinary pronominal agent, and in both psychoanalytic dimensions—search and reconciliation—the structure of the analytic process drives back to its Kantian origin, one that underlies the entire enterprise: (1) agency is not defined, only the conditions of knowing, (2) the reasoning faculty, which remains autonomous to follow its own course, again is left undetermined other than constitutive to ego-function, and (3) (from chapter 4) consciousness serves a neurophysiological observing function that processes inputs from unconscious forces through a representational language-like faculty, which translates these "sensory" data into meaningful understanding through the means of psychoanalysis. (This last feature freed Freud from Brentano's constraints and permitted the development of the psychoanalytic "science of the mind.")

From the vantage of later developments, we might better understand why the "self" (as such) was not a category Freud considered.[19] In terms of his psychology, the focus on drives, defenses, repressions, and so on, represents full attention on the individual, whose relationships serve as the métier of experience, but are hardly constitutive to personal identity. For Freud, the patient's "voice" focused his efforts as he probed the inner workings of the psyche, and in the process, the wider domain of personhood eclipsed his attention. Further, we have no evidence that Freud had any interest in understanding the *philosophical* question of personal identity. Nothing in his writings suggests that the issue ever arose, and thus we may fairly conclude that a commonsense notion of personal identity sufficed for his purposes. And even if he wished a clearer definition of selfhood, he would have little guidance from the leading philosophers of his own era—namely, Nietzsche (in one tradition) and Wittgenstein (in another; see chap. 4, note 2).

Nevertheless, an implicit understanding of personal identity operates throughout Freud's opera, one that sustains the authority of autonomous individuals to probe their inner emotion and thought, and as a result of this introspection, a new understanding of that experience conferred by a more acute self-consciousness opens the possibility of a therapeutic outcome. Indeed, the reflexive component of psychoanalytic self-consciousness becomes the means of achieving a revised sense of personal history and identity, as the ego, the pronominal agent-possessor of rationality, becomes increasingly self-aware of options and choices as a result of insight and reconstruction. Here we find the heart of Freud's humanist conception of human potential, and as discussed in the next chapter, the full moral dimension of psychoanalysis, in which the evolution from patient to liberated soul constitutes both a psychological project and an ethical venture. We conclude our study by characterizing Freud's moral mission.

Chapter Seven

The Ethical Turn

> Freud denied that psychoanalysis has "moral" implications
> beyond those of the scientific attitude in general ([Freud]
> 1933, pp.158 ff). Yet any comprehensive vision of human
> nature such as he provides must have implications for the
> nature of happiness, and for the relations of man's natural
> capacities to his normal or ideal state.
> —Ronald de Sousa (1974, 196)

THE CONTROVERSIES SWIRLING AROUND psychoanalysis for over a century may be reduced to the nature of its truth claims. Freud believed he followed strong empiricist methods in his analysis of signs and symptoms, and within the clinical tradition in which he trained and worked, he sought to achieve the same clinical status for psychoanalysis afforded other schools of psychiatry (Jones 1953–57; Decker 1977; Clark 1980; Gay 1988; Breger 2000; Makari 2008). The scientific standing of Freud's theory has suffered for many reasons, not the least of which results from the success of modern psychiatry in transforming itself into a molecular discipline. Supplied with sophisticated pharmacological agents and diagnostic techniques, mental illness has now been framed in various biochemical, biophysical, and anatomical formats conceptually comparable to other nonnervous diseases. In that molecular paradigm, "talking cures" have been relegated to the less severe adjustment and neurotic conditions, and there psychoanalysis has found its current home, albeit a waning method of intervention.

Because the scientific paradigm seems ill-suited for evaluating psychoanalysis as a clinical treatment, other criteria have been proposed (e.g., Edelman 1988), and in that reevaluation, the same basic questions have arisen about *what* was being studied and *how* Freud's techniques "worked," if they indeed were effective. Such discussions have applied interpretative philosophies that had been developed to examine the human sciences and address more general questions of the sociology of knowledge. Accordingly, in abandoning the problematic scientific question, some contemporary defenders of Freud have maintained that psychoanalysis embraces an entirely different agenda—a form of autobiography.

The analytic process relies on the skill, imagination, and creativity of the analyst and analysand in crafting a narration, which captures a reinterpreted life. This is not "science" as Freud presented his project, nor does it qualify as history or devolve into fiction. Instead, psychoanalysis becomes a means of individualization by serving to (1) identify a person freed of unwanted repressions and dysfunctions; (2) define articulated autonomous choices and goals; and (3) provide a moral compass by which values and self-identifications are established. In the psychoanalytic scenario, the ruling ego becomes both a subject of discourse and an object of control and change. This latter stage (the reflective assessment) occurs at a meta-level and is accomplished by constructing a story—a *meaningful* story—that establishes the reasons for behaviors, feelings, and choices of an ego living in the social world of interactions—benign and conflicted. In the relational context, the "I" then becomes "an interpretation: I become what I take the world to be" (Lear 1990, 162). On this view, psychoanalysis first presents a psychological description, and second, an interpreted narrative directed by a search for meaning. Narratives, of course, must be authored.

In the case of Freudian analysis, the narrative becomes a joint project, a collaboration of analysand and analyst. The personal chronicle, told and retold, interpreted and reinterpreted, follows a humanistic logic— human-valued, human-centered, human-derived, human-constructed, and human-intended—all oriented by human need. This humanistic orientation underlies psychoanalytic technique, a procedure that was devised to extract the elements of personal development and experience in order to reconfigure their significance and derive new meanings. From that insight, neurosis might be alleviated and even a revised notion of personal identity understood. Accordingly, the analysand becomes the protagonist of a psychic drama, playing a character whose history is revealed as a story. Autobiographical narrations carry certain commitments: a historical structure; an interpretative framework; a telos, which embeds a purpose or moral. Finally, linking this theme to the previous chapter, narration helps define and determine anticipated action, orient self-conscious thought, and unify notions of personal identity as a center of agency in relation to others (Oatley 2007).

Here we come to the inflection in our understanding of psychoanalysis, having shifted from a scientific venture to an ethical one. Each of these aspects of narrative may be contextualized ethically, and such a moral undertaking in the psychoanalytic setting points to a version of personal healing or, more generally, towards some perfectionist ideal. Interpretation and application of psychoanalytic knowledge occurs in a moral therapeutic framework not only through achieving self-knowledge, but also through a new ability to heighten self-awareness. In regarding the analysand's insight as an ethical project, we appreciate how Freud fulfilled his earliest humanistic aspirations, which in turn opens new pathways into his thought.

Freud's Narrative Project

In recent years, *narrative medicine* has emerged as a specialty interest of those seeking more effective humane approaches to patients, and from this base, "storytelling" has generated some analytic interest as a formal way of thinking about the analysand's autobiography (Rudnytsky and Charon 2008). This movement is a variant of an older and more broadly applied interpretative tradition, in which the psychoanalytic case history is understood as a *construction* (Spence 1992; Schafer 1985; Moore 1999), just as Freud had observed (1937a, 258–59). In the context of our discussion, the constructivist argument, in its broadest understanding, claims that the various forms of knowledge cannot be segregated from the complex cognitive and linguistic structures, nor the economic and political forces that support their activities, but are, in fact, heavily indebted to them. When personal reflection is added to this recipe, the constructivist perspective seems compelling. Accordingly, "what is" (i.e., the reality as described by the analytic narrative) cannot be understood independently from *how* that reality is reconstructed.[1] After all, knowledge formation is "filtered" through various conceptual and cognitive sieves, so that the interpretative claims become hopelessly conflated with the "facts" derived from recalled memory or the retelling of everyday conscious events or feelings. These issues were vociferously debated during the "memory wars" (Crews 1995), which contested the very core of the psychoanalytic rationale: Objective recollection lay beyond the individual, and thus reconstructed history is hopelessly mired in personal mythmaking that may serve any number of needs. Of course, rebuttals appeared in various forms (e.g., Edelson 1988; Forrester 1997; Lear 1998; Gomez 2005).

The constructivism debate has been heated because of the stakes: How might reality be conceived? This literature—both sympathetic and otherwise—has complemented another series of comments about the narrative structure of psychoanalysis, and that critique falls within a larger discussion about the character of interpretation. If the modern period witnessed a shift from domineering metaphysical questions to a primary concern with the possibility and nature of knowledge in the "epistemological turn," and twentieth-century Anglo-American philosophy preoccupied itself with the structure of language, word-world relationships, and analysis of meaning in the "linguistic turn," then the philosophical themes that dominated a major branch of contemporary European philosophy might be dubbed the "interpretive turn" (Hiley, Bohman, and Shusterman 1991). Indeed, Nietzsche's resolute epistle—"All is interpretation!"—fell on receptive ears and much of twentieth-century philosophy, criticism, and the arts followed his lead.[2] Where Freud might be situated in that story is not my specific concern here, and suffice it to note simply that psychoanalytic theory had both a profound influence *on* the application of hermeneutics to literary theory, the arts, cinema, and so on, and at the same time Freud's opus became the subject *of* important hermeneutical critiques.

From the hermeneutic point of view, both psychoanalytic theory and practice are seen as conceiving a life history outlining the dynamics of behavior, which follows a logic of its own interiority and whose validity is decided by criteria of its own coherence and veracity. For instance, Paul Ricoeur (1970; 1984; 1988; 1994) applied hermeneutical principles to argue that the psychoanalytic narrative sets itself the task of holding the ego's requirement for coherence (e.g., Freud 1913b, 95), consistency (e.g., Freud 1926c, 159), and constancy (Ricoeur 1988, 246–47), while

at the same time overcoming the resistances that would allow reinterpreted life experience and present behaviors.[3] Jacques Lacan developed
the narrative character of psychoanalysis as a linguistic series, in which
analytic technique is understood as "oriented in a field of language and
ordered in relation to the function of speech" (2002, 39). Accordingly,
the unconscious functions linguistically (rather than symbolically or
instinctually) and thus becomes a kind of linguistic organ (Dor 1998),
which in dialogue "engages" with other language centers (interpretative
or expressive). So from the Lacanian perspective, psychotherapy may
be understood

> not as a search for a mythical "self" or "truth," but as a set of discourses which
> overlap and interpenetrate, and continually refer to themselves. Psychoanalysis
> has the merit of being sensitive to its own discourses and their interrelations;
> in other words the analyst and the patient are able in the end to ask the compel-
> ling question: "Who is talking?" (Horrocks 2001, 17)[4]

As discussed in the previous chapter, the subject of the narrative, and the
selfsame author, have different personifications, but here we are concerned
only with the rational, interpretative ego. That agent remembers, reconstructs, and revises her personal history as analysis proceeds. The autobiography evolves slowly and piecemeal as different parts coalesce to signify
different understandings, and as each part assumes its respective role, the
whole takes on revised character, and, of course as the whole changes, so
do the meanings of the various parts. This is hermeneutics at work.

From this perspective, psychoanalysis "rewrites" the analysand's autobiography, and in the process strives for a therapeutic success. The process of revising a narrative based on analytic insight follows an analogous
strategy used by Otto Neurath to describe theory construction in science:
"We are like sailors who have to rebuild their ship at sea, without ever
being able to dismantle it in dry-dock and reconstruct it from the best
components" (1983, 92). In other words, new boards (interpretations)
must take their place with older planks that eventually will be discarded,
but until then, the new structures must be built piecemeal, and as new interpretations take hold, further revisions then require further remodeling.

This "shipbuilding" designed to arrive at some narrative truth was explicitly developed by Freud's concept of *Nachträglichkeit* (Freud 1985;

Modell 1990; Moore 1999), which refers to the reconstruction of memory to serve a current psychic state.[5] In a remarkable letter to Fliess (December 6, 1896), Freud explained how memory is reconfigured according to such emotional requirements:

> As you know, I am working on the assumption that our psychic mechanism has come into being by a process of stratification: the material present in the form of memory traces being subjected from time to time to a *rearrangement* in accordance with fresh circumstances—to a *retranscription*. Thus what is essentially new about my theory is the thesis that memory is present not once but several times over, that it is laid down in various kinds of indications. (1985, 207)

The plasticity of memory results from the tenet that "*consciousness and memory are mutually exclusive*" (1985, 208). One reading of these claims is that memory and consciousness occupy distinct sectors of the mind, and "translations" must occur to bring the historical domain into the present. Accordingly, the past may be recalled by the psychic rules governing conscious behavior, while analysis is designed to uncover a more accurate psychic history by piercing memory's isolation. In this letter Freud went on to posit that as individuals progress through their lives, periodic recalibrations of the life history are required, and if such "translations" are unsuccessful or unaddressed, then lingering psychic material remains behind. Thus "a failure of translation" is a "repression," which results from an avoidance of "unpleasure" (1985, 208). (He further postulated that painful memories follow either normal or pathological courses, a clinical appraisal we need not further consider.)

Thus the analysand's life history and the psychic defenses shielding that history mold memory for presentation to consciousness, which in turn rescrutinizes memory as the object of its own inquiry. As Freud wrote to Fliess a few months later,

> Everything goes back to the reproduction of scenes. Some can be obtained directly, others always by way of fantasies set up in front of them. The fantasies stem from things that have been *heard* but understood *subsequently* [*nachträglich*], and all their material is of course genuine. They are protective structures, sublimations of the facts, embellishments of them, and at the same time serve for self-relief. (1985, 239)

Thus, reason probes memory to draw out revised and even new remembrances, which, in the course of action, rewrite the psychic story. Freud himself recognized that the reconstruction was, at best, an approximation of earlier events and experiences, inasmuch as the original dream, trauma, or conflict is no longer accessible. Sifting the evidence—albeit partial or distorted—a reconfigured story emerges (one guided by Ricoeur's principles of ego coherence, consistency, and constancy [1970]), whose legitimacy is ultimately verified in therapeutic terms. Admitting to the mythic character of this revision, Freud commented,

> If the analysis is carried out correctly, we produce in him an assured conviction of the truth of the construction which achieves the same therapeutic result as a recaptured memory. The problem of what the circumstances are in which this occurs and of how it is possible that what appears to be an incomplete substitute would nevertheless produce a complete result—all of this is a matter for a later enquiry. (Freud 1937a, 265–66)

That later requirement was explored by Freud's followers within the psychoanalytic context, which would be buffeted by those who argued that language *failed* to effectively capture reality (most pointedly the personal reality of experience and thought), because language either ensnared thought (Wittgenstein), created obstructions between Dasein and its world (Heidegger), fixed meaning *between* language and thought/experience in *différance* (Derrida), and most directly relevant to our own consideration, failed in fully representing psychic reality (Lacan). Thus what Freud had perceived as illusionary interpretations offered by the capture of experience in some incomplete, if not distorting, second manifold, similarly appeared concomitantly as a deep philosophical imbroglio in both analytical and continental schools of twentieth-century philosophy.

Derrida dubbed the quest to overcome this fundamental discrepancy between language and the reality it describes the "singular desire of the philosopher":

> All communicative acts are anchored by a fundamental reference to a lost but coveted origin.... [This fact points to] the danger of an illusion at the heart of much philosophical thought and the distinction between reproducing that illusion and revealing it as illusion.... That illusion ... is that the possibility of pure

repetition promised by the signifier can in fact be redeemed in reality.... Inauthentic thinking, in this view, is a thinking founded on that illusion. [In contrast,] duplicitous truth recognizes its own duplicity.... Those interpreters who understand the object of interpretation to be itself not an object in the world, an imaginary answer to a symbolic question, but rather the constantly renewed product of an interpretation already at work making the world—those interpreters have read the philosopher's singular desire and seen in it their own. (Egginton 2007, 4–6)

Emmanuel Levinas's quip, "The best thing about philosophy is that it fails" (1986, 22) succinctly points to both the conundrum of the philosopher's desire and, in terms of our own considerations, the elusive character of the signified explored by psychoanalysis. On this view, psychoanalysis may well take its place among those philosophies that recognize the character of interpretation as an ongoing, endless pursuit of the real, whose inquiry not only must remain ever-mindful that language, and self-conscious thought itself, can only approximate capturing "the true," since ultimately language fails in that endeavor.[6] Freud did not think of *language* as restrictive, but rather that the *signs* of the unconscious and the *methods* for comprehending it left the analyst with weak means of decipherment. After all, the unconscious follows its own laws, and translating them into conscious understanding must be indirect and ultimately interpretative. Indeed, for Freud, "The [fundamental] work of analysis involves an *art of interpretation*" (1925a, 41). Note his word choice: *art*.

Although interpretation, as Freud observed, assumes the most fundamental tenet of a new psychology, *narration* per se appears rarely in Freud's writings. He certainly was aware that narration compromised the radically objective scientific report sought:

I have not always been a psychotherapist. Like other neuro-pathologists, I was trained to employ local diagnoses and electro-prognosis, and it still strikes me as strange that the case histories I write should read like short stories and that, as one might say, they lack the serious stamp of science. I must console myself with the reflection that the nature of the subject is evidently responsible for this, rather than any preference of my own. The fact is that local diagnosis and electrical reactions lead nowhere in the study of hysteria, whereas a detailed description of mental processes such as we are accustomed to find in the words

of imaginative writers enables me, with the use of a few psychological formu-
las, to obtain at least some kind of insight into the course of that affection.
(Breuer and Freud 1895, 160–61)

Freud thus resigned himself, and psychoanalysis, to the limitations of
"the nature of the subject" and recognized that the delimiting element
was the analysand himself. Therapeutic results thus depend on "the subject's *disposition* for narration" (Reeder 2002, 102). The story is never
completed, for the "talking cure" is an elusive, interminable task, coter-
minous with life, an autobiography continuously rewritten (Goldberg
1988,135, 169). Indeed, the interpretative process itself, eschewing any
finality, becomes the focus of the analysis. "Therefore the personal narrative can have only *one* fundamental form: *Incessant gathering* oscillating
between decomposition (analysis) and synthesis" (Goldberg 1988, 105).
Or from another vantage, "The truth of psychoanalysis is nothing other
than deconstruction, and vice versa (Egginton 2007, 11).

The "truth" attained through analysis serves a particular purpose:
personal narration becomes part of a new creation, where experience is
gathered and framed within an overarching theme directed towards dis-
tilling meaning (discussed below). A new *story* becomes constitutive to a
new *life* (Bruner 1987). The inquiry then is directed to answer the basic
moral question, Who am I? In this sense, the very act of interpretation,
the movement of conscious thought that captures unconscious intention
and derives meaning, constitutes an ethical act (Rieff 1959; Reeder 2002;
2004; Egginton 2007). With the new rendition, there occurs a shuffling of
the psychic foundations, which never settle into their old configuration,
and with that shift, self-understanding prompts a revised view of oneself
and the social-psychic world one inhabits. The moral inquiry beginning
with the identity question has been altered, deeply and fundamentally.
(Of course, the authenticity or honesty of the endeavor is never given, so
the "truth" of the interpretation is always in question, but for our discussion, the moral inquiry is an assumed "best faith" effort, and must be
judged on that basis.)[7]

If we ask *why* the analytic pursuit occurs in the first place, we can easily
follow the ancient's own dictum: the "philosopher's desire" to know the
real and to glimpse the truth. That imperative is captured in the psycho-

analytic credo, "Wo Es war, soll Ich werden" (Freud 1940a, 86), which the *Standard English* translation renders, "Where id was, there ego shall be" (Freud 1933, 80). A more accurate translation, "Where it [Id] was, I *must* become" (Egginton 2007, 12; emphasis added), moves psychoanalysis from an epistemological endeavor to a moral one: *Soll* implies "duty" or "obligation," and Freud thereby invoked an ethical imperative to explain the entire thrust of psychoanalysis. *Why* one is so obliged remains unsaid, but here an inference seems fair: If Freud was, indeed, the reluctant philosopher I have portrayed, then I surmise that he understood (or at least intuited) that *constitutive* to the ego's role of mediating the reality principle, summoning controls and making choices, the ethical must be invoked. At one level, the superego becomes the judge and jury of the ego's choices and actions and thus assumes the dominant role in character formation, or in another parlance, in establishing an ego ideal (Rendon 1986). (See above, Introduction, note 4.) However, as a result of self-reflection and a new assessment of this unconscious source of authority, the ego, through *rational* analysis, may come to a different moral understanding, one that modulates and controls the demands of a superego at variance with newfound purpose and potential. Just as libidinal forces are channeled and controlled through successful psychoanalysis, so might authoritarian ones be as well.

The Moral Dimension

Whatever claims made by the superego, id, or social mores, the essential function of the ego is to know the world and navigate it within the strictures imposed by external contingencies, the so-called reality principle. Among those choices, ethics plays a fundamental role, and in this sense, the "obligation" to know how the unconscious influences the ego's life becomes part of a morality play in which the ego, in any case, *must* fulfill its assigned role. For Freud, to *know* the demands of unconscious desires and drives fulfilled the primary function of consciousness, namely, to arrive at informed, rational decisions. And that role is fundamentally an ethical one, inasmuch as in the galaxy of options, ethical value and rational insight guide the enlightened agent.[8] And more, the ego works as the agent of normative constraint not just because the reality principle

206 of 344 is grounded

is grounded in social controls, but because the self-conscious, self-aware analysand must assert self-responsibility for the expressions of his or her unconscious life (Trilling 1972). Freud thus again declared a major precept of Western morality. To control the passions constituted a major theme of ancient Greek philosophy, and in that context, to act morally was to act with moderation and constraint on the basis of intelligible understanding (Naussbaum 1994). In the contemporary setting, psychoanalysis provides an articulation of the same goals and seeks to guide the search for emancipation with the same telos of self-understanding. These considerations segue into the most fitting philosophical setting for Freud, namely, ethics.

With the freedom psychoanalysis affords the successful analysand, the personae presented to the world drop away under the scrutiny of analysis. No longer content with comforting rationalizations and stories, the analytic process demands acknowledgment of trauma and disappointment; conflict and fear; disguise and deception. Jurgen Reeder refers to this movement, from the opaque state of inquiry to the clarity of acceptance, as "the ethical moment"—the meeting point not only of acknowledging who one is, but a *reconciliation* with that "person within." This shift represents a profoundly *moral* transposition: "The ethical dimension of reconciliation resides in the fact that after all the stories have been told and retold, a demand for responsibility arises—the obligation to respond and carry the full weight of his [the analysand's] self-understanding" (Reeder 2002, 244). The analytic question, "Who am I?" has thus been partially answered with the acknowledgment, "This too is me" (247).[9]

If introspective analysis yields a reconceived notion of personal identity, then a revised understanding of what an individual has been subject to, and is now responsible for, heralds a realignment of choices—ethical choices. Decisions are no longer dictated by a tyrannical superego or cunning unconscious drives, but instead emerge from a moral domain relatively freed of emotional shackles applied in an earlier history. In radically new terms, Freud presented another means of defining personhood, and in that reconceptualization, he offered a portrait of moral agency that defies the simple determinism with which he is so often accused. He acknowledged this reading in a call to arms: The analysand "must find the *courage* to direct his attention to the phenomena of his illness. His illness itself must no longer seem to him contemptible, but must become an enemy worthy of his *mettle*, a piece of his personality" (1914b, 152; emphasis added). From that battle, resolve and reconciliation, distinctly nonepistemic activities, constitute the "end game" of psychoanalysis, where the "science" leading to analytic insight provides the forum in which the battle takes place.

The battle itself is the subject of ethical action, in which the analysand chooses "himself over his own alienation" (Reeder 2002, 235–36). Indeed, the subject of ethical action is always at work, for unlike the analytic process, "where everything must take place in a deferred mode— *nachträglich—after* the event, *after* the experience, *after* the anticipation" (Reeder 2002, 244), reconciliation occurs in the *present*. The emphasis on the lived present moment, the so-called ethical moment, turns the analytic interpretation from a historical reconstruction (a narrative) into an ongoing recognition of a psychic reality lived in the present. Accordingly, successful psychoanalysis moves beyond what has been learned, to what has been accomplished, or as Reeder writes, it is "not *what* I have realized, but the fact that I have *done* so" (244). The doing is dependent upon autonomous reason, which is not only committed to the inquiry but also in acknowledging its result, takes the responsibility of accepting the consequences of those discoveries (Lear 1990, 168–77).[10] So Freud, like Aristotle before him, would ask not, What shall I *do*? but rather, What shall I *be*?

Ironically perhaps, this ethical dimension concerning moral agency remained latent in Freud's writings. However, summarizing the ethics of psychoanalysis is hardly a difficult task. As a first approximation, "moral" is used here to capture the understanding that psychoanalysis seeks personal improvement, self-definition, and the freedom of choice independent from coercive factors; further, this healthier state falls on a continuum of human evaluations structured by a set of values. Indeed, values define the character of one's life experience, so to pose behaviors as neurotic, for instance, already assumes a certain spectrum of normal. However, as Freud observed,

> a normal ego ... like normality in general, [is] an ideal fiction.... Every normal
> person, in fact, is only normal on the average. His ego approximates to that of
> the psychotic in some part or other and to a greater or lesser extent; and the
> degree of its remoteness from one end of the series and of its proximity to the

other will furnish us with a provisional measure of what we have so indefinitely termed an "alteration of the ego." (1937b, 235)

Therapy directs itself to help shift the analysand towards that "normal" pole, but more fundamentally towards a state of living that fulfills personal goals and potentials. Indeed, *normal* is not the issue, *health* is.

Psychoanalysis, as a *therapeutic* intervention, commits itself to limiting perversity, relieving anxiety, converting neurotic behavior to more ordinary life activities, and so on, and each of these parameters of psychic function must in turn be "tuned" to a functional standard. So Freud, by the necessity of his clinical logic, defined, diagnosed, and treated *pathological* psychic behaviors. Necessarily, his descriptions were subject to relative and personal factors: Standards of *function*—again, in a normative construal—must be established, and within these standards, interpretative (individual, and perhaps idiosyncratic) evaluations are operative. Because function is so overdetermined by human evaluations and judgments about those functions, that is, within the context of social and psychological factors, the criteria of "pathological" must remain flexible inasmuch as standards shift historically and culturally (e.g., Canguilhem 1989; Caplan 1993; Caplan, McCartney, and Sisti 2004). Disease, especially mental illness, has notorious cultural determinants, which may change over time, and with those shifts, redefinitions of what constitutes significant dysfunction may also be reconceived (e.g., Kleinman 1988; Shorter 1992). Indeed, Freud himself could not escape this judgment,[11] and the bias of his views has highlighted how hidden prejudice and cultural standards may determine clinical appraisals. In this reevaluation, the subjective character of the clinical narrative has been emphasized, as well as its "success." That the interpretation was "correct" could, in any final accounting, only be established by the achievement of some therapeutic assessment, which also suffers contextualization by the very same criteria that defined the pathological in the first place. In short, Freud's theory cannot escape subjective value judgments, which include determining the success of therapeutic outcomes themselves.[12]

After all, psychoanalytic practice must proceed in a normative cultural universe, where *normal* is inextricable from the value structure bequeathed by family, culture, historical forces, and political identities, to name the most prominent. Value refers to the way one thinks about choices among various options that fulfill some chosen intention. Simply, human choice is fundamentally value-based, and while the ethics of common experience remain largely undeclared, they order the ever-present challenges of the way we live and express our being. In the world of the neurotic, those choices become even more pressing. Psychoanalysis must pursue its craft within this complex value structure pitting individual desires and needs against communal requirements and standards. Freud's project cannot be conceived as somehow immune to this social context that makes psychoanalysis a most *human* science.

Freud thus employed a complicated moral calculus. On the one hand, he rejected the notion of "normal," as some idealized category: "We have been compelled to conclude that for the judgment of psychic events the category normal-pathological is as inadequate as the earlier all-inclusive category good-bad" (Freud and Bullitt 1967, xv). On the other hand, as the pathological became the focus of interest, "normal" could hardly be ignored inasmuch as the entire pathological axis has been characterized through descriptions of ideal character types, developmental achievements, and normal personality organization (Macklin 1973). To further complicate the issue, seemingly closely aligned concepts of abnormal and pathological demand multi-dimensional considerations inasmuch as the normal and the pathological do not necessarily fall along the same axis (e.g., homosexuality, which might be construed as abnormal, is not necessarily pathological [Robinson 2000]). The critical point for Freud was not to pass moral judgment on his patients but to help them live more satisfying lives. After all, morality and mental health are not necessarily coincident (Rieff 1959; Hartmann 1960).

Psychoanalytic strategy thus couples a method to define the history and psychic forces that brought the individual to the couch, an object of scrutiny, and an ethical telos, one where self-analysis itself became a moral venture—to free the analysand from debilitating repressive mechanisms of one sort or another. This search is governed by an "ethic of honesty" (Rieff 1959) pursued with a finely tuned "Stoic-Epicurean notion of balance" (Wallace 1986, 118). Drawing on these formulations, Freud devised a method that employs self-consciousness to create a narrative in which the analysand might live relieved of neurotic anxiety and other emotional dysfunctions. Psychoanalysis thus strives to achieve functional criteria, which cannot be reduced to abstract deontological principles or standard cultural mores. Freud's psychology champions the analysand's individuality, and this too represents a particular choice, one grounded in a liberal ideology and a humanist perspective.

For Freud, consistent with his positivist ideals, human personality is the topic of psychology; human character is the domain of ethics. Only later post-Freudians promoted an ethics of analysis, which were explicitly framed by humanistic values, namely, psychic growth and self-fulfillment (Fromm 1947; Horney 1950) and existentialist themes (Binswanger 1963; Weisman 1965); or framed by a linguistic account (Lacan 1992) or a relational notion of otherness (Ricoeur 1994). From these later perspectives, uncovering and deciphering the instinctual character of the unconscious, while comprising the thrust of Freudian *analysis*, cannot account for the moral influence of his theory, which ultimately was directed at human freedom (albeit, limited by the ongoing negotiation demanded by social realities [Meissner 1996]). This view then subordinates defining the role of the superego, tracking the biological basis of morality, establishing the psychodynamics of ethical behaviors, or negotiating the interests of the individual against competing demands of a challenging sociocultural environment. While each set of problems obviously pertains to understanding the ethical dimension of psychoanalysis, I wish to emphasize another aspect of psychoanalysis's moral project, namely *the process itself* as the moral rationale of the entire endeavor.

On this view, Freud's technique proceeds by constructing a historical narrative through various interpretations offered by a self-conscious ego in answer to the social and existential question, Who am I? The "answer" paradoxically follows Nietzsche's proclamation to "become what one is" while not having "the faintest idea of *what* one is" (Nietzsche 1967b, 254). Identity is thus both *discovered and created* as an ongoing project without firm prescription or dictates. This more encompassing project radically shifts perspective from the analysand as object of inquiry, to the subject who inquires and creates both understanding and identity; in short, the experiencing person, who becomes an individual. Indeed, "Psychoanalysis discovered that individual freedom requires freedom to become an individual.... Being an individual is a psychological achievement" (Lear 1990, 22). Thus, from the Freudian point of view, achieving personal autonomy completes the psychoanalytic investigation (see Introduction, note 4).

This focus on the individual as autonomous captures the analysand in a configuration where disabling neurotic impediments have been dispelled. After all, it is the *me* who acts; it is the *he* who makes choices; it is the *she* who establishes the values that guide behavior to the extent that behavior is selected and self-consciously evaluated. Epistemological criteria are obviously operative, but the *philosophical* question of personal identity from the perspective of personal action becomes a *moral* identification, not an epistemological one. The individualization of the person, the achievement of autonomy (at least from the Kantian-Freudian understanding) is the basis of ethics. "Moral" in this sense refers to (1) the value structure upon which identity becomes manifest, (2) the ways in which an agent makes choices and assumes responsibility for his or her actions in the context of personal identity, and (3) how an individual is identified socially or self-understood psychologically. In short, personal identity emerges in the identification by the selfsame ego and relationship to others through his or her behavior and speech acts. And underlying all of these aspects is the very possibility of moral action as residing in a self-conscious sense of autonomy and self-responsibility.

Psychoanalysis thus offers its own contribution to the ancient precept of the Delphi oracle, "Know thyself," which Socrates gave specific method and moral form: "The unexamined life is not worth living" (*Apology*). His critical pursuit has served as the guiding tenet of Western philosophy since the ancients, and while Freud's seminal contributions to contemporary thought may be traced into various avenues, I emphasize this moral sector of self-knowledge, which derives from the theory's central dogma of suspicion (Ricoeur 1970): If humans are strangers to themselves and psychoanalysis is dedicated to finding the person within, then analysis becomes an ethical venture, one in which an ongoing process of discovery, acceptance, and possible reform converge to reconfigure self-understanding and identity by

> the replacing of what is unconscious by what is conscious, the translation of what is unconscious into what is conscious.... [W]e lift the repressions, we

remove the preconditions for the formation of symptoms, we transform the pathogenic conflict into a normal one for which it must be possible somehow to find a solution. All that we bring about in a patient is this single psychical change. (Freud 1916–17, 435)

The psychoanalytic venture thus eventuates in a new life story, one reexamined historically and redirected into a purposeful future. Freud wrote of this movement in his *Introductory Lectures*: "The neurotic who is cured has really become another man, though at bottom, of course, he has remained the same; that is to say, he has become what he might have become at best under the most favorable conditions" (1916–17, 435).

In the resulting self-identification, *the I* becomes an interpreting faculty, whose articulation of thought into speech forms the nexus of human *being*. As a seeker of *be-ing,* meaning assumes the organizing telos. "To be more specific, we could say that *meaning is the dedicated 'intention' informing and guiding the act of interpreting*" (Reeder 2002, 55).[13] Indeed, how does the psychoanalytic experience affect human *being*, or more plainly, how does the analytic process result in placing the analysand within his or her larger world?

For Freud, science, with its claims to certainty and truth, offered at least a partial means of addressing (and perhaps providing an answer) to the dilemma of how the world might be understood. Given his enthusiastic embrace of science as truth-seeking, he thought that its methods might profitably be applied to other social endeavors as models of inquiry and standards for truth claims. Indeed, Freud was one of those who attempted to apply scientific standards in service to this larger project, and as we have already discussed, he did so for both epistemological and moral reasons: *Truth* was scientific truth, which meant not only that science captured *reality*, it did so correctly, and here we see the epistemological project slipping into the moral discourse. "Right" equals *correct* epistemologically, and "right" equals *good* in ethical terms. So, beyond the rhetorical power of invoking scientific methods, Freud was firmly committed to certain criteria of objective study for the authority—epistemological and moral—that clinical science offered the budding new field. Note that Freud rejected a false choice—knowledge *or* romance, science *or* narrative—and instead presented a synthesis. Both modes of experience are crucial in fulfilling his quest for psychic reality. The "ethics" of *understanding* drives the quest to know. This moral venture of "seeing"—one developed, exercised, and pursued—becomes an act of self-actualization, an act of self-definition. Psychoanalytic knowledge obviously remains in the employ of that agenda, so Freud's own notion of science belied the more profound purpose of self-knowledge. On this view, scientific knowledge was in the employ of this deeper moral agenda (Tauber 1999).

In the Freudian universe, unified reason would bequeath a unified moral vision, because knowledge leads to, or provides the basis for, moral choice. The value one sets on kinds of knowledge and their respective placement in a hierarchy of significance had been prominent issues of debate since the Romantics, who had identified the narrow confines in which positivism would ensnarl human experience. *Meaning*, they insisted, must be sought outside an objective knowledge of nature. Freud might well have explicitly "humanized" his project, and instead of presenting the analytic setting as a modified scientific laboratory, he could have deliberately sought the pathways by which objectivity can be mixed with the personal and thereby achieve what Michael Polanyi later called "personal knowledge" (1962; Tauber 2009). On this view, science *and* narrative are vehicles of knowing or expressing. One might assign them as tools of an interpretative faculty, which confers *meaning*. From this perspective, meaning cannot directly arise from epistemology or any of its branches, but rather arises from a dynamic synthesis—the moral orientation of the knower who weaves facts into their fabric of signification (Tauber 2001; 2009). Thus the epistemological and ethical components of Freud's theory must be scrutinized separately and then put back together into a moral epistemology (Tauber 2001; 2005; 2009). Psychoanalysis joins these two domains in a complex dialectic, where the standing of knowledge depends on the fixture of values arising from, and responding to, human need. Indeed, psychoanalytic facts become elements in a narrative created by a constellation of subjective interpretations, and in this sense, Freud offered the analysand the opportunity to create his or her own narrative—an autobiography based upon return, recognition, and reconciliation. Thus the rigid separation of facts and values collapses on the analytic couch, for no psychic fact exists independent of its interpretation.

According to this perspective, Freud fits within the orbit of those who sought a more inclusive epistemology than championed by the positivists, for in the larger philosophical context of his time, he practiced a form of investigation in which the subject-object divide, formed in radical opposition, was countered with an attempt to integrate human nature in terms of human value (as discussed in chapter 3). He thereby joined twentieth-century philosophers in their own synthetic efforts, while at the same time ostensibly committed to positivist tenets:[14] On the one hand, Freud sought to establish a science of the mind, and on the other hand, psychoanalysis directs itself towards its ethical mandate, one that is inseparable from the epistemology that drives it. This integrative project rests at the foundation of Freud's ambitions.

And while Freud left much clinical work for others to complete, the moral project continues essentially as he formulated it. This interpretation finds grounding in a philosopher Freud might have profitably read, John Dewey. According to Dewey, who wrote at about the same time Freud published *The Ego and the Id* (1923), all sciences

> are a part of disciplined moral knowledge so far as they enable us to understand the conditions and agencies through which man lives.... Moral science is not something with a separate province. It is physical, biological and historic knowledge placed in a human context where it will illuminate and guide the activities of men. (2002, 296)

Thus for Dewey, no firm demarcation between moral judgments and other kinds were possible, for "every and any act is within the scope of morals, being a candidate for possible judgment with respect to its better-or-worse quality" (279). He thus widened the scope of "morals" to value judgments writ large: "Morals has to do with all activity into which alternative possibilities enter. For wherever they enter a difference between better and worse arises" (278).[15] On this view, Freud's science must be seen as part of a larger moral enterprise; namely, the science Freud so passionately followed only becomes meaningful within the context of this human universe.

The necessity of revising positivism's hold on the imagination of human investigation of the natural and human worlds arises from addressing the metaphysical schism of the self peering *at* the world. Intuitions of wholeness, integration, and coherence suggest, perhaps require, some reconfigured relationship of the knowing agent and her object of inquiry. From this point of view, psychoanalysis might well offer a response to Dewey's acute diagnosis:

> The problem of restoring integration and cooperation between man's beliefs about the world in which he lives and his beliefs about the values and purposes that should direct his conduct is the deepest problem of modern life. It is the problem of any philosophy that is not isolated from that life. (1984, 204)

And this is why Dewey strikingly maintained that "meaning is wider in scope as well as more precious in value than is truth" (1931, 4). In demoting the centrality of "truth," he insisted on its *use* in the service of meaning. On this view, psychoanalysis enlists in that pursuit, one that reaches into the deepest metaphysics of personhood. Instead of a science of the mind narrowly conceived, Freud's project then becomes discovering and then defining a person's moral standing. Perhaps a general intuition of those possibilities has resisted the scientism that would place psychoanalysis in the ashbin of discarded psychologies. Philosophers would do well to further explore the portals Freud opened, not so much to justify his own efforts or the theory's truth claims, but for the common purpose of better defining the human predicament and exploring the possibilities for its rescue, despite Freud's pessimistic prognostication.

On my view, what remains central and enduring in the Freudian legacy is the ethics he left in the wake of his theory. The interaction of two psychic centers—an unconsciousness pitted against the acknowledged and authorized identity of the self-conscious analysand—serves as the foci of psychoanalysis, and from the intercourse drawing from these dual loci a refracted life emerges, one disassembled and then reconstructed and retold as an identity markedly altered from the pre-analytic ego. This process is moral in several ways: (1) the analysis is structured by certain normative values, (2) the process itself carries an ancient ethical precept, "Know thyself," and (3) from that position self-awareness permits, even commands, self-responsibility. With such an orientation, a philosophical critique of psychoanalysis entails probing the relationship of the epistemological character of the knowing agent with the agency of moral expression. When psychoanalysis is understood in these terms, it becomes an *ethical* project in the manner Ricoeur (1970) and Taylor (1989) have explored.

Ironically perhaps, Freud's "scientific" project became a moral endeavor. Regarded in this light, Freud, "the reluctant philosopher," assumes his most favorable philosophical standing as a moralist. The original scientific project is then eclipsed, because the moral agent cannot be objectified, nor her rationality understood other than in its phenomenological expressions. So on this reading, the particulars of Freud's psychological descriptions may be subordinated to a larger ethical enterprise: He created the most influential depiction of human beings offered in the twentieth century, one that has guided contemporary understandings well beyond the couch and past the strictures of his own biological and anthropological commitments. That description depends on rational insight, moral purpose, and ultimately a promissory note of personal redemption.

So Freudianism may be understood as a response to Nietzsche's challenge: In the most general sense, a "self-overcoming" guides a renewed human life, in which the growth and development of self-defined potentials capture the creativity and vigor of health. In Nietzsche's manifesto, false constraints must be shed, and part of that liberation includes a transvaluation of values and ethics. Morals are no longer bestowed by authority, tradition, theological dogma, or ideology, but must be conceived in terms of personal responsibility. That tradition, so clearly declared by Kierkegaard, extended by Nietzsche, and further developed by Heidegger (Ruti 2006, 121ff.), embraces a romantic hope of human growth and possibility, which underlies Freud's own vision. Once posed in these terms, a fundamental split opens: On one side, analysis allows humans degrees of freedom as conferred by their autonomous reason and through their putative free will; deliberate choices assume personal authority. We might call this the *therapeutic triumph* or *Nietzsche's credo*, because beyond the particulars of Freud's theory and methods, this visionary promise relies on the successful (i.e., optimistic) outcome of the analysis.

On the other side of the chasm, "therapy" is doomed from the outset. Putting aside Freud's detractors, who debunked the very legitimacy of Freud's psychiatry, a diverse critical chorus contests the possibility of attaining the self-authority psychoanalysis offered. Most famously, Foucault argued that the extent of autonomous choice and self-definition is fraught with illusion because of group political and cultural constraints that cannot be shed. Insight then becomes, at best, rationalization, and at worst, confirmation of the ruling ideology or social metaphysics (Foucault 1970). When extended to psychological maladies, these too were products of the culture, and diagnosis became a means of control (i.e., defining the normal and punishing the aberrant) (Foucault 2003; 2006a; 2006b). Let us call this position the *illusion of freedom* or *Foucault's pessimism*.[16]

Another path, one that meanders down one side of the cliff and then ascends an elusive trail, factors out the issue of therapeutic efficacy altogether, at least in its most direct clinical meanings. This alternative pathway construes the freedom conferred by analysis similar to Spinoza's conception of insight's power: While deterministic elements forever lodged in the psyche may still command the analysand, *knowledge of* those dark forces is liberation in itself, that is, knowing the extent and the means by which one's frustration or illusion about free will may be accounted. By this calculus, the analysis itself is freedom enough. This we will call *Spinoza's dictum*. I endorse this perspective, because from the *ethical* standpoint, the inquiry, irrespective of its therapeutic effectiveness, confers a compelling moral purpose to psychoanalysis.

Spinoza, much like Freud, fully acknowledged that because humans are part of nature, the moralist must be a naturalist, and thus understanding "the passions" comprised the first step in living an ethical life (Hampshire 1962, 121ff). Accordingly, dissecting the emotional basis of human behavior firmly places the moral project in its appropriate naturalistic setting. From this perspective, Freud closely follows Nietzsche's basic construction of human motive and higher intentions and, moreover, he adopted the commitment to self-overcoming as a moral imperative *derived* from a biological characterization of human nature.[17]

The second step, in which understanding frees humans from enslavement to those emotions, is, of course, the core of Freud's own project, which Spinoza famously describes in the preface of part 4 of the *Ethics*:

> Man's lack of power to moderate and restrain the affects [emotions] I call
> Bondage. For the man who is subject to affects is under the control, not of

himself, but of fortune, in whose power he so greatly is that often, though
he sees himself the better for himself, he is still forced to follow the worse.
(1985, 543)

But in what sense can understanding confer freedom? How, if humans
are fundamentally organic, might they liberate themselves from the determinism of the natural world? As I have discussed, this issue became
pivotal for Kant's philosophical project, which was based precisely on
moral action freed from naturalistic determinism. The autonomy of
Reason served as the explicit lynchpin of Kant's entire enterprise, and
similarly for Freud, reason's capacity to remove itself from the causative
chain imposed by the unconscious enabled judgment and choice to be
exercised. From Spinoza's point of view, to understand causes can never
be perfect, and thus freedom of the will cannot be complete, but to the
extent understanding is attained, insight mitigates the conflict and pain
inflicted by unknown and unbridled passions. Further, comprehension
directs those destructive forces to avenues better controlled through rational understanding. This same position served as the bedrock of Freud's
own formulation of psychoanalysis (Frank 1977).

Finally, neither Spinoza nor Freud would pass moral (i.e., cultural)
judgment on what they saw as clinical malfunctions (i.e., arising from the
natural domain). This formulation does not mean neuroses or deviant
behaviors are "normal," but rather they become dysfunctions that are
understood as *natural* aberrancies and thus not subject to culture-based
value judgments. So whether a metaphysician or physician, whether
living in a mechanical universe or Darwinian, both Freud and Spinoza
subscribed to the scientific study of human behavior as a means of deciphering objective psychological cause. Accordingly, if only our science
advanced enough, a specifically human science would emerge to explain
human actions. This was Spinoza's belief and Freud's grand aspiration.
Furthermore, their shared dream was based on the same *philosophical*
motivation.

Thus, acknowledging the influences of Schopenhauer and Nietzsche,
Hegel and, of course, Kant, Freud's overall ethical commitment most
closely coincides with Spinoza's position expressed at the end of part 4
of his *Ethics*:

Human power is very limited and infinitely surpassed by the power of external causes. So we do not have an absolute power to adapt things outside us to our use. Nevertheless, we shall bear calmly those things which happen to us contrary to what the principle of our advantage demands, if we are conscious that we have done our duty, that the power we could not have extended itself to the point where we could have avoided those things, and that we are a part of the whole of nature, whose order we follow. If we understand this clearly and distinctly, that part of us which is defined by understanding, i.e. the better part of us, will be entirely satisfied with this, and will strive to persevere in that satisfaction. For insofar as we understand, we can want nothing except what is necessary, nor absolutely be satisfied with anything except what is true. Hence, insofar as we understand these things rightly, the striving of the better part of us agrees with the order of the whole of nature. (Spinoza 1985, 593–94)

Freud also embraced this ongoing pursuit of wisdom, which both acknowledges what *is* and accepts the individual's placement in the world. Such a universe is never stable or finite, and thus it always is subject to further examination, in which Socrates' dictum prevails: "I know nothing except the fact of my ignorance" (Diogenes Laertius, *Lives of Eminent Philosophers*). To have Socratic wisdom, an intuition of the limits of knowledge, yet rely on reason's capacity for self-criticism, is to fulfill human potential and the quest for freedom. I would not venture beyond Socrates to make philosophy's existential claims, and only remind that beneath all philosophical arguments, the metaphilosophical concern is the inquiry itself, and to that end, the fundamental ethos of philosophy becomes its own inquiry, which never ceases. On this view, the analysand becomes one of philosophy's exemplar "alter egos," and psychoanalysis attains a therapeutic standing as a philosophical activity in the sense suggested by Foucault's revised "care of the self" (McGushin 2007), Nietzsche's self-proclaimed role of "physician to culture" (Ahern 1995), or Wittgenstein's version of philosophy as therapy (Peterman 1992).

Freud the Humanist

We conclude by asking, how might we understand Freud's moral vision, or in other words, what guides his ethical course? To answer this query, we must place him in a humanist context, which frames much of his thought and provides the general outline of a moral philosophy. So after amplifying the failings of "Freud, the reluctant philosopher," and accepting the limits of "Freud, the compromised scientist," and highlighting "Freud, the moralist," allow me to tie together these various personae. I appreciate that in seeking some common denominator I risk reducing the complexity of his thought to simple formulaic slogans. Nevertheless, I still believe that we can outline an orientation by which psychoanalysis might be regarded as a philosophy, not one that conventionally fills the criteria of the contemporary professional discipline, but as a form of thinking that reaches back to the origins of analytic thought.

Freud's preoccupation with the Greeks and their myths is no curious aspect of an eclectic mind, but rather provides us with an essential clue to how he conceived human being. Oedipus in orthodox Freudian theory assumes a particular psychosexual role; on the larger stage of psychoanalytic philosophy, Oedipus follows the Delphic oracle to know himself. That precept directed the first philosophers as well and remains the steadfast Western precept of heroic tragedy and philosophical inquiry. Freud followed that line of dramatists and philosophers to present the Oedipal inquiry in terms that caught the imagination of his time and continues to influence our own. He did so as a humanist and as a tragedian by writing myths that captured the deepest intuitions of our own self-understanding. In creating a language and intellectual structure for elucidating that self-appraisal, Freud became a principal architect of the modern mind.

Because psychoanalysis originated in the clinical setting (and thus required therapeutic options), the psychiatric parameters of Freudianism have dominated critical philosophical assessments. However, if the discussion moves to wider concerns, a different conceptual framework appears in which an ethics of self-responsibility (and more specifically the exercise of free will) becomes the central interest. Freud arrived at the meta-position of free will and analytic liberation not through philosophy, but rather through his abiding allegiance to Romantic and Enlightenment ideals, and beyond these to an even older humanism. In seeking means to liberate the neurotic through reasoned inquiry, he assumed the mantle of a champion of human freedom and the fulfillment of creative human potential. Accordingly, his clinical interests may be understood as inspired by the promise of some therapeutic triumph. That optimism drew from both the biomedical model (one that Freud himself was heavily invested) and the political meliorism of liberal Austria.[18]

However, as important a role as various sociocultural elements obviously played in creating Freud's worldview, beneath each of them, and in fact organizing them *in toto*, lies an older tradition, *humanism*. I am using that designation not only in the cultural sense in which we identify Freud's political identity, urbane wit, and classical knowledge, but also in the sense in which humanism offers an ethical point of view, where humans, residing in a secular world and exercising genuine personal freedom, might determine their own meanings and judge their own actions (Lamont 1993, 13). He drew his humanism from several sources, including a rich endowment of German romanticism (Ellenberger 1970, 534–43; Kirschner 1996; Ferguson 1999, 186–92); a deep appreciation of poets and dramatists from Sophocles and Euripides to Goethe and Schiller (Gay 1988, 128); and a firm disavowal of religion and reliance instead on human rationality as an Enlightenment ideal (Freud 1927b). And most saliently, Freud's own belief in free will and self-reliance finds its ethical expression in his *moral* commitment to an image of humans as legislators to themselves, which is, of course, a central tenet of humanism. Note that this position conflicted with the content of Freud's clinical science, where his understanding of psychic determinism dominates the psychoanalytic conception of human nature. Yet Freud coupled that orientation with a Kantian formulation that would invoke reason's independence of cause and thus assert rationality's autonomy.

Freud's underlying presupposition, namely, that humans have moral responsibility that requires free will, works its way into his psychology, where, although a naturalism putatively rules, the "end game" results in a nonnaturalist understanding of reason's role. Thus Freud's unresolved conundrum of melding psychic determinism with autonomous choice results in an ambiguity at the base of psychoanalytic theory: How, or to what extent, does analytic insight translate into a therapeutic result, or in other words, how does reasoned free will trump the determinism of the unconscious?

In the free will–determinism debate, Freud must be viewed as a member of the "compatibilist" camp of Hobbes, Locke, Hume, and John

Stuart Mill, who found no conflict between commonsensical notions of human choice and the determinism of the natural world.[19] Although he did not explain that position, he followed one of the major tropes of Western thought, not by a philosophical argument, but rather a moral assertion: Reason, operating to attain human self-understanding, permits choice and self-responsibility, and thus he joined a rich humanistic tradition that regarded humans as potentially self-willed and responsible for their fate, a sentiment perhaps best described by Giovanni Pico della Mirandola in 1486:

> Thou, like a judge appointed for being honorable, art the molder and maker of thyself; thou mayest sculpt thyself into whatever shape thou dost prefer. Thou canst grow downward into the lower nature which are brutes. Thou canst again grow upward from thy soul's reason into the higher natures which are divine. (1965, 5)

For Freud, that achievement was attained through self-knowledge.

The humanist message, reiterated in various contexts and with differing meanings, is clearly stated in a remarkable essay published in 1917, where Freud sought to explain the challenge of psychoanalysis and the ordinary resistance he encountered in its acceptance. For him, the insights offered by his methods were the third of three critical assaults on humankind's narcissism: (1) displacement from the center of the universe (Copernicus)—a cosmological blow; (2) recognition of human descent from animals (Darwin)—a biological blow; and (3) most wounding, *"The ego is not master in its own house"*—a psychological blow (Freud 1917b, 143). He summarized psychoanalytic findings as residing in two cardinal tenets: "Sexual instincts cannot be wholly tamed" and "Mental functions are unconscious," and thus the conscious mind possesses only incomplete and untrustworthy perceptions. Accordingly, "you behave like an absolute ruler" with only partial or distorted information. After this succinct admonishment, Freud declares, like the philosophers of old, *"Turn your eyes inward, look into your own depths, learn first to know yourself!"* (1917b, 143; emphasis added).

For Freud, the knowing, reflective ego becomes a moral agent, who takes in hand the project of self-inquiry to exercise choice over unconscious forces. Those choices, informed and deliberate, are guided by values and goals arising, perhaps even chosen, from the psychoanalytic experience. These then move the analysand from hostage to the unconscious to one who might work and love autonomously. From this perspective, the primacy of self-knowing conjoins emotional recognition, interpretative insight, and acceptance to generate "truth," a truth defined in subjective terms. Thus the self-reflection, assessment, judgment, aspirations, and motivations that go into processing the desiderata of analytic mining take hold within a humane construct, and *truth* moves from its objective lodgings to where it becomes personally *meaningful*. And that is the gist of the entire psychoanalytic enterprise.

Freud's science also may also be encompassed by this construction, inasmuch as psychoanalysis reaches back to its earliest philosophical roots, before natural philosophy became "science." In that history, where philosophical questions guided early experimentalists, two motives drove their research: the mastery of nature *and* the metaphysical wonder of placing humans in their natural order (Tauber 2009). Here, at their junction, a moral vision guided them—a vision of divine order—that by the end of the secularized nineteenth century had generated another relationship: humans alienated from nature (Tauber 2001; see above chap. 6, note 10). The key metaphysical problem of that era, one that deeply affected the young Freud (Trosman 1976) and continued to haunt him, revolved around the imbroglio of reenchanting the universe, which science had stripped of human value (Schiller 1993, 121). The profound influence of Feuerbach (Boehlich 1990, xvi–xvii) and the struggle with religious identity (Klein 1985; Gay 1987; Gresser 1994) Freud countered with a firm atheism; the appropriation of figures and themes from mythology and the preoccupation with the ancients (Scully 1997; Armstrong 2005) were balanced against a pedagogical anthropology (Kitcher 1992); the disappointment with the speculative philosophies ready-at-hand, and the search for truth in its most direct expression (positivism), each reflect dual commitments of Freud's bisected weltanschauung. Yet Freud effectively tapped into a humanism that marshaled an individualism based on meaningful insight to pursue self-defined goals and follow self-chosen values. So on this reading, while Freud worked with a bivalent worldview, the therapeutic orientation ultimately directed him to the promise of freedom.

The humanist-scientistic division was explicitly bridged once Freud felt psychoanalysis had achieved its basic insights. Confident of his conclusions, he then proceeded with the greater project, the one antedating his scientific career. Note the logic of this move: Freud establishes psychoanalysis on the basis of therapeutic successes documented in *individual* patients discovering *subjective*, meaningful truths about themselves to sweeping extrapolated *universal* theories of culture, religion, and history presented as scientifically *objective*. Putting aside the logic of this move (highly suspect), we can understand it in terms of Freud's biography. When he applied his findings to problems of war, religion, social structure, and creativity, he sought to reenter the larger intellectual world that he had abandoned as a young university student. Extending psychoanalysis to biography (Freud 1910b; Freud and Bullitt 1967), cultural and religious history (Freud 1939), and complex social dynamics (Freud 1913b), Freud clearly announced his greater ambitions, ones originating at a time in his life when he thought philosophy might have afforded him ways to study those deeply perplexing social and existential questions. So in turning from philosophy to clinical science, he began a long trek that eventually returned him to his original interests, whereby these cultural-historical works represent the expression of his earliest yearnings to comment on the history and culture in which he lived. He accomplished that mission not as a *philosopher*, but rather as a *humanist*.

Freud was no less challenged than earlier Romantic critics by a hegemonic reason divorced from the realities of human need and value. He too struggled with fitting the scientific mode of knowing within the broader agenda he set himself. For Freud, science did not function solely as some kind of separate intellectual or technical activity to study the natural world, but rather became an instrument to help define *human* realities in the humane quest of knowing the world in order to place ourselves within it. So despite Freud's commitment to empiricism and the scientific objectivity he claimed for his method, he began and ended his career with responses to perplexing questions about the nature of man, the history of culture, and the place of religion in the face of humanity's search for meaning. Further, he sought to reenchant human life, much in response to Schiller's earlier indictment. "Instead of helping to deprive the world of its magic, charm, and poetry, Freud made our psychic life more poetic—more poetic and more rational at the same time" (Kaufmann 1980, 104). He could not escape the duality he assigned himself, and thus what Walter Kaufmann called the "poetic," and what I refer to as "humanism," directed Freud's greater efforts, which he strikingly declared to his confidant Binswanger in 1927:

> I could scarcely believe my ears when I heard him say, "Yes, the spirit is everything," even though I was inclined to surmise that by "spirit" he meant in this case something like intelligence. But then Freud continued: "Mankind has always known that it possesses spirit; I had to show it that there are also instincts." (Binswanger 1957, 81)

Freud went on to decry "religion"; that is, religion was a poor way of attending to "spirit."[20]

The scope and breadth of Freud's creation still appears dazzling, because he tapped into the deepest sources of Western identity and reexpressed its key tenets in terms that we might effectively apply to ourselves. His supreme accomplishment thus resides in his picture of humans as natural (i.e., primitively willed) *and* humane in possessing an acute self-consciousness that not only informed them of their "alien" (natural) character, but also the means of attaining self-knowledge and control of their destiny. Freud thus exemplified the "natural philosopher" in the broadest and most noble tradition: to *know* nature; to define human beings *within* nature; to control nature in order to *direct* human destiny. To label Freud a scientist in this way is to recognize his genius in its most expansive expression.

Freud's systematic thinking and ordering of psychic manifestations leads to a synthesis, a processing, an education, a recounting, an *interpretation,* which brings the psychic "data" together into the analytic truth of self-recognition and reconciliation. The emotional truths attained at this juncture serve as the fundamental goal of psychoanalysis, whose therapeutic success might not be certain, but whose centrality for human *being*—the inner inquiry itself—remains a legitimate claim for those so committed. Achieving this plateau of self-understanding follows Spinoza's judgment, the one that also served as Freud's own credo: "Man's greatest happiness and peace of mind (*acquiescentia animi*) comes only from this full philosophical understanding of himself" (Hampshire 1962,

121). Here, the various streams of Freud's thinking converge: a commitment to autonomous reason (Kant); a hope for individual liberation (Nietzsche); and through insight, freedom *within* one's personal (psychic) fate (Spinoza).

We are heirs to how Freud saw and heard his patients with eyes pierced by skepticism and ears tuned by suspicion. He taught that to see ourselves anew requires fracturing molded figurines and critically listening to what *we say* and observing what *we do*. That is all, but that is enough, because he then turned that way of seeing from a dispassionate description to a deeply personal account of human living. Guided by a perfectionist ideal, whereby insight might convert neurotic afflictions into productive and happier lives, Freud expanded the Romantic and Enlightenment hopes for human fulfillment. He did so with a formulation that resonated with much of Western twentieth-century culture and at the same time pushed those despairing elements aside to make room for a paradoxical hope in a most unhappy century: We are determined, yet free. Philosophers have yet to exhaust that rich mine. Indeed, contemporary philosophy has largely left Freud's metaphysical inquiry for other pursuits. Accordingly, the sequel to my study might be *Freud **and** the Reluctant Philosophers*, which would explore why those disinclined to probe the questions that drove Freud's own humane venture considered his project misconceived, and how, at the same time (appearing averse), they have pursued Freud's general agenda in different ways. For now, the suggestion will have to suffice.

Notes

Preface

1. The assignment of Freud to the positivists is resisted by some critics. For instance, H. Stuart Hughes (1961) aligns Freud with "a revolt against positivism" in the fin de siècle movement to liberate thought from scientism and promote a greater legitimacy to subjectivism. That characterization misrepresents a more complex agenda, because Freud falls on both sides of the positivist divide: On the one hand, as a scientist, all of his clinical work reflects positivist ideals, and on the other hand, he contributed to the humanistic movement of the period. This bivalency makes Freud's assignment to one camp or the other a distortion of a complex intellectual personality, as I will amply document.

2. Thomas Mann, on the occasion of Freud's eightieth birthday, spoke about Freud's relationship to philosophy, and in those comments Mann captured much of my own sentiment about philosophy, and more specifically, how Freud misunderstood the role of philosophy: Freud "does not esteem philosophy very highly. His scientific exactitude does not permit him to regard it as a science. He reproaches it with imagining that it can present a continuous and consistent picture of the world; with overestimating the objective value of logical operations; with believing in intuitions as a source of knowledge and with indulging in ... the magic of words and the influence of thought upon reality. But would philosophy really be thinking too highly of itself on these assumptions? Has the world ever been changed by anything save by thought and its magic vehicle the Word? I believe in actual fact philosophy ranks before and above the natural sciences and that all method and exactness serve its intuitions and its intellectual and historical will.... Scientific freedom from assumptions is or should be a moral fact. But intellectually it is, as Freud points out, probably an illusion. One might strain the point and say that science has never made a discovery without being authorized and encouraged thereto by philosophy" (1947, 419).

3. James Edwards underscores a key theme explored here by placing Freud in the philosophical tradition he sought to deny: "Freud is a philosopher, in the way in which a fin-de-siècle Viennese Jewish physician was taught to be a philosopher, that is, as a natural scientist and cultural theoretician, one who 'adds one construction to another' ... trying to explain his own odd world ... by means of discovering the 'true' one that lies behind it" (2004, 130). (Why Freud qualifies as a metaphysician is explained in chapter 2 and further developed in chapter 3.) To praise or indict Freud as a metaphysician hardly settles the issues with which I deal (nor, for that matter, does doing so condemn or rescue him), but this characterization allows us to proceed with assessing the philosophical structure of psychoanalysis and defining Freud's philosophical debts.

4. In this regard, Stephen Toulmin made an unerringly astute observation, one that proved to be prescient for the next half century: "Philosophy has always flourished on half-fledged sciences. The great periods in the history of Western philoso-

phy have been periods in which new modes of thought and new ways of reasoning were being developed, and their history is at least partly a record of the teething-troubles of these new instruments. As long as new ideas remain unfamiliar, their scope and nature tend to be misunderstood, and their use hampered by misplaced and fruitless controversy. At the best, the result is Descartes; but a great deal of the more transitory kind of philosophy trades on these misunderstandings, and satisfies the public taste for conjuring, mystification, paradox by a fine display of technicalities, which on closer examination are found simply to sugarcoat a series of dotty answers to screwy questions. In the past this has happened chiefly to physics and biology, but nowadays the main victim is psycho-analysis" (1954, 132).

Introduction
Psychoanalysis as Philosophy

1. I follow in the wake of renewed philosophical interest in psychoanalysis. Beyond the juxtaposition with Schopenhauer and Nietzsche (Lehrer 1995; Assoun 2000), Freud's influence on, or interpretation by, other philosophers (e.g., Wittgenstein: Bouveresse 2001) provides rich comment; a hermeneutical approach has been extensively developed by Ricoeur (1970) and Habermas (1971), and disputed by others (Messer, Sass, and Woolfolk 1988; Saks 1999; Gomez 2005); analytic philosophers and philosophers of mind have found psychoanalysis a fruitful ground to furrow (e.g., Cavell 1993; Levy 1996; Levine 2000; Mills 2004); and the challenge of characterizing Freud's conception of the unconscious and its philosophical import has generated a rich literature (e.g., Sartre 1956 [see chap. 7, note 7]; MacIntyre 1958; Rorty 1986; 1993; Gardner 1993; Smith 1999b; Boothby 2001). More general descriptions of psychoanalysis (e.g., Hanly and Lazerowitz 1970; Wollheim and Hopkins 1982; Dilman 1984; Lear 1990; 1998; 2005; Farrell 1994; Wollheim 1999) have renewed Freud's presence in diverse philosophical venues.

2. "The unconscious" has several identities in Freudian theory: neuro-corporeal (never accessible to analysis), repressed (available upon introspective analysis), and a more superficial stratum in which a "preconsciousness" serves as a ready reservoir for the ego in the forms of words or images. In this book, each of these strata of unconsciousness is used, and the context of the discussion should make the meaning clear. In regards to the "ego," again a complex structure was hypothesized: In the last formulation (1933, 78), Freud diagrammed the ego as having both conscious and unconscious domains, which reflected the embodied concept of the ego as developing from, and integrated with, deeper strata of the unconscious. Despite these considerations, I will discuss the ego as the rational agent or faculty, which discerns the unconscious and draws judgment upon it in fulfilling the primary function of mediating unconscious drives with social realities.

3. Yet an implicit self appears as the voice of the analysand, and in Freud's later writings on the ego, the structural dynamics that had so dominated his earlier work began to make way for a fledgling object-relations theory, where the hitherto latent self explicitly appears when developed through interpersonal rela-

tionships. Of course the Oedipal complex addresses the interpersonal, but even in that context, an integrated notion of the self remains outside Freud's purview. The dynamics occur in the unconscious realm, leaving the unknowing ego ignorant and befuddled. To the extent an ego psychology develops, it is, again, distinctive and separate: repression, denial, and other ego defense mechanisms are posted against the forces of the unconscious, but appear only as instrumental means of negotiating the reality of the ego in its social world. The self became a fixture in the world of psychology by the 1970s (see chap. 6, note 19), which corresponded to its placement as a locus of cultural criticisms (e.g., Foucault 1970; 1983; Mauss 1985; Martin 1994; Rose 1990; 1998; Morris 1994; Mackenzie and Stoljar 2000), which extended to biology as well (Tauber 1994a; 1994c; 1999b).

4. Nancy Kobrin (1993) notes that *autonomie* is found only once in the original German (in regards to separating the erotogenic zones [Freud 1908, 188]), and otherwise "autonomy," in the context of setting boundaries, marked off, and distinct, appears in the *Standard Edition* as a translation of the German equivalents of "independent" or "independence"—*selbständig, Selbständigkeit,* and *Unabhängigkeit.* Kobrin identifies four cases in which the English "autonomy" has been substituted: the body compartmentalized; the question of ego autonomy; Moses as a representation of autonomy; and in descriptions of the superego. To the extent that the judicial or philosophical understanding of autonomy appears as a theoretical construct, Freud reserved it for his description of the superego, which he proposed must be independent to allow for conscience and self-observation. Such an autonomous function is distinct from the ego, which he described as merging (thus losing an autonomous, unitary character) by drifting "inwards, without any sharp delimitation, into an unconscious mental entity which we designate the id and for which it serves as a kind of facade" (1930, 66). Thus the ego's apparent sharp lines of demarcation fail to provide the necessary self-scrutiny required for a moral life, and another agency, the superego, assumes that role, inasmuch as "it is where human nature meets morality. Autonomy goes hand in hand with processes and degrees of identification; the superego bridges the intrapsychic and the social" (Kobrin 1993, 211). Thus Freud never uses "autonomous Ich," a term coined by Heinz Hartmann in 1939, but employed instead "coherent ego" (Freud 1922, 121) in reference to self-sufficiency or an independent self in relation to others. Consequently my argument about reason's autonomy does not rely on any explicit use of the term "autonomy" in Freud's theoretical or clinical writings, a matter fully discussed in chapter 4.

5. Note that I have deliberately framed Freud in his own Germanic intellectual culture, and while one might argue about the extent of the influence of Anglo-American notions of empiricism, utilitarianism and associationism, I have made my case based on the dominant tides of Freud's own era and culture. These are the most direct influences, and thus most relevant.

6. In April 1922, Abraham Kardiner (age 30), then in the midst of a five-month analysis with Freud, asked Freud to evaluate himself as an analyst. He received a forthright reply: "I'm glad you ask, because, frankly, I have no great interest in therapeutic problems, I am much too impatient now" (Lohser and Newton 1996,

38). Freud went on to describe his "handicaps" as being too much of a father figure; being too preoccupied with theoretical issues; and lacking patience with investing too heavily in a few analysands, for not only did he "tire of them," but he also wanted to "spread my influence." Kardiner, who later became a founder of the New York Psychoanalytic Society, disagreed, and thought Freud a great analyst, whose brilliance and intuition effectively focused upon subtle psychic material.

7. The psychoanalytic variants retained key features of Freudian psychoanalysis. Stripping away the particulars of any of the post-Freudian theoretical positions or alternative techniques reveals a psychology imprinted on Freud's teachings. *Psychoanalytic* therapists of every stripe work *within* the psychoanalytic tradition and align themselves with the basic precepts advocated from the beginning. Precisely identifying these basic tenets cannot be accomplished, for even Freud himself identified them in various ways. Typically, he stressed the scientific aspects:

> Psycho-analysis is the name (1) of a procedure for the investigation of mental processes which are almost inaccessible in any other way, (2) of a method (based upon that investigation) for the treatment of neurotic disorders and (3) of a collection of psychological information obtained along those lines, which is gradually being accumulated into a new scientific discipline. (1923b, 235)

In the same article, he also employed a phenomenological description:

> The assumption that there are unconscious mental processes, the recognition of the theory of resistance and repression, the appreciation of the importance of sexuality and the Oedipus complex—these constitute the principle subject-matter of psychoanalysis and the foundations of its theory. No one who cannot accept them all should count himself a psychoanalyst. (247)

At other times he identified the theory of dreams (1933, 7) and the twin phenomena of transference and resistance (1914c, 16) as key. Note that he did not place his metapsychological conceptualizations (the economic, topographical, and dynamic models) in such august standing and allowed that these theoretical models and speculations, as opposed to his empirical (i.e., clinical) findings, were open to review and future emendation if not outright rejection (Fulgencio 2005).

8. The complex and profound place the Oedipus myth held for Freud is thoroughly examined by Peter Rudnytsky (1987), who traces possible influences in Freud's own development and identifies prominent Germanic artistic, intellectual, and cultural uses of the myth in Freud's writings.

9. In his attempt to characterize psychoanalysis and unify some of its diverse elements, Jonathan Lear observes that one of Freud's great achievements was to begin "a science of subjectivity," an idea whose full force Freud himself "never came to grips with" (1990, 5), and which in some sense we still do not understand (3). Lear, in seeking to recast psychoanalysis under science's banner, would change the definition of science to integrate the knowledge psychoanalysis affords. While not willing to expand science to make such an accommodation, I agree that psychoanalysis offers a valid form of knowledge and so must be understood on its

own terms. That Lear goes on to argue that *love* represents the central trope of
Freudianism supports our mutual appreciation that the domain in which analysis
works is subjective and guided by humane pursuits.

10. Roy Schafer (1970) usefully parsed the psychoanalytic vision between four
versions of the analysand's quest: the comic, the romantic, the tragic, and the
ironic (albeit with some overlap of these categories). He concluded that these
visions each contribute to framing the fact-finding and the fact-organizing of the
psychoanalytic experience, and in this sense the schema proposes a structure by
which the analysand might organize his or her own self-image and self-identity.

Chapter 1
The Challenge (and Stigma) of Philosophy

1. As analysand and therapist engage at both conscious and unconscious levels,
the subjective element—love and hate, desire and guilt—rises to the fore, and
only later did psychoanalysts begin to appreciate the bi-directionality of such
exchange. Consider Freud's own description of the analyst's objective stare:

> I cannot advise my colleagues too urgently to model themselves during psycho-
> analytic treatment on the surgeon, who puts aside all his feelings, even his
> human sympathy, and concentrates his mental forces on the single aim of per-
> forming the operation as skillfully as possible.... The justification for requiring
> this emotional coldness in the analyst is that it creates the most advantageous
> conditions for both parties: for the doctor the desirable protection for his own
> emotional life and for the patient the largest amount of help that we can give
> him today. (1912a, 115)

See Paul Stepansky (1999) for discussion of the surgery motif in Freud's writings, which describes Freud's attempt to model psychoanalysis on the medical
encounter, one that emphasized objectivity and neutrality. While Freud's clinical
technique papers seem to emphasize this attitude, testimonies from his patients
suggest that this austere image did not always hold (Lohser and Newton 1996).
At least in the last two decades of his life, Freud permitted himself more active
exchanges with analysands-in-training by sharing personal information, introducing his wife and children, offering gossip and opinion of other analysts, and
encouraging analysands to discuss among themselves how to allocate clinical
hours and thereby allow their own social intercourse. The apparent inconsistency
between an objectivist and more personal attitude towards Freud's analysands
reflects the diversity of his patients and the shift in his interests over five decades
of clinical experience. (See note 9, below.)

2. A comprehensive overview of Freud's ambivalent attitude towards philosophy is given by Richard Askay and Jensen Farquhar (2006, 16ff.), who cite the
key remarks Freud made about philosophy throughout his career and then show
the various philosophical influences on him from the ancients to Nietzsche in
six dense chapters. Having demonstrated that Freud was well educated in philosophy, they then offer a critique of psychoanalysis in the context of existential

phenomenology. Their emphasis on Husserl, Heidegger, Sartre, and Merleau-Ponty is an important addition to the philosophical literature on psychoanalysis and complements my own portrayal of Freud as a moral philosopher. However, neither "ethics" nor "moral" (or any of their conjugates) appears in Askay and Farquhar's index, and while I see moral issues throughout their text, such matters remain muted and rarely explicitly identified and discussed by them.

3. While the general consensus concurs that Freud was judicious in not publishing this work, others regard the *Project* as not only a prelude to Freud's metapsychology, but more broadly a contribution to modern neuropsychology (Pribram and Gill 1976).

4. The reductionists were initially a group of German physiologists led by Hermann Helmholtz, who in the 1840s openly declared their manifesto of scientific inquiry (Galaty 1974). They did not argue that certain organic phenomena were not unique, only that all causes must have certain elements in common. They connected biology and physics by equating the ultimate basis of their respective explanations in physical laws, and proceeded to analyze organic processes within the framework of attractive and repulsive forces in order to link the physical sciences to the biological. Thus the reductionists sought unifying principles for all phenomena, which might have been interpreted as fodder for a materialist position (discussed in chapter 3). The reductionists' position was driven, at least in part, in reaction to romanticism's lingering attachment to vitalism, the notion that life possessed a special "life force." A new scientific ethos had taken over the life sciences by the 1860s. Helmholtz was the leader of that triumph. In the ascendancy of the reductionist strategy and its obvious advances, physiology assumed a new hegemony on claims of biological knowledge.

5. Beyond Ernst Mach's positivist aspirations for a unification of the sciences (1959), his influence on Freud's epistemology has been the subject of some comment (Assoun 1990; Fulgencio 2005). Mach's suspension of the "ego" and the focus on sensations as the subject of psychology (Mach 1959) resonates with Freud's own focus on manifest behavior as the subject matter of psychoanalysis. In this sense, they shared an empiricist commitment, albeit within vastly different psychological conceptions.

6. Others have also noted Freud's persistent philosophical interests and the ambivalence of his putative rejection of philosophy. See McGrath (1986), Brady (1986), Herzog (1988), Szaluta (1996), and Brunner (2002).

7. Why Freud chose to follow the path of science and not philosophy has been the subject of some debate. Ernest Jones and Fritz Wittels believed that Freud chose science over philosophy because of the fear of speculative tendencies that would only be checked by a career in medical science (Jones 1953–57, 1:29). Patricia Herzog (1988) disputes that claim and argues that Jones projected his own antiphilosophical biases, and that, more to the point, Freud was driven to the laboratory because of (1) the problematic status of his Jewishness, (2) the economic insecurity inherent in waiting for an unlikely professorship, and (3) most intriguing, Freud's likely underlying intellectual insecurity and self-doubt that he could become a successful philosopher in light of his admiration of Brentano's genius. In this dispute I side with Herzog, with the extra ingredient, as discussed,

that Freud simply could not abide the wild metaphysical speculation of the day, which seemed to put philosophy in disarray. As explored in later chapters, other philosophical options were open to him, if he was so inclined.

8. The rejection of idealism as a philosophy does not mean that Freud was immune to its wider influence. As Rudnytsky so richly illustrates (1987, 93–198), Freud's adoption of the Oedipus myth and the constellation of ideas swirling around mythic depictions of human nature and the metaphysics of freedom and fate cannot divorce Freud from the romantic philosophers he took such efforts to reject.

9. Transference and countertransference compromise the positivist requirements of subject-object separation, which by the 1920s was acknowledged in psychoanalytic theorizing as a problem for Freud's teachings. For instance, Georg Groddeck observed that the unconscious exchange between patient and analyst compromises the objectivist conceit, a critique that softened Freud's own staunch claims of (ego) objectivity (Groddeck 1976; Rudnytsky 2002; 2008, 141ff.). Indeed, transference became the lynchpin of a successful analysis and counter-transference the lurking danger. So beyond the indeterminacies of interpretation, Freud struggled with how to reconcile the emotional exchange between analyst and patient within the scientific context of objectivity he espoused. (See note 1, above.)

10. Stan Draenos similarly sees that Freud's early commitment to science at the expense of metaphysics was eventually reversed in his metapsychology by transforming "his science of the unconscious into the mythology of Eros and death instincts" (1982, 147). Indeed, all of the applications of psychoanalytic theory to culture, from *Totem and Taboo* (1913b) to *Moses and Monotheism* (1939), represent a "metapsychology" taking its place in the philosophical domain in which Freud placed his earliest ambitions.

11. Freud referred to Brentano only once in his published writings, and that citation in a footnote pertained to a discussion of condensation, where he used Brentano's riddles (published in 1879) as examples of the use of association in the condensation mode (Freud 1905a, 32; discussed by the editors 237–38). Note that beyond the normal associations used in analysis of inner perception, Brentano included dreams, insanity, and strange mental phenomena in his discussion of associative ideas, but to reiterate, Freud makes no reference to this work. Nevertheless, Freud's early interest in Brentano has long been noted, but largely ignored by Freud's general biographers (e.g., Jones 1953; Clark 1980; Gay 1988; Breger 2000), and even those who have focused on Freud's early life and genesis of his thought have not given sufficient attention to Brentano's formative influence (e.g., Wollheim 1981; Holt 1989). Notable exceptions include William McGrath (1986), who maintains that Freud held to a Brentanean vision of psychology, and Herzog, who subtly explores Freud's psychological relationship with his mentor, which is also commented on by Peter Newton (1995, 68–71) and Siegfried Bernfeld (1951).

The two most extensive studies of the infuence of Brentano on Freud available in English are doctoral dissertations by James Barclay (1959) and Aviva Cohen (1998). While indebted to Barclay and Cohen, my interpretation of the Brentano-

Freud relationship is considered within a larger philosophical context than they consider, and while I concur with some of Cohen's conclusions, especially the role of intentionality in orienting Freud's thought, the placement of Freud in relation to a critique of his theory and juxtaposed to other philosophers who contributed to his intellectual Zeitgeist clearly differentiates my interpretation from hers.

12. Whether Freud actually discussed with Brentano the basis for accepting or rejecting the notion of "the unconscious" or "unconsciousness" as a property of the mind cannot be determined, but the impressionable student did report to Silberstein Brentano's disparaging opinion of Johann Friedrich Herbart's views as "untenable" (Freud 1990, 102), which might well have included his adversary's endorsement of unconscious psychic phenomena (Brentano 1973, 165). In Brentano's *Psychology* (1973), Herbart frequently appears as representative of views Brentano rigorously rejects.

13. Wundt's *Principles of Physiological Psychology* effectively placed him as the "father" of German experimental psychology, a science he defined as the study of *conscious* processes (1904, 3). Thus Brentano, from a philosophical angle, joined the dominant German psychologists in framing their respective studies as the examination of consciousness. As detailed, Freud attacked this position as assuming an unwarranted definitional restriction that failed empirical evidence (Freud 1900, 611–12; 1912b, 260; 1925a, 31–32; 1940c, 286).

14. "The task of 'ascertaining the basic elements of mental phenomena' Brentano later assigned to 'descriptive psychology,' and the laws governing their coming into existence, duration, and passing away, to the investigations of 'genetic psychology,' which is then predominantly physiological in character. But before he had separated the two *disciplines*, he had already sharply discriminated between descriptive and genetic *questions*" (Oscar Kraus [ed. 1924 edition], in Brentano 1973, 7 n. 5).

15. While physical phenomena lack such psychic references, "every mental phenomenon includes something as object within itself" (Brentano 1973, 88), which should be "understood literally: the sound I hear is part of my hearing it, the thought that I am hearing the sound has both my hearing and the sound as parts, and my delight in hearing the sound has the thought and the hearing and the sound as ever more mediate parts. The sound on the other hand, is just a sound, it has nothing in it, and so is just a physical phenomenon" (Simons 1973, xviii). Donald McIntosh offers this example: "Beethoven's Third Symphony can be taken to mean, (a) a set of mental representations in the mind of Beethoven or a person reading the score (intentional contents), or, (b) a set of sounds produced by violins, horns, etc., as defined by the score (intentional object), or, (c) an actual performance of the work (actual object). The point is that in its main meaning as an intentional object, Beethoven's Third Symphony is neither a set of ideas in someone's head nor an actual performance of the work" (1986, 437). This construction, which attempts to define the distinction and relation between the intentional and the actual, was formulated by the medieval scholastics (Hedwig 1979) and served as a source of continued dispute that dates at least to Kant (Sassen 2000, 28–29). For an analysis of Brentano's concept of intentionality

as central to his empirical psychology, resisting analytic and phenomenological critiques, see Bartok (2005).

16. Without going into detail about Brentano's classification of psychical acts (i.e., representations, judgments, and emotion), it is important to note that he differentiated between primary and secondary objects or referents:

> The primary object is the one outside to which the psychological phenomenon refers; the secondary one is the psychical phenomenon itself. This double reference makes it possible for him to maintain that, while there may be no primary referent to certain psychical phenomena [such as moods that have no referents, in contrast to desires and perceptions], there always has to be a secondary one; otherwise the phenomenon would not even be conscious. This raises of course the question how far reflexive consciousness is essential to all the phenomena which psychology rightfully covers. Brentano's somewhat sweeping answer is that unconscious psychological phenomena are self-contradictory, hence fictitious[!] (Spiegelberg 1982, 38) (See note 21, below.)

17. "Brentano later acknowledged that the way he attempted to describe consciousness here, adhering to the Aristotelian tradition which asserts 'the mental inexistence of the object,' was imperfect. The so-called 'inexistence of the object,' the immanent objectivity, is not to be interpreted as a mode of being the thing has in consciousness, but as an imprecise description of the fact that I have something (a thing, a real entity, substance) as an object, am mentally concerned with it, refer to it" (Simons 1973, 89 n. 11).

18. Richard Wollheim described Freud's use of intentionality as a "philosophical *assumption* that Freud retained throughout his work and probably derives from ... Brentano.... And that assumption is that every mental state or condition can be analyzed into two components: an idea, which gives the mental state its object or what it directed upon; and its charge or affect, which gives it its measure of strength or efficacy" (1981, 20–21; emphasis added).

19. A. Vergote, "L'Intérêt philosophique de la psychanalyse freudienne," *Archives de philosophie*, January–February 1958, 38.

20. Brentano identified numerous other targets, but perhaps none with more relish than Eduard von Hartmann, whose *Philosophy of the Unconscious* went through eleven editions from 1869 to 1904 (the English translation, 1931, is based on the ninth edition). According to Brentano (1973, 107-9), von Hartmann's grand philosophy of the unconscious was a metaphysical enterprise quite at odds with the new scientism most enthusiastically embraced by positivists of all stripe, but also endorsed in a different fashion by the neo-Kantians (as discussed in chapter 3). Indeed, von Hartmann proffered the kind of metaphysics that focused much of the anti-idealist philosophies at the end of the nineteenth century. Brentano, of course, had his own deep disagreements with an ontology that was, at least on his view, wildly speculative. His criticism was directed at the religious overtones of Hartmann's *Philosophy of the Unconscious* and is noteworthy largely in placing in context Brentano's own conflicts over religion. (Brentano began his career as a Catholic priest, which he abandoned with much

ado and suffered political consequences, including the loss of his professorship
[Spiegelberg 1982, 28–30].) The attention paid to von Hartmann represents a
minor flank of Brentano's own campaign, the others represented by the physiologists and his close allies (like Maudsley), the empiricists inspired by Locke, the
positivists such as John Stuart Mill, and of course Kant and his later followers.
We saw above that Maudsley served as the principal whipping boy of Brentano's
own commitments to a scientific psychology, and in turning to von Hartmann we
witness how easily Brentano rejected a metaphysics that might pose a threat to
his philosophical construction. Freud, of course, was similarly averse to a metaphysically inspired philosophy.

21. Brentano included a fourth issue: In seeking the source of conscious
thought, either an unconscious source must be postulated or an infinitely complex recursive process of self-consciousness ensues (1973, 105). He described the
apparent imbroglio of a simple mental presentation as follows:

> First of all, no mental phenomenon is possible without a correlative conscious-
> ness; along with the presentation of a sound we have a presentation of the
> presentation of this sound at the same time. We have therefore, *two* presenta-
> tions, and presentations of two different sorts at that. If we call the presentation
> of sound "hearing" we have, in addition to the presentation of this sound, a
> presentation of the hearing, which is as different from hearing as hearing is
> from sound. (1973, 121)

Add to this duality in the presentation of hearing the accompaniment of some
consciousness of the hearing, and a third level is introduced, which in turn evokes
a self-consciousness of itself and so on. In short, hearing involves a regress: "a
presentation of sound, a presentation of the act of hearing, and a presentation
of the presentation of this act" (121), which may go on infinitely unless it ends
in some unconscious bedrock. Brentano avoids this construction (and thereby
rejects the logical basis of unconsciousness) by referring to an unstated assumption: "The act of hearing and its object are one and the same object, insofar as
the former is thought to be directed upon itself as its own object, then 'sound'
and 'hearing' would be merely two names for one and the same phenomenon"
(122). The dilemma is solved using Brentano's basic tenet about the intentionality of mental acts; i.e., the object of inner presentation and the presentation itself
belong to the same mental act, or as he writes,

> In the same mental phenomenon in which the sound is present to our minds we
> simultaneously apprehend the mental phenomenon itself. What is more, we
> apprehend it in accordance with its dual nature insofar as it has the sound as
> content within it, and insofar as it has itself as content at the same time. We can
> say that the sound is the *primary object* of the *act* of hearing, and that the act
> of hearing itself is the *secondary object*. Temporally they both occur at the same
> time, but in the nature of the case, the sound is prior. (127–28)

The mental act is thus divided in two, (1) a direct awareness of the fact
that one is engaged in a mental act (the "secondary object") and (2) an indirect
awareness of the object toward which the mental act is directed (the "primary

object") (Cohen 2000, 112). Here we witness Brentano's essential structure of the mind applied most directly to the very possibility of unconsciousness. (See note 16 above.)

Chapter 2
Distinguishing Reasons and Causes

1. As noted above, Freud understood the difference between the clinical facts and their interpretation, namely the metapsychological speculations. Beyond the topography or dynamics of the mind, which readily appear as schemas, even the basic notion of *Trieb* (drive, instinct) served Freud as a convention, which he described as "still somewhat obscure but which is indispensable to us in psychology" (1915b, 118).

2. Norman O. Brown offered a genealogy of Freud's understanding of the instincts to explain the final opposition of Eros and the death instinct:

> Freud began by borrowing from the romantic poets the antithesis of hunger and love, which, translated into scientific terminology, gave him the antithesis of the sexual and the self-preservation instincts.... [These] correspond to the antithesis of the pleasure-principle and the reality-principle, which is, in Freud's earlier theory, the cause of repression. At the same time they can plausibly be regarded as present in all organisms or at least in all animals, the sexual instincts working to preserve the species and the self-preservation instinct working to preserve the individual.... This first theory of repression was upset by developments in the exploration of the sexual instinct (libido). The antithesis of sex and self-preservation was undermined when empirical facts forced on psychoanalysis the recognition of the narcissistic character of the sexual instinct; for narcissistic libido cathects the self, and there was no way of distinguishing narcissistic libido from the self-preservation instinct ... [Because of] the convertibility of ego-libido into object-libido and vice versa, this duality was not firm enough.
>
> Hence, again looking for a dualism, Freud turned to the ambivalence of love and hate, an ambivalence prominent, like hunger and love, in romantic philosophy and poetry, and also prominent in ... case histories. But again the empirical facts ... showed that sexual and aggressive instincts were not an ultimate duality, ... [since] love can turn into hate. So, to obtain a firm enough duality, Freud turns for inspiration to the biological antithesis of life and death, and links the hypothesis of a universal biological death instinct with the psychological phenomenon of masochism.
>
> Now he is able to postulate an irreconcilable conflict between Eros, seeking to preserve and enrich life, and the death instinct, seeking to return life to the peace of death.... Sadism represents an extroversion of the innate death instinct. (Brown 1959, 79–80)

Lear observes more critically: "Freud invoked the death drive to explain human aggression and destructiveness. Aggression, Freud argued, was an attempt to direct this force outward, away from the self. However, Freud admitted that the ground for postulating the death drive did not arise from within psychoanalytic observation and thinking, but from biology [Freud 1920, 37–61; 1923a, 40; 1923b, 258].... Freud knew there was not a shred of evidence for the death drive. It is thus fair to say that Freud did not succeed in giving a distinctively psychoanalytic account of aggression. He tried to *derive* aggression from a more fundamental biological source, and thus he violated his own 'fundamental rule': to give a psychological account of psychological phenomena" (1990, 14–15).

3. Given the importance of the word "assuming," I checked the original German manuscript, which is stored in the Library of Congress in Washington, D.C. This German paper has not been published; the history of the English version is summarized by the editors of the *Standard Edition* (1926b, 261–62). On page 7 of the handwritten manuscript, Freud writes *Annahme*, which means "assume." (I am indebted to Michael Toch of Hebrew University for deciphering Freud's nearly unintelligible handwriting.) Freud also uses *Annahme* in the passages considered below from his *New Introductory Lectures*.

4. The rationality of psychoanalysis has been the subject of much discussion, for example, its diversity of forms of reason (Goldberg 1988), its conjectural process (Ginzburg 1983), its hermeneutics (Ricoeur 1970), its appreciation of reality (e.g., Schafer 1970; 1985; Sugarman 1998); its analytic logic (Flew 1954; Toulmin 1954; Sherwood 1969). On my view, "abduction" or "inference to the best explanation" (Lipton 1991) best characterizes the basic strategy of Freud's *clinical* reasoning. Abduction was proposed by Charles Sanders Pierce (1839–1914) as part of a tripartite schema for organizing scientific evidence. He used abduction to denote an inference from otherwise unexplained phenomena, or in other words, a kind of theory forming or interpretative inference (Josephson and Josephson 1994, 5ff.). Deduction and induction are then employed together to strengthen the inference from a conjecture to a hypothesis that is well grounded. The idea of inference to the best explanation might be regarded as a loose means to orient scientific investigation, and represents, as it were, an accounting of findings that seek a parsimonious or coherent schema from which predictions might be made. Generally, abduction does not seek to account for all the data but serves as a proto-theory and represents the logic by which medicine, law, and other everyday decision-making is guided (see, e.g., Achinstein 2001; 2005).

5. MacIntyre does not elaborate on this interesting aside. This idealistic issue is thoroughly explored by Marcia Cavell in her own reading of Freud's notion of *ideas* as mental entities (1993).

6. Wittgenstein's criticisms of psychoanalysis were made in the context of a deep ambivalence about Freud's achievements (Rhees 1966, 41–52; McGuiness 1982) and ranged from measured admiration (e.g., Rhees 1981, 151) to disparagement (e.g., Wittgenstein 1980a, 19, 36, 56, 87). That he took Freud to be worthy of comment attests to his intrigue with psychoanalysis, which belied his dismissals. Rush Rhees reported that soon after 1919, Wittgenstein discovered that Freud "had something to say," and later, Wittgenstein would speak of himself at times as "a disciple of Freud" and "a follower of Freud" (Rhees 1966, 41). In 1936 Wittgenstein even considered practicing lay analysis, but quickly disabused himself of the idea, both because of inhibitions to reveal his own secret life and

because of the danger of analysis producing "infinite harm" (Rhees 1981, 151). Perhaps more importantly, Wittgenstein recognized parallels between Freudian analysis and his own philosophical "therapeutic" project (Lazerowitz 1977; Peterman 1992; Bouveresse 1995, 3–21), albeit with a rich emotional overlay (Monk 1991; Mancia 2002).

7. Two major accounts provide Wittgenstein's views—summaries of lectures reported by his colleague G. E. Moore (1993) and reports of conversations with Rush Rhees (1966). These are supplemented with passages from various lectures (Wittgenstein 1958), occasional notes written between 1931 and 1948 (Wittgenstein 1980a), accounts of lectures concerning the philosophy of psychology (1980b; 1992), and some casual comments in conversation (e.g., Bouwsma 1986). Despite the apparent cursory character of these observations, much has been written on Wittgenstein's philosophical comments about Freud and psychoanalysis (e.g., MacIntyre 1958; Levy 1983; Johnston 1993, 225–33; Bouveresse 1995; Cioffi 1998b). Moore's summation of a short critique (offered in the early 1930s) concerning the purported conflation of cause and reason frames this discussion, which directly pertains to Freud's efforts to secure a scientific standing for psychoanalysis, and more specifically, the preoccupation with Brentano's challenge of causation.

8. At about the same time, in the "Blue Book" lectures of 1934, Wittgenstein elaborated the point:

> The proposition that your action has such and such a cause, is a hypothesis. The hypothesis is well-founded if one has had a number of experiences which, roughly speaking, agree in showing that your action is the regular sequel of certain conditions which we then call causes of the action. In order to know the reason which you had for making a certain statement, for acting in a particular way, etc. no number of agreeing experiences is necessary, and the statement of your reason is not a hypothesis. The difference between the grammars of "reason" and "cause" is quite similar to that between the grammars of "motive" and "cause." Of the cause one can say that one can't *know* it but can only *conjecture* it. On the other hand one often says: "Surely I must know why I did it" talking of the *motive*. When I say: "we can only conjecture the cause but we *know* the motive" this statement will be seen later on to be a grammatical one. The "can" refers to the logical possibility.
>
> The double use of the word "why," asking for the cause and asking for the motive, together with the idea that we can know, and not only conjecture, our motives, gives rise to the confusion that a motive is a cause of which we are immediately aware, a cause 'seen from the inside,' or a cause experienced.— Giving a reason is like giving a calculation by which you have arrived at a certain result. (1958, 15)

Recounting conversations with Wittgenstein between 1942 and 1946, Rhees reports the same general points, although the philosophical argument of contrasting causes and reasons was not explicitly invoked, but rather various aspects of the indeterminancy (or underdetermination) of the correct solution (Rhees 1966, 41–52).

9. Later commentators, Donald Davidson most notably, challenged Wittgenstein's categorical separation of cause and reason to argue that reasons could, in many instances, be fairly construed as causes. In a famous paper published in 1963, "Actions, Reasons, and Causes," Davidson argued that an action might be rationalized by a reason and in this sense cause is established: "A reason rationalizes an action only if it leads us to see something the agent saw, or thought he saw, in his action—some feature, consequence, or aspect of the action the agent wanted, desired, prized, thought dutiful" (1980a, 3). The explanatory role of what Davidson calls a "primary reason" is a rational construct that allows for teleological behaviors. In this sense, primary reasons order both simple and complex actions, and Davidson thus attempted to recapture the commonsense attitude that "the agent performed the action *because* he had the reason" to do so (1980a, 9). Perhaps it is perfectly legitimate to frame the action of turning on a light in a room as caused by the desire to find a book, and in this context the "search for the book" is the reason *and cause*, of going to the room and finding the book. That particular action, of course, falls into a larger causal chain (e.g., why do I want this book?—for a reference—for a larger intellectual project—for professional advancement—for self-esteem, and so on, endlessly), and this regress problem carries its own conundrum, but to confine the causal action within prescribed boundaries, reason may serve as cause, or as Davidson wrote elsewhere, "A reason is a rational cause" (1980c, 233).

Davidson's argument, however, is a bit tangential to Wittgenstein's, inasmuch as the question pertains not to reasons as causes in the sense Davidson allows, but rather the question of establishing *a*, or *the*, reason for a given behavior or action, one whose antecedents have no boundaries, and whose potential interpretations are myriad. The issue in psychoanalysis is how to establish reason, validate it, and ultimately define the precipitating cause in some ordered pattern of sequential psychic events that has no prescribed (discerned) order. The point is that cause and effect must be directly coordinated to fulfill Wittgenstein's objections, and as discussed, Freud could not establish psychoanalytic reasons by such criteria. A psychoanalytic "reason" was always one of several candidates, each of which resided in a fluid array of various "reasons" with diverse effects. In short, according to Wittgenstein, psychoanalytic "cause" was radically undetermined by diverse reasons and could not be understood in the common fashion that Davidson attempted to capture in an "ordinary language" philosophical approach. For further discussion, see MacIntyre (1958), Hart and Honré (1959), and Sherwood (1969, 146–79).

10. According to Wittgenstein, Freud "has not given a scientific explanation of the ancient myth. What he has done is to propound a new myth" (Rhees 1967, 51), so while Freud claims to explain myth psychologically, in reality, says Wittgenstein,

He is portraying psychology mythically.... The myth presents those psychological dynamics dramatically and in narrative.... But doesn't Freud in his explanations do exactly the same? ... [Freudian] characterization holds the same charm for us as the ancient myths it is supposed to explain and replace....

Freud's explanations derive their force not from their powers of empirical prediction and control, and not from the careful collection of evidence that led to their adoption, but from what Wittgenstein calls their *charm*. (Edwards 2004, 120)

Freud himself admitted to creating a myth (1932, 211; see my Introduction, above), but he was hardly defensive about such a designation, since he maintained that all science is based on mythology, by which he meant a metaphysics (whose import is discussed in the next section and the next chapter).

11. Consider Wittgenstein's notebook passage written in 1948:

In Freudian analysis a dream is dismantled, as it were. It loses its original sense *completely*. We might think of it as a play enacted on the stage, with a plot that's pretty incomprehensible at times, but at times too quite intelligible, or apparently so; we might then suppose this plot torn into little fragments and each of these given a completely new sense. Or, we might think of it in the following way: a picture is drawn on a big sheet of paper which is then so folded that pieces which don't belong together at all in the original picture now appear side by side to form a new picture, which may or may not make sense. (This latter would correspond to the manifest dream, the original picture to the "latent dream thought.") ...

What is intriguing about a dream is not its causal connection with events in my life, etc., but rather the impression it gives of being a fragment of a story—a very *vivid* fragment to be sure—the rest of which remains obscure.... What's more, if someone now shows me that this story is not the right one; that in reality it was based on quite a different story, so that I want to exclaim disappointedly, "Oh, *that's* how it was? ... The original story certainly disintegrates now, as the paper is unfolded: the man I saw was taken from over *here*, his words from over *there*, the surroundings of the dream from somewhere else again; but all the same the dream story has a charm of its own, like a painting that attracts and inspires us. (Wittgenstein 1980a, 68e–69e)

12. Jacques Bouveresse further explains: "A reason is characterized by the capacity to be recognized as such by the person whose reason it is, and not on the basis of an inductive inference. Freud ... proposes and imposes reasons, and the acceptance of a reason has nothing to do with the acceptance of an explanatory hypothesis of the causal type, or for that matter with any hypothesis at all" (1995, 69–70).

13. This strong empirico-logical orientation was opposed not only by Heidegger, but also by neo-Kantians such as Ernst Cassirer, who argued that language, myth, art, *and science* must be regarded as *expressions* of the human mind and language, inasmuch as each is a way of apprehending and recording a reality structured on humans' cognitive faculties (Cassirer 1953–57). Beyond the Kantian strategy of offering a priori categories by which humans might know a formless and incoherent nature, "the world" is partly, but inextricably, the product of human self-expression (Wolterstorff 1990). (This is what Cassirer referred to as "functional" a priori categories.)

14. In his last remarks, collected in *Philosophical Investigations* (1968), Wittgenstein disallowed language as a "representation" of the world, and thus he dispelled any notion that language serves as a direct correspondence to reality. Language (coincident with the mind) could not mirror nature. Further, he discounted the ability to discern any formal language rules for natural languages, because natural languages do not take a form analogous to formal language. For Wittgenstein, actions or behavior defines language, and its "logical" basis emerges solely in the ordinary course of communication. Accordingly, he maintained that only particular kinds of empirical questions were meaningful and qualified as warranting *certain* answers, and his last writings are rift with skepticism and guarded statements about scientific knowledge, the standing of beliefs, the individual status of certainty, the logical basis of empirical propositions, and so on (Wittgenstein 1969, especially 24–31). Indeed, when he wrote, "The difficulty is to realize the groundlessness of our believing" (1969, 24e), he reiterated the uncertainty of even empirical claims, and thereby straddled the fine line that separates solipsism and public discourse: "I act with complete certainty. But this certainty is my own" (1969, 25e). Wittgenstein's later views have had lasting effect in contemporary philosophy and beyond, but for our present purposes in setting the philosophical context of Freudian psychoanalysis, the earlier Wittgenstein is the crucial one in terms of how he influenced the philosophy of science during the first half of the twentieth century. (The above discussion of Wittgenstein's philosophy of language has been adapted from Tauber 2009, 105, 199–200.)

15. Mathematical and logical statements are analytical (tautologies) and true by definition. Such propositions are helpful in organizing cognitively meaningful statements, but are not verifiable by examining the world and thus say nothing about the world. In contrast, synthetic truths are empirical. The analytic/synthetic division may be dated to Leibniz and Hume, but it is most clearly stated by Kant, who argued in the first *Critique* that sensory experience required mental (cognitive) synthesis, while analytic statements were tautological and rested within their own internal logic and definition. For instance, the truth of the statement, "All unwedded men are bachelors," depends solely on the definition of "bachelor" and thus is an analytic statement. "I dropped the ball" is a synthetic statement and its truth content is assessed by determining whether I actually dropped a physical sphere, and if not, whether my statement refers to having failed an assignment or responsibility, or some other referent. In short, synthetic judgment requires some interpretative, empirical operation. This distinction was overturned by Willard van Orman Quine, who dismantled the positivist program to open philosophy of science to a radical deconstruction led by Thomas Kuhn, Michael Polanyi, and Paul Feyerabend (Zammito 2004; Tauber 2009).

16. With that position, analytic philosophy was born (Hylton 1990; Giere and Richardson 1996; Tait 1997), largely in revolt against the idealism that dominated philosophy at the turn of the century (see Reichenbach 1938; 1951; Frank 1960; and various papers in Ayer 1959).

17. After observing that Freud's theory possessed explanatory power and appeared to be verified by observations, Popper goes on to write that each case example "had been interpreted in the light of 'previous experience,' and at the

same time counted as additional confirmation. What, I asked myself, did it con-firm? No more than that a case could be interpreted in light of the theory. But this meant very little.... I could not think of any human behaviour which could not be interpreted in terms of either [Freud's or Adler's] theory. It was precisely this fact—that they always fitted, that they were always confirmed—which in the eyes of their admirers constituted the strongest argument in favour of these theories. It began to dawn on me that this apparent strength was in fact their weakness" (1963, 35).

Chapter 3
Storms over Königsberg

1. In either case, the subject-object dichotomy, the Cartesian-Lockean concep-tion of the knowing agent, remained intact. The more radical approach followed by Heidegger was to reconfigure the subject-object dichotomy by redefining the ontology of the subject altogether as Dasein (Bambach 1995).

2. Hermeneutics, as formulated by Friedrich Schleiermacher two generations earlier, was initially used as a tool to assess texts (literary texts, codes of law, his-torical documents, contracts, etc.), but Dilthey radically expanded the interpreta-tive method to "life" itself. "Every part of life ... has significance for the whole. And, in turn, the whole determines the significance of each part. Life expresses itself to us within a context of meaning whose unity is based on this part-to-whole relationship, following a hermeneutical structure.... In seeing the human world in this way, Dilthey radically altered the meaning of hermeneutics within German philosophy. Whereas hermeneutics had been ... a methodological tool used to guarantee the scientific rigor of philological and historical understanding, for Dilthey it became an essential part of the foundations of the human sciences" (Bambach 1995, 164).

3. A Hegelian stream enters with Dilthey's commitment to historicism, in his placing reason within a historical context, which meant for him that if all knowl-edge was an expression of human "life" (holding a particular meaning in Dilthey's philosophy [Zaner and Heiges 1977, 4–11; Betanzos 1988, 12–16]; see previous note), then knowledge was historically contingent. He thus opened himself to charges of historical relativism, and while committed to obtaining an objective view of human life, the effort of finding some meeting point (as he himself recog-nized) seemed doomed (Bambach 1995, 176ff; Gadamer 1990, 218ff.).

4. The admission by Dilthey and Windelband of what was essentially a failure of metaphysics became a rout with Heidegger's "recasting the historicist's epis-temological question about the objectivity of historical knowledge [as] an onto-logical question about the meaning of historical being" (Bambach 1995, 184). Heidegger overturned the very framework of discussion by arguing that Dilthey's theory of knowledge was still conceived as a theory of "method" aimed at sci-entific objectivity (Bambach 1995, 181–85). For Heidegger, "method" was not a mode of investigation but rather a metaphysical concept, inasmuch as *method*, understood since Descartes's *Discourse*, was a way to define *truth* (Heidegger

1979). Truth on this view establishes itself in the certitude of self-consciousness (as opposed to revelation, for instance), and this certainty thus rests on human assessment, measurement, and ultimately, interpretation. This Cartesian formulation, however, is not conceived simply as "subjective" feelings, desires, beliefs, etc., but rather resides in what Heidegger calls, a "subjectivist" attitude. Simply, once the knowing subject is firmly grounded in its own self-consciousness, the world then confidently becomes an object of scrutiny. Kant further developed this key modernist tenet by presenting the world through the a priori conditions of the human mind, which provides the preconditions for experiencing objects at all. The end of the twentieth century witnessed this fundamental argument continued in various guises, notably by Thomas Kuhn (1991), Jürgen Habermas (1971), Richard Rorty (1991), Karl-Otto Apel (1994), and many others.

5. Of the figures discussed here, Friedrich Albert Lange is associated with the Marburg School; his lineage is more directly traced not so much to his philosophical position as through his mentorship of Hermann Cohen, who was followed by Paul Natorp and Ernst Cassirer, each of whom was more Kantian than Lange himself. Lange dealt most directly with the issue of scientific epistemology and was heavily influenced by the physiologist Hermann Helmholtz. Windelband entered the neo-Kantian school through the Baden (or southwest German) School, which was preoccupied with value theory. Windelband studied with Rudolph Lotze and Kuno Fischer. Fisher's two-volume study of Kant, *Geschichte der neueren Philosophie* (1860–61), became a landmark in the genesis of neo-Kantianism through its renewed criticism of Kantian epistemology (albeit from a Hegelian point of view) (Könke 1991, 40–57). Lotze, although hardly a direct forerunner of neo-Kantianism, was a pivotal figure in the struggle against Hegelianism and materialism (Könke 1991, 59–68). Windelband returned to "Kantian-Cartesian questions of methodology and epistemology as a strategy for assuring the certitude of the sciences" (Bambach 1995, 58), and his philosophy reflects an indebtedness to both: To Lotze, Windelband attributed his primary interest in the concept of value (Windelband 1921, 209), and to Fischer, Windelband credited his basic Fichtean approach to the epistemology of selfhood, i.e. the primacy of consciousness (Windelband 1921, 282).

6. In barest outline, realism is "commonsensical" (Miller 2002, 13), and although it comes in several varieties (Horwich 2004b; Fine 1998; Alston 2002), its basic tenets maintain that facts of the world exist and those facts do not owe their existence to our ability to appreciate them, or even the possibility of knowing them. Following Hilary Putnam (1983; 1990), philosophers more broadly refer to this belief as "metaphysical realism." A simplified definition states that the picture science offers of the world *corresponds* to reality and is therefore true and faithful, so that the entities postulated *really exist as described*. In its simplest form, truth then corresponds to a human-independent reality.

In contrast to the realist, a more skeptical antirealist position hedges her bets. Despite the assertions of the commonsensical position of the realist, profound philosophical conundrums concerning the relation of mind with the material world arise from the antirealist challenge. While the realist maintains that the world exists independent of human mind, the antirealist asserts that such claims are meaningless, because the world can *only be known* cognitively (through mind functions). Accordingly, one might "accept the well established theories of science (even about unobservable) as (probably) true, but that this should not be understood as accepting the 'metaphysical realist' (Putnam's term) view that the statements which constitute those theories correspond to reality" (Boyd 2002). After all, empiricism holds that all knowledge of fact (as opposed to logic or mathematics) is based on experience, but if such knowledge is mediated as the antirealist argues, the consequences of such mediation must be understood.

Antirealism, like realism, is not a single philosophy, but rather captures a variety of critiques opposing the cluster of opinions that comprise realism. A schematic approach would divide the matter into three approaches:

    a. Ontologically, antirealism does not dispute the existence of things. Simply, antirealists see an irredeemable conflict between the autonomy of facts (that facts exist independent of us) and their accessibility (the possibility of our gaining knowledge of them) (Horwich 2004a).

    b. Epistemologically, the scientific antirealist asserts that the paradigm of *knowledge* is on *observed* facts, which are dependent on human cognition. Such facts may be reformulated and used as theoretical terms, but once an attempt is made to extend such knowledge into a distinct realm of unobservable facts, insuperable obstacles arise, "for how could we ever recognize such facts, or even so much as comprehend them?" (Horwich 2004a, 35). In other words, "theoretical facts" are those that are postulated but not observed.

    c. Finally, a semantic version of the debate shifts the argument from the ontological and epistemological theaters: Following Michael Dummett (1963), realism and antirealism clash over opposed theories of meaning. The realist understands meaning in terms of truth conditions (the situations that must obtain if they are to be true), while the antirealist maintains that meanings are understood under the conditions in which we are justified in asserting them. "*Semantic* realism is a theory about how to interpret a certain set of sentences; it is a theory about the *meaning* of our words. *Metaphysical* realism is a theory about the ultimate nature of reality; it is a theory about our *ontological* commitments.... Obviously, the truth of metaphysical realism does not entail semantic realism, nor does the converse hold. It might turn out that metaphysically real objects exist but that the statements that we utter about the external world do not in fact express a commitment to these objects. Alternatively, it might turn out that although our statements about the external world assert the existence of mind-independent objects, we are somehow being deceived and none of the objects to which we are committed does in fact exist." (Anderson 2002, 132)

Adapted from Tauber 2009, 201–5.

7. We might concur that the degree of epistemological agreement between individual knowers must be very high (because of adaptive evolution, the commonality of language, and the overwhelming evidence of practice), yet because

of the "other minds" problem and the uncertainty of noumena, Kant, inadvertently, opened the doors of skepticism and relativism in a new way. Science has, of course, always made a privileged claim on objectivity, but if one extrapolates the Kantian position from individual perceptions to instruments, on the one hand, and social factors (including language, cultural values, political organization, etc.) on the other hand, then "constructivism" in science becomes a problem of degree. In short, the argument hinges on the degree to which science's privileged epistemological position protects its cognitive content from contamination by confounding elements not factored into the calculus of ideal objective knowing. Presumably that critical judgment is tempered by human experience bumping into nature and accommodating itself to those realities (Tauber 2009, 60, 100–102).

8. As already discussed, for the realist, truth is grounded in some ultimate reality, while for the antirealist, in any format, cautiously claims that the aims of science can be well served without encumbering it with truth criteria that cannot be met. In other words, instead of proclaiming a theory to be true, this "modest realist" would simply display it, and enumerate its virtues, which may include the empirical values of adequacy, simplicity, comprehensiveness, coherence, predictability, etc. (van Fraassen 1980; see n. 6 above and Tauber 2009, 102–4, 123–29).

9. Helmholtz's mature assessment of his epistemology in relation to Kant (and his most comprehensive philosophical paper) was given in 1878, "The Facts of Perception," where he firmly distanced himself from transcendental speculation, which he regarded as aptly applied to mathematics but inapplicable to an epistemology based on *experience*, by which he meant scientific investigation (Helmholtz 1971a, 407). Experience, of course, was based on the Kantian precept that the mind ordered perceptions by its own laws (Helmholtz 1971b, 77).

10. Joining that effort, Lange became an enthusiastic proponent of Kantianism, stating that "the physiology of the sense-organs is developed or corrected Kantianism" (Lange 1950, book 2, third section, 202), i.e., "our senses determine, in a restricted way, the nature of appearances for us" (Stack 1991, 35), and he even went so far as equating "the reality of the phenomenal world [with] ... the physiology of the sense-organs" (Lange 1950, book 2, first section, 158). In this sense, Lange was a close devotee of Kant: He equated Kant's (1) metaphysical epistemology with a scientific epistemology ("the whole of our world of appearances depends on our organs" [Lange 1950, book 2, first section, 217]); (2) "transcendental method with psychological analysis of the mind" (Willey 1978, 88); and (3) "categories of knowing" with the psycho-physiological structures of the brain (Willey 1978, 102). Thus experience is a compound physiological occurrence, where "experience is no open door through which external things ... can wander in to us, but a process by which the appearance of things arises within us" (Lange 1950, book 2, first section, 188).

11. Of many instances, consider this comment characteristic of Lange's antimetaphysical stance: "Perhaps some day the basis of the idea of cause may be found in the mechanism of reflex action and sympathetic excitation; we should then have translated Kant's pure reason into physiology, and so made it more easily conceivable. But the question ["How is experience possible?"] essentially

continues to be the same; for when once simple faith in the reality of the phenomenal world is expelled, the step from the physical to the intellectual element
will always remain unknown, just because we can only conceive it in sensuous
images" (Lange 1950, book 2, first section, 211).

12. Since Lange's idealism is epistemic, rather than ontological, he did not
speculate on the "being" or transcendental conditions of either the phenomenological or noumenal realm but, rather, sets out only to define their boundaries. According to "Kant's own view ... the 'thing-in-itself' is a mere idea of limit" (Lange
1950, book 2, first section, 216), from which Lange argued that the noumenal
can only be thought of as a mental (imaginary) approximation of an elusive yet
ever-present anchor to an objective world forever inaccessible to us.

13. Lange was skeptical of belief in all Ideas, even belief in a "unified 'ego'"
(Stack 1991, 38). More generally, "While Kant held that objects of knowledge
were conceived of in terms of the application of the category of unity, Lange
argued that there are no pure unities in the natural world.... [Indeed they are]
... fictitious," and "categories such as unity, substance, being, object, cause, etc.,
were basically convenient hypothetical notions that have practical value but no
ontological reference" (Stack 1991, 38).

14. "Some attempt has recently been made (by Stumpf, Brentano, &c.) to eliminate 'unconscious' or 'latent' ideas out of psychology.... There is ... assuredly a
material error in Brentano, if he proposes to explain everything by ideas which
have been conscious but have been forgotten. Comp. especially the inadequate
way in which Brentano tries to dispose of Maudsley's views as to unconscious
intellectual labour" (Lange, 1950, book 2, third section, 193 n. 60).

15. This line of criticism assumes wide-ranging relevance considering the normative structure of psychiatric thinking (Sadler 2004; Bolton 2008). Putting aside
the antipsychiatry critics (Laing 1960; Szasz 1961; Foucault 2006a; 2006b), unpacking psychoanalysis's normative value system remains a philosophical challenge, namely, explicating how "value" and "facts" are inextricably intertwined
as a complex array, in which diverse values both create knowledge and apply it.
I have previously explored this issue in different contexts (Tauber 1999a; 2001;
2005; 2009), and here again, defining the amalgamation of facts and values underlies my own method of untangling the various epistemological and moral
strands of psychoanalytic theory and practice, a matter considered in detail in
chapter 6.

16. Freud goes on to observe with some circumspection, "The fact that a theory is psychologically determined does not in the least invalidate its scientific
truth" (1913a, 179). Interesting that he used the word "scientific."

17. Note that while objectivity has lost its rarified status, Windelband hardly
discarded it. He bypassed the concern with the objective content of the noumenal
world because the "thing-in-itself remains a postulated nothing, to which no real
definition and no formal relation can be applied" (1921, 195). He also understood Kant's noumena only "as *limiting conceptions* of experience" (Windelband
1919, 547), but even though they are not knowable, noumena "must be thought"
(548) if philosophical inquiry is to have any reference point at all. Thus, Windelband posited the theoretical existence of absolute value and transcendental

normativity to conclude that "the existence of a stable world stands or falls by the constancy and similarity of factual impressions based on such values" (Picard 1920, 142). At this nexus, the transcendental, "normal" relationship between the world and man's impressions must be sought. Thus Windelband's notion of normativity serves as a placeholder in his skeptical idealism.

For Windelband, the philosopher's task is to strive toward an understanding of the transcendental values that unite historical and scientific data, and it is the task of each society to determine its own (relatively) transcendental values, its own "relative norms" (Hodge 1896, 635). Freud (with Nietzsche) took one further step: it is the moral task of each individual to determine his own values, norms, and motivating factors. Further, these norms were relative. Note that while admitting that standards vary as they arise in different cultures and historical periods (Windelband 1921, 307–8), Windelband nevertheless fiercely opposed relativism. His insistence on the existence of objective values lies in the belief that "'natural man' has no immediate awareness of his moral duty or of how to order his thinking correctly: it is the discipline of history that has trained the peoples in both of them" (Könke 1991, 238, quoting Windelband). So from a philosophical study of history, humans might eventually discover the logically necessary foundation of morality. A prominent historical consciousness informed this project. For Windelband, the return to Kant was built on a merger of criticism with the historicist perspective, so prevalent at this time, to create an invigorated new idealism (Kiernan 1961, viii). Accordingly, the necessary forms of thought must transcend the individual (the empirical) and therefore are only to be found through a study of *all* of the sciences (Kiernan 1961, 68) in hopes that the "the logical thought-form" (Windelband 1961, 24) might be revealed.

18. Windelband defined philosophy as the search for "the absolutely real" (1921, 39), which he based on a "science of values which are universally valid" (1919, 680). While he presupposed the *existence* of absolute values, he never feigned knowledge of *what*, exactly, those values are, and instead of formulating such a schema, his *Introduction to Philosophy* (1921) largely takes the form of a series of criticisms of numerous dogmatic positions.

19. According to Windelband, rather than attempt to salvage something objective in experience, objectivity is to be sought in the study of what transcends and unites experience. In other words, given the Kantian idealist tenets, he dismissed the realist position of the positivist, and instead assigned himself the task of better grounding knowledge and the epistemological agent within the constraints of human cognition. On this path, he followed Lange's epistemological direction and observed that "*the only object of human knowledge is experience*, i.e. phenomenal appearance; and the division of objects of knowledge into phenomena and noumena, which has been usual since Plato, has no sense. A knowledge of things-in-themselves through 'sheer reason,' and extending beyond experience, is a nonentity, a chimera" (Windelband 1919, 546).

20. The rationale for positing a moral imperative is the same as that of Kant. If "the requirement of the moral command [in a general sense] must be propounded and fulfilled solely for its own sake" (Windelband 1919, 552), then a prerequisite of free moral agency must be an augmented understanding of the mysterious

norms that motivate and unify human actions and experiences. Windelband read Kant's categorical imperative as a system in which each "submit[s] his will to a law, a command, and tells him[self] that this command is entirely independent of whatever tendencies the individual finds already present in his will" (Windelband 1921 236–37).

Chapter 4
The Paradox of Freedom

1. This matter has, of course, a rich scholarly literature organized around the problem of psychic determinism, which I previously considered around the Wittgensteinian differentiation of "cause" and "reason." I have made no further attempt to elucidate the various interpretations of drives, instincts, desires, wishes, and so on, nor the more specific (and possibly germane) decipherment of the various psychodynamic theories pertaining to their control other than in the very narrow sense of the philosophical role of reason, further developed below. For treatment of the determinism in the psychoanalytic context issue see, for example, Arlow (1959), Holt (1972), Rosenblatt and Thickstun (1977), Wallace (1985), and Meissner (1995; 1999).

2. As Freud explained, "We know two things about what we call our psyche (or mental life): firstly, its bodily organ and scene of action, the brain (or nervous system), and on the other hand, our acts of consciousness, which are immediate data and cannot be further explained by any sort of description. Everything that lies between is unknown to us, and so the data do not include any direct relation between these two terminal points of our knowledge. If it existed, it would at most afford an exact localization of the processes of consciousness and would give us no help towards understanding them" (1940b, 144–45). In that opinion, Freud joined good company. For instance, William James, in his magisterial *Principles of Psychology* (1890), wrote extensively *about* consciousness, but eschewed a definition, and further, he would "discard all curious inquiries about its certainty as too metaphysical" (James 1983, 185). Then, as James moved from a scientific orientation to a philosophical one, a nagging sore opened. In "Does Consciousness Exist?" (first presented as a lecture in 1905), he observed,

> For twenty years past I have mistrusted "consciousness" as an entity; for seven or eight years past I have suggested its non-existence to my students, and tried to give them its pragmatic equivalent in realities of experience. It seems to me that the hour is ripe for it to be openly and universally discarded.... Let me then immediately explain that I mean only to deny that the word stands for an entity, but to insist most emphatically that it does stand for a function. (1996, 3)

From this position, James went on to develop a functional thesis of the mind, and much of later twentieth-century philosophy of mind argued this issue. Needless to say, Freud did not. He resided comfortably with the James of 1890, and there matters stood.

From a different tradition altogether, Wittgenstein espoused a similar end-point. For Wittgenstein, the "self," while a useful linguistic tool, refers to a metaphysical construction. In the *Notebooks 1914–1916*, he mused, "The thinking subject is surely mere illusion. But the willing subject exists. If the will did not exist, neither would there be that centre of the world, which we call the I, and which is the bearer of ethics. What is good and evil is essentially the I, not the world. The I, the I is what is deeply mysterious! The I is not an object" (Wittgenstein 1979, 80e), and later in the *Tractatus* he argued:

5.63   I am my world. (The microcosm)

5.631 The thinking, perceiving subject does not exist…. (or: The thinking, presenting subject; there is no such thing)

5.632 The subject does not belong to the world but is the boundary [limit of the world….

5.633 Where *in* the world could a metaphysical subject be? …

5.641 … The philosophical I is not the human being, not the human body, not the human soul with which psychology deals. The philosophical self is the metaphysical subject, the boundary—nowhere in the world. (Wittgenstein 1998, 38–39)

G.E.M. Anscombe (1959, 68) explains that the "I" "is not something that can be found as a mind or soul, a subject of consciousness, one among others; there is no such thing to be 'found' as the subject of consciousness in this sense. All that can be found is what consciousness is of, the contents of consciousness: 'I am my world' and 'The world and life are one.' Hence this 'I,' whose language has the special position, is unique; the world described by this language is just the real world: 'Thoroughly thought out, solipsism coincides with pure realism'" ([*Tractatus*] 5.640). In other words, "There is no 'I,' no ego or subject, that stands alone in the world and sees and thinks and confers sense on what it sees and thinks. But there is a language of thought, and 'I' is the formal point of reference for it" (Heaton and Groves 1994, 49). See also Wittgenstein's remarks in *The Blue and Brown Books* (1958, 60ff.)

3. Criticism of representationalism underlying Freud's philosophy of mind has been made on the basis that (1) the unconscious can only be known through its expression in affect and thus separate from the realm of representation (Henry 1993); (2) psychoanalytic meaning is generated from an interactional conception of mind, which highlights the competing visions between a neurophysiological reductionism and a view of psychological explanation directed by meaning and purpose (Cavell 1988); and (3) representationalism has been critiqued generally by contemporary philosophers (reviewed in the psychoanalytic context by Levin 1995).

4. Famously, Freud abandoned the "seduction theory" as a result of recognizing that he could no longer "distinguish between truth and fiction" in the unconscious (Freud 1986, 264; letter to Fliess, September 21, 1897), which indicated that normal cause-effect relationships and categories of association do not adhere to the logic of everyday experience. That does not mean that Freud could not discern the workings of unconscious desires, but the strategies of investigation

and interpretation required a sleuth-like procedure given the limitations imposed by "the psyche [that] can only be approached obliquely, [through] ... 'signals'" (Green 2005, 11) or clues (Ginzburg 1983).

5. Various alternative orientations have been adopted to interpret Kant's conception (and use) of reason: (1) part of the skeptical attack of discrediting speculative metaphysics; (2) a vindication of, or allowance for, metaphysics; (3) a rejection of scientific realism; (4) a refutation of Humean skepticism by establishing a transcendental defense of objectivity and science; (5) a characterization of reason as teleological (Velkley 1989). This last theme orders the précis of Kant's project that follows (the capacity of reason to direct itself towards some good).

6. "The antimony of pure reason" in Kant's first *Critique* provides the argument for reason's autonomy (1998, 484–87 [B474–75]). There he attempts to solve the contradiction of comprehending causal (natural) law of the world as something universal by positing that "causality through freedom" lies not in the empirical domain, but in the "intelligible character" of the agent; i.e., freedom is not an empirical concept. (The argument is schematized by Allison 2004, 378 and 382 and by Watkins 2005, 306 and 308.) So the world of appearances and the intelligible world are governed by noncontradicting types of causality, an argument that rests on Kant's fundamental neumonon/phenomenon distinction (Kant 1998, 535–36 [B566–67]). For different interpretations of how Kant presented his case, see Guyer (1987, 411–12), Allison (2004, 376ff.), and Watkins (2005, 304–16).

7. The problematic status of the "mental," in the sense discussed here, was forcefully expounded by Quine, who sought "to demolish the ontology of mental states altogether" (Zammito 2004, 38). His overriding commitment to naturalism drove him to assert that he could discriminate a "fact of the matter" for physical theory, which could not be achieved for mental states.

> By postulating the ontology of current natural science, Quine believes he can anchor epistemology as much as it can be anchored, since there is no first philosophy, no foundationalism. There is a "fact of the matter" about the world for Quine, because he adopts as his ontology the views of contemporary natural science. Physicalism postulates that all there is, ultimately, is the world of physics, the world physics as a research science has unearthed, or the world according to the latest theory of physics. (Zammito 2004, 42)

Thus Quine was radically committed to a naturalized epistemology, and the ontology of mental states simply does not conform to those standards; i.e., they do not adhere to physical concomitants and thus are not *facts*.

8. Ernst Tugendhat comes to a similar conclusion (one that is developed further in chapter 6): "It is striking that Freud not only does not refer to the ordinary way of talking about the 'I' but also does not even speak of a relation of oneself to oneself. The ego is an objective power within the psychical reality .. reduced to an anonymous organization with an integrative function. In so doing he discards precisely that aspect which was the basis for the orientation toward the expression *I*: the relation of oneself to oneself" (1986, 131).

9. Of course, the relationship Freud's ideas had with Kant's depends on how Kant is construed and employed. Predictably, then, scholars disagree on this assessment (e.g., MacIntyre 1958, 31, 71; Pettigrew 1990, 67–88; Rozenberg 1999; Fulgencio 2005, 108–10; Askay and Farquhar 2006). Most germane to my own point of view, Alasdair MacIntyre comments on Freud's use of autonomy in the Kantian context. He makes the point that two versions of the ego appear in Freud's opus; i.e., the ego is "in heteronomous thrall to the It and the Superego" and has the "task of becoming autonomous" (MacIntyre 2004, 10). MacIntyre sees the same paradox of an ego-as-autonomous and ego-as-determined that I have explicated, and he offers the following qualifications for such an ego to be theoretically sustainable: a rational agent must (1) be undeceived by reasons and motives, (2) have a conception of his own good, and (3) be able to articulate that good and subject it to scrutiny (MacIntyre 2004, 12). In due course, we will consider these characteristics and whether the paradox is resolved or not.

Bettina Bergo and I explore similar epistemological parallels between Kant and Freud, but we disagree that this relationship was self-evident to Freud himself; i.e., "Freud sought to go further than Kant had ventured," (Bergo 2004, 344). That is, "The unconscious was arguably more than Kant's noumenon, because it did not set a speculative limit to the possibilities of experience but instead opened certain types of experience to systematic investigation" (345). Furthermore she does not consider the wider moral impact of Kant's project on Freudianism.

Opposing these sympathetic readings, virtually every previous consideration of Freud's relationship to philosophy either ignores or pays scant attention to Kant, and some actively deny any connection (e.g., Kaufmann 1980; Decker 1977). Walter Kaufmann offers a good example of this latter position. He opined that Freud embraced a "deeply anti-Kantian conception of science" (1980, 79), which Kaufman characterizes as a "poetic science of the mind [that] constitutes his first major discovery" (1980, 109). As a poet-scientist, Freud, according to Kaufman, models himself after Goethe (1980, 16ff.; 32–45), an opinion shared by Fritz Wittels (Kaufman 1980, 38) and later commentators (e.g., Ellenberger 1970, 465–67). Kaufman's antipathy for Kant notwithstanding (1980, 42–43), he strangely saw Kant as "Goethe's great antipode" (13), when contrary testimony is plain and direct that Goethe saw himself fulfilling Kant's project (Goethe 1988b, 29; Tauber 2009, chap. 2). Beyond the shared sensibility of the aesthetic and the sublime, the rejection of positivism (the construction of reality by melding "mind" and "nature"), Goethe embraced Kant's characterization of reason. However, rather than divide reason as irredeemably separate, Goethe regarded them as emanating from a single root (Goethe 1988b, 29; Tauber 2009, chap. 2) (which Kant called the "unconditioned") and believed that they might be traced to their common origin and ultimately combined. This was, in fact, the guiding aspiration of Goethe's scientific investigations (Tauber 1993). So contrary to Kaufmann's appraisal, the Goethean-Freudian affinity offers further support to Freud's debts to Kant.

10. However, it is important to note that Kant did not mean by "autonomy a self-determination of the person as a person or of the I as an I, but a self-

determination of reason" (Tugendhat 1986, 133–34). Kant never refers to an autonomous self or an autonomous person or autonomous individual, but rather to the autonomy of reason, the autonomy of ethics, the autonomy of principles, and the autonomy of willing (O'Neill 2002, 83). Hence, so-called principled autonomy is not something one has, nor is it equated with personal independence or self-expression. Rather, it is the self-legislated moral behavior prescribed by principles that could be laws for all (Kant 1996c, 73 [4:421] and *passim*).

> Reasoning … is simply a matter of striving for principled autonomy in the spheres of thinking and of action. Autonomy in thinking is no more—but also no less—than the attempt to conduct thinking (speaking, writing) on principles on which all others whom we address could also conduct their thinking.… Autonomy in action is no more—but also no less—than the attempt to act on principles on which all others could act. Wood's dilemma is avoided because Kantian autonomy is neither derived from an antecedently given but unjustified account of reason (hence unreasoned), nor lacking in structure (hence willful and arbitrary); principled autonomy itself supplies basic structures of reasoning. (O'Neill 2002, 94)

Thus for Kant, moral agency is grounded in the ability to discern moral principles—to judge and choose, to act and execute according to what might reasonably be applied to others. In short, principled autonomy is a formulation of the basic requirements of all reasoning (O'Neill 2002, 90–91), and, accordingly, moral will is primary, not reason, and moreover, this will is the foundation of reason itself.

11. Stuart Hampshire clearly presented the argument against the very possibility of defining psychic determinism, in terms of the underdetermination of psychic sequences and influences (1975, 113ff.), and Donald Davidson (1980b) argued towards the same conclusion on the basis that mental and physical domains operate with different constitutive principles; i.e., mental states are not subject to the same scientific laws that govern physical events.

12. Of course, one could not draw any parallels between Kant's development of his explicit moral philosophy, embedded in the notion of a categorical imperative, with the Freudian construction that would deny any such idealistic formulation (Wallwork 1991, 239; Meissner 2003, 31–35). Indeed, in this context, Freud utterly rejected Kantian deontological ethics, but this is not the manner in which I have sought to chart Freud's debts to Kant. Further, as noted by an anonymous reviewer of the manuscript of this book, for Kant, "Moral reason is not based on freedom per se. Freedom is and remains a regulative ideal, rationally undemonstrable. It is even the object of an Antinomy in the first *Critique*. If it should be assumed in the practical sphere (along with an abiding, spiritual substance like the soul, and its creator: liberty, soul, God), it can never be demonstrated."

13. Nietzsche observed in an early notebook, "What a curious opposition, '*knowledge and faith*'! What would the Greeks have thought of this? Kant *was acquainted with no other opposition*, but what about us! A cultural need impels Kant; he wishes to *preserve* a domain *from knowledge*: that is where the

roots of all that is highest and deepest lie, of art and of ethics" (1979, 11). Given Nietzsche's sustained and relentless attack on Reason, this astute comment struck at the heart of Kant's project. For many reasons Nietzsche has been reckoned the first postmodernist, a title well deserved (Koelb 1990).

Chapter 5
The Odd Triangle: Kant, Nietzsche, and Freud

1. *Apperception* is the perception of one's own consciousness; *empirical apperception* is the ego's awareness of actual and changing states of consciousness, a function of the *empirical ego*, in contrast to the *pure ego*, which produces a transcendental apperception, the faculty that affixes the unchanging unity of consciousness. This pure ego precedes (is transcendent to) the content of human perceptions and makes possible their experienced order and meaning. This structured unity consists of (1) the intuitions of time and space, and (2) the categories of understanding. Transcendental apperception is thus the necessary condition for synthesizing experience into meaning (Angeles 1981, 16).

2. Kant also referred to apperception as a logical condition: for one to become conscious, it must be logically possible to ascribe representations. The objects of empirical consciousness are not the objects of the self or the mind. Thus there is a clear distinction between the world as object and the mind's ability to attend to its own representing activity as a distinct capacity. This is an important distinction between the Kantian "self" and the Cartesian. The Cartesian view is that all consciousness, including all Kantian experience, is a species of self-consciousness (Pippin 1989, 20). According to Kant, on the other hand, self-consciousness is a condition of experience, because the unity necessary to appreciate an object by an identical subject depends on the implicit ability to be self-aware. A subject that is "perceiving, imagining, remembering, and so on is an inseparable component of *what it is* to perceive, imagine, remember, and so on" (Pippin 1989, 21).

3. No effort to situate my discussion within the enormous contemporary literature on the philosophical and neuro-scientific character of consciousness is made here. However, the position charted by Daniel Wegner (2002) strikes me as a useful framework in which to place the problem: He proposes that self-consciousness and conscious will in particular (which constitutes my main concern) arose as an evolutionary mechanism to appreciate and remember what we are doing and, furthermore, to consider future action. If one becomes self-aware of options and choices, then action follows a kind of primitive reason or "cognitive feeling" (Clore 1992). On this view, self-consciousness serves as a means of monitoring states of the self in these deliberations. "Conscious will is the mind's compass"; serving "like a compass reading, the feeling of doing tells us something about the operation of the ship.... Just as compass readings do not steer the boat, conscious experiences of will do not cause human actions" (Wegner 2002, 317–18). Conscious will, then, appears as an "emotion of authorship" (318), which means that "the perception of control is not the same thing as actual control"

(332), so in the end, conscious will is a product of self-monitoring, a sense of the will's autonomy when in fact it is an epiphenomenon of a particular form of mental self-appraisal. Of course, the character of responsibility and the ethical framework in which one functions is not explained by this formulation, which only offers a way of thinking about how moral reasoning might be based upon this model of reflexivity.

4. Perhaps the clearest statement of Kant's understanding of self-reflection is found in his discussion of inner states as objects of thought in his *Anthropology from a Pragmatic Point of View* of 1798. There Kant clarified his notions of "inner sense" and "apperception":

> This difficulty [the objectification of inner states] rests entirely on the confusion of *inner sense* with *apperception* (intellectual self-consciousness), which are usually taken to be one and the same. The I in every judgment is ... an act of understanding by the determining subject as such, and the consciousness of oneself; pure apperception itself therefore belongs merely to logic (without any matter and content). On the other hand, the I of inner sense, that is, of the perception and observation of oneself, is not the subject of judgment, but an object. Consciousness of the one who *observes* himself is an entirely simple representation of the subject in judgment as such, of which one knows everything if one merely thinks it. But the I which has been observed by itself is a sum total of so many objects of inner perception that psychology has plenty to do in tracing everything that lies hidden in it. And psychology may not ever hope to complete this task and answer satisfactorily the question: "What is the human being?" (Kant 2006, 31.)

Interestingly, the "inner state" Kant refers to apparently only possesses a one-way vector in the healthy mind, for those states that seemingly arise spontaneously, that is, appear independently of self-conscious scrutiny or intelligible self-awareness, and then are brought to self-consciousness (namely to "spy upon one's self" [Kant 1996e, 17]), are of a dangerous sort:

> To observe the various acts of representative power in myself, *when I summon them*, is indeed worth reflection; it is necessary and useful for logic and metaphysics.—But to wish to eavesdrop on oneself when they come into mind *unbidden* and on their own (this happens through the play of the power of the imagination when it is unintentionally meditating) constitutes a reversal of the natural order in the faculty of knowledge, because then the principles of thought do not lead the way (as they should), but rather follow behind. This eavesdropping on oneself is either already a disease of the mind (melancholy), or leads to one and to the madhouse. He who knows how to describe a great deal about his *inner experiences* (of grace, of temptations) may, with his voyage of discovery in the exploration of himself, land only in Anticyra [a city where a medicinal against madness grew]. (Kant 2006, 22)

Thus the entire métier of psychoanalysis—free association and unbidden thoughts and emotions—repelled Kant's sense of mental propriety (Stone 1983), and this

difference from Freud's psychiatric pursuits cautions us to be cognizant of the
vast differences in their theories of psychology while exploring their deeper philosophical affinities.

5. Schopenhauer conceived the world (as did Kant) of which we have knowledge as a world of appearance or, to use Schopenhauer's concept, "representation" (*things*-in-themselves are unknowable). Although there *is* an empirical
world composed of spatiotemporal objects, that world is "exhausted" in what
the subject perceives as its object:

> The world is my representation ... [N]o truth is more certain, more indepen-
> dent of all others, and less in need of proof than this, namely that everything
> that exists for knowledge, and hence the whole of this world, is only object in
> relation to the subject, perception of the perceiver, in a word, representation....
> Everything that in a way belongs and can belong to the world is inevitably as-
> sociated with this being-conditioned by the subject, and it exists only for the
> subject. The world is representation. (1969, l:3)

In other words, all objects presuppose a subject, and it is the subject that confers
connectedness and identity on the world. This knowing subject is not conceived
as an individual, but rather as the necessary correlate of all objects; as such, the
knower is never an object itself (5). It follows that the subject of representations
is itself unknowable, "like an eye that cannot see itself" (Janaway 1989, 6), and
thus Schopenhauer presented a perplexing Fichtean-Kantian riddle: (1) of the self
as unknowable to itself, and (2) of the transcendental world as known only as the
self's representation:

> Without representation, I am not knowing subject but mere, blind will; in just
> the same way, without me as subject of knowledge, the thing known is not
> object, but mere will, blind impulse. In itself, that is to say outside the represen-
> tation, this will is one and the same with mine; only in the world as representa-
> tion . . . are we separated as known and knowing individual. (Schopenhauer
> 1969, 1:180)

Further, "The intellect is the secondary phenomenon, the organism the primary, that is the immediate phenomenal appearance of the will; the will is metaphysical, the intellect physical; the intellect, like its objects, is mere phenomenon,
the will alone is thing-in-itself" (2:201). As Simmel adroitly puts it: "Schopenhauer has reduced man to the denominator shared by the totality of the world"
(1991, 34).

The Will constitutes the thing-in-itself, and all appearances are manifestations
of will, knowable to the intellect through the application of Kantian categories.
But in contrast to knowledge of appearances, the Will is known "immediately,"
and not by the intellect, but rather *through* action. The will *in* humans is both
more powerful and more primary than the intellect, and thus knowledge of willed
actions, for Schopenhauer, is uniquely immediate (Janaway 1989, 7). This insight
into how action situates and reveals the subject provides access to the underlying
thing-in-itself as existing *within* humans rather than being external and forever
beyond one's grasp. With the denial of an inner or purely mental act of willing

as preceding action, Cartesian dualism is foreclosed, and subjects of will are thus embodied. As embodied Will, actions define or, better, expose that will, leading ultimately to its full recognition. In this scheme, self-consciousness "is the *self-knowledge of the will*" (Schopenhauer 1969, 2:259), which becomes the concluding step of self-exploration. Thus this process, a product of the self-conscious capacity to appreciate one's own nature, allows humans to recognize fundamental being as "will" (Tauber 1994a, 239–49).

Whereas Kant left the perceiving subject as a transcendental principle to unify representations, Schopenhauer asserted, first, that subject and object were necessary correlates, and more radically, the modes of organization of objects stemmed *from* the subject, rather than existing *in* themselves. Second, he firmly situated the subject in the biological domain, where both body and mind were manifestations of blind purposiveness, the primacy of the Will. This second element allowed Schopenhauer a teleological corollary, which he built into an elaborate explanation of human action that I have not discussed, but note its reincarnation in Brentano's notion of *intention*, a concept that was to have a rich history in later phenomenology. Most germane here is that the Kantian split between pure subject and mere object disappears in the Schopenhaurian context of the self-awareness of the Will, of purpose, of subjecthood. The willing subject is another manifestation of the substratum of Will, but unique in recognizing its own being.

6. As with Nietzsche, Freud respected Schopenhauer, but allowed for no direct influence. In Freud's *Autobiographical Study*, he wrote: "I was always open to the ideas of G. T. Flechner and have followed that thinker upon many important points. The large extent to which psycho-analysis coincides with the philosophy of Schopenhauer—not only did he assert the dominance of the emotions and the supreme importance of sexuality but he was even aware of the mechanism of repression—is not to be traced to my acquaintance with his teaching. I read Schopenhauer very late in my life. Nietzsche, another philosopher whose guesses and intuitions often agree in the most astonishing way with the laborious findings of psycho-analysis, was for a long time avoided by me on that very account; I was less concerned with the question of priority than with keeping my mind un-embarrassed" (Freud 1925a, 59–60). For fair (and generous) appraisals of Freud's reluctance to acknowledge previous philosophers, see Hughes (1961, 106), Roazen (1968, 84–86), and note 9 below.

7. "Not only the consciousness of other things, i.e. the apprehension of the external world, but also *self-consciousness* ... contains a knower and a known, otherwise it would not be *consciousness*. For *consciousness* consists in knowing, but knowing requires a knower and a known. Therefore self-consciousness could not exist if there were not in it a known opposed to the knower and different therefrom. Thus, just as there can be no object without a subject, so there can be no subject without an object, in other words, no knower without something different from this that is known. Therefore, a consciousness that was through pure intelligence would be impossible.... Therefore in self-consciousness the known, consequently the will, must be the first and original thing; the knower, on the other hand, must be only the secondary thing, that which has been added, the mirror" (Schopenhauer 1969, 2:202).

8. Nietzsche's skeptical position derives from his very different concept of Schopenhauerian Will. For Nietzsche, the Will was a multiplicity of forces in competition: Thinking is only the occasional manifestation of such activity, and it is coalesced by value-laden needs and drives. But most profoundly Nietzsche contended that there is no need to posit a thinking subject, nor even *a* subject *of* willing at all: "*My hypothesis*: The subject as multiplicity" (1967, 270). So instead of belonging to a single, unified agent that thinks, wills, and acts, the mind, according to Nietzsche, is in a perpetual state of becoming, and thus the self is viewed as a continuous process of becoming: "There are only interpretations, but there is no 'I' that is the subject of the interpretation. The 'I' is a fiction whose author is an aggregate of manifestations of the will to power" (Janaway 1989, 355).

9. Drawing parallels and contrasts between Freud and Nietzsche dates to Freud himself, and, not surprisingly, a diverse literature has developed around the topic (e.g., Mazlish 1968; Waugaman 1973; Roazen 1991; Karwautz, Wöber-Bingöl, and Wöber 1995; Lehrer 1995; 1996; Assoun 2000; Greer 2002). Although Freud was undoubtedly well aware of Nietzsche's philosophy (indeed, he bought Nietzsche's collected works in 1900 and took them with him upon emigrating to England [Trosman and Simmons 1973]), he deliberately denied any direct influence (see note 6 above). He assumed this detachment in the face of having read Nietzsche as a young student and citing his guidance (Gay 1988, 45–46; Scavio, Cooper, and Scavio Clift 1993). Part of the reason for aloofness may have been Freud's commitment to science (as opposed to philosophy) and part to a reluctance to subtract anything from his own originality. Nevertheless, he quotes Nietzsche (Gay 1988, 129), and, more to the point, he shared with his erstwhile competitor two cardinal ideas about human agency: (1) a general orientation to believing in the primacy of unconscious drives, and (2) an understanding of human autonomy quite distinct from Kant's views. However, Nietzsche and Freud assemble each characteristic in different fashion, as discussed below.

10. Numerous commentators have dealt with various aspects of Nietzsche's biological conceptions relevant to this discussion, including evolution and Darwinism in particular (e.g., Mostert 1979; Smith 1986; 1987), Nietzsche's concepts of forces (e.g., Deleuze 1983; Moles 1990), the role of the body in Nietzsche's philosophy (e.g., Warren 1988; Foucault 1984; Kogaku 1991; Blondel 1991), and more specific issues regarding the unconscious (e.g., Ellenberger 1970; Golumb 1989; Jung 1988).

11. As David Levin observes, "Nietzsche comes within a breath of recognizing something like a corporeal intentionality, i.e., a 'functioning intentionality' of the body which is anterior to acts of 'judgment' and makes them possible: 'Before judgment occurs,' he writes, 'there is a cognitive activity that does not enter consciousness,' but which operates through the living body [1967, 289]. Nietzsche even hints ... at a cognitive functioning of the body which is able to unify its field of being and constitutes a personal identity without the intervention of a transcendental ego [1967, 270–71, 281, 294–95]" (Levin 1985, 35).

12. Recall from chapter 2 the discussion of the epistemological standing of Freud's empirical findings as distinguished from his frankly speculative metapsychological theorizing. The latter included his notion of instincts, and so when

discussing the standing of the death instinct specifically, he admitted that while its postulation addressed certain clinical phenomena (e.g., hypochondria, narcissism, sadism), that heuristic value must be balanced against skeptical doubts about the model's empirical standing (see above chap. 2, note 2).

13. *Trieb* and *Instinkt* may be differentiated: the former is speculative, while the latter has an objective referent (Fulgencio 2005); nevertheless Freud never differentiated them as such, nor compared them (Laplanche 2000).

14. The metaphysics derived from this organic orientation go in several directions. Nietzsche distinguished what would appear to be a guiding principle of biological processes, that of development and evolution—what he called becoming—from being. Becoming, that which is never complete or finished, always tentative and subject to change, is contrasted with being. That manifesto is a recurrent theme, but most succinctly stated as, "To impose upon becoming the character of being—that is the supreme Will to Power" (Nietzsche 1967a, 330). Thus the Will is engaged in the ontological project. This is not to deny "becoming," and in a different moral setting, Nietzsche uses precisely that terminology as the basis of a new ethic. Thus, depending on the context, there may be confusion concerning the concepts of becoming and being. On the one hand, his expounded ethic of living the full moment, man's full being in the present, appears in conflict with the basic notion of the self in constant strife, always in conflict, overcoming; as Zarathustra says, "Become what you are." The basic active drive will not allow self-satisfaction, but it does allow rapture, self-fulfillment. As Heidegger wrote, "All being is for Nietzsche a becoming" (1979, 7). But Nietzsche rejects a final state. Let there be no confusion: the changes wrought by time are self-apparent, but he imposes restrictions that redefine the moral dimension of becoming, and in the process of growth, demands that we recognize experience as *is*.

> Becoming must be explained without recourse to final intentions; becoming must appear justified at every moment ... [T]he present must absolutely not be justified by reference to a future, nor the past by reference to the present. To this end it is necessary to deny a total consciousness of becoming a "God," to avoid bringing all events under the aegis of a being who feels and knows but does not *will*. (Nietzsche 1967a, 377)

Zarathustra thus proclaims "God is dead" from this fundamental metaphysical orientation, and the prophet then builds upon this position to critique modern man: degenerate, disoriented, and diseased—and perhaps most devastating, crippled by nihilism.

15. Art was conceived by Schopenhauer as a means to escape the ruthless will (Simmel 1991, 75–104; Magee 1983, 164–88; Hamlyn 1980, 110ff.; Janaway 1989, 275–79), and Nietzsche would follow Schopenhauer's lead in viewing art as a means for self-transfiguration (Young 1992). Of course Freud saw art as an important conduit for sublimation, and he himself had diverse interests in art to the point that some have argued that his art resonates with his theories (Burke 2006), and that beyond his profound influence on art criticism, Freud himself should be considered an artist, albeit a repressed one (Chamberlain 2000).

16. On this reading, Freud, in terms of the sustained commitment to reason, remained a modernist, while Nietzsche proclaimed the postmodern (Koelb 1990; Behler 1991): If the classical object is characterized as given, independent of a subject, and the modern (i.e., Kantian) object is known only by its attributes bestowed by a knowing subject, the postmodern confounds the subject-object relationship as a wavering exchange (Tauber 1994a, 280–83). Nietzsche actively propounded the collapse of such distinctions ("'Subject,' 'object,' 'attribute'— these distinctions are fabricated" [1967a, 294]), and in the process he proposed a radical psychology: By removing the body as an *object* (and thus opposing Schopenhauer), Nietzsche firmly establishing it as the *basis* of selfhood and eschewed the disjointed Cartesian mind-body duality through a discourse that fuses the subjective "I" to its biological, i.e., instinctual or emotional identity (Tauber 1994b). Notwithstanding the appeal of this conception, Nietzsche appreciated the complexity and challenges of biological models to describe such an identity. But precisely in his multi-perspectivism, the schema might be refracted from many different angles, which of course is his philosophy's strength—and weakness.

17. I have argued that Freud relied on reason's autonomy to effect the distance and perspective on unconscious influences and thereby free a tortured ego. Does an inconsistency loom? David Hume argued that determinism was compatible with *liberty* and any confusion was the result of a linguistic snarl. "Liberty" and "necessity" are often paired as opposites, but the true opposite of "liberty" is "compulsion," and necessity's opposing pair is "chance" or "randomness" (Lindley 1986). Actions, including human actions, may be explained as "necessary" in the sense they do not occur at random. And "liberty" should be understood as any act performed without compulsion, i.e., against individual choice. A prisoner may be forced to act in a certain way; whether I get up and leave my house or not is freely chosen according to my will (Hume 1975, 95). Autonomy then corresponds to Hume's understanding of liberty, namely choices that seem reasonable.

18. Much of twentieth-century criticism concerning freedom of moral choice follows this orientation. Accordingly, not only is rationality often considered a conceit and incapable of assuring moral responsibility, but to even believe that ethical actions are reducible to insular reason ignores the complex array of social, existential, and emotional factors that go into play in any decision. The Humean position has been extended not only by psychoanalytic theory, but by Foucault's theories of power and agency (1970; 1983), feminist theories of sexual difference and otherness (Butler 1990), and various twentieth-century philosophical schools ranging from phenomenology to post-Wittgensteinian analytics. What holds these various perspectives on the "critique of the subject" together is the recognition that the ideal self is hardly self-transparent, psychically unified (or rational), or able to achieve self-mastery (Mackenzie and Stoljar 2000). *Reason* becomes highly problematic when the moral agent is depicted as conflict-driven, often self-deluded, fundamentally opaque, and driven by archaic drives and desires of which she is unaware and consequently cannot control. These forces may be intrapsychic (Freud) or social (George Herbert Mead), i.e., persons constituted within and by regimes, discourses and power of which they have little knowledge or control (Rose 1990; 1998), or by historically specified cultural ideals that

masquerade as universal norms (Butler 1990). In any case, following these views, moral-driven self-will (self-determining free choice) is a delusion of unrecognized configurations of psychic, political, or historical forces, and thus Freud's understanding of the autonomous individual, one who might strive for psychological emancipation, ironically no longer exists. Accordingly, "The sweeping changes in advanced industrial society are accompanied by equally basic changes in the primary mental structure" (Marcuse 1970, 59) leading to the collectivization of identity and the obsolescence of Freud's ego ideal and the autonomy that underlies it. More, "Freedom becomes an impossible concept, for there is nothing that is not prescribed for the individual in some way or another. And in fact freedom can be defined only within the framework of domination ... in which the means provided satisfy the needs of the individual" (2). Thus the autonomy, rationality, and conscience Freud considered fundamental to health has vanished into history (if ever existing at all). (See ch. 6, note 18 below.)

19. The Nietzschean I has little explicit concern for the social, or perhaps better stated, the I functions within the social domain in a spirit of self-aggrandizement. Nietzsche's philosophy fails to satisfactorily account for the Other and establish the basis of relation—a subject with another. The "self-centered" structure of his thought actually precludes consideration of a social ethics, because the individual is (1) affirmed as primary and self-sufficient, and (2) held captive to itself. Because the relation between persons is only described in terms of conflict and hierarchical control, cooperative intersubjectivity remains outside Nietzsche's concern (Tauber 1999a).

Chapter 6
Who Is the Subject?

1. "The positing of the self is a truth that posits itself; it can be neither verified nor deduced; it is at once the positing of a being and of an act; ... Fichte called this first truth the *thetic* [arbitrary, given] judgment" (Ricoeur 1970, 43).

2. A note on Freud's social morality: Politically, he identified as a liberal, for example he supported efforts to provide psychoanalytic services to the economically disadvantaged in free clinics that opened in ten European cities between 1920 and 1938 (Danto 2005). In another context, he applied psychoanalytic insights to explain social morality in works ranging from *Totem and Taboo* (1913b) to *Civilization and its Discontents* (1930) and "Why War?" (1932). Such essays principally were concerned with understanding human nature within the social milieu. This tributary of his thought—wide-ranging and highly speculative—has not received the same attention as the more narrow clinical applications, but nevertheless represents an important part of Freud's opus (Roazen 1968).

Some have argued for the essential political character of psychoanalysis, inasmuch as Freud viewed both the psyche and society as constellations of power and domination, and he saw their interplay as constitutive to each (Brunner 2001). After all, the relationship between individual and society, a relationship that is both internalized and resisted by the individual, underlies much of Freud's notions of ego function and reality mediation (Gabriel 1983). However, such social themes remain muted in Freud's writings, and only with the theory's radical revisions in the 1960s did the social import of psychoanalysis receive full attention. For instance, Thomas Szasz (1965) argued that psychotherapy, at best, was a form of social action (as opposed to healing) and that its function putatively served the goal of increasing the patient's self-knowledge and thereby personal autonomy. Since he argued that "mental illness" was a misapplied category of an extrapolated medical model, he, like Foucault (2003; 2006a; 2006b), also regarded psychotherapy as a tool of the state (Szasz 1961). Whether liberating or controlling, psychoanalysis in both modalities served a social function, namely, control.

Marxist theorists pushed psychoanalysis towards a more radical politics that reflected an ethics principally concerned with the individual situated within a larger collective in which persons might find a more optimal social world in which to live (e.g., Marcuse 1955). Utopian political critiques that arise from the psychoanalytic tradition also have various contemporary apostles (e.g., Rose 1990; 1998). More recent critiques following different lines of argument but arriving at a similar destination may be found in Horwitz (2002) and Bracken and Thomas (2005), with a critical overview by Pickering (2006).

The larger psychological issue, whether emotional problems are a function of misalignments of the ego or the appropriate response to a diseased or malevolent culture, obviously underlies the entire issue of social adjustment, appropriate ego reality testing, delinquency and so on, matters that lie at the heart of contemporary social psychology, ego psychology, and psychoanalysis. Interestingly, Freud had little comment on such questions, and as explained in the previous chapter, his interests remained for the most part focused on the individual's inner psychic dynamics.

3. Hegel's dispute with Kant follows many paths, but here the metaphysical argument focuses upon *reflexion*. For Hegel, *reflexion* especially as used by Kant (according to Hegel), maintains separation of contrasts, e.g., faith and reason, or finite and infinite, whereas reason serves to synthesize and integrate (Hegel 1984, 205–6). Accordingly, speculative philosophy apprehends or establishes the unity that reflection breaks. One might readily appreciate how crucial this schema is for his attack on Kantian idealism with its inherent dualisms. Hegel argued that self-relation (self-consciousness) cannot be understood on empirical or rational grounds and, more, that it was empty if considered apart from intersubjectivity or outside its historical community (Pippin 1989, 158). The dialectical synthesis, and more specifically the evolution of *Geist*, directed itself precisely at this seeming defect of Kant's philosophical program. In short, whereas Kant's transcendental idealism is interpreted as embodying irreducible dualisms, Hegel sought synthesis through reason (Tauber 2006).

4. This schema sets the stage for later dialectical constructions. Generally, *alterity* refers to an understanding of the self as defined in opposition to, or engaging with, an "other"—God, man, nature, self-reflection, society—and in the self's response to the other, identity is configured. Briefly, the self, to the extent that

it can be actualized, is defined by the other, a view continued in the twentieth century through many paths (see, for example, Theunissen 1984; M. C. Taylor 1987). One might trace the self's dependency on the other, and more specifically its radical social contingency, to Hegel's social theory (Neuhouser 2000), and more deeply to his metaphysics (M. C. Taylor 1980), which in turn was prefigured by Fichte's account of mutual recognition.

5. Hegelian self-consciousness requires "awareness of oneself as an inhabitant among others of a world informed by spirit" (Inwood 1992, 122). This dawning of I-awareness, awareness of one's identity, is not only the beginning of self-consciousness, but it portends the final evolution of *Geist*, whose manifestation in the natural and human worlds is only fully conceived at the culmination of history at the height of philosophical Reason. Thus *Geist* and human self-awareness evolve in tandem. So, while alterity establishes the conditions of identifying the self, this encounter serves as only the initial step in the synthetic process leading to History's evolution, which sweeps each individual in its path.

6. Recent critics (Herman 1993; Korsgaard 1996) dispute such a radical distinction and see in Kant's ethics a deep social commitment, where private morality, governed by some private, atomistic individuality, moves to a public domain in which autonomous individuals buy into public reason and cash out ethical behavior (discussed in Tauber 2005, 98–100).

7. John Locke attempted to construct "the self" as an autonomous legal unit to fulfill certain seventeenth-century liberal political goals. To do so he extrapolated from a philosophical invention employed in constructing the early modern scientific persona: the isolated knowing subject totally divorced from the world in order to objectify it (Fox-Keller 1994; Daston 2000). Under the same conditions, the self itself also became a subject of scrutiny, so that ordinary experience might be seen from afar—objectified, and thereby controlled.

8. Science's instantiation of the Cartesian subject/object divide places the observer outside the world to peer at it, and at oneself. Always aware of separation, and appropriately so, since science would purge itself of subjective contamination, this "subjectless subject" (Fox-Keller 1994) faces the metaphysical challenge of finding itself *in* the world defined without the individual. This epistemological structure refers to shifting the human "stare" *at* the world to human placement *within* it. Simply, the modernist stance poses the challenge of how to mend the world, to make the world—humans and nature—whole again. Taking their lead from Goethe (1988a; Tauber 1993), twentieth-century continental philosophers, most notably Heidegger (1977a; 1977b), Weber (1946), Husserl (1970), and Sartre (1956) repeatedly addressed this imbroglio and provided commentaries about a reality depicted "objectively," i.e., a world in which humans self-consciously reside separated from that world. For better or for worse, Heidegger set the argument in the starkest terms by attacking the very basis of objectification and the pursuit of what he referred to as "object-ness." Indeed, the central task of *Being and Time* (1996) was to dispense with the "subject" altogether and to place Dasein in a historical world. In that move, the structure of the subject-object divide would be replaced by a construction in which human beings are

constituted by their "being-in-the-world." Heidegger's views converged with
that of others who generally agreed on the inability of the then current expectations of science to provide a comprehensive worldview, and a basis by which
knowledge might be unified under its auspices. Among these philosophical allies
was Edmund Husserl, who dramatically posed the challenge in *The Crisis of the
European Sciences* (1970) in the same period Freud composed *Civilization and its
Discontents*. (See note 10 below.)

9. In the early 1830s, the word "individualism" was independently coined by
two French commentators, Alexis de Tocqueville and Michael Chevalier, to describe Americans. Tocqueville observed that individualism embedded conflicting
social values: on the one hand, Americans prided themselves as independent in
their psychological and political personas; and on the other hand, because of the
loss of strong government or social hierarchy, they also exhibited a strong sense
of social dependence (Shain 1994, 90–92; see also 112ff.). He concluded that
because of the dominant influence of the mass community, individuals in democ-
racies lost independence of mind. In opposition, Henry David Thoreau asserted
radical individuality and sought a life to exemplify it (Tauber 2001).

Emerson, who had inspired Thoreau, became the spokesman of a new individuality. Living during the major cultural upheaval of the Jacksonian era, he
revised expectations concerning personal autonomy and redefined moral agency.
By proselytizing the "divine sufficiency of the individual" (Parrington 1987, 390),
Emerson must be credited with the successful articulation of this new individualism within these shifting social and political contexts (Tauber 2003). In terms of
influence, Emerson's celebration of individualism would generate a much wider
command than his espousal of a distinct American ideal. In the European theater,
that influence is traced to Nietzsche, whose own emphasis on individual responsibility and self-assertion is a direct outgrowth of Emersonian concepts of the
individual (Stack 1992). What in Nietzsche became the Will to Power (see chapter
5) is in Emerson a more muted declaration of self-reliance and growth (Emerson
1979, 40–41); man "must learn to walk alone" (Emerson 1883a, 118), for "man
was made for conflict, not for rest. In action is his power; not in his goals but in
his transitions man is great" (Emerson 1883b, 55). An Emerson-Nietzsche-Freud
axis does not gainsay the vast labyrinth of influences that converged on Freud's
own understanding of an ego ideal, but the Nietzschean ethos quickly seeped into
the Austro-Germanic culture in which Freud matured, and the character of that
identity powerfully resonates with a Darwinian orientation in which individualistic striving captures the essence of human nature.

10. Nineteenth-century naturalism bequeathed its own unique challenge:
Metaphysically, the self-conscious peering self works from a conflicted agenda: it
both establishes a firm and abiding relation with nature, even a union, and also
recognizes that this engagement is fraught with a dangerous dissolution of that
self as an agent. So, on the one hand, some students of the Romantics see the
poetic quest as transfiguring an alienated nature to one redeemed, while others
see an unreconciled, alienated, nature whose pursuit is tragic. But, in fact, both
Romantic themes are played as a complex counterpoint, which Harold Bloom de-

scribes as a widened consciousness that seeks not a union with nature or even the divine, but rather a "self-less self" (1971, 26). In this posture, a common response, one embraced by Nietzsche and Freud, bestowed a deep insecurity when linked to the radical autonomy they each espoused. (See note 8 above.)

11. A comprehensive treatment of this passage is given by Arnold Come (1995), who compares the various English translations and offers a detailed analysis in the context of several of Kierkegaard's key works. In summary, Kierkegaard turns reflexivity upon itself in an endless regress, only to turn it outward. That reversal originates with recognition of the Other (i.e., God), and in this sense he follows the basic structure elaborated by Hegel (Tauber 2006). So according to Kierkegaard, full actualization requires an existential acceptance of the absurd leap of faith that identifies man in relation to God. In this last phase of an individual's development (from aesthetical and ethical forerunners), the recursive self-reflection ends. By turning reflexivity outward to engage another, a bond is established: an ethical metaphysics holds the self and other together in a dyad that defines the subject. "To be oneself" thus becomes an abiding ethical demand, which is attained by "consciousness of an infinite self" (Kierkegaard 1980, 67–68). The vectors then overlap: one directed inward in self-consciousness, and the other directed outward towards the infinite. Once recognized, a synthesis may be chosen or rejected. It is a choice governed by the absurd, but to make that choice exhibits, for Kierkegaard, the final expression of freedom that completes the turn of the reflexive spiral. There, authentication is achieved. Thus reflexivity, both through its moral mandate and by its own nature, defines the very essence of selfhood through this assertion of choice. The tensions within his philosophy might be considered a response to an existential insecurity of self-identity framed by an ethos of individuality. By declining the Hegelian idea of persons identifying themselves within the collective, and alternatively championing a self-centered individualism, Kierkegaard set the stage for Nietzschean and later existentialist formulations of personal responsibility and moral self-determination.

Despite a commitment to individualism, Kierkegaard saw the ethical limits of self-conscious exploration and recognized the critical turn that must occur to avoid moral solipsism. By following the road of self-consciousness, he outlined the boundaries of self-knowledge, revealed the irony of self-reliance, pushed towards the limits of individuality, and flung open the portals of self-responsibility. But during a period still infatuated with the promise of Reason, he went further by explicitly recognizing the "impossibility" of philosophy's fulfilling its own ambitions (Kierkegaard 1985c, 140, 143).

The theological context provided a cogent description of reason's limits. For Kierkegaard, the suspension of rational control (in the form of the leap of faith required to respond to divine command) led to an authentic life, one in which moral choice arises from individual action. Whether "absurd" or otherwise, *choice* is the critical parameter. For Kierkegaard, fundamentally, "the self is freedom" (1980, 29). But unlike Kantian freedom, freedom does not depend on the exercise of rationality. Indeed, freedom requires the suspension of reason and relies instead on the absurd, or arational, leap of faith. Just as the renunciation of reason as arbiter of the Will plays a dominant role in Nietzsche's thought, so too would Kierkegaard exercise self-determination and freedom of self-overcoming (Kierkegaard 1985c, 169).

Kierkegaard's "anxiety" coincides with Western consciousness, and cannot be regarded as an issue unique to his era (or our own). Indeed, we may discern the roots of this conundrum in earlier epochs—in Augustine, Descartes, Rousseau—and easily follow the course of its exploration in late-nineteenth-century psychology, postanalytic philosophy, and post-1945 art and literature. As Jonathan Dollimore cogently observes, "What we might now call neurosis, anxiety and alienation with the subject in crisis are not so much the consequence of its recent breakdown as the very stuff of its creation, and of the culture—Western European culture—which it sustains" (1997, 254). Kierkegaard clearly enunciated the despair that so easily follows self-conscious awareness, and his response, both heroic and tragic, appeals to an existential credo: Humans exist as moral agents who assume responsibility for choices taken. That freedom, whether real or illusionary, is the basis of self-identity.

12. William James makes important distinctions in the notion of selfhood, dividing its constituents into the "pure ego," and the material self, social self, and spiritual self. The last "is a reflective process, the result of our abandoning the outward-looking point of view, and of our having become able to think of subjectivity as such, *to think ourselves as thinkers*" (James 1983, 284).

13. As others have also noted (e.g., Guntrip 1971, 74), "the self" has been translated alone (not as a element of one of the conjugates, e.g., "self-confident," "self-deception," "self-punishment," etc., that appear hundreds of times) in five places in the English *Standard Edition* (Guttman 1984): In *The Interpretation of Dreams*, Freud quotes someone else (1900, 67); in the 1915 essays, "Repression" and "Instincts and Their Vicissitudes," Freud refers to the capacity of instincts to turn "round upon the subject's own self" (1915b, 126; 1915c, 147); in *Beyond the Pleasure Principle*, again in a passing footnote about the Upanishad origin of Plato's myth in the *Symposium*, where Aristophanes describes the male/female composition of humans before they were split into separate sexes by Zeus (1920, 57); and in the *Ego and the Id*, "self" only appears in a footnote: "In fact, on our view it is through the agency of Eros that the destructive instincts that are directed towards the external world have been diverted from the self" (1923a, 46). Interestingly, in only this last instance does Freud actually use the word *Selbst*: "Nach unserer Auffassung sind ja die nach außen gerichteten Destruktionstriebe durch Vermittlung des Eros vom eigenen Selbst abgelenkt worden" (*Gesammelte Werke*, 13:275). What Freud means when using the word "self" here is never elaborated. The other translations are *inaccurate*: The 1915 essays employ "die eigene Person" (*Gesammelte Werke*, 10:219, 250), and in *Dreams*, he writes of "dein Inneres" (*Gesammelte Werke*, 2–3:70), like a noun made from "inner," "inside," or "interior." (I am indebted to Jurgen Reeder for helping me with this lexical survey.)

14. For example, Harry Guntrip maintains that "Freud takes the whole self for granted and nowhere discusses it specifically as one psychic phenomenon that matters most of all" (1971, 74). Part of the problem of selfhood pertains to

a semantic fluidity in Freud's writings. Donald McIntosh offered the following topography for personal identity in the Freudian opus (1986, 430–31): *Die Person* connotes the individual as a whole, mental and physical, as both subject and object. The term is also used in a reflexive sense, *Die eigen Person*, "the own person." *Das Ich* conforms to the person as a subject who acts, thinks, feels, desires, suffers, etc. A second sense of *Das Ich* refers to the "I" we think about, perceive, i.e., as an object. This is the dominant usage and exemplified in Freud's early writings. Indeed, "In experiential terms, the conscious 'I' of ordinary language finds its centre and core in the system-structure ego" (McIntosh 1986, 433). In contrast, the essay on narcissism employs *Das Ich* differently than in the later system's "ego": In 1914, the ego becomes an object of libidinal investment. Further, in contrast to the essays on sexuality where a single libidinal instinct is at play, now Freud posits an "ego instinct," which is directed at preserving the ego as a person. This totalizing construction suffices for McIntosh as a "self," and thus he places the missing *Selbst* (by inference) principally in Freud's metapsychological papers (e.g., 1914–17). In contrast, the third designation, *Der Charakter* (1905b) refers to the character of the individual, a set of traits that describe the thoughts and actions of a person. Here, a third-party appraisal of character or personality is made and assumes a different scope of describing personal identity than those terms employed to describe psychodynamics and psychic structure. One must also factor into this last designation the role of the superego in character formation. See above, introduction, note 4.

15. "If I were pressed to say what the ego is, as Freud understood it, I would say that it is the subject of intentional actions and decisions, as well as of perceptions and knowledge, the object of shame and guilt, the recipient of impulses, urges, and dreams, and the sufferer of fear and anxiety. It is also involved, in logically more complex ways, in those cases where we speak of self-regard, pride, self-love and self-pity, and also self-deception, as well as of self-restraint and self-control. The concept in question is intimately connected with our use of the first person pronoun 'I' in a wide range of cases. It is in fact more or less equivalent to what we mean by 'the self' or 'selfhood'" (Dilman 1984, 106).

16. Bruno Bettelheim argued that where the English *Standard Edition* uses "ego," a better translation is "the I" (*ich* or *das Ich*), and from there an intimate sense of personal identity emerges (1982, 53–55; see Lear 1990, 156–82). According to Bettelheim, the translation of *Ich* and *Es* into their Latin equivalents— "ego" and "id"—rather than "I" and "it" "turned them into cold technical terms, which arouse no personal associations," whereas Freud deliberately chose them to facilitate "an intuitive understanding of his meaning" (Bettelheim 1982, 53). "To mistranslate *Ich* as 'ego' is to transform it into jargon that no longer conveys the personal commitment we make when we say 'I' or 'me'" (53). Indeed, the mistranslation turns "an introspective psychology ... into a behavioral one, which observes from the outside" (54).

17. A complex psychic fugue—between inner psychic forces and external reality— is played between the ego and superego (classically the heir of the Oedipus complex [Freud 1924, 167]). According to Freud, the superego's influence in establishing character draws not only from parental superego content, but cultural

sources as well. Freud saw the moral agent as some amalgam between the ego and
the superego in creating "the higher nature of man" (Freud 1923a, 37; Kobrin
1993).

18. Twentieth-century postmodernists (more specifically, poststructuralists)
highlighted the contingency of the self's construction. From this perspective, no
claims might be held regarding the "natural" state of cultural structures (e.g., language, kinship systems, social and economic hierarchies, sexual norms, religious
beliefs) that would define the self, and indeed, a rich anthropological literature
on the particular notion of Western selfhood revealed its idiosyncratic character
(e.g., Roland 1988; Morris 1994; Reiss 2002; Biehl, Good, and Kleinman 2007),
which resides well beyond the social configuration of the members of a society,
to the very basis of consciousness itself (Throop and Laughlin 2007). Since no
transcendental significance to limit "meanings" existed, late-twentieth-century
commentators spoke of the self's "indeterminacy"—a "decentered" subject. No
longer an origin or a source, it becomes only the contingent product of multiple
historical, social, and psychological forces (Lewis 1952; Foucault 1970; 1983;
Mauss 1985 and commentaries in Carrithers, Collins, and Lukes 1985; Rose
1998; 1999) with radical reconfigurations of self-identity (e.g., Borch-Jacobsen
1988; Kristeva 1987; Rose 1998; Derrida 2007). (See above ch. 5, note 18.)

Despite the demurral of postmodernists, who would argue that Foucauldian
power relations reduced the self to a cultural construct, useful for political and social manipulation, existentialists asserted that choice and responsibility conferred
individual authenticity, irrespective of the self's contingency or construction for
political control. Thus an existentialist theme counterbalances the postmodern
one in the twentieth century, and it stems, in large part, from Kierkegaard. (This
existentialist theme also has been traced by Kojève (1980) to Hegel, based on a
very different orientation, and some would say a very idiosyncratic reading).

19. Freud's understanding of the ego as configured by object relations shifts
throughout his career, albeit much controversy has swirled around the explicit
character of those dynamics and the theoretical basis of accounting for external
demands on the ego (e.g., Guntrip 1971; Mitchell 1988; Holt 1989, 137–39; and
most fairly summarized by Greenberg and Mitchell 1983, 233–36). Generally,
most agree that object relations have a fast hold on Freud's theory in the *Three
Essays on the Theory of Sexuality* (1905b), where the object is one of the constituents of the drive; in a different sense during the metapsychology phase, most
explicitly in his discussion of narcissism (1914a) and melancholia (1917a), where
in his discussion of mourning Freud asserts that when the individual is "faced
with the loss of a love-object, the object is incorporated within the psyche in the
form of an identification." Object identification further develops in Freud's late
papers on female sexuality (Freud 1931; 1933, 112–35; Horrocks 2001, 95–96,
126ff.), and in this last phase, Freud shifted his notion of the ego as derivative
of the id and considered the ego as a structure in its own right. In "Analysis,
Terminable and Interminable" (1937b), Freud observed that in personality development "in addition to the factors of native drive endowment and traumatic
frustrations in infancy, the ego must be predisposed innately to certain lines of

development" (Rubovits-Seitz and Kohut 1999, 5), albeit Freud hardly develops this notion (Freud 1937b, 240ff.).

In the writings of Ronald Fairbairn, Melanie Klein, and Harry Stack Sullivan a more obvious theoretical inflection occurs, a "psychology of object relations that put the individual's need to relate to others at the center of human development" (Scharff 1996, 3). The object-relations school they founded developed its own distinctive program by reconfiguring psychoanalysis from a "science of the unconscious" to "the theory of the whole person, of the personal ego in personal object-relations, good and bad, growing either mature or basically disturbed" (Guntrip 1971, 80). On this platform, the analysand is *basically* an ego, endowed with both its own constitution and, to varying degrees and ways, formed by seminal relationships. So in place of an ego acting in a vise between unremitting unconscious forces and the reality principle, a self emerges with its own standing and telos. In that scenario, the ego is subject to various relationships, and analysis is devoted to deciphering the emotional factors to which the patient responds (for example, the Oedipal complex and transference) by offering explanations of how and why such behaviors developed from those relationships.

The object-relations movement has several origins, but clearly Harry Stack Sullivan's substitution of an instinct-based psychology with "personality" serves as a useful focal point. In moving from a biological model to one based on interpersonal relationships, Sullivan had been arguing since the mid-1920s that

> the field of psychiatry is neither the mentally sick individual, nor the successful and unsuccessful processes that may be observed in groups and that can be studied in detached objectivity. Psychiatry, instead, is the field of interpersonal relations, under any and all circumstances in which these relations exist. It was seen that *a personality* can never be isolated from the complex of interpersonal relations in which the person lives and has his being. (Sullivan 1953, 10)

On this view Freud's achievement served as an early stage for the development of an ego-based psychology: "Freud revealed the experiential origin of specific limitations of personal awareness. By this achievement, he cleared the way for the scientific study of people, in contradistinction to mind, or society, or brain, or glands" (Sullivan 1953, 9). By subordinating the id as the focus of attention, Sullivan opened the way for an exploration of object-relations theory, which was developed from different theories and practice by Klein, Fairbairn, Erich Fromm, Karen Horney, D. W. Winnicott, and Erik Erikson, who made the ego's development an explicit subject of inquiry. With Heinz Kohut, an explicit "psychology of the self" was expounded in the late 1970s. Kohut sought to extend psychoanalysis to a more holistic consideration of the individual, namely one whose *identity* becomes a focus of concern.

The theoretical constructions of the psychology of the self differ among the various proponents of an interpersonal perspective, but the common element is a general shift of attention from Freud's distinctive formulation of an ego preoccupied with its relation to its own psyche to a Kohutian universe, where both self-awareness—a relation of oneself as a self (i.e., an individual)—and relation to others become *constitutive* to the individual's psychology (much in the spirit of

Hegel's formulation). Thus in Kohut's writings, the self becomes a hub of psycho-analytic interest in terms that constitute successful formation of personal identity: a reflective self-awareness, cohesive in space and enduring in time, a center of initiative and a recipient of impressions (Kohut 1977, 99). Accordingly, "The self is no longer a representation, a product of the activity of the ego, but is itself the active agent; it therefore carries more theoretical weight than the earlier views.... Kohut grants the self a functional role, bringing its relational origins right to the theoretical core" (Greenberg and Mitchell 1983, 353). Yet, and this represents an irony of sorts, Kohut made no attempt at defining "the self" and simply acknowl-edged an implicit understanding based on empirical observations (what he called, "psychological manifestations"): "My investigation contains hundreds of pages dealing with the psychology of the self—yet it never assigns an inflexible meaning to the term self, it never explains how the essence of the self should be defined.... Demands for an exact definition of the nature of the self disregard the fact that 'the self' is not a concept of an abstract science, but a generalization derived from empirical data" (1977, 310–11). What that "generalization" might be beyond the pronominal "I" or "me" cannot be derived from Kohut's psychology. Indeed, what he means by a "generalization" escapes me. From a philosophical point of view, I regard this lacuna as problematic (Tauber 1999b).

Of note, American pragmatism takes up this relational theme for both socio-logical constructions of personal identity and ethics (Diggins 1994). In particu-lar, John Dewey (1997, 187; 1984, 208) and George Herbert Mead propounded the social character of persons as constitutive to personal identity, inasmuch as the mind "can never find expression, and could never come into existence at all, except in terms of a social environment" (Mead 1934, 223), and Mead then linked his position to Hegel (unacknowledged) because of the very construc-tion of self-consciousness:

> The existence of private or "subjective" contents of experience does not alter the fact that self-consciousness involves the individual's becoming an object to himself by taking the attitudes of other individuals toward himself within an organized setting of social relationships, and that unless the individual had thus become an object to himself he would not be self-conscious or have a self at all. Apart from his social interactions with other individuals, he would not relate the private or "subjective" contents of his experience to himself, and he could not become aware of himself as such. (225–26)

Chapter 7
The Ethical Turn

1. A definition of *constructivism* begins with "X is said to be constructed if its produced by intentional human activity" (Kukla 2000, 3), and thus human artifacts or social activities are easily recognized as products of human invention. The constructivist arguments possess complexity because of the varying positions adopted. Constructivists may argue a *metaphysical* thesis about the facts describ-

ing the world in which humans live; an *epistemological* thesis concerning what
can be known about the world; and a *semantic* thesis regarding what can be said
about the world (Kukla 2000, 4). Some confusion exists in the literature over
what these various positions maintain, and more pointedly on whether constructivism is invariably associated with relativism, whether ontological or epistemological (Kukla 2000, 4–6).

Philosophically, Kant was most influential in presenting a constructive picture
of the world, inasmuch as the transcendental deduction conceived of human cognitive faculties processing phenomena through the mind's basic categories (see
chapters 4 and 5). Such data then progresses to higher cognitive functions and
reality thus becomes a product of the mind *and* nature, however, not constructed
by a universal reason as Kant thought, but composed with varying rules, historical and culturally developed and thus contingent to time and place: Some cognitive rules may present themselves precisely, while others less so, and some remain
seemingly nonspecific, their full character shrouded as the faculties of human
explanation and understanding weave the threads of experience into whole cloth,
all the while oblivious to analytic attempts to discern them.

In the contemporary debates of our own era, arguments have raged as to
what extent scientific *concepts,* paragons of objective appraisals of reality, are
constructed (Tauber 2009). In other words, does science discover natural kinds
(whereby conceptual schemes just carve nature at its preexisting joints and these
are then regarded as discovered, not invented) and assemble theories from some
sacrosanct objectivity? Argument about constructivism served as the theme of the
Science Wars of the 1990s, which in the simplest formulation, concerned the character of scientific truth claims, where those holding to a scientific realism fought
a defensive battle against those who regarded scientific knowledge as exhibiting
various degrees of construction and thus hardly able to offer some final objective
account of reality. The challenge to ponder the claims of the scientific vision, not
only of its characterization of nature, but of society and human kind, had broad
significance. Indeed, this divisive controversy over the sociology of knowledge
(i.e., the values of science, the relation of science to its supporting culture, the
nature of scientific reasoning, etc.) was perceived as vital to intellectual inquiry,
generally, and consequently the debate carried over to other disciplines, including history (Fay, Pomper, and Vann 1998) and literary studies (Adams and Searle
1986), where arguments over the veracity of historiographical integrity and deconstruction of texts, respectively, held center stage. Although largely an academic affair, the repercussions of the controversy reached into many corners—the
judiciary, public policy, education, and beyond. Thus with the rise of this new
criticism, intellectual territories were marked and divided not by different academic traditions and subjects of inquiry, but rather over how one regarded the
character of knowledge, rationality, and objectivity. Similar debates, spawned by
the constructive works of Donald Spence (1982) and Roy Schafer (1992b), took
place in psychoanalytic circles as well (e.g., Sass and Woolfolk 1988; Leary 1989).

2. On this view, the hermeneutics created by Nietzsche asserted *interpretation* as a ubiquitous feature of all human activity ("hermeneutic universalism"),
where "there can be no appeal to experience, meaning, or evidence that is in-

dependent of interpretation or more basic than it" (Hiley, Bohman, and Shusterman 1991, 7). Critically, interpretation must occur within some context or background ("hermeneutic contextualism"), "such as webs of beliefs, a complex of social relations, tradition, or the practices of a form of life" (7). The power of this orientation—built upon Nietzsche's notions of perspectivism—effectively undermined the dream of a universal method, a universal reason, and a system of unified knowledge, so that by the second half of the twentieth century, the positivist philosophies founded on these ideals would suffer defeat at the hands of Nietzsche's descendants (Zammito 2004; Tauber 2009).

3. Jürgen Habermas's *Knowledge and Human Interests* (1971) soon followed Ricoeur's *Freud and Philosophy* (1970), which together, most influentially applied a critical hermeneutic interpretation to Freud's theory. Beyond psychoanalysis, they had a wide impact on critical thought in literary and culture studies. Ricoeur and Habermas see hermeneutics as part of a wider ethics of interpretation. Useful overviews are found in Gomez (2005) and Saks (1999).

4. Lacan's construction of the subject arises from his structuralist understanding of language, where the human psychic structure is produced through the signifier:

> There is no subject without language, Lacan wants to say, and yet the subject constitutively lacks a place in language.... [T]he subject is not an object capable of being adequately named within a natural language, like other objects can be ("table," "chair," or [*sic*] so on). It is no-thing.... Lacan articulates his position concerning the subject by way of a fundamental distinction between the ego or "moi"/"me," and the subject intimated by the shifter "je"/"I." The subject is a split subject ... it has consciousness and an unconscious. When Lacan says the subject is split, he means also that, as a subject of language, it will always evince the following two levels. The first is the ego, or subject of the enunciated. This is the self wherein the subject perceives/anticipates its imaginary unity. Since the ego is an object, according to Lacan, it is capable of being predicated about like any other object. I can say of myself more or less truthfully that "I am fat," or "honest," or anything else. What my enunciated sentence will speak about in these cases, for Lacan, is my ego. But this is to be distinguished from a second "level" of subjectivity: the subject of the enunciation.... The subject of the unconscious is the subject of the enunciation, Lacan insists. This is one way he expresses the elementary Freudian hypothesis that, in symptoms and parapraxes, the subject says more than s/he intended to say. What s/he intended will usually be captured in the explicit content of what s/he has enunciated. (Sharpe 2006)

Given our considerations of the previous chapter, Lacan must be counted among the postmodernists who would discount the notion of selfhood, and from this perspective, he took what he perceived as latent Freudian inclinations into a fully developed "alternate" psychology (Lacan 1968; Ragland-Sullivan 1986; Weber 1991).

5. "*Nachträglichkeit* is usually translated as 'deferred action' or 'deferred effect,' although the literal meaning is something like 'the quality of carrying on

after the event.' With this concept, Freud claims that memory is itself a creative act, for in deferred action one retrospectively ascribes significance to an event or a situation which it did not possess at the time" (Horrocks 2001, 65). Oliver Sacks (2000, 232–33) notes that this conception of memory was also articulated during the 1930s by the experimental psychologist Fredrick Bartlett, who emphasized the reconstruction of memory as fulfilling present needs and cultural context of the subject (Bartlett 1995).

6. Recent commentaries by Reeder (2002) and William Egginton (2007) have brilliantly explored this issue, the former within a hermeneutical construction and the latter from a Lacanian-Derridian perspective.

7. Sartre, in chapter 2 of *Being and Nothingness* (1956), attacked Freud precisely on these grounds in terms of formulating a psychology on "bad faith" by splitting the psychic whole into two components, and thereby "represent self-deception as the deception of one person, or sub-person, by another" (Dilman 1984, 89). The philosophical argument about this matter and other issues of repression and self-deception have been discussed by many. For a variety of philosophical critiques, see Needleman (1967, 96–97, 132–35), Pears (1974), Fingarette (1982), Dilman (1984, 89ff.), Gardner (1991, 151–53; 1993, 36–38, 87–88), Sherman (1995), Cavell (2001, 73–74).

8. William Meissner has extensively explored the relationship of what he calls "will"—the capacity of being rational and fulfilling reasoned decisions—and selfhood (1986; 1993; 2003). Meissner (2003) maintains that if we can accept that Freud held a set of ethical convictions that persisted throughout the corpus of his writings and seem to run in parallel with his psychoanalytic thinking (both of these points are well demonstrated), the tensions between these lines of thought demand resolution. If such is the case, how would psychoanalytic theory be rethought to accommodate these vying viewpoints? In contrast, Ernest Wallwork (1991) employs psychoanalysis as a vehicle to develop a contemporary ethical theory, and thus his book addresses another agenda: psychoanalysis is being used to develop an argument about ethical choice and moral agency. While offering valuable insight into the moral structure of Freud's theory, Wallwork is concerned with *applying* Freudian insight to contemporary moral philosophy, while Meissner is primarily concerned with *elucidating* the ethics of Freudian theory.

9. Reeder has argued in later work (2008) that psychoanalysis as fundamentally an ethical venture finds itself in conflict with contemporary medicine, which continues to appropriate a positivist orientation despite the obvious failings of this approach in the clinical setting (Tauber 1999; 2005; 2009)—not only for the basic therapeutic encounter, but even more for the analytic exchange. The drug-driven society devolves upon a reductionist view of the mind coupled to a political-economic reality that has made health care a commodity governed by the same market forces that regulate other industries. The ethical component then is subsumed beneath a larger materialistic culture. Reeder asserts that psychoanalysis must align itself with philosophy and reinvent itself as a contemplative moral project, an undertaking closely akin to my own position.

10. We might understand such choice as following a 'procedural' theory, which employs a structural description of moral choice—a hierarchical organization of

various desires, emotions, traits, values, objectives, and the like—to describe how autonomy is exercised. Influentially promoted by Harry Frankfurt (1971) and expanded by Gerald Dworkin (1988), this understanding of autonomy is based on a conception of a person as having potentially conflicting forces that must be aligned and coordinated by higher-order desires to achieve morally autonomous actions (Christman 1989, 6–8). In other words, as rational beings, humans are endowed with the capacity to reflect on their wants and beliefs, and ultimately these yearnings must be stratified, so that some impulses will be acted upon immediately, some deferred, and some ignored (Lindley 1986, 64–66). But such a schema hardly suffices for the psychoanalytic scenario, where so-called choices may still be dictated by unexamined coercive elements, whether inner-driven or environmental (Lear 1990, 187–89).

11. From this perspective, Freud's own cultural heritage has been carefully scrutinized to explain the genesis and workings of his theory, albeit with widely divergent opinions (e.g., Roazen 1968; Trosman 1976; Schorske 1980, 181–207; Clark 1980; Marcus 1984; Zanuso 1986; Gay 1988; Breger 2000; Zaretsky 2004), and given the relativism of psychiatric diagnosis, recent reexaminations of Freud's reports have found some major misalignments with current thinking, especially about the psychology of women (see various views in Schafer 1992a; Bernheimer and Kahane 1990; Chodorow 1991; Makari 1991; Skues 2009), his relationship with his mother (Sprengnether 1990; Breger 2000), and conflicts with his father (Balmary 1982; Krüll 1986; Shengold 1993).

12. The literature on this topic is immense and falls along a wide spectrum from the memory fantasies decried by Frederick Crews (1995) to the defending hermeneutists, who, as discussed below, embrace the challenge of interpretation. Of this latter genre see representative views in Messer, Sass, and Woolfolk (1988) and Lowenberg (2000), and a critical defense by Edelson (1988).

13. In *Being and Time,* Heidegger neatly captures an understanding of meaning and the interpretative process in the sense discussed here: "Meaning [*Sinn*] is that wherein the intelligibility [*Verständlichkeit*] of something maintains itself. That which can be articulated in a disclosure by which we understand, we call 'meaning.' ... Meaning is the 'direction'—based upon a fore-having, a fore-sight, and a fore-conception—belonging to a project, and making something be intelligible as something" (Heidegger 1996, 193; emended; quoted by Reeder 2002, 85–86).

14. These comments are directed towards Freud's moral enterprise, for when we consider his epistemology, the notion that all human experience comprised some integrated whole simply eclipsed his philosophical concern. In this sense, Windelband remained true to a larger philosophical cause (see chapter 3) and Freud adopted the common philosophical position of the "natural philosopher" (scientist) of a particular kind. Freud's basic orientation in this regard is completely consistent with his allegiance to positivism. The positivists' position formally originates with Hume's proclamation that one cannot infer an "ought" from an "is." This means, simply, that a moral case cannot be deduced from a natural fact. The critique is sometimes referred to as Hume's Law and is famously stated in his *A Treatise of Human Nature* (book 3, part 1, section 1), where

he is attacking the apparent rationality of various ethical or religious positions (Hume 1978, 469–70). Thus the so-called fact/value distinction originated in an argument against the illogical deduction of religious belief from natural facts and morality from similar constructions derived from natural law or other systems of supposed rational basis (Putnam 2002). Hume argued instead that ethics are grounded in human emotions, needs, and caprices that are rationalized into moral justifications (Lindley 1986). The ethical dimensions of Hume's position will be considered in detail below, but the salient point for now is that Hume's philosophy supported Freud's scientific aspiration of objectivity, i.e., facts divorced from contaminating personal values, and upon that platform the moral structure of psychoanalysis would be built. Ironically, as a "science" conceived on a biological model, where normative standards define the quality of function, psychoanalysis could not escape value judgment, albeit subsumed beneath a scientific banner. This inner tension underlies the dilemma of psychoanalytic theory, which endeavors to attain a putative objective investigation and yet must be guided by an implicit set of normative values. How that dilemma has been approached characterizes much of Freudianism's history.

15. For Dewey and Putnam, morals are "objective" in the sense that consensus and considered judgment deliberate the better choice of dealing with the world or drawing inferences from it. A Platonic ideal of "objective" or "real" or "true" then is replaced with a pragmatic assessment adjudicated by the rules of human flourishing. Indeed, as MacIntyre cogently confirms: "To be objective, then, is to understand oneself as part of a community and one's work as part of a project and part of a history. The authority of this history and this project derives from the goods internal to the practice. Objectivity is a moral concept before it is a methodological concept, and the activities of natural science turn out to be a species of moral activity" (1978, 37; see also MacIntyre 1984, 56ff.).

16. So the very notion of an identity that not only possesses itself but might freely make choices in its social world becomes a construction of the "effects" of technologies and the power relations operative in a particular society, which, in turn, require their own critique and therapy (Foucault 2003; 2006a; 2006b). Accordingly, the analysand, configured within the larger individual-society construction, has no autonomy, and so-called clinical insight represents a delusion. This account, however, did not prevent Foucault late in his life from offering his own version of psychic therapy in a renewed study of philosophy, where the "care of the self" might assume new possibilities for self-renewal (McGushin 2007).

17. Spinoza's concept of *conatus* approximates Freud's conception of the libido (Hampshire 1962, 141–42), but given the vastly different scientific metaphysics in which each lived, I do not pursue this parallel.

18. Many have observed how Freud's thought reflected the secular, liberal culture in which he lived (Schorske 1980, 181–207; Marcus 1984) and the professional world in which he competed (e.g., Clark 1980; McGrath 1986; Gay 1988), which was marked by anti-Semitism and professional animosity (Sachs 1944, 18ff.; Gay 1978; Beller 1989; Gilman 1993b).

19. The compatibilism argument (which Kant famously called a "wretched subterfuge" [1996b, 216; 5:96]), defines freedom as the ability to exercise choice

without constraints or impediments. On this view, actions are free or not depending on the kinds of causes they have (some causes enhance freedom, others hinder). *Cause* of course remains inasmuch as character, context, and experience are determinative in varying degrees. Accordingly, free actions are unconstrained, not uncaused (Strawson 1998; Kane 2005, 12–21).

20. While some have made similar observations about Freud's humanism (e.g., Mann 1947; Trosman 1976; Loewald 1978; Kaufmann 1980; Bettelheim 1982; Goldberg 1988; Brown and Richards 1999), most of Freud's biographers, and certainly his critics, have subordinated, and more often ignored, what appears to me the crucial component for understanding the overall thrust of his thought.

References ————————————————————————

Achinstein, P. 2001. *The Book of Evidence*. Oxford: Oxford University Press.
———, ed. 2005. *Scientific Evidence: Philosophical Theories and Applications*. Baltimore: Johns Hopkins University Press.
Adams, H., and L. Searle, eds. 1986. *Critical Theory since 1965*. Tallahassee: Florida State University Press.
Ahern, D. 1995. *Nietzsche as Cultural Physician*. University Park: Pennsylvania State University Press.
Allison, H. 1983. *Kant's Transcendental Idealism*. New Haven: Yale University Press.
———. 1990. *Kant's Theory of Freedom*. Cambridge: Cambridge University Press.
———. 2004. *Kant's Transcendental Idealism: An Interpretation and Defense*. New Haven: Yale University Press.
Alston, W. P., ed. 2002. *Realism and Antirealism*. Ithaca, N.Y.: Cornell University Press.
Anderson, D. L. 2002. "Why God Is Not a Semantic Realist." In *Realism and Antirealism*. Ed. W. P. Alston. Ithaca, N.Y.: Cornell University Press, 131–48.
Angeles, P. A. 1981. *Dictionary of Philosophy*. New York: HarperCollins.
Anscombe, G.E.M. 1959. *An Introduction to Wittgenstein's Tractatus*. Philadelphia: University of Pennsylvania Press.
Apel, K.-O. 1994. "Perspectives for a General Hermeneutic Theory." In *The Hermeneutics Reader*. Ed. K. Mueller-Vollmer. New York: Continuum, 320–45.
Arlow, J. A. 1959. "Psychoanalysis as Scientific Method." In *Psychoanalysis, Scientific Method, and Philosophy*. Ed. S. Hook. New York: New York University Press, 201–11.
Armour-Garb, B. P., and J. C. Beall, eds. 2005. "Deflationism: The Basics." In *Deflationary Truth*. Ed. B. P. Armour-Garb and J. C. Beall. Chicago: Open Court, 1–29.
Armstrong, R. H. 2005. *A Compulsion for Antiquity: Freud and the Ancient World*. Ithaca, N.Y.: Cornell University Press.
Askay, R., and J. Farquhar. 2006. *Apprehending the Inaccessible: Freudian Psychoanalysis and Existential Phenomenology*. Evanston, Ill.: Northwestern University Press.
Assoun, P.-L. 1990. *Introduction à l'épistémologie freudienne*. Paris: Payot.
———. 2000. *Freud and Nietzsche*. Trans. R. L. Collier, Jr., London: Continuum.
Ayer, A. J., ed. 1959. *Logical Positivism*. Glencoe, Ill.: Free Press.
Babitch, B., ed. 1999. *Nietzsche, Epistemology, and Philosophy of Science: Nietzsche and the Sciences*. Dordrecht: Kluwer Academic.
Balmary, M. 1982. *Psychoanalyzing Psychoanalysis: Freud and the Hidden Fault of the Father*. Trans. N. Lukacher. Baltimore: Johns Hopkins University Press.
Bambach, C. R. 1995. *Heidegger, Dilthey, and the Crisis of Historicism*. Ithaca, N.Y.: Cornell University Press.

Barclay, J. 1959. "Brentano and Freud: A Comparative Study in the Evolution of Psychological Thought." Ph.D. diss., University of Michigan.

———. 1964. "Franz Brentano and Sigmund Freud." *Journal of Existentialism* 5:1–36.

Bartlett, F. C. 1995. *Remembering: A Study in Experimental and Social Psychology.* Cambridge: Cambridge University Press.

Bartok, P. J. 2005. "Brentano's Intentionality Thesis: Beyond the Analytic and Phenomenological Readings." *Journal of the History of Philosophy* 43:437–60.

Behler, E. 1991. *Confrontations: Derrida, Heidegger, Nietzsche.* Trans. S. Taubeneck. Palo Alto: Stanford University Press.

Beiser, F. C. 2005. *Schiller as Philosopher: A Re-examination.* Oxford: Oxford University Press.

Beller, S. 1989. *Vienna and the Jews, 1867–1938: A Cultural History.* Cambridge: Cambridge University Press.

Bergo, B. 2004. "Psychoanalytic Models: Freud's Debt to Philosophy and His Copernican Revolution." In *The Philosophy of Psychiatry: A Companion.* Ed. J. Radden. New York: Oxford University Press, 338–50.

Bernfeld, S. 1951. "Sigmund Freud, M.D., 1882–1885." *International Journal of Psycho-analysis* 32:204–16.

Bernheimer, C., and C. Kahane, eds. 1990. *In Dora's Case: Freud—Hysteria—Feminism.* 2nd ed. New York: Columbia University Press.

Betanzos, R. J. 1988. "Wilhelm Dilthey: An Introduction." In *Introduction to the Human Sciences: An Attempt to Lay a Foundation for the Study of Society and History.* Trans. R. J. Betanzos. Detroit: Wayne State University Press, 9–63.

Bettelheim, B. 1982. *Freud and Man's Soul.* London: Penguin.

Biehl, J., B. Good, and A. Kleinman, eds. 2007. *Subjectivity: Ethnographic Investigations.* Berkeley: University of California Press.

Bilder, R. M., and F. F. Lefever, eds.1998. *Neuroscience of the Mind on the Centennial of Freud's "Project for a Scientific Psychology."* New York: New York Academy of Sciences.

Binswanger, L. 1957. *Sigmund Freud: Reminiscences of a Friendship.* Trans. N. Guterman. New York: Grune and Stratton.

———. 1963. *Being-in-the-World: Selected Papers of Ludwig Binswanger.* Trans. with a critical introduction by J. Needleman. New York: Basic Books.

Blondel, E. 1991. *Nietzsche: The Body and Culture.* Trans. S. Hand. Stanford: Stanford University Press.

Bloom, H. 1971. "The Internalization of Quest Romance." In *The Ringers in the Tower: Studies in Romantic Tradition.* Chicago: University of Chicago Press, 13–35.

Boehlich, W. 1990. "Introduction." In *The Letters of Sigmund Freud to Eduard Silberstein, 1871–1881.* Trans. A. J. Pomerans and ed. W. Boehlich. Cambridge: Harvard University Press, xiii–xvii.

Bolton, D. 2008. *What Is Mental Disorder? An Essay in Philosophy, Science, and Values.* New York: Oxford University Press.

Boothby, R. 2001. *Freud as Philosopher: Metapsychology after Lacan.* New York: Routledge.

Borch-Jacobsen, M. 1988. *The Freudian Subject*. Trans. F. Roustang. Stanford: Stanford University Press.

Bouveresse, J. 1995. *Wittgenstein Reads Freud: The Myth of the Unconscious*. Trans. C. Cosman. Princeton: Princeton University Press.

Bouwsma, O. K. 1986. *Wittgenstein Conversations, 1949–1951*. Ed. J. L. Craft and R. E. Hustwit. Indianapolis: Hackett.

Bowlby, R. 2007. *Freudian Mythologies: Greek Tragedy and Modern Identities*. Oxford: Oxford University Press.

Boyd, R. N. 2002. "Scientific Realism." *The Stanford Encyclopedia of Philosophy*. Summer 2002 edition. Ed. Edward N. Zalta. http://plato.stanford.edu/archives/sum2002/entries/scientific-realism/.

Bracken, P., and P. Thomas. 2005. *Postpsychiatry: Mental Health in a Postmodern World*. New York: Oxford University Press.

Brady, D. 1986. "Freud's Distaste for Philosophy: A Hint of an Explanation." *Journal of the American Academy of Psychoanalysis and Dynamic Psychiatry* 14:297–307.

Brandt, R. B. 1979. *A Theory of the Good and the Right*. Oxford: Oxford University Press.

Breger, L. 2000. *Freud: Darkness in the Midst of Vision*. New York: John Wiley and Sons.

Brentano, F. 1973. *Psychology from an Empirical Standpoint*. 1874. Trans. A. C. Rancurello, D. B. Terrell, and L. L. McAlister. London: Routledge.

Breuer, J., and S. Freud. 1895. *Studies on Hysteria*. In *The Standard Edition of the Complete Psychological Works of Sigmund Freud*. Vol. 2. Trans. and ed. James Strachey et al. London: Hogarth Press and The Institute of Psychoanalysis, 1955.

Brook, A. 1995. "Explanation in the Hermeneutic Science." *International Journal of Psycho-analysis* 76:519–32.

Brown, J., and B. Richards. 1999. "The Humanist Freud." In *Freud 2000*. Ed. A. Elliott. New York: Routledge, 235–61.

Brown, J.A.C. 1964. *Freud and the Post-Freudians*. New York: Penguin.

Brown, N. O. 1959. *Life against Death: The Psychological Meaning of History*. Middletown, Conn.: Wesleyan University Press.

Bruner, J. 1987. "Life as Narrative." *Social Research* 54:11–32.

Brunner, J. 2001. *Freud and the Politics of Psychoanalysis*. New Brunswick, N.J.: Transaction Publishers.

———. 2002. "Freud's (De)construction of the Conflictual Mind." *Thesis Eleven* 71:24–39.

Buller, D. J. 2006. *Adapting Minds: Evolutionary Psychology and the Persistent Quest for Human Nature*. Cambridge: MIT Press.

Burke, J. 2006. *The Sphinx on the Table: Sigmund Freud's Art Collection and the Development of Psychoanalysis*. New York: Walker.

Butler, J. 1990. *Gender Trouble: Feminism and the Subversion of Identity*. New York: Routledge.

Campbell, J. 1949. *The Hero with a Thousand Faces*. Princeton: Princeton University Press.

Canguilhem, G. 1989. *The Normal and the Pathological*. Trans. C. R. Fawcett. New York: Zone Books.

Caplan, A. L. 1993. "The Concepts of Health, Illness, and Disease." In *Companion Encyclopedia of the History of Medicine*. Ed. W. Bynum and R. Porters. London: Routledge, 1:233–48.

Caplan, A. L., J. J. McCartney, and D. A. Sisti, eds. 2004. *Health, Disease, and Illness*. Washington, D.C.: Georgetown University Press.

Carrithers, M., S. Collins, and S. Lukes, eds. 1985. *The Category of the Person: Anthropology, Philosophy, History*. Cambridge: Cambridge University Press.

Cassirer, E. 1953–57. *The Philosophy of Symbolic Forms*. 1923–29. Trans. R. Manheim. 3 vols. New Haven: Yale University Press.

Cavell, M. 1988. "Interpretation, Psychoanalysis, and the Philosophy of Mind." *Journal of the American Psychoanalytic Association* 36:859–79.

———. 1993. *The Psychoanalytic Mind: From Freud to Philosophy*. Cambridge: Harvard University Press.

———. 2001. "Seeing through Freud." *Annual of Psychoanalysis* 29:67–82.

———. 2006. *Becoming a Subject: Reflections on Philosophy and Psychoanalysis*. Oxford: Clarendon Press.

Chamberlain, L. 2000. *The Secret Artist: A Close Reading of Sigmund Freud*. New York: Seven Stories Press.

Chodorow, N. A. 1991. "Freud on Women." In *The Cambridge Companion to Freud*. Ed. J. Neu. Cambridge: Cambridge University Press, 224–48.

Christman, J. 1989. "Introduction." In *The Inner Citadel: Essays on Individual Autonomy*. Ed. J. Christman. Oxford: Oxford University Press, 3–23.

Churchland, P. M. 1991. *Neurocomputational Perspective: The Nature of Mind and the Structure of Science*. Cambridge: MIT Press.

Cioffi, F. 1998a. *Freud and the Question of Pseudoscience*. Peru, Ill.: Open Court.

———. 1998b. *Wittgenstein on Freud and Frazer*. Cambridge: University of Cambridge Press.

Clark, R. 1980. *Freud: The Man and the Cause*. New York: Random House.

Clore, G. 1992. "Cognitive Phenomenology: Feelings and the Construction of Judgment." In *The Construction of Social Judgments*. Ed. L. L. Martin. Hillsdale, N.J.: Erlbaum, 133–63.

Cohen, A. 1998a. "The Impact of Franz Brentano's Early Intentionality." Ph.D. diss., University of Essex.

———. 1998b. "Franz Brentano: L'inspirateur philosophique de Freud." In *Aux Sources de la psychoanalyse: Une analyse des premiers écrits de Freud (1877–1900)*. Ed. F. Geerardyn and G. Van de Vijvers. Paris: Éditions L'Harmattan, 111–22.

———. 2000. "The Origins of Freud's Theory of the Unconscious: A Philosophical Link." *Psychoanalytische Perspectieven* 41–42:109–22.

Cohen, R. S., ed. 1970a. *Ernst Mach: Physicist and Philosopher*. Dordrecht: Reidel.

———. 1970b. "Ernst Mach: Physics, Perception and the Philosophy of Science." In *Ernst Mach: Physicist and Philosopher*. Dordrecht: Reidel, 126–64.

Come, A. B. 1995. *Kierkegaard as Humanist: Discovering My Self*. Montreal: McGill-Queens University Press.

Crews, F. 1986. *Skeptical Engagements*. Oxford: Oxford University Press.

———. 1995. *The Memory Wars: Freud's Legacy in Dispute*. New York: New York Review of Books.

Danto, E. A. 2005. *Freud's Free Clinics: Psychoanalysis and Social Justice, 1918–1938*. New York: Columbia University Press.

Daston, L. 2000. "Wordless Objectivity." In *Little Tools of Knowledge: Historical Essays on Academic and Bureaucratic Practice*. Ed. P. Becker and W. Clark. Ann Arbor: University of Michigan Press, 259–84.

Davidson, D. 1980a. "Actions, Reasons, and Causes." 1963. In *Essays on Actions and Events*. Oxford: Clarendon Press, 3–19.

———. 1980b. "Mental Events." 1970. In *Essays on Actions and Events*. Oxford: Clarendon Press, 207–27.

———. 1980c. "Psychology as Philosophy." 1974. In *Essays on Actions and Events*. Oxford: Clarendon Press, 229–39.

Decker, H. S. 1977. *Freud in Germany: Revolution and Reaction in Science, 1893–1907*. New York: International Universities Press.

Deleuze, G. 1983. *Nietzsche and Philosophy*. Trans. H. Tomlinson. New York: Columbia University Press.

della Mirandola, G. P. 1965. *On the Dignity of Man and Other Works*. Trans. C. G. Wallis. Indianapolis: Bobbs-Merrill.

Depew, D. J., and B. H. Weber. 1995. *Darwinism Evolving: Systems Dynamics and the Genealogy of Natural Selection*. Cambridge: MIT Press.

Derrida, J. 2007. *Psyche: Inventions of the Other*. Vol. 1. Stanford: Stanford University Press.

de Sousa, R. 1974. "Norms and the Normal." In *Freud: A Collection of Critical Essays*. Ed. R. Wollheim. Garden City, N.Y.: Anchor, 196–221.

Dewey, J. 1931. "Philosophy and Civilization." In *Philosophy and Civilization*. New York: Capricorn Books, 3–12.

———. 1984. *The Quest for Certainty*. 1929. Carbondale: Southern Illinois University Press.

———. 1997. "The Ethics of Democracy." 1888. In *Pragmatism: A Reader*. Ed. L. Menand. New York: Vintage, 182–204.

———. 2002. *Human Nature and Conduct: An Introduction to Social Psychology*. 1922. Amherst, N.Y.: Prometheus Books.

Diggins, J. P. 1994. *The Promise of Pragmatism: Modernism and the Crisis of Knowledge and Authority*. Chicago: University of Chicago Press.

Dilman, I. 1984. *Freud and the Mind*. Oxford: Blackwell.

Dilthey, W. 1976. "The Construction of the Historical World in the Human Studies." 1906. In *Selected Writings*. Ed. and trans. H. P. Rickman. Cambridge: Cambridge University Press, 170–245.

———. 1977. "Ideas concerning a Descriptive and Analytic Psychology." 1894. In *Descriptive Psychology and Historical Understanding*. Trans. R. M. Zaner and K. L. Heiges. The Hague: Martinus Nijhoff, 23–120.

———. 1988. *Introduction to the Human Sciences: An Attempt to Lay a Foundation for the Study of Society and History*. 1883. Trans. R. J. Betanzos. Detroit: Wayne State University Press.

Dollimore, J. 1997. "Death and the Self." In *Rewriting the Self: Histories from the Renaissance to the Present*. Ed. R. Porter. London: Routledge, 249–61.

———. 1998. *Death, Desire, and Loss in Western Culture*. New York: Routledge.

Doolittle, H. 1971. *Tribute to Freud*. 1956. South Winksey, Oxford: Carcanet Press.

Dor, J. 1998. *Introduction to the Reading of Lacan: The Unconscious Structured Like a Language*. New York: Other Press.

Draenos, S. 1982. *Freud's Odyssey: Psychoanalysis and the End of Metaphysics*. New Haven: Yale University Press.

Dummett, M.A.E. 1963. "Realism." In *Truth and Other Enigmas*. London: Duckworth, 145–65.

Dworkin, G. 1988. *The Theory and Practice of Autonomy*. Cambridge: Cambridge University Press.

Edelson, M. 1988. *Psychoanalysis: A Theory in Crisis*. Chicago: University of Chicago Press.

Edwards, J. C. 2004. "From Myth to Metaphysics: Freud and Wittgenstein as Philosophical Thinkers." In *Psychoanalysis and the Limit: Epistemology, Mind, and the Question of Science*. Ed. J. Mills. Albany: State University of New York Press, 117–37.

Egginton, W. 2007. *The Philosopher's Desire: Psychoanalysis, Interpretation, and Truth*. Stanford: Stanford University Press.

Ellenberger, H. F. 1970. *The Discovery of the Unconscious: The History and Evolution of Dynamic Psychiatry*. New York: Basic Books.

Emerson, R. W. 1883a. "Character." In *Lectures and Biographical Sketches*. Vol. 10 of *Emerson 's Complete Works*. Cambridge: Riverside Press, 91–121.

———. 1883b. "Natural History of Intellect." In *Natural History of Intellect and Other Papers*. Vol. 12 of *Emerson's Complete Works*. Cambridge: Riverside Press, 1–59.

———. 1963. *The Journals and Miscellaneous Notebooks of Ralph Waldo Emerson*. Vol. 3, *1826–1832*. Ed. W. H. Gilman and A. R. Ferguson. Cambridge: Harvard University Press.

———. 1979. "The Over-soul." In *Essays: First Series*. Vol. 2 of *The Collected Works of Ralph Waldo Emerson*. Cambridge: Harvard University Press, 157–75.

Erdelyi, M. H. 1985. *Psychoanalysis: Freud's Cognitive Psychology*. New York: W. H. Freeman.

Eysenck, H. J. 1985. *The Decline and Fall of the Freudian Empire*. New York: Viking.

Fancher, R. E. 1977. "Brentano's Psychology from an Empirical Point of View and Freud's Early Metapsychology." *Journal of the History of Behavioral Science* 13:207–27.

Farrell, B. A. 1981. *The Standing of Psychoanalysis*. Oxford: Oxford University Press.

———, ed. 1994. *Philosophy and Psychoanalysis*. New York: Macmillan.

Fay, B., P. Pomper, and R. T. Vann, eds. 1998. *History and Theory: Contemporary Readings*. Malden, Mass.: Blackwell.

Feigl, H. 1958. "The 'Mental' and the 'Physical.'" In *Concepts, Theories, and the Mind-Body Problem*. Ed. H. Feigl, M. Scriven, and G. Maxwell. Minneapolis: University of Minnesota Press, 370–497.

Ferguson, H. 1999. "Freud and the Dynamics of Modernity." In *Freud 2000*. Ed. A. Elliott. New York: Routledge, 169–203.

Fine, A. 1998. "Scientific Realism and Antirealism." In *Routledge Encyclopedia of Philosophy*. Ed. E. Craig. London: Routledge, 8:581–84.

Fingarette, H. 1982. "Self-Deception and the 'Splitting of the Ego.'" In *Philosophical Essays on Freud*. Ed. R. Wollheim and J. Hopkins. Cambridge: Cambridge University Press, 212–27.

Fleck, L. 1979. *Genesis and Development of a Scientific Fact*. 1935. Chicago: University of Chicago Press.

Flew, A. 1954. "Psychoanalytic Explanation." In *Philosophy and Analysis*. Ed. M. Macdonald. Oxford: Basil Blackwell, 139–48.

Forrester, J. 1997. *Dispatches from the Freud Wars: Psychoanalysis and Its Passions*. Cambridge: Harvard University Press.

Foucault, M. 1970. *The Order of Things: An Archeology of the Human Sciences*. New York: Vintage.

———. 1983. "The Subject and Power." In *Michel Foucault: Beyond Structuralism and Hermeneutics*. 2nd ed. Ed. H. L. Dreyfus and P. Rabinow. Chicago: University of Chicago Press, 229–52.

———. 1984. "Nietzsche, Genealogy, History." In *Foucault Reader*. Ed. R. Rabinow. New York: Pantheon, 76–100.

———. 2003. *Abnormal: Lectures at the Collège de France, 1974–1975*. New York: Picador.

———. 2006a. *History of Madness*. New York: Routledge.

———. 2006b. *Psychiatric Power: Lectures at the Collège de France, 1973–1974*. London: Palgrave Macmillan.

Fox-Keller, E. 1994. "The Paradox of Scientific Subjectivity." In *Re-thinking Objectivity*. Ed. A. Megill. Durham, N.C.: Duke University Press, 313–31.

Frampton, M. F. 1991. "Considerations on the Role of Brentano's Concept of Intentionality in Freud's Repudiation of the Seduction Theory." *International Review of Psycho-analysis* 18:27–36.

Frank, I. 1977. "Spinoza, Freud, and Hampshire on Psychic Freedom." In *Thought, Consciousness, and Reality*. Ed. J. H. Smith. New Haven: Yale University Press, 257–309.

Frank, P. 1960. *Modern Science and Its Philosophy*. 1941. New York: Collier.

———. 1977. "Psychoanalysis and Logical Positivism." in *The Freudian Paradigm: Psychoanalysis and Scientific Thought*. Ed. M. Mujeeb-ur-Rahman. Chicago: Nelson-Hall, 101–5.

Frankfurt, H. G. 1971. "Freedom of the Will and the Concept of a Person." *Journal of Philosophy* 68:5–20.

Freud, A. 1967. *The Ego and the Mechanisms of Defense*. 1936. Vol. 2 of *The Writings of Anna Freud*. New York: International Universities Press.

Freud, S. 1894. "The Neuro-psychoses of Defence." In *The Standard Edition of the Complete Psychological Works of Sigmund Freud*. Trans. and ed. James

Strachey in collaboration with A. Freud, assisted by A. Strachey and A. Tyson. London: Hogarth Press and The Institute of Psycho-analysis, 1953–74. 3:45–61.

Freud, S. 1900. *Interpretation of Dreams. Standard Edition*, 4–5.

———. 1901. *The Psychopathology of Everyday Life. Standard Edition*, 6.

———. 1905a. *Jokes and Their Relation to the Unconscious. Standard Edition*, 8.

———. 1905b. *Three Essays on the Theory of Sexuality. Standard Edition*, 8.

———. 1908. "'Civilized' Sexual Morality and Modern Nervous Illness." *Standard Edition*, 9:181–204.

———. 1909a. "Notes upon a Case of Obsessional Neurosis." *Standard Edition*, 10:151–320.

———. 1909b. "Analysis of a Phobia in a Five-Year-Old boy." *Standard Edition*, 10:5–149.

———. 1910a. *Five Lectures on Psycho-Analysis. Standard Edition*, 11:3–55.

———. 1910b. *Leonardo da Vinci and a Memory of his Childhood. Standard Edition*, 11:63–137.

———. 1912a. "Recommendations to Physicians Practicing Psycho-analysis." *Standard Edition*, 12:111–20.

———. 1912b. "A Note on the Unconscious in Psychoanalysis." *Standard Edition*, 12:255–67.

———. 1913a. "The Claims of Psycho-analysis to Scientific Interest." *Standard Edition*, 13:165–90.

———. 1913b. *Totem and Taboo. Standard Edition*, 13:1–161.

———. 1914a. "On Narcissism: An Introduction." *Standard Edition*, 14:73–102.

———. 1914b. "Remembering, Repeating and Working-through. (Further Recommendations on the Technique of Psycho-analysis II)." *Standard Edition*, 12:147–56.

———. 1914c. "On the History of the Psycho-analytic Movement." *Standard Edition*, 14:7–66.

———. 1915a. "The Unconscious." *Standard Edition*, 14:166–215.

———. 1915b. "Instincts and their Vicissitudes." *Standard Edition*, 14:109–40.

———. 1915c. "Repression." *Standard Edition*, 14:146–58.

———. 1916–17. *Introductory Lectures on Psycho-analysis, Standard Edition*, 15 and 16.

———. 1917a. "Mourning and Melancholia." *Standard Edition*, 14:243–58.

———. 1917b. "A Difficulty in the Path of Psycho-analysis." *Standard Edition*, 17:137–44.

———. 1918. *From the History of an Infantile Neurosis. Standard Edition*, 17: 7–136.

———. 1919a. "The 'Uncanny.'" *Standard Edition*, 17:219–52.

———. 1919b. "Preface to Reik's *Ritual: Psycho-analytic Studies*." *Standard Edition*, 17:259–63.

———. 1920. *Beyond the Pleasure Principle. Standard Edition*, 18:7–64.

———. 1922. "Group Psychology and the Analysis of the Ego." *Standard Edition* 18:3–64.

———. 1923a. *The Ego and the Id. Standard Edition*, 19:12–59.

———. 1923b. "Two Encyclopedia Articles." *Standard Edition*, 18:235–59.

———. 1924. "The Economic Problem of Masochism." *Standard Edition*, 19:159–70.

———. 1925a. "An Autobiographical Study." *Standard Edition*, 20:7–74.

———. 1925b. "Resistances to Psychoanalysis." *Standard Edition*, 19:213–22.

———. 1926a. "The Question of Lay Analysis: Conversations with an Impartial Person." *Standard Edition*, 20:183–250.

———. 1926b. "Psychoanalysis, Freudian School." *Standard Edition*, 20:263–70.

———. 1926c. *Inhibition, Symptom and Anxiety. Standard Edition*, 20:87–174.

———. 1927a. "Postscript to the Question of Lay Analysis." *Standard Edition*, 20:251–58.

———. 1927b. *The Future of an Illusion. Standard Edition*, 21:5–56.

———. 1930. *Civilization and its Discontents. Standard Edition*, 21:64–145.

———. 1931. "Female Sexuality." *Standard Edition*, 21:223–46.

———. 1932. "Why War?" *Standard Edition*, 21:203–15.

———. 1933. *New Introductory Lectures on Psycho-analysis. Standard Edition*, 22.

———. 1935. "An Autobiographical Study, Postscript." *Standard Edition* 20:71–74.

———. 1937a. "Constructions in Analysis." *Standard Edition* 23:255–70.

———. 1937b. "Analysis, Terminable and Interminable." *Standard Edition* 23:216–53.

———. 1939. *Moses and Monotheism: Three Essays. Standard Edition* 23:7–137.

———. 1940a. *Neue Folge der Vorlesungen zur Einführung in die Psychoanalyse.* 1933. *Gesammelte Werke.* Vol. 15. London: Imago.

———. 1940b. *An Outline of Psycho-analysis. Standard Edition*, 23:144–207.

———. 1940c. "Some Elementary Lessons in Psycho-analysis." *Standard Edition*, 23:279–86.

———. 1955. *Project for a Scientific Psychology.* 1895. *Standard Edition*, 1:295–387.

———. 1960. *The Letters of Sigmund Freud.* Trans. T. Stern and J. Stern and ed. E. L. Freud. New York: Basic Books.

———. 1985. *The Complete Letters of Sigmund Freud to Wilhelm Fliess 1887–1904.* Trans. and ed. J. M. Masson. Cambridge: Harvard University Press.

———. 1987. *A Phylogenetic Fantasy: Overview of the Transference Neuroses.* Ed. I. Grubrich-Simits and trans. A. Hoffer and P. T. Hoffer. Cambridge: Harvard University Press.

———. 1990. *The Letters of Sigmund Freud to Eduard Silberstein, 1871–1881.* Trans. A. J. Pomerans and ed. W. Boehlich. Cambridge: Harvard University Press.

Freud, S., and W. C. Bullitt. 1967. *Thomas Woodrow Wilson: A Psychological Study.* Cambridge: Houghton Mifflin.

Friedman, M., and A. Nordmann, eds. 2006. *The Kantian Legacy in Nineteenth-Century Science.* Cambridge: MIT Press.

Fromm, E. 1947. *Man for Himself: An Inquiry into the Psychology of Ethics.* New York: Holt.

Fulgencio, L. 2005. "Freud's Metapsychological Speculations." *International Journal of Psycho-analysis* 86:99–123.

Gabriel, Y. 1983. *Freud and Society*. London: Routledge and Kegan Paul.

Gadamer, H.-G. 1990. *Truth and Method*. 2nd ed. New York: Crossroad.

Galaty, D. H. 1974. "The Philosophical Basis for Mid-Nineteenth-Century German Reductionism." *Journal of the History of Medicine and Allied Sciences* 29:295–316.

Gardner, S. 1991. "The Unconscious." In *The Cambridge Companion to Freud*. Ed. J. Neu. Cambridge: Cambridge University Press, 136–60.

———. 1993. *Irrationality and the Philosophy of Psychoanalysis*. Cambridge: Cambridge University Press.

Gay, P. 1978. *Freud, Jews, and Other Germans: Masters and Victims in Modernist Culture*. New York: Oxford University Press.

———. 1987. *A Godless Jew: Freud, Atheism, and the Making of Psychoanalysis*. New Haven: Yale University Press.

———. 1988. *Freud. A Life for Our Time*. New York: Norton.

Giere, R. N., and A. W. Richardson, eds. 1996. *Origins of Logical Empiricism*. Minneapolis: University of Minnesota Press.

Gill, M. M. 1994. *Psychoanalysis in Transition: A Personal View*. New York: Analytic Press.

Gilman, S. L. 1993a. *Freud, Race, and Gender*. Princeton: Princeton University Press.

———. 1993b. *The Case of Sigmund Freud: Medicine and Identity at the Fin de Siècle*. Baltimore: Johns Hopkins University Press.

Ginzburg, C. 1983. "Clues: Morelli, Freud and Sherlock Holmes." In *The Sign of Three: Dupin, Holmes, Peirce*. Ed. U. Eco and T. A. Sebeok. Bloomington: Indiana University Press, 81–118.

Glymour, C. 1991. "Freud's Androids." In *The Cambridge Companion to Freud*. Ed. J. Neu. Cambridge: Cambridge University Press, 44–85.

Goethe, J. W. von. 1988a. "The Experiment as Mediator between Object and Subject." 1792. In *Scientific Studies*. Trans. and ed. D. Miller. New York: Suhrkamp, 11–17.

———. 1988b. "The Influence of Modern Philosophy." 1817. In *Scientific Studies*. Trans. and ed. D. Miller. New York: Suhrkamp, 28–30.

Goldberg, S. E. 1988. *Two Patterns of Rationality in Freud's Writings*. Tuscaloosa: University of Alabama Press.

Golumb, J. 1989. *Nietzsche's Enticing Psychology of Power*. Ames: Iowa State University Press.

Gomez, L. 2005. *The Freud Wars: An Introduction to the Philosophy of Psychoanalysis*. New York: Routledge.

Gould, S. J. 1977. *Ontogeny and Phylogeny*. Cambridge: Harvard University Press.

Green, A. 2005. *Psychoanalysis: A Paradigm for Clinical Thinking*. Trans. A. Weller. London: Free Association Books.

Greenberg, J. R., and S. A. Mitchell. 1983. *Object Relations in Psychoanalytic Theory*. Cambridge: Harvard University Press.

Greer, S. 2002. "Freud's Bad Conscious: The Case of Nietzsche's *Genealogy.*" *Journal of History of the Behavioral Sciences* 38:303–15.

Gresser, M. 1994. *Dual Allegiance: Freud as a Modern Jew.* Albany: State University of New York Press.

Groddeck, G. 1976. *The Book of the It.* 1923. New York: International Universities Press.

Grünbaum, A. 1984. *The Foundations of Psychoanalysis: A Philosophical Critique.* Berkeley: University of California Press.

Guntrip, H. 1971. *Psychoanalytic Theory, Therapy, and the Self: A Basic Guide to the Human Personality in Freud, Erikson, Klein, Sullivan, Fairbairn, Hartmann, Jacobson, and Winnicott.* New York: Basic Books.

Guttman, S. A. 1984. *The Concordance to the Standard Edition of the Complete Psychological Works of Sigmund Freud.* New York: International Universities Press.

Guyer, P. 1987. *Kant and the Claims of Knowledge.* New York: Cambridge University Press.

———. 1992. "The Transcendental Deduction of the Categories." In *The Cambridge Companion to Kant.* Ed. P. Guyer. Cambridge: Cambridge University Press, 123–60.

———, ed. 2006. *The Cambridge Companion to Kant and Modern Philosophy.* Cambridge: Cambridge University Press.

Habermas, J. 1971. *Knowledge and Human Interests.* Trans. J. J. Shapiro. Boston: Beacon Press.

Hamlyn, D. W. 1980. *Schopenhauer.* London: Routledge and Kegan Paul.

Hampshire, S. 1962. *Spinoza.* London: Penguin.

———. 1975. *Freedom of the Individual.* Expanded edition. Princeton: Princeton University Press.

Hanly, C., and M. Lazerowitz, eds. 1970. *Psychoanalysis and Philosophy.* New York: International Universities Press.

Hanna, R. 2001. *Kant and the Foundations of Analytic Philosophy.* Oxford: Oxford University Press.

Hart, H.L.A., and A. M. Honré. 1959. *Causation in the Law.* London: Oxford University Press.

Hartmann, H. 1960. *Moral Values in Psychoanalysis.* New York: International Universities Press.

Heaton, J., and J. Groves. 1994. *Introducing Wittgenstein.* New York: Totem Books.

Hedwig, K. 1979. "Intention: Outlines for the History of a Phenomenological Concept." *Philosophy and Phenomenological Research* 39:326–40.

Hegel, G.W.F. 1977. *The Difference between Fichte's and Schelling's System of Philosophy.* 1801. Albany: State University of New York Press.

———. 1984. *Lectures on the Philosophy of Religion,* 1832. Vol. 1, *Introduction and the Concept of Religion.* Berkeley: University of California Press.

———. 1999. *Hegel's Phenomenology of Self-Consciousness: Text and Commentary.* 1807. Ed. L. Rauch and D. Sherman. Albany: State University of New York Press.

Heidegger, M. 1977a. "The Age of the World Picture." 1954. In *The Question Concerning Technology and Other Essays*. Trans. W. Lovitt. New York: Harper Torchbooks, 115–54.

———. 1977b. "Science and Reflection." 1954. In *The Question Concerning Technology and Other Essays*. Trans. W. Lovitt. New York: Harper Torchbooks, 155–82.

———. 1979. *Nietzsche*. 1961. Vol. 1. Trans. D. F. Kressl. San Francisco: Harper.

———. 1996. *Being and Time*. 1927. Trans. J. Stambaugh. Albany: State University of New York Press.

Helmholtz, H. von. 1971a. "The Facts of Perception." 1878. In *Selected Writings of Hermann Helmholtz*. Ed. R. Kahl. Middleton, Conn.: Wesleyan University Press, 366–408.

———. 1971b. "Über das Sehen des Menschen." 1855. In *Philosophische Vorträge und Aufsätze*. Ed. H. Hörz and S. Wollgast. Berlin: Akademie-Verlag.

———. 1995. "On Goethe's Scientific Researches." 1853. Trans. E. Atkinson. In *Science and Culture: Popular and Philosophical Essays*. Ed. D. Cahan. Chicago: University of Chicago Press, 56–74.

Henry, M. 1993. *The Genealogy of Psychoanalysis*. Trans. D. Brick. Stanford: Standford University Press.

Herman, B. 1993. *The Practice of Moral Judgment*. Cambridge: Harvard University Press.

Herzog, P. 1988. "The Myth of Freud as Anti-philosopher." In *Freud: Appraisals and Re-appraisals: Contributions to Freud Studies*. Ed. P. E. Stepansky. New York: Analytic Press, 2:163–89.

Hiley, D. S., J. F. Bohman, and R. Shusterman, eds. 1991. *The Interpretive Turn: Philosophy, Science, Culture*. Ithaca, N.Y.: Cornell University Press.

Hobson, J. A. 1988. *The Dreaming Brain*. New York: Basic Books.

Hodge, C. W. 1896. "Windelband on 'The Principle of Morality.'" *Philosophical Review* 56:623–27.

Holt, R. R. 1972. "Freud's Mechanistic and Humanistic Images of Man." *Psychoanalysis and Contemporary Thought* 1:3–24.

———. 1989. *Freud Reappraised: A Fresh Look at Psychoanalytic Theory*. New York: Guilford Press.

Hook, S., ed. 1959. *Psychoanalysis, Scientific Method, and Philosophy*. New York: New York University Press.

Horney, K. 1950. *Neurosis and Human Growth*. New York: Norton.

Horrocks, R. 2001. *Freud Revisited: Psychoanalytic Themes in the Postmodern Age*. New York: Palgrave.

Horwich, P. 2004a. "Realism and Truth." 1996. In *From a Deflationary Point of View*. Oxford: Clarendon Press, 32–44.

———. 2004b. "Three Forms of Realism." 1982. In *From a Deflationary Point of View*. Oxford: Clarendon Press, 7–31.

Horwitz, A. V. 2002. *Creating Mental Illness*. Chicago: University of Chicago Press.

Hughes, H. S. 1961. *Consciousness and Society: The Reorientation of European Social Thought, 1890–1930*. New York: Vintage.

Hume, D. 1975. *Enquiry concerning Human Understanding*. 1748. Ed. P. H. Nidditch. Oxford: Oxford University Press.

———. 1978. *A Treatise of Human Nature*. 1739. Oxford: Clarendon Press.

Hussain, N.J.Z. 2005. "Friedrich Albert Lange." *The Stanford Encyclopedia of Philosophy*. Ed. E. N. Zalta. http://plato.stanford.edu/entries/friedrich-lange/.

Husserl, E. 1970. *The Crisis of European Sciences and Transcendental Phenomenology*. 1935. Evanston, Ill.: Northwestern University Press.

Hylton, P. 1990. *Russell, Idealism, and the Emergence of Analytical Philosophy*. Oxford: Clarendon Press.

Inwood, M. 1992. *A Hegel Dictionary*. Malden, Mass.: Blackwell.

Jacob, A. 1992. *De Naturae Natura: A Study of Idealist Conceptions of Nature and the Unconscious*. Stuttgart: Franz Steiner Verlag.

Jacquette, D., ed. 2004a. *The Cambridge Companion to Brentano*. Cambridge: Cambridge University Press.

———. 2004b. "Brentano's Conception of Intentionality." In *The Cambridge Companion to Brentano*. Ed. D. Jacquette. Cambridge: Cambridge University Press, 98–130.

James, W. 1983. *The Principles of Psychology*. 1890. Cambridge: Harvard University Press.

———. 1996. "Does Consciousness Exist?" In *Essays in Radical Empiricism*. Lincoln: University of Nebraska Press, 1–38.

Janaway, C. 1989. *Self and World in Schopenhauer's Philosophy*. Oxford: Clarendon Press.

Jasanoff, S., G. E. Markle, J. C. Petersen, and T. Pinch, eds. 1995. *Handbook of Science and Technology Studies*. Thousand Oaks, Calif.: Sage.

Jeanes, H. 1656. *A Mixture of Scholastic Divinity*. Oxford: Printer to the University.

Johnston, P. 1993. *Wittgenstein: Rethinking the Inner*. London: Routledge.

Jones, E. 1953–57. *The Life and Work of Sigmund Freud*. 3 vols. New York: Basic Books.

Josephson, J. R., and S. G. Josephson. 1994. *Abductive Inference: Computation, Philosophy, and Technology*. Cambridge: Cambridge University Press.

Joyce, R. 2007. *The Evolution of Morality*. Cambridge: MIT Press.

Jung, C. G. 1988. *Nietzsche's Zarathustra*. 2 vols. Princeton: Princeton University Press.

Kane, R. 2005. *A Contemporary Introduction to Free Will*. New York: Oxford University Press.

Kant, I. 1987. *Critique of Judgment*. 1790. Trans. W. S. Pluhar. Indianapolis: Hackett.

———. 1996a. "Conflict of the Faculties." 1798. In *Religion and Rational Theology*. Trans. and ed. A. Wood and G. di Giovanni. Cambridge: Cambridge University Press, 247–93.

———. 1996b. *Critique of Practical Reason*. 1788. In *Practical Philosophy*. Trans. M. J. Gregor. Cambridge: Cambridge University Press, 139–271.

———. 1996c. *Groundwork of the Metaphysics of Morals*. 1785. In *Practical Philosophy*. Trans. M. J. Gregor, Cambridge: Cambridge University Press, 49–108.

Kant, I. 1996d. "What Is Enlightenment?" 1784. In *What Is Enlightenment?* Ed. J. Schmidt. Berkeley: University of California Press.

———. 1996e. *Anthropology from a Pragmatic Point of View*. 1798. Trans. V. L. Dowdell. Carbondale: Illinois Southern University Press.

———. 1998. *Critique of Pure Reason*. 1787. Trans. P. Guyer and A. W. Wood. Cambridge: Cambridge University Press.

———. 2006. *Anthropology from a Pragmatic Point of View*. 1798. Ed. and trans. R. B. Louden. Cambridge: Cambridge University Press.

Kaplan, A. 1977. "Psychoanalysis and Modern Philosophy." In *The Freudian Paradigm: Psychoanalysis and Scientific Thought*. Ed. M. Mujeeb-ur-Rahman. Chicago: Nelson-Hall, 75–99.

Karwautz, A., C. Wöber-Bingöl, and C. Wöber. 1995. "Friedrich Nietzsche and Sigmund Freud." *British Journal of Psychiatry* 166:825–26.

Kaufmann, W. 1980. *Freud, Adler, and Jung: Discovery of the Mind*. Vol. 3. New York: McGraw-Hill.

Keller, P. 1998. *Kant and the Demands of Self-Consciousness*. Cambridge: Cambridge University Press.

Kierkegaard, S. 1980. *The Sickness unto Death*. 1980. Trans. H. V. Hong and E. H. Hong. Princeton: Princeton University Press.

———. 1985a. *Fear and Trembling*. 1843. Trans. A. Hannay. Harmondsworth: Penguin.

———. 1985b. *Philosophical Fragments*. 1844. Trans. H. V. Hong and E. H. Hong. Princeton: Princeton University Press.

———. 1985c. *Johannes Climacus*. 1844. Trans. H. V. Hong and E. H. Hong. Princeton: Princeton University Press.

Kiernan, T. P. 1961. "Introduction." In *Theories in Logic*, by W. Windelband. New York: Citadel Press.

Kirschner, S. R. 1996. *The Religious and Romantic Origins of Psychoanalysis*. Cambridge: Cambridge University Press.

Kitcher, P. 1992. *Freud's Dream: A Complete Interdisciplinary Science of the Mind*. Cambridge: MIT Press.

———. 2006. "Kant's Philosophy of the Cognitive Mind." In *The Cambridge Companion to Kant and Modern Philosophy*. Ed. P. Guyer. New York: Cambridge University Press, 169–202.

Kite, J. V. 2008. "Ideas of Influence: The Impact of the Analyst's Character on the Analysis." *Psychoanalytic Quarterly* 77:1075–1104.

Klein, D. B. 1985. *Jewish Origins of the Psychoanalytic Movement*. Chicago: University of Chicago Press.

Kleinman, A. 1988. *The Illness Narratives: Suffering, Healing, and the Human Condition*. New York: Basic Books.

Knorr Cetina, K. 1999. *Epistemic Cultures: How Science Makes Knowledge*. Cambridge: Harvard University Press.

Kobrin, N. 1993. "Freud's Concept of Autonomy and Strachey's Translation: A Piece of the Puzzle of the Freudian Self." *Annual of Psychoanalysis* 21: 201–23.

Koch, S., and D. Levy. 1992. *A Century of Psychology as a Science*. Washington, D.C.: American Psychological Association.

Koelb, C., ed. 1990. *Nietzsche as Postmodernist: Essays Pro and Con*. Albany: State University of New York.

Kōgaku, A. 1991. "The Problem of the Body in Nietzsche and Dōgen." In *Nietzsche and Asian Thought*. Ed. G. Parkes. Chicago: University of Chicago Press, 214–25.

Kohut, H. 1977. *The Restoration of the Self*. New York: International Universities Press.

Kojève, A. 1980. *Introduction to the Reading of Hegel: Lectures on the Phenomenology of Spirit*. 1947. Ithaca, N.Y.: Cornell University Press.

Könke, K. C. 1991. *The Rise of Neo-Kantianism: German Academic Philosophy between Idealism and Positivism*. Trans. R. J. Hollingdale. Cambridge: Cambridge University Press.

Korsgaard, C. M. 1996. *The Sources of Normativity*. Cambridge: Cambridge University Press.

Kristeva, J. 1987. *Tales of Love*. New York: Columbia University Press.

Krüll, M. 1986. *Freud and His Father*. Trans. A. J. Pomerans. London: Hutchinson.

Kuhn, T. 1991. "The Natural and the Human Sciences." In *The Interpretive Turn: Philosophy, Science, Culture*. Ed. D. S. Hiley, J. F. Bohman, and R. Shusterman. Ithaca, N.Y.: Cornell University Press, 17–24.

Kukla, A. 2000. *Social Constructivism and the Philosophy of Science*. London: Routledge.

Küng, H. 1990. *Freud and the Problem of God*. New Haven: Yale University Press.

Lacan, J. 1968. *Speech and Language in Psychoanalysis*. Trans. A. Wilden. Baltimore: Johns Hopkins University Press.

————. 1992. *The Seminar of Jacques Lacan. Book VII: The Ethics of Psychoanalysis*. Trans. D. Porter. New York: Norton.

————. 2002. "The Function and Field of Speech and Language in Psychoanalysis." In *Ecrits: A Selection*. Trans. B. Fink. New York: Norton, 31–106.

Laing, R. D. 1960. *The Divided Self: An Existential Study in Sanity and Madness*. London: Tavistock.

Lakoff, G., and M. Johnson. 1980. *Metaphors We Live By*. Chicago: University of Chicago Press.

Lamont, C. 1993. *The Philosophy of Humanism*. 2nd ed. New York: Continuum.

Lange, F. A. 1950. *The History of Materialism and Criticism of Its Present Importance*. 1873–75. 2nd ed. Trans. E. C. Thomas. London: Routledge and Kegan Paul.

Laplanche, J. 2000. "Interview." *Radical Philosophy*, issue 102. http://www.radicalphilosophy.com/default.asp?channel_id=2190&editorial_id=10027.

Laplanche, J., and J. B. Pontalis. 1973. "Ego." In *The Language of Psycho-analysis*. Trans. D. Nicholson-Smith. New York: Norton, 130–43.

Latour, B. 1993. *We Have Never Been Modern*. Cambridge: Harvard University Press.

Mach, E. 1959. *The Analysis of Sensations*. 1897. Trans. C. M. Williams and S. Waterlow. New York: Dover.

MacIntyre, A. C. 1958. *The Unconscious*. Bristol: Thoemmes Press.

———. 1978. "Objectivity in Morals and Objectivity in Science." In *Morals, Science, and Sociality*. Ed. H. T. Engelhardt, Jr. and D. Callahan. Hastings-on-Hudson, N.Y. : Hastings Center, Institute of Society, Ethics, and the Life Sciences, 21–39.

———. 2004. "Preface to the Revised Edition." In *The Unconscious: A Conceptual Analysis*. Rev. ed. New York: Routledge, 1–38.

Mackenzie, C., and N. Stoljar. 2000. "Introduction." In *Relational Autonomy: Feminist Perspectives on Autonomy, Agency, and the Social Self*. Ed. C. Mackenzie and N. Stoljar. New York: Oxford University Press, 3–31.

Macklin, R. 1973. "Values in Psychoanalysis and Psychotherapy: A Survey and an Analysis." *American Journal of Psychoanalysis* 33:133–50.

Macmillan, M. 1997. *Freud Evaluated: The Completed Arc*. Cambridge: MIT Press.

Magee, B. 1983. *The Philosophy of Schopenhauer*. Oxford: Clarendon Press.

Makari, G. 1991. "German Philosophy, Freud, and the Riddle of the Woman." *Journal of the American Psychoanalytic Association* 39:183–213.

———. 1994. "In the Eye of the Beholder: Helmholtzian Perception and the Origins of Freud's 1900 Theory of Transference." *Journal of the American Psychoanalytic Association* 42:549–80.

———. 2008. *Revolution in Mind: The Creation of Psychoanalysis*. New York: HarperCollins.

Mancia, M. 2002. "Wittgenstein's Personality and His Relations with Freud's Thought." *International Journal of Psychoanalysis* 83:161–77.

Mann, T. 1947. "Freud and the Future." 1936. In *Essays of Three Decades*. Trans. H. T. Lowe-Porter. New York: Alfred A. Knopf, 411–28.

Marcus, S. 1984. *Freud and the Culture of Psychoanalysis*. Boston: George Allen and Unwin.

Marcuse, H. 1955. *Eros and Civilization: A Philosophical Inquiry into Freud*. Boston: Beacon Press.

———. 1970. *Five Lectures: Psychoanalysis, Politics, and Utopia*. Trans. J. J. Shapiro. Boston: Beacon Press.

Margolis, J. 2004. "Reflections on Intentionality." In *The Cambridge Companion to Brentano*. Ed. D. Jacquette. Cambridge: Cambridge University Press, 131–48.

Martin, E. 1994. *Flexible Bodies: Tracking Immunity in American Culture from the Days of Polio to the Age of AIDS*. Boston: Beacon Press.

Maudsley, H. 1867. *Physiology and Pathology of the Mind*. London: Macmillan.

Mauss, M. 1985. "A Category of the Human Mind: The Notion of Person; the Notion of Self." In *The Category of the Person: Anthropology, Philosophy, History*. Ed. M. Carrithers, S. Collins, and S. Lukes. Cambridge: Cambridge University Press, 1–25.

Mazlish, B. 1968. "Freud and Nietzsche." *Psychoanalytic Review* 55:360–75.

McAlister, L. L. 1982. *The Development of Franz Brentano's Ethics*. Amsterdam: Rodopi.

McAlister, L. L. 2004. "Brentano's Epistemology." In *The Cambridge Compaion to Brentano*. Ed. D. Jacquette. Cambridge: Cambridge University Press, 149–67.

McGrath, W. J. 1986. *Freud's Discovery of Psychoanalysis: The Politics of Hysteria*. Ithaca, N.Y.: Cornell University Press.

McGuiness, B. 1982. "Freud and Wittgenstein." In *Wittgenstein and His Times*. Ed. B. McGuiness. Oxford: Blackwell, 27–43.

McGushin, E. F. 2007. *Foucault's Askēsis: An Introduction to the Philosophical Life*. Evanston, Ill.: Northwestern University Press.

McIntosh, D. 1986. "The Ego and the Self in the Thought of Sigmund Freud." *International Journal of Psycho-analysis* 67:429–48.

Mead, G. H. 1934. "A Contrast of Individualistic and Social Theories of the Self." In *Mind, Self, and Society*. Chicago: University of Chicago Press, 222–26.

Megill, A. 1985. *Prophets of Extremity: Nietzsche, Heidegger, Foucault, Derrida*. Berkeley: University of California Press.

Meissner, W. W. 1986. "Can Psychoanalysis Find Its Self?" *Journal of the American Psychoanalytic Association* 34:379–400.

———. 1993. "Self-as-Agent in Psychoanalysis." *Psychoanalysis and Contemporary Thought* 16:459–95.

———. 1995. "The Economic Principle in Psychoanalysis. 3. Motivational Principles." *Psychoanalysis and Contemporary Thought* 18:261–92.

———. 1996. *The Therapeutic Alliance*. New Haven: Yale University Press.

———. 1999. "The Dynamic Principle in Psychoanalysis. 1. The Classic Theory Reconsidered." *Psychoanalysis and Contemporary Thought* 22:3–40.

———. 2003. *The Ethical Dimension of Psychotherapy: A Dialogue*. Albany: State University of New York Press.

Merlan, P. 1945. "Brentano and Freud." *Journal of the History of Ideas* 6:375–77.

———. 1949. "Brentano and Freud—a Sequel." *Journal of the History of Ideas* 10:451.

Messer, S. B., L. A. Sass, and R. L. Woolfolk, eds. 1988. *Hermeneutics and Psychological Theory: Interpretative Perspectives on Personality, Psychotherapy, and Psychopathology*. New Brunswick, N.J.: Rutgers University Press.

Miller, C. 2002. "Realism, Antirealism, and Commonsense." In *Realism and Antirealism*. Ed. W. P. Alston. Ithaca, N.Y.: Cornell University Press, 13–25.

Mills, J. 2002. *The Unconscious Abyss: Hegel's Anticipation of Psychoanalysis*. Albany: State University of New York Press.

———, ed. 2004. *Psychoanalysis and the Limit: Epistemology, Mind, and the Question of Science*. Albany: State University of New York Press.

Modell, A. H. 1990. *Other Times, Other Realities: Toward a Theory of Psychoanalytic Treatment*. Cambridge: Harvard University Press.

———. 1993. *The Private Self*. Cambridge: Harvard University Press.

———. 2006. *Imagination and the Meaningful Brain*. Cambridge: MIT Press.

Moles, A. 1990. *Nietzsche's Philosophy of Nature and Cosmology*. New York: Peter Lang.

Monk, R. 1991. *Ludwig Wittgenstein: The Duty of Genius*. New York: Penguin.

Moore, G. E. 1993. "Wittgenstein's Lectures in 1930–1933." 1954, 1955. In *Ludwig Wittgenstein: Philosophical Occasions, 1912–1951*. Ed. J. C. Klagge and A. Nordmann. Indianapolis: Hackett, 46–114.

Moore, R. 1999. *The Creation of Reality in Psychoanalysis: A View of the Contributions of Donald Spence, Roy Schafer, Robert Stolorow, Irwin Z. Hoffman, and Beyond*. Hillsdale, N.J.: Analytic Press.

Morris, B. 1994. *Anthropology of the Self: The Individual in Cultural Perspective*. London: Pluto Press.

Mostert, P. 1979. "Nietzsche's Reception of Darwinism." *Bijdragen lot de Dierkunde* 49:235–46.

Moulines, C. U. 1981. "Hermann von Helmholtz: A Physiological Theory of Knowledge." In *Epistemological and Social Problems of the Sciences in the Early Nineteenth Century*. Ed. H. N. Jahnke and M. Otte. Dordrecht: D. Reidel, 65–73.

Natsoulas, T. 1984. "Freud and Consciousness. I. Intrinsic Consciousness." *Psychoanalysis and Contemporary Thought* 7:195–232.

———. 1985. "Freud and Consciousness. II. Derived Consciousness." *Psychoanalysis and Contemporary Thought* 8:183–220.

Needleman, J. 1967. "A Critical Introduction to Ludwig Binswanger's Existential Psychoanalysis." In *Being-in-the-World: Selected Papers of Ludwig Binswanger*. Ed. J. Needleman. New York: Harper Torchbooks, 7–145.

Neiman, S. 1994. *The Unity of Reason: Rereading Kant*. New York: Oxford University Press.

Neuhouser, F. 2000. *Foundations of Hegel's Social Theory: Actualizing Freedom*. Cambridge: Harvard University Press.

Neurath, O. 1983. "Protocol Statements." 1931. In *Philosophical Papers, 1913–1946*. Ed. R. S. Cohen and M. Neurath. Dordrecht: Reidel, 91–99.

Newton, P. M. 1995. *Freud: From Youthful Dream to Mid-life Crisis*. New York: Guilford Press.

Nietzsche, F. 1959a. *Twilight of the Idols*. In *The Portable Nietzsche*. Ed. and trans. W. Kaufmann. New York: Penguin, 463–563.

———. 1959b. *The Antichrist*. In *The Portable Nietzsche*. Ed. and trans. W. Kaufmann. New York: Penguin, 568–656.

———. 1959c. *Thus Spoke Zarathustra*. In *The Portable Nietzsche*. Ed. and trans. W. Kaufmann. New York: Penguin, 112–439.

———. 1959d. *Nietzsche contra Wagner*. In *The Portable Nietzsche*. Ed. and trans. W. Kaufmann. New York: Penguin, 661–83.

———. 1966. *Beyond Good and Evil*. Trans. W. Kaufmann. New York: Vintage.

———. 1967a. *The Will to Power*. Trans. W. Kaufmann and R. J. Hollingdale. New York: Vintage.

———. 1967b. *Ecce Homo*. Trans. W. Kaufmann. New York: Vintage.

———. 1967c. *On the Genealogy of Morals*. Trans. W. Kaufmann and R. J. Hollingdale. New York: Vintage.

———. 1974. *The Gay Science*. Trans. W. Kaufmann. New York: Vintage.

———. 1979. *Philosophy and Truth: Selections from Nietzsche's Notebooks of the Early 1870's*. Trans. and ed. D. Breazeale. Atlantic Highlands, N.J.: Humanities Press.

———. 1982. *Daybreak*. Trans. R. J. Hollingdale. Cambridge: Cambridge University Press.

Nussbaum, M. 1994. *The Therapy of Desire*. Princeton: Princeton University Press.

Oatley, K. 2007. "Narrative Modes of Consciousness and Selfhood." In *The Cambridge Handbook of Consciousness*. Ed. P. D. Zelazo, M. Moscovitch, and E. Thompson. Cambridge: Cambridge University Press, 375–402.

O'Donnell, J. J. 2004. *Augustine: A New Biography*. San Francisco: Harper.

O'Neill, O. 1992. "Vindicating Reason." In *The Cambridge Companion to Kant*. Ed. P. Guyer. Cambridge: Cambridge University Press, 280–308.

———. 2002. *Autonomy and Trust in Bioethics*. Cambridge: Cambridge University Press.

Parfit, D. 1984. *Reasons and Persons*. Oxford: Oxford University Press.

Parisi, T. 1989. "Freud's Phylogenetic Fantasy: An Essay Review." *Biology and Philosophy* 4:483–94.

Parrington, V. L. 1987. *Main Currents in American Thought*. Vol. 2, *The Romantic Revolution in America, 1800–1860*. 1927. Norman: University of Oklahoma Press.

Paul, R. A. 1996. *Moses and Civilization: The Meaning behind Freud's Myth*. New Haven: Yale University Press.

Pears, D. 1974. "Freud, Sartre and Self-deception." In *Freud: A Collection of Critical Essays*. Ed. R. Wollheim. Garden City, N.Y.: Anchor Books, 97–112.

Peterman, J. F. 1992. *Philosophy as Therapy: An Interpretation and Defense of Wittgenstein's Later Philosophical Project*. Albany: State University Press of New York.

Pettigrew, D. E. 1990. "The Question of the Relation of Philosophy and Psychoanalysis: The Case of Kant and Freud." *Metaphilosophy* 21:67–88.

Phillips, A. 2000. *Darwin's Worms: On Life Stories and Death Stories*. New York: Basic Books.

Picard, M. 1920. *Values Immediate and Contributory*. New York: New York University Press.

Pickering, N. 2006. *The Metaphor of Mental Illness*. New York: Oxford University Press.

Pippin, R. B. 1989. *Hegel's Idealism: The Satisfaction of Self-Consciousness*. New York: Cambridge University Press.

Polanyi, M. 1962. *Personal Knowledge: Towards a Post-critical Philosophy*. Corrected edition. Chicago: University of Chicago Press.

Poli, R. 1998. "The Brentano Puzzle: An Introduction." In *The Brentano Puzzle*. Ed. R. Poli. Aldershot, Hampshire: Ashgate, 1–14.

Popper, K. R. 1959. *The Logic of Scientific Discovery*. 1935. New York: Harper Torchbooks.

———. 1963. *Conjectures and Refutations: The Growth of Scientific Knowledge*. New York: Harper Torchbooks.

Pribram, K. H., and M. M. Gill. 1976. *Freud's "Project" Re-assessed: Preface to Contemporary Cognitive Theory and Neuropsychology*. New York: Basic Books.

Putnam, H. 1981. *Reason, Truth, and History*. Cambridge: Cambridge University Press.

———. 1983. "Why Isn't There a Ready-Made World?" In *Realism and Reason*. Vol. 3 of *Philosophical Papers*. Cambridge: Cambridge University Press.

———. 1990. "Why Is a Philosopher?" In *Realism with a Human Face*. Ed. J. Conant. Cambridge: Harvard University Press, 105–19.

———. 2002. *The Collapse of the Fact/Value Dichotomy and Other Essays*. Cambridge: Harvard University Press.

Quine, W.V.O. 1980. "Two Dogmas of Empiricism." In *From a Logical Point of View*. 2nd ed. Cambridge: Harvard University Press, 20–46.

Ragland-Sullivan, E. 1986. *Jacques Lacan and the Philosophy of Psychoanalysis*. Urbana: University of Illinois Press.

Rank, O. 2004. *The Myth of the Hero: A Psychological Exploration of the Myth*. 1904. Baltimore: Johns Hopkins University Press.

Reeder, J. 2002. *Reflecting Psychoanalysis: Narrative and Resolve in the Psychoanalytic Experience*. London: Karnac.

———. 2004. "Narration as a Hermeneutical Relationship to the Unconscious." *Scandinavian Psychoanalytic Review* 27:118–23.

———. 2008. "The Enigmatic 'Nature of the Subject': With Philosophy at the Interface of Psychoanalysis and Society." *Scandinavian Psychoanalytic Review* 31:114–21.

Reichenbach, H. 1938. *Experience and Prediction: An Analysis of the Foundations and the Structure of Knowledge*. Chicago: University of Chicago Press.

———. 1951. *The Rise of Scientific Philosophy*. Berkeley: University of California Press.

Reiss, T. J. 2002. *Against Autonomy: Global Dialectics of Cultural Exchange*. Stanford: Stanford University Press.

Rendon, M. 1986. "Philosophical Paradigms in Psychoanalysis." *Journal of the American Academy of Psychoanalysis and Dynamic Psychiatry* 14:495–505.

Rhees, R. 1966. "Conversations on Freud." In *Wittgenstein: Lectures and Conversations on Aesthetics, Psychology, and Religious Belief*. Ed. C. Barrett. Berkeley: University of California Press, 41–52.

———. 1981. *Ludwig Wittgenstein: Personal Recollections*. Totawa, N.J.: Rowman and Littlefield.

Rickert, H. 1962. *Science and History: A Critique of Positivist Epistemology*. Trans. G. Reisman. Princeton, N.J.: Van Nostrand.

Rickman, H. P. 1976. "Introduction." In *Selected Writings*, by W. Dilthey. Ed. and trans. H. P. Rickman. Cambridge: Cambridge University Press, 1–31.

Ricoeur, P. 1970. *Freud and Philosophy: An Essay on Interpretation*. 1965. New Haven: Yale University Press.

———. 1984. *Time and Narrative*. Vol. 1. 1983. Chicago: University of Chicago Press.

Ricoeur, P.. 1988. *Time and Narrative*. Vol. 3. 1985. Chicago: University of Chicago Press.

———. 1994. *Oneself as Another*. 1990. Chicago: University of Chicago Press.

Rieff, P. 1959. *Freud: The Mind of the Moralist*. New York: Viking Press.

———. 1966. *The Therapeutic Triumph: Uses of Faith after Freud*. New York: Harper-Row.

Ritvo, L. B. 1990. *Darwin's Influence on Freud: A Tale of Two Sciences*. New Haven: Yale University Press.

Roazen, P. 1968. *Freud: Political and Social Thought*. New York: Alfred A. Knopf.

———. 1975. *Freud and His Followers*. New York: Alfred A. Knopf.

———. 1991. "Nietzsche and Freud: Two Voices from the Underground." *Psychohistory Review* 19:327–49.

Robinson, P. 2000. "Freud and Homosexuality." In *Whose Freud? The Place of Psychoanalysis in Contemporary Culture*. Ed. P. Brooks and A. Woloch. New Haven: Yale University Press, 144–49.

Rockmore, T. 2006. *In Kant's Wake: Philosophy in the Twentieth Century*. Malden, Mass.: Blackwell.

Roland, D. 1988. *In Search of Self in India and Japan*. Princeton: Princeton University Press.

Rorty, R. 1986. "Freud and Moral Reflection." In *Pragmatism's Freud: The Moral Disposition of Psychoanalysis*. Ed. J. H. Smith and W. Kerrigan. Baltimore: Johns Hopkins University Press, 1–27.

———. 1991. "Inquiry as Recontextualization: An Anti-dualist Account of Interpretation." In *Objectivity, Relativism, and Truth*. Vol. 1 of *Philosophical Papers*. Cambridge: Cambridge University Press, 93–110.

———. 1993. "Centers of Moral Gravity: Commentary on Donald Spence's 'The Hermeneutic Turn.'" *Psychoanalytic Dialogues* 3:21–28.

Rose, N. 1990. *Governing the Soul: Shaping the Private Self*. London: Routledge.

———. 1998. *Inventing Ourselves: Psychology, Power, and Personhood*. Cambridge: Cambridge University Press.

———. 1999. *Powers of Freedom: Reframing Political Thought*. Cambridge: Cambridge University Press.

Rosenblatt, A. D., and J. T. Thickstun. 1977. *Modern Psychoanalytic Concepts in a General Psychology*. New York: International Universities Press.

Rozenberg, J. J. 1999. *From the Unconscious to Ethics*. New York: Peter Lang.

Rubovits-Seitz, P.F.D., and H. Kohut. 1999. *Kohut's Freudian Vision*. Hillsdale, N.J.: Analytic Press.

Rudnytsky, P. L. 1987. *Freud and Oedipus*. New York: Columbia University Press.

———. 2002. *Reading Psychoanalysis: Freud, Rank, Ferenczi, Groddeck*. Ithaca, N.Y.: Cornell University Press.

———. 2008. "Introduction." In *Psychoanalysis and Narrative Medicine*. Ed. P. L. Rudnytsky and R. Charon. Albany: State University of New York Press, 1–22.

Rudnytsky, P. L., and R. Charon, eds. 2008. *Psychoanalysis and Narrative Medicine*. Albany: State University of New York Press.

Ruti, M. 2006. *Reinventing the Soul: Posthumanist Theory and Psychic Life*. New York: Other Press.

Sachs, H. 1944. *Freud: Master and Friend*. Cambridge: Harvard University Press.

Sacks, O. 2000. "The Other Road: Freud as Neurologist." In *Freud, Conflict and Culture: Essays on His Life, Work, and Legacy*. Ed. M. S. Roth. New York: Viking, 221–34.

Sadler, J. Z. 2004. *Values and Psychiatric Diagnosis*. New York: Oxford University Press.

Saks, E. R. 1999. *Interpreting Interpretation: The Limits of Hermeneutic Psychoanalysis*. New Haven: Yale University Press.

Sartre, J.-P. 1956. *Being and Nothingness: An Essay on Phenomenological Ontology*. 1943. Trans. H. E. Barnes. New York: Philosophical Library.

Sass, L. A., and R. L. Woolfolk. 1988. "Psychoanalysis and the Hermeneutic Turn: A Critique of Narrative Truth and Historical Truth." *Journal of the American Psychoanalytic Association* 36:429–53.

Sassen, B. 2000. "Introduction." In *Kant's Early Critics: The Empiricist Critique of the Theoretical Philosophy*. Cambridge: Cambridge University Press, 1–49.

Scavio, M. J., A. Cooper, and P. Scavio Clift. 1993. "Freud's Devaluation of Nietzsche." *Psychohistory Review* 21:295–318.

Schafer, R. 1970. "The Psychoanalytic Vision of Reality." *International Journal of Psycho-analysis* 51:279–97.

———. 1985. "Interpretation of Psychic Reality, Developmental Influences, and Unconscious Communication." *Journal of the American Psychoanalytic Association*, 33:537–54.

———. 1992a. "Problems in Freud's Psychology of Women." In *Retelling a Life. Narration and Dialogue in Psychoanalysis*. New York: Basic Books, 59–81.

———. 1992b. *Retelling a Life: Narration and Dialogue in Psychoanalysis*. New York: Basic Books.

Scharff, D. E. 1996. *Object Relations Theory and Practice: An Introduction*. Lanham, Md.: Rowman and Littlefield.

Schiller, F. 1993. *Letters on the Aesthetic Education of Man*. 1801. Trans. E. M. Wilkinson and L. A. Willoughby. In *Essays*. Ed. W. Hinderer and D. O. Dahlstrom. New York: Continuum, 86–178.

Schnädelbach, H. 1984. *Philosophy in Germany, 1831–1933*. Cambridge: Cambridge University Press.

Schneewind, J. B. 1992. "Autonomy, Obligation, and Virtue: An Overview of Kant's Moral Philosophy." In *The Cambridge Companion to Kant*. Ed. P. Guyer. Cambridge: Cambridge University Press, 309–41.

———. 1998. *The Invention of Autonomy: A History of Modern Moral Philosophy*. Cambridge: Cambridge University Press.

Schopenhauer, A. 1969. *The World as Will and Representation*. 1819. 2 vols. Trans. E.F.J. Payne. New York: Dover.

———. 1974a. *The Fourfold Root of the Principle of Sufficient Reason*. 1813. Trans. E.F.J. Payne. LaSalle, Ill.: Open Court.

———. 1974b. *Parerga and Parilipomena: Short Philosophical Essays*, 1851. Trans. E.F.J. Payne. 2 vols. Oxford: Oxford University Press.

———. 1999. *Prize Essay on the Freedom of the Will*. 1839. Trans. E.F.J. Payne. New York: Cambridge University Press.

Schorske, C. E. 1980. *Fin-de-Siècle Vienna: Politics and Culture*. New York: Vintage.

Scruton, R. 1982. *From Decartes to Wittengenstein: A Short History of Modern Philosophy*. New York: Harper Colophon.

Scully, S. 1997. "Freud's Antiquities: A View from the Couch." *Arion* 5:222–33.

Seigel, H. 2005. *The Idea of the Self: Thought and Experience in Western Europe since the Seventeenth Century*. Cambridge: Cambridge University Press.

Seligman, A. 2000. *Modernity's Wager: Authority, the Self, and Transcendence*. Princeton: Princeton University Press.

Shain, B. A. 1994. *The Myth of American Individualism: The Protestant Origins of American Political Thought*. Princeton: Princeton University Press.

Sharpe, M. 2006. "Jacques Lacan." *The Internet Encyclopedia of Philosophy*. http://www.iep.utm.edu/l/lacweb.htm#H4.

Sherman, N. 1995. "The Moral Perspective and the Psychoanalytic Quest." *Journal of the American Academy of Psychoanalysis and Dynamic Psychiatry* 23:223–41.

Sherwood, M. 1969. *The Logic of Explanation in Psychoanalysis*. New York: Academic Press.

Shengold, L. 1993. *"The Boy Will Come to Nothing." Freud's Ego Ideal and Freud as Ego Ideal*. New Haven: Yale University Press.

Shorter, E. 1992. *From Paralysis to Fatigue: A History of Psychosomatic Illness in the Modern Era*. New York: Free Press.

Simmel, G. 1991. *Schopenhauer and Nietzsche*. 1907. Trans. H. Loiskandl, D. Weinstein, and M. Weinstein. Urbana: University of Illinois Press.

Simons, P. 1973. "Introduction" and editorial notes in *Psychology from an Empirical Standpoint*, by F. Brentano. 1874. Trans. A. C. Rancurello, D. B. Terrell, and L. L. McAlister. London: Routledge, xiii–xxii.

Skues, R. A. 2009. *Sigmund Freud and the History of Anna O.: Reopening a Closed Case*. New York: Palgrave Macmillan.

Smith, C.U.M. 1986. "Friedrich Nietzsche's Biological Epistemics." *Journal of Social and Biological Structure* 9:375–88.

———. 1987. "Clever Beasts Who Invented Knowing: Nietzsche's Evolutionary Biology of Knowledge." *Biology and Philosophy* 2:65–91.

Smith, D. L. 1999a. "Sigmund Freud's Programme for a Science of Consciousness." *British Journal of Psychotherapy* 15:412–24.

———. 1999b. *Freud's Philosophy of the Unconscious*. Dordrecht: Kluwer Academic Publishers.

Smith, R. 1997. *The Norton History of the Human Sciences*. New York: Norton.

———. 2007. *Being Human: Historical Knowledge and the Creation of Human Nature*. Manchester: Manchester University Press.

Sober, E., and D. S. Wilson. 1998. *Unto Others: The Evolution and Psychology of Unselfish Behavior*. Cambridge: Harvard University Press.

Spence, D. 1982. *Narrative Truth and Historical Truth: Meaning and Interpretation in Psychoanalysis*. New York: Norton.

Spiegelberg, H. 1982. *The Phenomenological Movement: A Historical Introduction*. 3rd ed. The Hague: Martin Nijhoff.

Spinoza, B. 1985. *Ethics*, in *The Collected Works of Spinoza*. Ed. and trans. E. Curley, Vol. 1. Princeton: Princeton University Press, 408–617.

Sprengnether, M. 1990. *The Spectral Mother: Freud, Feminism, and Psychoanalysis*. Ithaca, N.Y.: Cornell University Press.

Stack, G. J. 1991. "Kant, Lange, and Nietzsche: Critique of Knowledge." In *Nietzsche and Modern German Thought*. Ed. K. Ansell-Pearson. New York: Routledge, 30–58.

————. 1992. *Nietzsche and Emerson*. Athens: Ohio University Press.

Steiner, R. 1995. "Hermeneutics or Hermes-mess?" *International Journal of Psychoanalysis* 76:435–45.

Stepansky, P. E. 1999. *Freud, Surgery, and the Surgeons*. Hillsdale, N.J.: Analytic Press.

Stewart, J. 2003. *Kierkegaard's Relations to Hegel Reconsidered*. Cambridge: Cambridge University Press.

Stone, A. A. 1983. "A Brief Note on Kant and Free Association." *International Review of Psycho-analysis* 10:445.

Strawson, G. 1998. "Free Will." In *Routledge Encyclopedia of Philosophy*. London: Routledge, 3:743–53.

Sugarman, S. 1998. *Freud on the Acropolis: Reflections on a Paradoxical Response to the Real*. Boulder, Colo.: Westview Press.

Sullivan, H. S. 1953. *Conceptions of Modern Psychiatry*. New York: Norton.

Sulloway, F. J. 1979. *Freud, Biologist of the Mind*. New York: Basic Books.

Szaluta, J. 1996. "Sigmund Freud's Phiosophical Ego Ideals." In *Psychoanalysis and the Humanities*. Ed. L. Adams and J. Szaluta. New York: Brunner/Mazel Publishers, 5–28.

Szasz, T. S. 1961. *The Myth of Mental Illness: Foundations of a Theory of Personal Conduct*. New York: Dell.

————. 1965. *The Ethics of Psychoanalysis: The Theory and Method of Autonomous Psychotherapy*. New York: Delta.

Tait, W. W, ed. 1997. *Early Analytic Philosophy: Frege, Russell, Wittgenstein*. Chicago: Open Court.

Tauber, A. I. 1993. "Goethe's Philosophy of Science: Modern Resonances." *Perspectives in Biology and Medicine* 36:244–57.

————. 1994a. *The Immune Self: Theory or Metaphor?* Cambridge: Cambridge University Press.

————. 1994b. "A Typology of Nietzsche's Biology." *Biology and Philosophy* 9:24–44.

————. 1994c. "The Immune Self: From Theory to Metaphor." *Immunology Today* 15:134–36.

————. 1995. "On the Transvaluation of Values: Nietzsche contra Foucault." In *Science, Mind and Art: Papers in Honor of Robert Cohen*. Ed. K. Gavroglu and M. Wartovsky. Dordrecht: Kluwer Academic Publishers, 349–67.

————. 1999a. *Confessions of a Medicine Man: An Essay in Popular Philosophy*. Cambridge: MIT Press.

————. 1999b. "The Elusive Immune Self: A Case of Category Errors." *Perspectives in Biology and Medicine* 42:459–74.

————. 2001. *Henry David Thoreau and the Moral Agency of Knowing*. Berkeley: University of California Press.

Tauber, A. I. 2003. "The Philosopher as Prophet: The Case of Emerson and Thoreau." *Philosophy in the Contemporary World* 10:89–103.

———. 2005. *Patient Autonomy and the Ethics of Responsibility*. Cambridge: MIT Press.

———. 2006. "The Reflexive Project: Reconstructing the Moral Agent." *History of the Human Sciences* 18:49–75.

———. 2009. *Science and the Quest for Meaning*. Waco, Tex.: Baylor University Press.

Tauber A. I., and S. H. Podolsky. 1999. "Nietzsche's Conception of Health: The Idealization of Struggle." In *Nietzsche, Epistemology, and Philosophy of Science: Nietzsche and the Sciences II*. Ed. B. Babich. Dordrecht: Kluwer Academic Publishers, 299–311.

Taylor, C. 1989. *Sources of the Self*. Cambridge: Harvard University Press.

Taylor, M. C. 1980. *Journeys to Selfhood: Hegel and Kierkegaard*. Berkeley: University of California Press.

———. 1987. *Alterity*. Chicago: University of Chicago Press.

Thalberg, I. 1982. "Freud's Anatomies of the Self." In *Philosophical Essays on Freud*. Ed. R. Wollheim and J. Hopkins. Cambridge: Cambridge University Press, 241–63.

Theunissen, M. 1984. *The Other: Studies in the Social Ontology of Husserl, Heidegger, Sartre, and Buber*. Trans. C. Macann. Cambridge: MIT Press.

Throop, C. J., and C. D. Laughlin. 2007. "Anthropology of Consciousness." In *The Cambridge Handbook of Consciousness*. Ed. P. D. Zelazo, M. Moscovitch, and E. Thompson. Cambridge: Cambridge University Press, 631–69.

Thulstrup, N. 1980. *Kierkegaard's Relation to Hegel*. Princeton: Princeton University Press.

Toulmin, S. 1954. "The Logical Status of Psychoanalysis." In *Philosophy and Analysis*. Ed. M. Macdonald. Oxford: Basil Blackwell, 132–39.

Trilling, L. 1972. *Sincerity and Authenticity*. Cambridge: Harvard University Press.

Trosman, H. 1976. "Freud's Cultural Background." In *Freud: The Fusion of Science and Humanism. The Intellectual History of Psychoanalysis*. Ed. J. E. Gedo and G. H. Pollock. New York: International Universities Press.

Trosman, H., and R. D. Simmons. 1973. "The Freud Library." *Journal of the Psychoanalytic Association* 21:646–87.

Tugendhat, E. 1986. *Self-Consciousness and Self-Determination*. Trans. P. Stern. Cambridge: MIT Press.

van Fraassen, B. 1980. *The Scientific Image*. Oxford: Clarendon Press.

Velkley, R. L. 1989. *Freedom and the End of Reason: On the Moral Foundation of Kant's Critical Philosophy*. Chicago: University of Chicago Press.

Volberg, J. J. 2007. *Dream, Death, and the Self*. Princeton: Princeton University Press.

von Hartmann, E. 1931. *Philosophy of the Unconscious*. 9th ed. Trans. W. C. Coupland. London: Kegan Paul, Trench.

von Unwerth, M. 2005. *Freud's Requiem: Mourning, Memory, and the Invisible History of a Summer Walk*. New York: Riverhead Books.

Wallace, E. R. 1985. *Historiography and Causation in Psychoanalysis: An Essay on Psychoanalysis and Historical Epistemology.* Hillsdale, N.J.: Analytic Press.
———. 1986. "Freud as Ethicist." In *Freud: Appraisals and Reappraisals.* Ed. J. Stepansky. Hillsdale, N.J.: Analytic Press, 83–141.
Wallwork, E. 1991. *Psychoanalysis and Ethics.* New Haven: Yale University Press.
Warren, M. 1988. *Nietzsche and Political Thought.* Cambridge: MIT Press.
Watkins, E. 2005. *Kant and the Metaphysics of Causality.* Cambridge: Cambridge University Press.
Waugaman, R. 1973. "The Intellectual Relationship between Nietzsche and Freud." *Psychiatry* 36:458–67.
Weber, M. 1946. "Science as a Vocation." 1919. In *From Max Weber: Essays in Sociology.* Trans. and ed. H. H. Gerth and C. W. Mills. New York: Oxford University Press, 137–56.
Weber, S. 1991. *Return to Freud: Jacques Lacan's Dislocation of Psychoanalysis.* Cambridge: Cambridge University Press.
Webster, R. 1995. *Why Freud Was Wrong: Sin, Science, and Psychoanalysis.* New York: Basic Books.
Wegner, D. M. 2002. *The Illusion of Conscious Will.* Cambridge: MIT Press.
Weisman, A. D. 1965. *The Existential Core of Psychoanalysis: Reality Sense and Responsibility.* Boston: Little, Brown.
Westen, D., J. Weinberger, and R. Bradley. "Motivation, Decision Making, and Consciousness: From Psychodynamics to Subliminal Priming and Emotional Constraint Satisfaction." In *The Cambridge Handbook of Consciousness.* Ed. P. D. Zelazo, M. Moscovitch, and E. Thompson, Cambridge: Cambridge University Press, 673–702.
Whewell, W. 1840. *Philosophy of the Inductive Sciences.* London: J. W. Parker.
Whitehead, A. 1925. *Science and the Modern World.* London: Macmillan.
Willey, T. E. 1978. *Back to Kant: The Revival of Kantianism in German Social and Historical Thought, 1860–1914.* Detroit: Wayne State University Press.
Wilson, T. D. 2002. *Strangers to Ourselves: Discovering the Adaptive Unconscious.* Cambridge: Harvard University Press.
Windelband, W. 1919. *A History of Philosophy.* 1900. Trans. J. Tufts. New York: Macmillan.
———. 1921. *An Introduction to Philosophy.* 1895. Trans. J. McCabe. New York: Henry Holt.
———. 1961. *Theories in Logic.* 1901. New York: Citadel Press.
———. 1980. "History and Natural Science." 1894. Trans. G. Oakes. *History and Theory* 19:169–85.
Wittgenstein, L. 1958. *The Blue and Brown Books.* 1933–34. New York: Harper and Row.
———. 1968. *Philosophical Investigations.* 3rd ed. Trans. G.E.M. Anscombe and trans. D. Paul and G.E.M. Anscombe. New York: Macmillan.
———. 1969. *On Certainty.* Ed. G.E.M. Anscombe and G. H. von Wright. New York: Harper Row.
———. 1979. *Notebooks 1914–1916.* 2nd ed. Ed. G. H. von Wright and G.E.M. Anscombe and trans. G. E. M. Anscombe. Chicago: University of Chicago Press.

Wittgenstein, L. 1980a. *Culture and Value*. Ed. G. H. von Wright and trans. P. Winch. Chicago: University of Chicago Press.

———. 1980b. *Remarks on the Philosophy of Psychology*. Ed. G.E.M. Anscombe and G. H. von Wright. 2 vols. Chicago: University of Chicago Press.

———. 1992. *Last Writings on the Philosophy of Psychology*. Vol. 2, *The Inner and the Outer*. Ed. G. H. von Wright and H. Nyman and trans. C. G. Luckhardt and M. A. E. Rue. Oxford: Blackwell.

———. 1998. *Wittgenstein's Tractatus* [*Tractatus Logico-Philosophicus*]. 1921. Trans. D. Kolak. Mountain View, Calif.: Mayfield.

Wollheim, R. 1981. *Sigmund Freud*. Cambridge: Cambridge University Press.

———. 1999. *The Thread of Life*. New Haven: Yale University Press.

Wollheim, R., and J. Hopkins, eds. 1982. *Philosophical Essays on Freud*. Cambridge: Cambridge University Press.

Wolterstorff, N. 1990. "Realism vs. Anti-realism." In *Reality in Focus*. Ed. P. K. Moser. Englewood Cliffs, N.J.: Prentice-Hall, 50–64.

Wright, G. H. von 1971. *Explanation and Understanding*. London: Routledge and Kegan Paul.

Wundt, W. M. 1904. *Principles of Physiological Psychology*. Trans. Edward Bradford Titchener. New York: Macmillan.

Young, J. 1992. *Nietzsche's Philosophy of Art*. Cambridge: Cambridge University Press.

Zammito, J. H. 2004. *A Nice Derangement of Epistemes: Post-positivism in the Study of Science from Quine to Latour*. Chicago: University of Chicago Press.

Zaner, R. M., and K. L. Heiges. 1977. "Introduction." In *Descriptive Psychology and Historical Understanding* by W. Dilthey. Trans. R. M. Zaner and K. L. Heiges. The Hague: Martinus Nijhoff, 3–20.

Zanuso, B. 1986. *The Young Freud: The Origins of Psychoanalysis in Late Nineteenth-Century Viennese Culture*. Oxford: Basil Blackwell.

Zaretsky, E. 2004. *Secrets of the Soul: A Social and Cultural History of Psychoanalysis*. New York: Alfred A. Knopf.

Zoeller, G. 1993. "Main Developments in Recent Scholarship on the *Critique of Pure Reason*." *Philosophy and Phenomenological Research* 53:445–56.

Brentano, Franz (*cont'd*)
  Herzog; Maudsley; McGrath; Newton;
    von Hartmann; Wollheim
Brown, Norman O., xvi, 8, 12, 165, 170,
  237n.2
Brücke, Ernst, 27, 29, 30, 40, 155. *See also*
  reductionism
Büchner, Ludwig 98. *See also* materialism

Cartesian. *See* Descartes
cause, 2, 66, 85, 157, 246n.11, 247n.13,
  254n.9, 276n.19; natural, 6, 10, 18,
  100, 111, 116, 148; psychic, Freudian,
  9, 16, 51–52, 56–57, 59, 63–64, 66, 82,
  85, 104, 120–21, 123, 141, 158, 165,
  170, 237n.2, 250n.4; psychic deterministic, Freudian, 6, 18, 22, 34, 66, 127,
  133, 143–44, 171, 206, 221, 249n.1,
  253n.11. *See also* Brentano: intentionality; Brentano: psychic cause; determin-
  ism/free will paradox; free will; Kant:
  free will; Wittgenstein: cause differentiated from reason
Cavell, Marcia, 12, 37, 121, 131, 185,
  228n.1, 238n.5, 250n.3, 273n.7. *See*
  also Freudianism: philosophical
  critique of
Claus, Carl, 163. *See also* Darwinism;
  Freud, scientist: Darwinian
cognitive science, 1, 83
Cohen, Aviva, 233-34n.11, 237n.21. *See*
  also Brentano
Comte, August, 31, 77, 86
consciousness, 4, 30, 35, 40, 47, 68, 77,
  89, 94, 98–99, 111–13, 123, 146, 149,
  150, 160, 175, 179, 180, 183, 184,
  192, 234n.13, 244n.5, 250n.2, 254n.3,
  265n.10, 265n.11, 268n.18, 272n.4. *See*
  also Brentano: consciousness; Freud,
  philosopher: philosophy of mind; mental activity: conscious; mental activity:
  pre-conscious; mental activity: unconscious; selfhood, philosophy of: Freud;
  Schopenhauer: consciousness; self-consciousness; unconscious, the constructivism, 12, 46, 58-59, 65–66, 77, 96, 97,
  100, 104, 116, 127, 162, 173, 178, 182,
  193, 188, 195, 197, 198–202, 207, 210,
  215, 227n.3, 246n.7, 252n.9, 268n.18,
  270n.19, 270-71n.1, 275n.16. *See also*

Kant; realism, antirealism; Schafer;
    Science Wars; Spence
Copernicus, Nicolas, 222
Crews, Fredrick, 7, 67, 192, 199, 274n.12.
  See also "memory wars"

Darwinism, 27, 60, 95, 115, 144, 151, 154,
  162–64, 173, 258n.10, 264n.9. *See also*
  Freud, scientist: Darwinian
Davidson, Donald, 240n.9, 253n.11. *See*
  also Wittgenstein
della Mirandola, Giovanni Pico, 222
Derrida, Jacques, 202, 268n.18
Descartes, René, 20, 146, 175, 179,
  228n.4, 243n.4, 244n.5, 263n.8,
  266n.11; concept of mind, 44, 68–69,
  87, 111, 113, 147, 174, 177, 254n.2;
  selfhood, 20, 68, 87, 129, 146, 147–48,
  160, 168, 174, 175–76, 179, 181, 186,
  187, 194, 243n.1, 244n.4, 254n.2,
  260n.16, 263n.8
determinism. *See* cause; determinism/free
  will paradox; free will; Freudian psychoanalysis, theory of: psychic cause
determinism/free will paradox, 18, 111,
  139-40; Freud, 7, 18, 21–22, 111, 115,
  139–40, 169, 221, 226, 252n.9; Hume,
  260n.17; Kant, 18, 139–40, 143, 218;
  Mill, 222; Schopenhauer, 157–58. *See*
  also free will
Dewey, John, xi, 214–15, 270n.19,
  275n.15
Dilthey, Wilhelm, 17, 88-89, 90, 92, 93,
  108, 243n.2, 243n.3, 243n.4. *See also*
  historicist; human sciences
Draenos, Stan, 67, 233n.10
du Bois-Reymond, Emil, 27. *See also*
  reductionism
Dummett, Michael, 245n.6
Dworkin, Gerald, 274n.10. *See also*
  free will

Edwards, James, 76, 227n.3, 241n.10.
  See also Freudianism: philosophical
  critique of
Egginton, William, 48, 202-3, 204, 205,
  273n.6
ego, Freudian psychoanalytic, 152, 187–88,
  229n.4, 267n.15, 266–67n.14, 267n.15,
  267n.16, 268–69n. 19; freedom of, 3–4,

314

INDEX